B.A.L.A.N.C.E.

nature's way to heal your body

by

Susan Manion Mac Donald

New World Publishing
P. O. Box 36075
Halifax, N.S., Canada B3J 3S9
1-877-211-3334
e-mail: nwp1@eastlink.ca
www.newworldpublishing.com

The suggestions outlined in this book are recommendations only and are not intended as medical advice. Persons who are ill or on medication who wish to change their diet would be well advised to consult a health care professional who understands the effects of diet on health. The same holds true for adding supplements, reducing medications, taking herbal preparations, and/or undergoing detoxification procedures, each of which could conflict with any current medications or supplements that an individual may be taking. It is always wise to consult a full range of health care practitioners, including your family physician, appropriate medical specialists, naturopath, nutritionist and/or pharmacist before embarking on any changes or adopting protocols outlined in this or any other book. This book is meant to teach, not diagnose or treat. The publishers also regret that under no circumstances can they refer any readers to any of the medical practitioners, natural therapists, or other specialists referred to in this publication.

Although all sources have been thoroughly researched to ensure the accuracy and completeness of the information contained in this book, we assume no responsibility for errors, inaccuracies, omissions, or any inconsistency included herein. Any perceived slights to individuals or organizations are unintentional

Published by: New World Publishing, P.O. Box 36075,
Halifax, N.S., B3J 3S9 Canada   1-877-211-3334

Copyright: © 2004 Susan [Manion] MacDonald; © 2007 New World Publishing

Managing Editor: Francis G. Mitchell
Editors: Francis Mitchell and editorial staff
Copy Editing: Virginia Houston
Content Proofing: Bruce Hayhoe and Susan M. MacDonald
Graphic Design, Typography & Layout: New World Publishing & Designs
Cover Concept: Susan M. MacDonald, Virginia Houston & Francis Mitchell

National Library and Archives Canada Cataloguing in-Publication Data:
MacDonald, Susan [Manion], 1949 -
B.A.L.A.N.C.E.: nature's way to heal your body
Includes bibliographic references, resource lists and index
ISBN 10 digit: 1-895814-32-4; ISBN 13 digit: 978-1-895814-32-0

1. Environmentally induced diseases -- Popular works. 2. Environmental health -- Popular works. 3. MacDonald, Susan [Manion]. 4. Cancer -- Patients -- Rehabilitation. I. Mitchell, Francis, 1942 - II. Title.

RA565.M33 2006   613'.1   C2006-904237-3

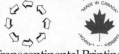

Printed and bound in Canada on 100% recycled paper by Transcontinental Printing..
Printings: 1   2   3   4   5   6   7   8   9   10

Dedication

To my husband, Jim, who accompanied me on my journey.

Your strength of character and integrity has always humbled me.

Thank you for being there, for loving me without question!!

To my three wonderful children Tammy, Charlene and Dan,

there is the potential for greatness in each of you

to discover and nourish. Each of you is unique.

There is magic in you, and collectively you embody

the foundation of a family with traditions and values

that make me proud to be called mom.

This book is also dedicated to my grandchildren,

Benjamin, Katherine, Gia, and Brady, as well as

step-grandchildren Adam and Carl.

May you seek to learn and set goals,

and when bumps in the road of life come along with the

power to shake you, that you can learn to see them as gifts.

That will ultimately make you stronger.

Balance always lives in the present!

SPECIAL THANKS

Dr. Bruce Hayhoe, naturopath, you were always there for me, far more than a paid professional, but a true health professional at all times. I would pitch my ideas and you would teach me even more. Your knowledge has enabled me to learn so much about how and why my body works the way it does. Your insights related to my thyroid, liver, lymph and bowels helped to keep chemotherapy at bay while I worked to detoxify my body and heal my cells. Thank you for giving me that time.

Aunt Frankie, your principles, organizational skills, traditions, and sense of family have been my guiding light. Our joint interest in politics added flavor to the mix. Growing up you treated me with the respect of an adult, giving me confidence and providing me with warmth. Your presence always made me feel like my Dad was close by after we lost him in 1980. Thank you for opening up your home and heart to me and mine!

Gil, Clare, and Chuck: you are my mentors. Your ability to trust, lead and empower gave me direction during those times when I wasn't even sure who I was. You had enough confidence in yourselves to allow me to shine and excel in what I was good at. Thank you!

Bill Casey, thank you for maintaining your integrity over the many years we worked together - as a political leader that can often be an insurmountable task. Your example has helped me to recognize, define and incorporate a sense of integrity in my life, which has helped to create the person I have become today.

Catherine March, your friendship, and direction in recommending me to Dr. Hayhoe, helped create a whole world of opportunity for me. Your smile is like the sun - warm and energizing to so many others, especially me.

To Cathy, my younger sister, please accept my apology for leaving home at sixteen and for not recognizing that you would be saddled with so much responsibility at such an early age. But like so many other things in life, those early experiences helped define our character and made us who we are today. And I like who we are. Terry, Mike, Bob and Margaret, I love each of you. Thank you for the part you play in my life today.

Debbie, as a friend for thirty years, we have seen a lot of changes in our bodies and in our lives. Helping you cope with changes in your life has helped strengthen and encourage what I do with mine. Thank you for your friendship!

Carolyn, as a friend and former co-worker, thank you for your help on my journey. Your words of encouragement and polite editing suggestions were crucial when I began writing this book. The loss of your brother to cancer during my own process of recovery helped fuel my vision to complete this work, and hopefully, provide others with the assistance they may require in making important changes in their lives.

Stephanie and Connie, you came along at the right moment in my life. There are no accidents in life. *The Way of the Heart* is more than a program, indeed it is a way of life. You are the keepers of the light, which has become a path to our hearts - a light that helped to release the joy, faith and trust buried deep inside each of us. Thank you for showing me the way.

Judit Rajhathy, your intuition, foresight and best-selling publication ultimately led me to Francis Mitchell, editor and publisher, New World Publishing. Thank you Francis for setting my dream in motion when you agreed to publish my book. You had the insight and knowledge to understand the importance of my story and the research gathered during my recovery. You also had the patience and skill to help me rewrite and edit my manuscript to produce a quality publication that would appeal to readers, enabling them to begin their own journeys towards wellness.

Annette Klein, Valerie Gaudet, Julie Savoie and Colleen Dwyer - it was a pleasure to know each of you. May your spirit shine upon us and guide us to a better place. Your courage empowers me.

I thank God for giving me patience while I searched and found that hidden quality within me that was essential before proceeding on my life's mission.

"Each person we meet along the road of life is there for a reason. It is our responsibility to determine those reasons and to complete the journey with the required knowledge and fortitude."

Susan

Table of Contents

Table of Contents

Foreword/Biography

Today, Susan Manion MacDonald is a thriving mother of three, a grandmother, sister and partner to husband Jim. She is currently living her dream of helping others through her work as a naturo-therapist and owner of the JTW Natural Health Guidance Centre. She has abundant energy and excellent health to meet all of her personal and family commitments, and live life to the fullest.

But it was not always that way!

Born Susan Manion in 1949 in Ottawa, the second of six children, she attended a variety of Roman Catholic schools in a host of cities and towns throughout Canada and the United States - as her father transferred constantly to new locations as a member of the Canadian Air Force. She learned to make friends quickly, but they did not last - and, as a result, her siblings became her real 'best' friends.

However, there was a lot of instability in an alcoholic home and she dropped out of school at age sixteen to marry her first love, and subsequently suffered eight years of mental and physical abuse for the sake of her first daughter. In hindsight that was a huge mistake as that relationship ended in violence, following which Susan jumped almost immediately into a new four year relationship that fared no better and ended badly as well.

By that time she had lost her family values, traditions and any semblance of self-esteem and balance - to the point of attempted suicide – and ended up on social assistance. And, if that was not enough, a fire destroyed their apartment and all of the family's possessions - she and her daughters were fortunate to escape with their lives.

But somehow she persevered and survived, as she now had two daughters to care for. She worked at several jobs and volunteered within the community, learning and growing more each day. Through these experiences, Susan developed new life skills and responsibility, as well as interpersonal and organizational skills - all of which contributed to her self-esteem and sense of self-worth. She was beginning to find stability in her life, and her sense of balance and personal worth was strengthened in 1978 when she met and married Jim MacDonald, a caring, trusting man who shared her values, traditions and love.

Life was good!

She continued to work at a variety of interesting jobs and career paths, including work as an assistant to the federal Member of Parliament, and as president of the provincial constituency association. She also completed high school, attained university credits, and earned a diploma in adult education.

She was on a lifetime high, but that would soon come to an abrupt halt in December, 2002 when she walked into her Doctor's office and heard those most dreaded of words: *"You have terminal cancer!"*

With no offer of viable treatment options, nor any words of hope, many people in the same situation might be crushed, but this was a new Susan. She faced the situation head on, and not only survived, but thrived through dogged determination, faith, and a profound commitment to research, which not only cured her cancer, but ultimately formed the basis for her life's work and this book.

It is a story worth reading. It is a model for how ordinary people can improve their health and the quality of their lives by emulating what Susan did, or by simply following her advice. Do not wait until you become ill before beginning to walk the walk - the advice in this book is both preventative as well as restorative. And do not forget to ask for help - everyone knows how to give advice, but often we do not have the skills or courage to seek assistance from others.

Francis Mitchell
Educator, Publisher

Introduction

I believe that each new life is blessed with a guiding light that emanates from the heart, along with a path to follow using one's instincts and intellect. That light can brighten or dim according to the physical, emotional or spiritual conditions individuals experience as they grow and mature. There are always choices: to accept or discard negative or positive conditions that affect one's ability to shine. Everyone has a purpose on earth - a 'life mission', but poor choices and unfortunate circumstances, including the quality of foods eaten, toxins encountered and emotions buried, have the ability to dim those guiding principles and one can become lost. Illness is merely a symptom of those conditions.

My purpose in writing this book is to help others increase their life force by attaining balance in their lives; through understanding nature's way to heal the body; and assisting readers as they embark on the most important journey of their lives. The book has a role in the prevention of illness, as well as for healing or recovery from disease. The body has an innate ability to heal itself, whether one has heart disease, diabetes, fibromyalgia, a single arthritic joint, or, as in my situation, terminal cancer.

In December 2002, when an oncologist presented me with the terminal diagnosis, my initial response was that life, as I knew it, was over! However, I not only had the support of family and friends, but a level of empowerment and courage wrought from early life experiences, which enabled me to move forward with hope. Early life lessons prepared me; the only question was what now? What was I expected to do with this new information?

Specialists said I was fortunate as the type of cancer was not as aggressive as many others. It took only a few moments to understand the impact of that statement - after all, a truck had not struck me. I had been given time - time to share my past with family; to leave a legacy for my husband, children, grandchildren and community; even perhaps enough time to conduct research and make a difference in someone else's life; as well as enough time to see the larger picture of life. The latter was especially true related to the important concept that each body is unique and if given the proper tools how it can heal itself. I also had enough time and support to find and follow what I now understand to be my life's purpose.

Early in the process of writing, I was unsure how to proceed with the manuscript and even wondered what qualified me to write it at all. In the end, I came to believe it is simply that my life experiences and a tenacity to overcome adversity, had given me a set of abilities, as well as an opportunity to guide others on a simpler path than that which I had experienced during my life. On the other hand, perhaps it was simply my way of giving thanks for what was given to me - my family and my life.

Past life experiences have assisted me in becoming the person I have developed into today. I believe that these events were also attempts by my soul to gain my attention, and unearth positive qualities hidden beneath the rubble, that would guide me on that 'life mission'. Before that eventful day in 2002, I had never taken the time to slow down and let the light guide me. Nor had I listened to my instincts. However, while I had steadfastly refused to become a victim, I had not allowed myself to experience the fullness of life.

In the end, I wound up with two stories in one manuscript. The first is my personal story of illness and recovery, while the second is not only an accumulation of the research required to heal myself, but it is much more. I continued well beyond the initial level of research to create information for workshops I had begun to present to others - in order to help them find a starting point and balance on their own road toward wellness.

Ultimately, with the help of mentors and my publisher, my personal story and research became this book.

B.A.L.A.N.C.E. is meant to be a guide. Each person is unique - with a unique body composition and set of life experiences that create positive or negative issues in one's life - and health. The common sense approach suggested in this book is to not proceed toward extremes where healing is concerned, as too much of one thing may well be as potentially damaging as too little. Unfortunately, when one is fearful for the very existence of life, it is easy to grasp at 'solutions' offered by family and friends, medical doctors, naturopaths, nutritionists, or through advertisements and books - clutching at straws with survival as an end in itself. Rather, the body needs to become balanced - overloading it with drugs, supplements (whether good quality or not) or food is not the answer.

Healing begins with you! The emergence or disappearance of a cancer tumor is not the marker that needs to be observed. The tumor is not the disease; it is a 'symptom' - a result of the disease process - a breakdown of the natural biological order. Once balance has been achieved, the body's immune system will search for, destroy and dispose of cancerous cells .

Initially, I was angry at the medical system for letting me down - for not recognizing that my serial illnesses and unfortunate incidents were part of a larger overall breakdown of my entire body, especially my immune system. In retrospect, and especially since I have attained balance in my life, both physically and emotionally, I consider the cancer to have been a gift. For without this disease, I might have not changed old habits, nor cleared past emotional wounds. Their removal has not only enabled me to become the person I am today, but, in addition, it has allowed me to follow a clear path towards my 'life's mission'. Perhaps the cancer was a wake-up call - my last opportunity to fulfil my then sub-conscious dreams.

Today, I understand that my purpose was not to change the medical system, but to teach others how to utilize their doctors to the best capacity, and to give readers the knowledge to take charge of their own bodies - to ultimately become responsible for their own health and lives. Once populations gain sufficient knowledge, they become empowered to act - and the health care system should begin to change to more of a partnership among the stakeholders, including family physicians, other health providers, such as naturopaths and nutritionists, pharmacists, and most important, you! Attaining and maintaining wellness must be a team effort.

My goal will have been achieved if you, the readers, use this book as a guide - as an example of how you can learn to reverse illness, and/or to ensure that you remain as healthy as possible for the time you have on this earth. You owe it to yourself and any others, such as your family, for whom you have responsibility. Remember wellness is far more than the mere absence of illness - it is attaining wholeness of body, mind and spirit.

Susan Manion MacDonald

Bridge Mandala[1]

Prescription for Life

As the earth circles 'round the sun,
Fire and water dance as one.

A planet of fire, a planet of water,
Circle together with infinite power.

The eternal flame, the liquid that quenches,
Creates new life, which the Universe embraces.

Two opposites combine,
Sustaining life throughout all time.

The wisdom of Sages
Passes through the ages.

Modern entwines with the old,
So the prescription can unfold.

1. Sketch and poem by Kathy Roy, Spirit Gardens Retreat, Stellerton, Nova Scotia, Canada. Check her website at: www.spiritgardensretreats.ca

Terminal illness is about
as far as one can travel
and is the longest road back!

Chapter One

Susan's Story

Introduction

Science has discovered that humans were 'designed' to live between 120 and 150 years. However, given the poor quality of nutrition and drinking water, as well as the ever-increasing levels of stress in our 'modern' world, that range has been shortened by at least one-third or more. Then human bodies had to deal with an onslaught of toxins, which after centuries of 'progress' has lead to record levels of cancer and heart disease in an all too toxic Western world. As a result, those pervasive toxins have further narrowed the spread between the potential for human longevity and actual life expectancies even more. But there is good news! Given the proper tools and conditions, the body has the ability to heal itself, beginning at the cellular level. As a result, life expectancies could rise again. And this improvement is not simply about longevity, but a better quality of life as well.

Unfortunately the human species does not get much help from modern medicine, which like many other aspects of the modern world, is not structured appropriately to improve the overall quality of our health. The current approach to health care is not proactive and preventative, but rather is primarily reactive in nature and based on a range of short-term or stopgap measures which often only postpones or delays the inevitable. Since the scourge of *AIDS/HIV* descended upon the world three short decades ago, science and modern medicine have learned a great deal about the role of the immune system in protecting individuals against disease, but governments and health agencies have not developed strategies to reduce illnesses by teaching people how to strengthen their immune function. It is well-known that individuals with compromised immune systems contract a wide range of deadly illnesses more easily (e.g., *SARS*, the *West Nile Virus*, *Legionnaire's Disease*), which rarely affect those with a strong immune function, but health care agencies and the medical industry have done little to educate the general population in this vital area. Why is that so? One could be cynical and suggest, for example, that the pharmaceutical industry has no financial incentive to do so as they sell the drugs that can 'cure' those diseases once contracted. However, one would assume that governments, health boards and HMOs[1] would be concerned, given the overburdened health care systems, limited public health dollars and the strain on health insurance programs everywhere. It would only make sense, both financially and logically to reduce illnesses and costs through better health prevention programs. Rather than giving the body opportunities and optimal conditions required for healing itself, health care in the 21st Century has focused on abating symptoms, masking them with drugs and painkillers, or on the removal of offending segments of the body via surgery.

The healing process cannot take a segmented or piecemeal approach to individual symptoms or conditions, but rather must focus on one that treats the body as a whole - an holistic approach based on quality nutrition, a cleaner environment and support for a stronger immune system. That is the kind of healing envisaged in this publication. To have proper healing take place, it must begin from the inside out, and then from the top down. As a result, the body begins to heal deep within at the cellular level, and the first external signs of wellness will begin at the top, so to speak, with thicker, shiny hair; clear, sparkling eyes; stronger teeth and gums; a healthier tongue; and, if applicable, a reduction in bad breath.

Why this book was written:
Consequently, the primary rationale for writing this book was to help readers obtain the tools and develop the skills required to heal their own bodies. Most of the information contained in this book is based on research, although my own personal healing, which paralleled the writing of this book, was, in part, driven by intuition as I traveled on a journey that ultimately meant life or death for me.

B.A.L.A.N.C.E. became a wonderful common sense approach to determine and monitor my own path to healing. The remarkable changes that occurred within my body ultimately gave me the courage to pass this

---

1. Health Management Organizations (more common in the USA than Canada)

information on to others, regardless of their current state of health. Some individuals may be in good health today and want a program to maintain it, while others may desire a preventative approach to ward off illness with advancing years; yet others, in a state of illness or disease, may require a restorative program to return them to a better quality of life. I truly believe that B.A.L.A.N.C.E. is a program for all of those situations - a program for everyone - and the principal reason I am not only alive today, but am living a quality of life, both physically and emotionally, that I had never known before. This story is a way of sharing my knowledge and experiences as I traveled on my own personal journey toward wellness.

Everyone has embarked on a significant journey at some point in his/her life. This book is about simplifying that process, as well as determining the best path for the most important journey of one's life. It also is about the connections between and among Body, Mind and Spirit, and the importance of balance among all three. This first chapter will detail my own story from the original diagnosis of terminal cancer to my current situation as a healthful, vibrant and energetic woman in the prime of her life. Chapter Two initiates the story of **B.A.L.A.N.C.E.**, beginning with **B**, a review of the operation of the human body and how vital it is to get to know it better, somewhat like having an owner's manual for the **body**. Negative symptoms that the body commonly experiences will be dealt with in this chapter, as well as in succeeding sections of this publication. It will also explain how symptoms can be obscured through medication, including over-the-counter and prescription drugs, which can ultimately create even more devastating conditions and symptoms of poor health in the future. If someone seeks a state of wellness as the ultimate destination, it is crucial not to mask symptoms, but to address the root causes of illnesses. That is what this book hopes to achieve.

Susan's Story begins:

In the past I enjoyed eating as most families of moderate means in North America did: home cooked meals; an occasional frozen entree; packaged meals in a box; refined and processed foods; plus a weekly visit to a take-out of choice. Since 1993, I had exercised regularly, including weight resistance training three times a week at the local YMCA, yet was still about forty pounds overweight with an increasing number of health issues. When I looked in the mirror, it reflected what I assumed was a relatively healthy, normal adult of fifty plus, but, in retrospect, I now understand what was happening inside my body, at the cellular level, was very troubling. Symptoms had accumulated over the years, some of which were explained away by medical doctors as a result of genetics, yet other indicators of my poor state of health were more difficult to diagnose or explain away so easily.

On **December 4, 2002**, after four years of allopathic medicine failing to explain the unusual sets of symptoms I had been experiencing, my perception of a healthy body was shattered! I was diagnosed with *terminal cancer*: *non-Hodgkin's lymphoma*[1], *low indolent follicular, stage 3a*. My condition was critical! Furthermore, a mere three weeks later, when all tests had been completed, my condition was downgraded even further - to the most acute diagnosis possible. Since the cancer was now in my bone marrow, it was determined to be 4b, the very last stage ultimately leading to death! Tumors were in my upper diaphragm: neck, shoulders, chest, and underarms, as well as in my lower diaphragm, including my stomach and groin. I was extremely fatigued, unable to sweep or wash the floor, or even carry a handbag. The abundance of tumors in the lymphatic nodes of my neck and shoulders even caused a dislocation of the joints, which only a chiropractic adjustment brought some relief from the unbearable pain in my arms.

Almost every evening, both during and immediately following the evening meal, I would experience symptoms of shock: diarrhea, nausea and vomiting; rapidly followed by alternating bouts of cold chills and hot flashes; as well as deepening anxieties and feelings of overwhelming panic. I subsequently learned, through research and the experience of detoxification, that those were symptoms of toxic attacks - and that the negative reactions were simply attempts by my body to warn me of an impending catastrophe. My liver was overloaded with toxins and, therefore, could not support the digestion of larger meals. In addition, one of the more than 500 functions of the liver is to balance the body's natural hormone levels, but the overload of toxins prevented this process from occurring effectively. As a result, anger became a part of my 'new character' - and it took months of additional searching to discover that this too was the result of a weakened and stressed liver. The loss of independence that this disease created had a profound effect upon me. My husband had not only become the maid, cook and chauffeur, but on many evenings, he often literally had to be my baby-sitter, as I could not be left alone due to the all consuming fear that threatened to overwhelm me.

The oncologist explained that low, indolent cancer meant that it was a slow moving cancer, and, normally, I would have had from five to seven years to live from the onset of this disease. That date was initially pegged as 2000, but I now understand that 1998 would have been a more accurate date, as that was the time my symptoms had become significantly more pronounced. The cancer was quite literally beyond

---

1. There are 29 known types of lymphomas.

the point where allopathic medicine could save me. Chemotherapy might be used to clear a blockage, or to relieve pain by reducing the size of a tumor, but this kind of lymphoma had a 'brain of its own' and a more virulent cancer would eventually return, sooner than later in another part of my body, most likely in my brain. Yet, I was still offered three choices: a low dose of chemotherapy in pill form; aggressive doses of chemotherapy by injection; or to take a 'wait and see' approach. The oncologist believed all three would get me to the same place at the same time - **death!** He predicted that a more aggressive form of cancer would return following each chemotherapy session, until it eventually killed me. I chose to wait. Conventional medicine was no longer a viable option for me.

During this process, it was easy to understand why someone without any prior knowledge of the dangers of chemotherapy might initially choose to go that route. My initial reaction was: "Get the cancer out of me now! I don't care how, just do it!" However, as my research continued, I gained more knowledge, and with that knowledge came empowerment. That process changed my initial knee-jerk reaction to one of calm and determination based on understanding. I learned that once the body's immune system is returned to peak performance, the tumors would completely dissolve. I needed to believe that; it was a real test of faith. In the meantime, detoxification would relieve some of the pressure on my liver, as well as reduce the anxieties and panic attacks that resulted from the accumulation of toxins. A lack of knowledge also created even more apprehension, as there were times when it felt as if the contrasting emotions of fear and courage were fighting a war within the confines of my body.

Looking back to **December 2002**, I now realize that I was in shock. The trip home was one of silence, accompanied by more than a few tears that escaped as droplets, running in slow motion down my cheeks. My husband, Jim, was rather stoic, but upon our arrival at home, held me in his arms tightly. It seemed as if he never wanted to let go. At the time, I recall asking if he were okay? His response was that it was not about him, but about me. Jim then suggested that he should call our three children. They were aware that I would have received the test results earlier that day and would be anxious to hear from us. Although the words *terminal cancer* had initially knocked me to my knees, many of my past life experiences had somewhat prepared me for that moment. At first I agreed, but within seconds replaced that initial response with an emphatic no! I reasoned that it was necessary for me to make those calls, as such an important call coming from Jim might have led them to believe I was really going to die of cancer, and I did not want to leave them with that rather bleak prognosis. With that more considered response, I had begun to achieve balance, to adjust my stance towards this disease.

My daughter, Tammy, was at work and called before we had the opportunity to contact her. After hearing the news, she quietly suggested that she would come over immediately with the grandchildren, Benji and Katie. Charlene, my other daughter, was a lot like her Dad; rather stoic, but I knew them both too well. Driving to our home, Charlene recalled thinking that whatever it took, she would be there for me. Our son, Dan, was taking an important test at work and could not be readily contacted, so I called his wife, Stacy. She had just lost her father to colon cancer only a few months earlier, and as a result, left work directly to join the rest of the family who were gathering at our home. When Dan arrived, his primary concern was whether I was suffering any pain. No doubt he was remembering the amount of pain that Junior, Stacy's father, had endured during the months that preceded his passing. Dan was quite relieved when I assured him that I was not in pain, while the others were buoyed that I was not depressed with the potentially devastating news received earlier that day. Quite the opposite, I was ready for the fight for my life!

In the beginning, writing this chapter was relatively easy from an emotional standpoint, but during the process of editing it became an important life lesson that I would never forget. Normally, I deal with most problems by working diligently, and in attaining knowledge in order to make more informed decisions. As a result, it was normal for me not to take hours or days before committing myself to a course of action. In this particular situation it was literally minutes after the original diagnosis that I began to ask questions - important questions about the possibility of finding other, perhaps more natural, ways of healing my body. Although the process of jumping immediately into a research mode was very beneficial in locating much needed answers, it was not one that encouraged facing life squarely and directly. To achieve fullness, life must be experienced and felt, but I did neither at that time. It took three years, and a progression through several other life-threatening health issues before I finally resolved the past and began to move forward. When I was diagnosed with *terminal cancer*, I had spent mere minutes in tears, then put away the pain and got on with life, things I had routinely learned to do since early childhood. As a consequence, the process of re-reading and editing my personal story developed into a nightmare that had to be faced - and resolved - before this illness annihilated me. It was necessary to let the tears flow, to permit pain and vulnerability to emerge, and allow anger to surface - within myself, with God and with a conventional health care system that I felt had failed me! Unfortunately, modern medicine tends to simply disguise or negate symptoms with medication or surgery, and in doing so often fails to correctly identify and eradicate the root causes of illness. That is what had happened to me! It was also critical to learn how to give permission to others to comfort me, something that had not been easy in the past. Unfortunately, I had learned those early lessons far too well, and had routinely put my feelings aside, as simply as returning a book to its place on a shelf.

On that watershed day in 2002, everyone was willing to join me in my battle. It was essential to locate as much information as possible about *non-Hodgkin's lymphomas*, especially the variety with which I had been diagnosed. My daughter-in-law was a real trouper. Having lost her father to cancer only a few months previously, she eagerly shared information learned through his illness and subsequent death to help guide me on my own journey. For example, her specific knowledge of an immune builder, *Tahitian Noni juice*, has been prominent in my recovery as well. Information on the body's immune functioning, and in my case, an absolute absence of functioning, was a beginning upon which to build - and that knowledge gave me hope.

To improve my immune function I immediately eliminated all refined, chemically altered or synthetic sugars[1] from my diet. As a consummate chocolate lover this was not an easy task, but the prospect of living beyond the sentence I had been given was a strong inducement for change. I also made many other nutritional changes within the month: the elimination of red meats, which the liver can have difficulty processing; all hydrogenated oils, which create free radicals; bleached flours with questionable nutritional value, unwanted chemical additives, as well as processed dairy products that could facilitate cellular growth, including cancer cells. As a result, my chocolate cravings soon became a non-issue. Once the initial cravings had passed, life without chocolate became quite tolerable. Today, for special holidays or events, I buy dark, organic Belgian chocolate, containing no dairy, waxes or sugars, to make almond clusters or other healthier chocolate treats for my family.

Changing my diet completely was not an easy task. In the beginning, there were many frustrating days on which I experienced alternating bouts of anger and depression. Fortunately that was only during the period of transition. As the weeks passed, my emotions became more balanced and stable. For those who find change or renewal difficult, remember that many changes can often be cemented into the subconscious if performed diligently for as little as three consecutive weeks. Cravings often become a non-issue and that makes it easier to implement other changes required to reduce or eliminate illness within the body.

1. It has been demonstrated that a single bottle of regular soda pop has the ability to suppress the immune system for up to six hours; and now (Halifax Herald, July, 2007) even moderate diet pop consumption has been implicated in five major areas of disease as well.

Within five days I had figured out what I absolutely needed to know to rid my body of cancer. Now I had to set this plan in motion - I must prevent toxins from entering my body in order for it to be able to work on those toxins already present. Then I had to devise a way to rid my body of fifty-plus years of toxins. Most of the frustration in the latter phase of my recovery centered on locating food and personal care products that did not contain toxins. In fact, I asked: "What in hell didn't?" However, I immediately stopped dyeing my hair, which I discovered was actually more white than grey. Today, the pigments are slowly returning due to a healthier body - the back and top of my head are now a darker color, while the sides and front are beginning to move in that direction as well. It is remarkable what proper nutrition can do.

Within the first month, I also ceased using nail polish, changed my shampoo, soap, toothpaste, laundry detergent, as well as many other household and personal care products. I also introduced rebounding to move my lymphatic fluid; experimented with several detoxification methods such as *Epsom salt soaks*, dry saunas, and dry brushing, as well as adding green tea to my daily regimen. I also drank four ounces of *Noni juice* daily, added two tablespoons of *flax oil* (an *essential fatty acid*) mixed with one-quarter cup of organic quark. Both had an unpleasant taste at first, but as my taste buds changed, I actually began to enjoy them.

Each day was spent reading yet another book, searching on the Internet, and communicating with others to learn as much as I could about cancer in general, chemotherapy, the body, and what I now have come to call 'natural medicine'. At the time, it was not an easy task as the daily toxic attacks were still occurring. There were times I would be wrapped in a blanket with a bowl at my side should I not make it to the bathroom in time to vomit. Those frailer moments were hidden from friends and family. Jim and my naturopathic doctor were the only ones who experienced these emotions first-hand, but there were times I was even able to hide them from myself. Dr. Bruce Hayhoe, my naturopath, who eventually became my teacher and mentor, supplied me with my first book: *How to Fight Cancer and Win* by William Fischer. The information in this publication taught me valuable lessons about protecting cells in the body through the inclusion of essential fatty acids (*EFAs*) in my diet. Later I learned more about the partnership between *EFAs* and quark (a German cottage cheese) and their combined role in increasing oxygen in the blood that had been stolen by cancerous cells. Subsequently, I was also able to teach others, including Dr. Hayhoe, with my common sense approach to the diagnosis. The entire world is a university if one utilizes all aspects of the wealth of knowledge that surrounds us, especially if a common sense approach is applied to the synthesis of information.

On **December 9, 2002**, while on a trip to Ottawa to visit my siblings, I gained additional strength. Each member of the family offered to be bone marrow donors, if required, although my brother Bob cajoled that he was so tired all the time it might be better to leave him until last! After that trip, I returned home with a very significant book that gave me even more hope: *Alternative Medicine: The Definitive Guide to Cancer* by Burton Goldberg. In that publication, thirty-seven physicians had researched and catalogued a wide range of safer, non-toxic, and successful (proven) treatments and practices for reversing cancer through natural, alternative or complementary medicine. I was both astounded and elated to find so many possible treatments in a single publication.

From **December 17th** to the **21st**, I made daily trips to the hospital for what seemed like every x-ray and scan known to man, from the top of my head to the tips of my toes. At least it seemed that they were being thorough! On **December 23, 2002** it was confirmed that the cancer was in my bone marrow, as well as throughout my body. As a result, it was difficult to focus on Christmas, an important event in our family life, with x-rays as daily reminders that this year might be one of my last. Christmas was always one of my favorite times of the year and it was especially meaningful that year - and has been ever since. It was not only the prospect of having, perhaps, only one or more Christmases together as a family, but my husband suggested another factor - I had given family members permission to spend more time and money that year - on me! On Christmas day, I cried when I saw the card attached to a gift from Jim. It was a digital camera. He knew that I loved photographs; the card read appropriately: "For those treasured moments caught in time".

The months from **January to April 2003** were spent combating daily bouts of depression with an exercise program, while the toxin attacks were reduced with detoxification methods described earlier in this chapter. In **2004**, I began using organic coffee enemas for liver detoxification, and by **2005** became more knowledgeable about cellular detoxification methods. Still **later in 2005**, I purchased an energy balance cellular detoxification machine for my own use, which I now employ in a new health-consulting venture. By that time, I was able to fill in some of the blanks between allopathic medicine and more natural approaches to healing. I was also frequenting health food stores, discussing new products with staff and customers, and contacting manufacturers via the Internet. I continued to read magazines such as *Vista*, *Canadian Health*, and *Alive*.

There were many setbacks and the path was not always smooth. For example, my dietary changes created power conflicts with my oncologist. During visits to his clinic, he would upset me with rather off-hand comments such as: "Why would you give up something you enjoy, when you are going to die anyway?" He then referred me to a registered dietician, as he did not believe in my protocols, or in the information I had obtained from a nutritionist. At first, the dietician seemed upset with my decision not to include dairy in my diet. That immediately put me on the defensive, and I had to summon up courage to defend that decision. At the time, I felt I had to convince her that my decision was a considered one, and that I was, in fact, eating properly. To make the visit more positive, I had produced a monthly chart of my food consumption, which made it more difficult for her to respond too negatively. In fact, as a consequence of our conversation, I came to believe that I was actually eating a more nutritionally sound diet than her. As a result, that appointment strengthened my resolve to continue on my chosen path. Subsequently, I have learned that many dieticians generally view standard food guides in relation to the average person's body according to age and sex, whereas most nutritionists or nutritional consultants take an approach that recognizes each person as unique and works with the person's symptoms in relation to their specific quality of nutrition required. The former is especially true of many hospital-based dieticians, but today, thankfully, there is a gradual increase in the number of dieticians who have begun to adopt the latter, more individualistic, approach when dealing with clients.

By **February 2003**, after learning that an acidic pH often creates a vacuum for disease, I was able to return my pH to a normal alkaline state. But in March I ran into a crisis that pushed my pH back to acidic levels. My mother had passed away on the eleventh day of that month. That change, combined with the toxins remaining in my body, caused me to become severely agitated, followed by bouts of anger and depression. When friends and relatives came to the funeral parlor to show their respect, I was physically too weak to stand and greet them. About that same time two new tumors also appeared, one on each side of my neck. I was frightened, devastated! I had learned through research that cancer, as well as other forms of illness and disease could be defeated by natural means, but had not found any specific references to the type of advanced stage lymphoma with which I had been diagnosed. Fortunately, I already knew the factors that influenced pH[1] readings, so it did not take long after this incident to do the necessary work to return my urine pH readings to a healthier alkaline level. However, what I did not realize at the time was that urine pH was not sufficient in itself as an indicator for wellness. It was only in **2004** that I discovered more about testing my salivary pH[2].

At **the end of February 2003**, it finally hit me - illness and disease in the body could be cured if the body were given the proper tools and conditions to do so. Subsequently, between February and May of that year, I developed a program entitled *A Journey to Wellness on B.A.L.A.N.C.E.: nature's way to heal your body* and began to deliver that program through the YMCA only three months later. Helping others to help themselves was gratifying - and that positive attitude benefited me physically as well. However, after working with the program for a while, I realized that four hours were insufficient to bring about change in a life that is filled with illness or disease, although it appeared to be optimum information for preventative health care, as well as a reasonable place from which individuals could begin to reverse disease. That is when, with God's guidance, I began to collate and organize materials to support the initial program with additional workshops. The latter ultimately led to the development of this book, written with the intent of developing material that would not confuse readers with unnecessary complexities or hidden agendas. What was required was a more direct approach with personal examples included as often as possible. However, during the attacks brought on by an overload of toxins, it was, at times, difficult to concentrate and extract common threads from the material I read. Thankfully, my past experiences, continuing research and problem-solving with others had given me the tools and tenacity to continue, so I soldiered on!

Early in April 2003, I ceased the consumption of all dairy products, except quark. By the middle of April, I began to notice a significant increase in my energy level, and eventually was relieved of anxieties created by toxins and/or allergies that I had accumulated since the early 1980s. I could even drive myself to appointments - the old Susan I used to know was nearly back! My body was exhibiting other signs of improved health: thicker hair, softer skin, and no more plaque on my teeth. Although my body was not where I wanted it to be ultimately, there were many promising signs, and I learned as I progressed.

May was a distressing month as I broke my big toe. To many this may seem a trivial event, but for someone already diagnosed with a major illness, it weighed heavily upon me, adding to the existing burden on my body, both physically and emotionally. When surgery, or in my particular case, a broken bone occurs, the body's immune system normally kicks in to repair the damage and as a result, it has less time to work on other issues, including the reduction of tumors in the body. In

1, 2. The concept of pH will be dealt with in greater detail in Chapter Three. See also Appendix C (pp. 281 -282) and Resources II (Web sites - pp. 315 - 6) for scientific explanations of pH and pH testing.

this situation I ended up with a virus, nausea and extreme pain on my right side. Unsure about the larger picture of my health, I was afraid, uncertain how to deal with this event. Still, my faith in conventional medical treatment had been ingrained in me from my past, so my first visit was to my family physician. He was somewhat apprehensive about my decision to use natural health approaches to healing and seemed rather unsure of what to do with me. As a result he recommended that I go to the hospital outpatients' clinic, where subsequent tests confirmed that I had actually contracted a virus. By that time, my bowels had ceased functioning for over twenty-four hours. A comment by the attending physician that I might eventually require surgery to unblock the bowel scared me. In fact, I was on the verge of panic! Most practitioners of *modern medicine* do not consider constipation a significant issue unless it persists for four or five days. But, I did not want to wait and took immediate action by obtaining an appointment with my naturopath, who immediately taught me how to massage my colon to relieve this condition. The massage began just below my diaphragm at the liver, then across the transverse colon and down the left side of my body. This procedure apparently moved the intestine away from an enlarged node blocking my intestines. My bowels eliminated in short order. Additional vitamin C, *Noni juice*, *Kyolic garlic* and exercise helped relieve the viral symptoms, while the pain in my right side eventually subsided. It also improved my mood, helping me through a rather difficult moment in time.

In **July 2003**, I was sent to a specialist to aspirate a cyst on my thyroid. It took three separate visits, as they were looking for indications of thyroid cancer, but found none. Again, I refused an anesthetic for this procedure in order to prevent further toxins from entering my body. The process was not painful, and when viewed in combination with an earlier experience during a bone marrow test, it supported my decision to avoid anesthetics and pain medications as much as possible, as many of them may not only have been unnecessary, but in my case would have likely increased the level of toxins in my body. **At this point I had drawn an absolute line in the sand with respect to toxins entering my body**. I also refused further x-rays[1], making a decision to opt for one only if my body experienced pain or impairment from a possible blockage – and only if more natural methods could not be utilized to help that situation. It took two visits to the oncologist before he understood that when I said no, I meant no!

Some readers may wonder why would I seek the services of an oncologist while going through natural healing. When the short-term medical coverage through my employment expired, it was necessary to establish a long-term disability claim in order to

---

1. See more on Diagnostic x-rays and radiation treatments in Chapter Five.

obtain the financial means to at least partially cover expenses for a naturopath and nutritionist; to ensure that death benefits were available; and to maintain, to some reasonable extent, our previous standard of living. Even with the modest compensation I received, nothing covered the additional costs of organic food, supplements or traveling considerable distances to seek the assistance of natural health practitioners. But both Jim and I felt these expenses were absolutely necessary for me to heal, as well as for our future together. In addition, if I really wanted to become healthy naturally, I was advised to take time off work to allow the body to heal. That further reduced our income at a time we really needed more, not less. Unfortunately, services provided by naturopathic doctors and nutritionists are not covered by provincial government Health Insurance Plans, and few of their services are covered to any extent by many private medical insurance plans. This is something that must change in the future.

I also applied to the health benefits section of the Canada Pension Plan, a federal government health insurance program. I had been paying premiums through employment insurance (EI) and Canada Pension (CPP) since I was sixteen. But both the Canada Pension Plan benefits program and the disability insurer denied these claims, stating that I was not sick enough according to their standards. Imagine that - after having received a letter from the oncologist who stated unequivocally that I was terminally ill and was going to die. It makes one wonder who is responsible for writing those regulations, and based on what logic?

Then, to obtain long-term disability, the insurers made an appointment for me with a psychiatrist. I was advised to keep that appointment, as they would no longer correspond with me on this subject if I did not. The psychiatrist was quite surprised with the response of the insurance company, but after he filed his letter of support, I was finally able to establish a claim.

I did not reapply for Canada Pension benefits as the entire fiasco was such a negative experience, and to heal naturally requires one to remain positive. That is difficult to do in today's world. To heal naturally one must visualize being healthy, but to access the funds I had worked so hard to acquire, I was forced to proclaim that I was not only disabled, but was going to die. That certainly was not positive, but rather the complete opposite of what was required for me to become healthy again It was a paradox that had to be overcome.

It is crucial to understand that when someone is informed that (s)he has a terminal disease, that such information is according to one tradition and one tradition only - that of allopathic medicine - and there may well be other alternatives to consider. When the subconscious is given no hope, an individual can move rapidly towards death, quite often without just cause. As stated earlier, the body can heal itself when the proper conditions and tools are available to do so. Finding those conditions with help from others, including medical doctors, naturopaths and nutritionists is crucial. Reducing toxins from all sources (including toxic medications), undergoing detoxification, the inclusion of proper nutrients, immune builders, and hope gives each person the best chance to live. And first on that list are toxins, which must be removed, not added to the body's burden.

At the beginning of my diagnosis for cancer, had the information gathered for the writing of this book been readily available to me (in a single book or location), without having to research and test each situation as I went along, perhaps what took me almost three years to learn could have occurred over a much shorter period of time, even as little as several months. That is what I hope to give to each reader of this book, much as Judit Rajhathy did with her seminal publication, *Free to Fly: a journey toward wellness*. Unfortunately, I did not have the advantage of reading Ms. Rajhathy's book until I was many months into my research and had already begun the detoxification process. While my liver would have required two years to completely regenerate, had I known about this book, as well as other information earlier, the process would certainly have been much less stressful. Although my emotional link to illness was only hinted at slightly in the beginning of this chapter, it was not until much later that I came to realize the critical impact that emotions[1] had on my health.

Reversing illness or disease is a unique process, somewhat akin to peeling an onion. Not only does the body heal itself from the top down and then inside out, but it also heals from the most recent illness (in my case, terminal cancer) through past stages in one's life. As each layer heals, the next one is ready to be worked upon. Each layer is hidden by symptoms from the previous stage and it is not until that layer is repaired, that the next becomes apparent. All illness or disease has an emotional attachment and those issues will often relate back to childhood situations. As such, resolution of an attached emotional issue must occur before moving forward through the next layer. To achieve this resolution I utilized several books, researched the Internet, located a spiritual medium, as well as a program entitled *The Way of the Heart*TM.

---

1. The subject of the emotional context for illness and coping skills to handle one's emotional responses is dealt with at some length in Chapter Seven.

I also had help from my naturopath and nutritionist, as well as self-analysis utilizing *muscle response testing (MRT)*. It is also necessary to come to terms with the illness or disease itself. The latter can be completed with the help of a health practitioner who can check one's subconscious levels through *MRT*.

Once the cancer was in remission, the next step on my journey was to begin to support a weakened *liver* and *pancreas*, which had created a pathway for body wasting, known as *cachexia*. After that I had to deal with a yeast condition (*Candidiasis*) that had caused digestive issues and another bout of acidic pH. After that there was *adrenal fatigue* that affected both the *thyroid* and *parathyroid*, which along with arsenic poisoning, eventually helped to create a blocked lymphatic capillary; as well as other health-related issues, including an *under-active stomach* and *parasitic infestations*. Re-building my immune system was a vital part in this process, along with the removal of environmental and emotional toxins, from childhood to the present. My journey was rather long, as I had to learn at each step. It was not found in a single place, in plain black and white to read and follow, but required many books and many sources of information from which to glean what was essential for me to heal.

The personal relationship with my husband also changed following the diagnosis for cancer. At first, I felt that he pulled away emotionally from me and became distant. It appeared as if Jim was subconsciously protecting his heart. If I died it would hurt, but if he slowly stepped away now, he may have unconsciously thought it would be less painful. But we were lucky. We had always communicated our feelings to one another, so we talked it out and then worked with the naturopath as a team. However, another aspect of our relationship was less fortunate - our sexual relationship had changed as well. At first Jim was afraid he might hurt me, and, perhaps, at a subconscious level, he also feared that he might 'catch' my disease. Then later, we could no longer be spontaneous with one another. The process of stopping long enough to assess the situation made us realize that each time we had intercourse my body received more of Jim's toxins. Due to the excess levels of toxins already in my body, each time we were intimate my body produced a negative response. Often a virus would appear and I would have to add extra *Noni juice* and *Kyolic garlic* to gain control again. At that point, we began to use condoms regularly and Jim began to detoxify his body on a regular basis.

Blood tests, observation of tumor growth and the regular analysis of symptoms became my constant companions, as well as guidelines and directions for the future. However, x-rays were not an option for me as a diagnostic tool. The body tells us what it needs on a daily basis, and cancer, although a very serious disease process, it is just as much a symptom of problems in the body as a headache or stomachache. Cancer is a symptom of a malnourished body due to many of the following: weakened cells, lack of appropriate amounts of pure water, excess protein intake, insufficient carbohydrates, environmental and emotional toxins, improper nutrition, as well as a lack of exercise, fresh air and sunlight.

The body is the first to warn us when something is wrong; it talks to us through the experiences of pain, pleasure, anxiety or even feelings of relaxation. Unfortunately, it is not always easy to take the time to listen to the body, and most people are not well versed in what their body is saying to them. They have not been trained or educated in this very important skill. The position one should adopt is to determine the cause for each symptom, and ascertain whether those causes can be reversed, rather than seeking out medications that may simply postpone or mask those symptoms.

Editor's Notes on reading and using this book:
A detailed chronology of the author's illness from her first benign tumor in 1976 to allergies and food poisoning in the early eighties, through an entire series of devastating symptoms during the later years of the last two decades, ultimately leading to the diagnosis of *terminal cancer* in 2002, is detailed in *Appendix A*. This appendix also chronicles a very real failure on the part of specialized or compartmentalized allopathic medicine, which unfortunately treated each episode or condition as separate incidents or illnesses, while her body gradually broke down, resulting in an inevitable slide into a state of chronic disease with the ultimate diagnosis of **4th stage terminal cancer**. This chronology not only describes each episode or stage of the disease process, but also presents a **retrospective analysis of the most likely cause or causes of each event or illness.**

Although it is fascinating reading, the information in this chronology overlaps much of Susan's personal story thus far, and is not essential before proceeding through the subsequent chapters of this book. Therefore, it has been placed as *Appendix A* of this publication, giving readers a choice of turning the page to proceed to Chapter Two (**B** for body, the first letter in **B.A.L.A.N.C.E.**) or reading *Anatomy of Illness and the Development of Cancer: a Chronology* on page 273 before doing so. Many readers may also find the latter chronology a good summary once the entire book has been read. It is a choice each reader gets to make!

The remainder of Susan's **personal story** is included, as relevant and appropriate, in each chapter of this publication. These personal anecdotes are intertwined with research on how readers can reverse disease if they are currently ill and live a healthier life in the future by following this advice. Susan's personal story, which relates to the content of each chapter, have been designated by placing the text between two *medieval garlands* as follows: Shorter passages were often placed in rectangular boxes within the body of the text to assist readers to maintain the connections and threads of the essential messages of the publication, as well as to explain Susan's progress, including setbacks, during her journey towards wellness.

The book not only includes one individual's personal recovery from the very brink of extinction in this mortal world, but also includes extensive research from the allopathic and 'alternative' medical literature, as well from the vast world of natural healing. We trust that the substantial amount of information and research contained in this publication has been presented as simply and clearly as possible, although we recognize that the scientific and medical information can be somewhat technical at times. The appendices, footnotes and references to web sites or reference books were included for those who want more detailed research - without interfering with the flow of the main story.

The chapters are inexorably linked to one another as they unfold to tell the story of Susan's recovery from cancer and triumphant return to wellness through BALANCE. **However, each chapter is also a complete concept in itself**, and some readers may wish to skip to a section that is particularly relevant to their own personal situations before proceeding to the remaining chapters. That will work as well. **The order is less important than eventually reading the entire book to uncover the intricate healing connections that result from knowing one's body well and giving it the support it requires to heal itself.** It is anticipated that this process will provide each reader with the information and tools required to travel from a state of illness to one of wellness, and to remain healthy and happy in the rather complex, but often toxic, world of the 21st Century.

Much of the material is relatively easy reading, albeit some information is rather complex and will require time to distill and incorporate into one's base of knowledge. That is why this publication has also been **indexed**: to enable readers to easily locate and/or to return to selected concepts or topics; to use this publication as a reference book on specific health-related issues or concerns; or, indeed, to use it to begin their own research on conditions or illnesses of particular interest to them. Such approaches will not only permit readers to emulate the processes followed by the author on her path to recovery, but should assist them in tailoring that research to their own situations.

So make your choice now.

"Nature is the healer of disease"
(Hippocrates, 460-377 BC)

Chapter Two

Body

The Role of Symptoms

Are symptoms diseases in themselves; are they warning signs for the body; or are they precursors of something more serious? The truth is they are primarily warning signs, but if ignored, misunderstood or covered up by medications, they could easily develop into a more serious disease process. Unfortunately, in our modern world, the first choice often is to treat symptoms as individual issues, and not assume they are signs of some larger problem within the body. Seldom do sufferers look for the root causes of illness or pain within the body, but rather begin immediately to search for ways to treat these symptoms - to allay or remove the negative experiences through medication. Consider the following example. How often do individuals choose an antacid for heartburn, or take pain medication as a first choice for a headache? The next time a headache comes along, listen to the body before popping pain medication. Take time to ask this question: "When was the last time the body was replenished with a glass of water?" Drink a glass or two (about one bottle) of water; then wait up to twenty minutes to see if the headache is still an issue, and, indeed, if pain medication is still required. In most cases, the additional water resolves the problem. If the pain remains, by all means, alleviate the pain temporarily with an appropriate medication, but if the symptom persists, begin your search for the source or cause of the headache. A similar procedure can be followed for back pain, as spinal discs are somewhat like sponges, which require appropriate amounts of water to function properly. The latter solution may take a few days of ensuring that proper amounts of water are consumed daily. (See more on the subject of water later in this chapter)

Coffee drinkers, as well as some who drink darker teas or colas, often suffer from cyclical headaches. In many cases, these headaches are symptoms of withdrawal from the caffeine contained in these drinks, as well as the effects of an increase in the level of dehydration of the body. Caffeine dehydrates the body, and rather than adding fluid, it actually depletes the amount of water in the body. So instead of the usual mid-afternoon coffee break, why not take a 'water break' instead to increase one's level of energy. So keep a bottle of water close by at all times.

Have you ever wondered why conditions such as *athlete's foot* or *jock itch* occur? Or do you simply apply a cream or spray to 'treat' these conditions without any thought about what those treatments actually accomplish? Do you love peanut butter (peanuts are also commonly known as ground nuts as they grow in the soil like tubers) or button mushrooms? They both contain fungus, which may be one reason why an individual may have increased levels of toxins in his or her body. Too much of either or both of these foods, or indeed many other fungus-containing foods, have been known to contribute to, or aggravate fungal infections such as athlete's foot, fungal nails or jock itch. If a fungal infection is suspected, try removing the potentially offending foods for a week; then re-introduce one food, followed by another about forty-eight (48) hours later, and observe the results. In most cases, the itch will first disappear, but return with the re-introduction of the food, a situation that occurred with my husband. Other common *fungal-bearing foods* include grapes, Brazil nuts, and many cheeses, especially aged ones. Natural treatments and allopathic medical therapies for dealing with fungal or yeast infections will be presented in subsequent sections of this publication. Readers may also wish to obtain a copy of *The Yeast Connection* or later publications on this topic by William Crook, M.D.

Take Charge of the Body: Deep breathing exercises

Begin by taking a good look at one's body! However, before beginning this process, it is important to relax and take some deep breaths. Deep breathing is very helpful if one is stressed due to illness, and especially so if it becomes difficult to concentrate without becoming anxious. This breathing technique will help the body to relax. A subsequent chapter, number seven, will include more on breathing, along with *visualization techniques* that can be most beneficial to one's health.

Take a deep breath through one's nose; not just from the lungs, but from one's entire being. Do this on the count of four; hold this breath for a count of seven; then release it through the mouth for an eight count. Repeat these steps for five to ten minutes. This exercise can be done almost anywhere, and it is very calming. Counting while breathing in this manner removes negative thoughts and reduces the stresses of everyday life, while enabling the mind to slip into and remain in the moment.

I often use the above technique to relieve stress, or to simply oxygenate my body. This breathing technique is also very useful when used in conjunction with visualization. In December 2002, the latter was crucial to help me get through a potentially painful *bone marrow procedure* referred to in Chapter One. Through my investigations, I had realized that this procedure was not a simple 'walk in the park'. Prior to my appointment, I was in a small cubicle with my husband, waiting my turn to walk through a door where an oncologist would then drill two small holes through my hipbones to draw out fluid. Nearby, another patient was having this same procedure performed on her, and within moments her muffled cries could be heard in the distance. Talk about scary! A bit later the woman appeared and had difficulty walking, but made a valiant attempt to compose herself, despite dabbing an occasional tear from her eyes.

In my mind, I repeated: "This will be fine, I can do this". When it was my turn to lay on the bed, on my side with my knees curled up in a fetal position, I began the breathing exercise described above, in conjunction with a visualization technique. My vision was of being with my husband Jim, on a white sandy beach in the Caribbean, gazing out across the bluest ocean, as we lay side by side, gently rocking back and forth in a hammock. Before long, the doctor said the procedure was completed and that I could leave. Some bruising was evident for a few days, but that was the extent of the pain. I had also refused the pain medication that was offered. I had felt it unnecessary and it would have only added to my toxic burden. This particular breathing technique was learned a few years back through reading Dr. Andrew Weil's books, *Eating Well For Optimum Health* and *Spontaneous Healing*.

The body visualization: beginning the journey
The body tells its story through the symptoms displayed. To learn how to really stop, look and listen carefully to the body may require the help of a friend or family member willing to give up a few minutes of their time to help one perform a close visual examination of one's body. Remember, that another person will generally see things more objectively during this process. In the course of a formal presentation on wellness, individuals often partner up with a stranger, and although it is a bit different in this context, readers may wish to give that a try. Ask someone that may be seated nearby on a bus or at the next table during lunch. Step out of the box; there is nothing to lose!

Listed below are negative symptoms related to the body visual examination, along with boxes to check as appropriate. A few spaces (marked as 'Other') have been left for items noticed that are not on the chart. Have a chosen partner take a good look at one's body. Help that partner by being objective and not overly sensitive at what is initially discovered. Choose a day when one's nails are not polished, and when lotions, creams or makeup have not been applied to the body.

Hair:	Mouth:	Lips:
☐ Thin	☐ Plaque	☐ Dry
☐ Dry/dull	☐ Receding gums	☐ Cold Sore
Eyes:	**Tongue:**	**Face:**
☐ Red	☐ Thick coated	☐ Dry
☐ Flaky eye lids	☐ Dry, rough	☐ Oily
☐ Dull	☐ Ridged edge	☐ Blemishes
☐ Seepage	☐ Deep crack in center of . . .	☐ Color off

Nails:	Overall appearance:	
☐ Thin/transparent	☐ Overweight	
☐ No half moons	☐ Underweight	
☐ Splitting	☐ Other _____	
☐ Spots/ridges	☐ Other _____	

What was learned about the body? Discuss what was learned with the person who helped with this examination. Prior to reading this section, would what was discovered during this exercise have been as important? Should it have been? These findings are the ways the body has to tell its story, and with the help of a naturopath or nutritionist, one can usually find answers to many complex health issues. Taking time to '*stop, look at, and listen carefully*' to one's body is a process that should be carried out on a regular basis. Each body is unique and time must be set aside to ensure that one's health is a priority. The conditions listed in the self-examination above do not constitute a healthy body.

One example: half moons (*lunula*) on the fingernails:

Healthy fingernails have a whitish half moon, known as *lunula* (based on their lunar shape) at the base of the nail. This feature is prominent on the thumb, index and middle finger, but is rarely seen on the ring finger, and almost never on one's pinky. Nails contain three layers of protein fiber, including keratin, which is the primary constituent. Keratin strengthens nails; prevents them from splitting; and utilizes B vitamins and zinc to keep them healthy. Missing half moons may be a symptom of a parathyroid issue. The parathyroid also regulates the calcium ion homeostasis of the blood, and an imbalance or lack of homeostasis can create more significant problems than simply missing half moons. This imbalance can result in painful muscle spasms and, ultimately, the destruction of bone. The parathyroid issue could also be the end result of adrenal fatigue, and once the fatigue has been resolved, the missing half moons may return.

The purpose of the 'stop, look and listen' exercise clearly demonstrates that symptoms occur long before full-blown health issues develop. However, even knowing this, it is still possible to miss signs (symptoms) as occurred during my own recovery. For example, an episode with bottled water, that had contained excess levels of arsenic resulted in anemia, ultimately producing a domino effect with my health. I knew that more symptoms had appeared, but did not take sufficient time to follow the impact of these changes to fruition, although, fortunately, the impact of this particular setback with arsenic was reversed rather quickly through juicing, rather than through a proposed blood transfusion. This incident and juicing will be discussed more fully in a subsequent section of this chapter.

A second example involved a situation where within an hour of eating a sandwich consisting of almond butter and sliced banana, I became so sleepy that I actually dozed off while standing in church. It was extremely difficult to think, as if my brain had just shut down. While dealing with the anemia and a blocked capillary, I had ignored this particular symptom until other, more troubling, symptoms had appeared. This included extreme fatigue upon waking or at three in the afternoon; craving salt and low blood pressure; and / or occasional 'weepy moments' for no apparent reason. A third symptom had also occurred many years earlier. I would often drive my car to go shopping, then get to the stop sign near my home and not remember why I was in the car or where I was going. I now realize that those events were caused by *adrenal fatigue*.

I had assumed the anemia had caused my blood pressure to drop and had activated the blocked capillary as well. To help relieve that symptom I would eat non-hydrogenated sea salt potato chips, perform a chest massage, and perform some light exercise. It was not until the lump caused by the blocked capillary had dissolved, and a subsequent attempt to remove the chips from my diet, that I recognized that eating them had been a craving based on a deficiency, and without the added salt, my blood pressure would actually drop again.

In hindsight, I now understand that the dozing off in church and other similar episodes of fatigue were actually symptoms of hypoglycemia. Separating the banana and almond butter worked to relieve the symptom, but I still had to find the cause. That opportunity came in the form of a short course on *adrenals* presented by the *Canadian School of Natural Nutrition*, which my daughter was attending. I was granted permission to attend this session as well, and at last, discovered an explanation for my own situation that finally made sense.

The stress that the excess levels of arsenic had on my body had affected my adrenals, which in turn, interfered with the production of cortisol, which regulates blood sugar, as well as the opening and closing of blood vessels and capillaries. The arsenic was a critical stressor that adversely affected my adrenal function, the resolution of which could well be a significant part of the wellness process for many individuals.

Once I knew which issue that produced each symptom, I began to work with the naturopath to resolve them. I took a homeopathic adrenal supplement that was checked for compatibility with my body via *MRT*, and rested in bed until seven am each day. I also included a morning and afternoon nap in my wellness regimen. Adrenal fatigue is one issue that individuals cannot work through, but rather must 'rest their way out of' to heal properly.

There are also relatively simple tests that individuals can perform at home to determine if they have an issue with their adrenals. (See *Appendix* E, pp. 284-286 for further information on adrenals and those tests.)

Genetics:

Is the assignment of blame and acceptance of genetically inherited factors (i.e., from parents, grandparents, or similar to siblings) the usual thought process one encounters when family-related illnesses or disease processes occur? While genetic factors do play a part, it is only when the body is imbalanced that symptoms such as cataracts, kidney stones, high blood pressure, or certain types of cancer, will appear. Illness will usually follow the weaker structures or connections within the body, but those connections are not inevitable paths that must be followed. Most people do have control of the extent to which many of these issues or diseases will affect them individually. Disease is not a foregone conclusion. Each body is unique, and each one has the ability to heal itself if given the appropriate conditions to do so.

At age 50, when I was diagnosed with cataracts, I questioned the ophthalmologist as to why this could have happened. His reply, "This is a result of your genetics". My mother had developed cataracts a few months previously and he suggested it simply ran in the family. However, with subsequent research, I discovered that an acidic pH, as well as an accumulation of heavy metals that were retained in my body as a result of many years of factory work, may have played a significant role in the development of these cataracts. They had likely contributed to kidney stones years earlier. Today, I would argue that utilizing the B.A.L.A.N.C.E. program, this condition could have been reversed and the cataract surgery might have been avoided. While the latter statement may seem somewhat sensational to some, the knowledge gained through research, as well as the changes I had experienced personally, has certainly reinforced this belief.

In 2005, I began a natural health-consulting venture to help individuals to bridge the gap between natural therapies and conventional allopathic medicine. I also performed energy balance cellular detoxification therapy, which is a process that removes toxins through the larger pores of the feet utilizing foot baths and a machine that first adds negative, then positive ions to the body, similar to the way in which magnets attract and repel. Sea salt is used as a conductor. When I first met one of my clients, she had a degenerative eye disease for some time. After only four detoxification sessions, as well as the addition of *essential fatty acids (EFAs)* to her diet, she commented that her eyes now had a definite sparkle in them. Before her next treatment, she went for an appointment with her ophthalmologist, who had expected to find further degeneration, but was surprised when the degenerative disease was, indeed, no longer present. Today, she has 20/20 vision. This is but one of many small '*miracles*' that can occur when toxins are removed and the body receives appropriate nourishment.

Harvey Diamond, author of *Fit for Life 3*, certainly got it right when he referred to the concept of seven stages of disease. Disease can be reversed at any of these stages, as long as no damage has been done to one's organs and that no vital part of the body has been removed via surgery. Stages may vary slightly in order, depending upon toxin levels and possible genetic predisposition or weaknesses. Illness begins from the inside out, then top down, as does the process of healing. Since it takes approximately two years to completely change old cells to new ones, the process of healing in this manner does takes time.

> The physical conditions and trauma experienced over the years prior to the diagnosis of cancer spoke to me on a very personal level, while others I met while compiling information for this book confirm that my case was not an isolated incident with respect to Dr. Diamond's concept.

When an exercise on this topic is presented to a group of participants, the seven stages of disease listed below are carefully reviewed with each participant utilizing a rather interesting process. A different colored post-it note is assigned for each stage, and if participants feel comfortable doing so, they raise their hands to indicate each stage of disease into which they believe they fit. Then an appropriately colored note that represents that stage is positioned on their body. It is quite revealing to see the number of colored post-it notes in the room once the list has been completed. More than a few individuals, who assumed they were rather healthy, and had only enrolled in the course to ensure they stayed that way, were somewhat shocked with these results. After this process, many were surprised to learn they were not as healthy as they would have liked to be or had assumed they were. It was a real wake-up call for many of them!

The Seven Stages of Disease[1]

1. *Energy* is the essence of life. When the body is unable to generate sufficient energy to eliminate toxins, warning signs appear. People are often described as being "tired, as well as sluggish", and begin to gain weight, which only adds to their burden.

2. *Toxemia*: toxins begin to saturate the blood, the lymphatic system as well as other bodily tissues. In this state, the body attempts to flush toxins and one experiences discomfort.

---

1. For more information on the 'Seven Stages of Disease', read *Fit For Life 3* by Harvey Diamond.

3. _Irritation_: the skin may become itchy, or nausea and queasiness may occur. Individuals become easily agitated, nervous, depressed, experience headaches, minor aches and pains, bad breath, or complexion problems.

4. _Inflammation_: In this stage the body is intensely trying to restore itself. This stage usually involves pain. Pain has a purpose; it is a warning sign, specifically designed to protect the body. Pain is the body's way to indicate that it has far too many toxins to deal with. Rather than working to remove toxins, most individuals simply take drugs, which actually increase the level of toxicity in the body. Conditions such as tonsillitis, appendicitis, arthritis, colitis, sinusitis, swollen glands, dermatitis, fibromyalgia, lupus, allergies, as well as specific heart conditions are but a few of the disease processes the body could exhibit at this stage.

5. _Ulceration_: At this stage cells are now being destroyed. Lesions occur inside, as well as on the surface of, the body. Cankers, ulcers, and psoriasis, are a few of these conditions found at stage five.

6. _Indurations_: Tissues harden to form tumors or cysts. Most are benign at this point.

7. _Cancer_: Research indicates that one in three people in North America currently develop cancer.

Remember to review the list of seven stages of disease and compare them with your own health issues. Note all the stages discovered, even if surgery has occurred in the past and that item is no longer an issue for you. Use the spaces below to document the results in order to retain the information for future reference.

1. _____

2. _____

3. _____

4. _____

5. _____

6. _____

7. _____

Were there any surprises? How did that feel? Remember, it is possible to reverse all seven stages of disease as long as organs are not damaged or have not been removed. Even then it is possible to become healthier, more energetic, and be a more active participant in life.

Looking inside the body:
Do not simply dismiss symptoms lightly as indicated in the following statement: "Oh, I get heartburn because I eat the wrong kinds of foods". A healthy body should be able to consume most foods in reasonable quantities and not experience undue distress. What about heat or cold? Do extreme temperatures affect one's body? For example, must the heat be turned up, and then down quite often or do readers constantly put on and take off layers of clothing?

> In my own case, I no longer experience 'heartburn', yet still eat the same vegetables that previously caused the indigestion. In the past, I would have been uncomfortable in any extreme temperature, but my inner thermostat is now fantastic. Previously I had found it difficult to remain in a sauna for more than five minutes, but now enjoy a fifteen to twenty minute session, and can go directly from the hot sauna into the cold air outside. I love the way the latter experience feels on my body.

Blood and urine tests:
The value of making appointments with medical doctors, a naturopath, and a nutritionist were explained in the introduction of this book. The information gathered through these visits, coupled with reading and research, can help individuals to become extremely knowledgeable about their own body and to act decisively upon that knowledge. It is an empowerment that comes from knowing one's body, but to know it fully, it is essential to have blood and urine tests performed. Recent tests results can be obtained through the medical doctor who requested them, but remember to ask for copies of past results as well. The cost to make photocopies of these results is usually nominal. Remember that medical doctors are only human, often overworked, and each doctor likely has different ways of dealing with patients. When lab tests are returned, some medical doctors review each report in detail, while others may just simply take a quick glance, looking for significant anomalies. In the latter situation, a single report might well be regarded as acceptable, but how many patients actually remember if the doctor compared the latest report with previous ones? Or how many patients raise questions about a report or take notice of the range of tests reported upon?

The diagnosis for terminal cancer, as well as the books I read, gave me the power to take responsibility for my own health. I requested copies of blood and urine tests over the past five years. At first, my doctor had been somewhat resistant to my request. Although he did not consent immediately, I knew my rights in asking for copies of my own personal information, so I persisted. Many medical practitioners often have legitimate concerns about giving patients that much information, fearing that it could lead to self-diagnosis, with the distinct possibility of worsening a health condition. While this may be true for some, it is important to consider each person as an individual and base such decisions on the competency of the patient or someone with power of attorney to act on their behalf. Viewing each person as a whole, rather than as a list of symptoms, should lead to a more partnered approach to healing.

After obtaining a complete set of these tests, I was able to compare my results over the last five years. My knowledge of computer spreadsheets enabled me to produce a graph that was much easier to comprehend and permitted me to spot trends. Medical journals on the Internet helped me obtain a precise definition and explanation for each test. What I discovered was a real eye-opener! First, only those lab reports that had an L for low, or an H for high beside a specific result, received particular attention from most medical doctors. Secondly, there was a definite trend over the past year. While a few of my tests had dropped only slightly each time, and no single report was, in itself, something to be particularly concerned about, when compared with other test results over that year, there was a definite pattern, and certainly enough of a pattern to suggest that my health was in a steady decline. I also noted my pH levels had dropped and asked my doctor why that fact had not been noticed. His response was similar to the above, in that changes in test results were not always noted unless L (for low), or H (for high) were indicated alongside the test result itself. Individual tests are important, but readers should also be aware of small changes that occur over time, as often it is those trends that are the more important indicators of one's overall health.

Conventional tests for the presence of heavy metals are costly and, therefore, are not normally requested by most medical practitioners. Neither are tests that evaluate the body's level of magnesium. Information in Chapter Six will clearly illustrate that lower levels of magnesium are commonly found in patients with serious disease processes, such as cancer, heart disease or diabetes. That is why it is so important to have these tests performed, especially if one has been employed in an industry that produced 'pre-VOC'[1] free' **(see footnote at bottom of page 44)** or lead-based paints, or used other products that contained metallic toxins, pesticides, or organic solvents. Prescription medications, especially ones that contain lithium are also of concern and those levels should be checked as well.

The following chart lists a number of conventional medical tests that are available through blood and urine samples. Take responsibility by reviewing those test results, and attempt to comprehend the meaning of each test in relation to the quality of one's health. Get assistance if required - it is the only body you have in this lifetime!

TEST	DESCRIPTION	NORMAL RANGE
pH	alkaline level	7.35 - 7.4
white cells (leukocytes)	protect cells in the blood by attacking bacteria through capillary walls	4.0 - 11
red cells	transport oxygen and removes carbon dioxide; contains iron in the hemoglobin	4.00 - 5.50
hemoglobin	iron rich protein component that carries oxygen to the body tissues	115 - 155
hematocrits	anemia or iron and vitamin deficiency	0.37 - 0.47
platelets	cells that help blood to clot	150 - 400
lymphocytes	part of the lymphatic system; white cells that fight bacteria, fungus, and disease	19.0 - 48.0
monocytes	made in the bone marrow; kills bacteria and regulates the immune response	3.4 - 9.0
neutrophils	white cells fight infection by forming pus; and are produced in the bone marrow	40.0 - 74.0
eosinophils	related to allergies; component of white cells that recognizes foreign bodies	0 - 7.0
absolute lymph	part of the white cell count	0.90 - 5.2
BUN	blood urine nitrogen (kidney function test); excess protein will cause high readings	2.5 - 6.4
bilrubin	digestion and bile test for jaundice, liver anemia and bile impairment(e.g., gall stones)	0 - 17
ALT (SGPT)	liver enzyme function test	30 - 65
AST (SGOT)	liver enzyme function test	15 - 37

1. VOCs are *volatile organic compounds* commonly found in paints and solvents prior to the 1990s. Today, due to federal and provincial or state legislation, most paints for home use do not contain VOCs, albeit there are many commercial products that still contain these compounds. These substances include many families of organic solvents such as many aldehydes, almost all ketones, many alcohols and ethers, plus most cyclic-ring compounds, PCBs, pesticides, including many aerosol sprays and some air fresheners Many are known cancer-causing agents, so great care must be exercised in using them.

Carbon Dioxide , bicarbonate and *LDH* (*Lactate Dehydrogenase*) levels:
Two rather important test results include one's carbon dioxide and bicarbonate levels, as they are indicators of the body's acid/base balance. High *LDH* readings, especially if it is in excess of 139 U/L on the standard scale, may well indicate the presence of specific types of cancer, stroke, advanced kidney and/or liver disease, Muscular Dystrophy, or even the presence of a parasitic infestation. Stress can create digestive problems, a systemic yeast infestation, or adrenal issues in the body, as well as increased levels of *LDH*. *Lactate Dehydrogenase* is an intra-cellular lactic enzyme that increases when the body is experiencing acute or chronic conditions causing tissue or cellular destruction. That situation allows *LDH* to be released into the bloodstream. The latter can also occur when elevated carbon dioxide and/or bicarbonate levels upset the acid-base balance of the body. The liver then processes the lactic enzyme and converts it to glucose. The presence of large amounts of glucose creates a vicious cycle, as even more *LDH* is released into the bloodstream. This continues at an accelerated pace as the cancer cells feed on the glucose. The liver becomes overburdened, causing many cancer patients to die from liver failure or body wasting. Conventional allopathic medicine suggests that the destruction of cells may be stopped by chemotherapy, which certainly can work in some situations, but for other forms of this disease, it is often only effective for a short period of time.

Always remember that natural medicine assessments should be balanced and confirmed with conventional allopathic medical tests and evaluations.

When cellular and tissue destruction occurs, high levels of *Lactate (Lactic Acid) Dehydrogenase (LDH)* are released into the bloodstream. Elevated levels of carbon dioxide (CO_2) and bicarbonates (HCO_3^{-1}) also indicated an acid-base imbalance that was likely caused, for the most part, by emotional stress, either conscious or subconscious. For my oncologist, those high levels were strong indicators that chemotherapy must be administered - and soon! However, given the parameters of allopathic medicine, and lacking knowledge of more natural approaches, my oncologist did not realize there might be other possible paths to consider. Although I knew of such possibilities from my own research into natural medicine, this new information had not completely replaced my own entrenched biases for modern medical approaches, and, as a result, I was even reluctant to discuss these test results with my naturopath at that time. That was a mistake! In 2002, I was informed that chemotherapy treatments would also likely activate cancer cells in other areas of my body, and, with or without chemotherapy, I would likely die. The latter was what challenged me to begin a more thorough research of natural approaches in the hope of finding other possible treatment alternatives. However, it was almost too late to find another way! Poor digestion and sluggish bowel elimination were the latest evidence of the ever-increasing destruction taking place within my body. I experienced indigestion, gas, burping, constipation and diarrhea. My stools smelled and sank rather than floated, and were yellow in color, not brown. Having had regular bowel movements for over a year, this new experience shocked me. A visit to a nutritionist was my first stop. She instinctively knew my body required beneficial bacteria to prevent gas, as well as sweet bitters for indigestion. She also suggested digestive enzymes to help digest food in my smaller intestine. Each of these processes helped me to overcome these negative experiences. (This topic will be covered in more depth in Chapter Seven.)

There are several approaches used in natural medicine to detect the presence of toxins, vitamin and minerals deficiencies, as well as to determine the presence of healthy cells. These include applied kinesiology or muscle response testing (MRT); iridology (using the eye to identify illnesses); hair analysis to determine levels of toxins and mineral deficiencies; *Dark-field Microscopy*, or *live blood cell analysis (LBA)*, as well as a visual inspection of the tongue . . . and more.

When signs of disease are present, standard blood and urine tests are often insufficient to obtain an accurate diagnosis, especially if a toxic overload is suspected. A combination of tests, including hair analysis, iridology or dark-field microscopy, as well as standard blood and urine samples would give a more complete picture of one's health at a particular point in time. It is important to look specifically, for example, for heavy metals, pesticides, and/or VOC contamination; as well as issues related to the body's immune function, including liver impairment.

Dark-field Microscopy or *Live Blood Analysis (LBA)* :

Since 1994, hundreds of clinics throughout North America have used *live blood analysis* to help prevent illness, enhance health and treat disease in its early stages. In this way, many disorders can be detected long before standard blood tests can recognize chemical changes in the cells. A finger prick blood sample produces thousands of live blood cells that can be observed by the patient through a video monitor, while the technician analyses it under a microscope. Samples can also be videotaped for future comparison. This particular test can detect circulation toxicity (metals), uric acid crystals, digestion issues (fats and proteins), immunity problems (white blood cells, allergies, yeasts and parasites), and the condition of red blood cells (e.g., vitamin/mineral deficiencies, as well as free radical damage). It is unfortunate that *LBA* is not available through family practitioners as this test is non-invasive and is a quick method, requiring only twenty minutes, to detect a wide range of burgeoning and/or potential medical issues. If readers wish more detailed information on *LBA*, read *Blood Never Lies* by Ted Aloisio.

After researching *LBA* quite extensively and locating a clinic nearby, I setup an appointment for my husband, daughter Tammy, and myself. Not only did I want to know about my own health, but as my husband Jim was beginning to show signs of distress, it was essential to have him checked as well. Jim's hands blistered easily, a sore on his leg was not healing properly, and recently, he seemed to have caught far too many viruses. His last two years had been spent helping me get well and I would have hated for a cruel twist of fate to claim my partner. Jim had supported me from the very beginning, and had eaten the same foods required to help me heal - other than a few items he refused to part with. But he had not taken the time to remove a lifetime of toxins that had accumulated from his years of factory work. I also sought a better assessment of Tammy's health status as she began her own search for wellness.

During the *LBA* procedure, my cells were mostly round, although a few had indentations, indicating free radical damage. In addition, every third cell was smaller than normal, suggesting an iron deficiency. My immune system had improved, but it was still not enough. What looked like broken glass turned out to be a crystal of uric acid, but due to the increased alkalinity of my body, the crystal had shattered. That was a good sign. There were also a few black dots, which represented the remaining toxins in my system.

My husband's blood analysis told a very different story. Jim had quite a few free radicals (cells shaped like old fashioned bottle caps) and many more toxins. In addition, his immune system was even more dormant than mine. His body also contained fungus, which showed up as light circles on the monitor. When Jim saw how healthy my blood was compared to his, he became a convert to, and supporter of, what I had been doing - and immediately embarked on a more intense detoxification program himself. He added extra greens to his list of foods and finally exchanged his peanut butter, containing fungus, for cashew butter. He added *Tahitian Noni juice* to clear up the immune system, and reduced refined sugars and high sugar-containing foods for the same reason.

Tammy's cells were linked together like sausages. These pictures, as well as what we had learned previously were clear indications that Tammy required supplemental enzymes as soon as possible. After reviewing the videos, we were also able to clearly see the differences among all three immune systems: Tammy's immune cells actually morphed from one shape to another; mine moved slightly, while Jim's had little motility. With direction from the naturopath who performed the analysis, I began a regimen of aerobic oxygen drops to further boost my immune system. (See more on this latter concept in Chapter Five). We were amazed at what we had learned during this session, and looked forward to being re-tested in a few months to measure our progress. It is hoped that by recounting these personal stories, readers may be helped to understand the importance of taking responsibility for their own bodies - and ultimately, their own health.

A number of years before we became involved in these natural approaches to health, Jim had been diagnosed with high blood pressure. At that time he was prescribed blood pressure medication that had to be taken on a daily basis. After a year on medication, Jim's blood pressure had actually increased, so his medical doctor felt that an even stronger dose was required. However, having become more skeptical than in the past, we took the prescription to a local pharmacist to inquire about the new dosage and its possible side effects. We were told it was a strong medication and that Jim would not be able to discontinue it without a medical doctor's assistance - or he could die! That frightened us. So rather than purchase the new medication at that time, we spent sixty dollars on a blood pressure monitor. Jim tested his pressure four times a day for a month and found that the readings were consistently low. This would explain why he felt cold most of the time while on this particular medication, and more importantly, suggested he might not have even required the original blood pressure medication.

So, what had been happening to Jim over the past few years? Further research on blood pressure proved to be a blessing as we discovered there was something known as the *'white coat syndrome'*. The blood pressure of certain individuals will actually rise when they visit a doctor or hospital and apparently that was what was happening with Jim. So, Jim took the month long documentation of his blood pressure readings to the doctor, along with the device itself. The doctor tested Jim on both instruments to ensure that those readings were accurate. It was determined that he likely had *'white coat syndrome'* and had not required the original prescribed medication, let alone a potentially more dangerous dosage. That is why it is critical to listen to the messages the body is sending us. Ask questions of the local pharmacist, as their knowledge of pharmaceutical medications is usually far more extensive than most medical doctors. Utilize all practitioners, including naturopaths and nutritionists, before beginning medications with potentially negative side effects. The removal of toxins from the body by various detoxification methods, including cellular detoxification therapy, has allowed many individuals to return to their family doctor to seek a reduction in their blood pressure medication. Toxins alone were the cause. Remember that high blood pressure is a symptom of an imbalanced system, and, for the most part, should not be treated as a medical condition in and of itself.

You only have one life to live, so take good care of it!.

During my own recovery, I had many fearful moments, and none more stressful than the time my red blood cells, both *hemoglobin* and *hematocrits*, had dropped to extremely low levels. My oncologist wanted me to have an immediate blood transfusion followed by chemotherapy, as he felt these low readings were definitely cancer-related. My family physician also had that same concern. He informed me that when blood hemoglobin readings drop as low as 80 g/L (or 9.4 gm/dL in USA) patients are always given a blood transfusion. However, I still believed they could have been mistaken, as my *blood platelets* and *neutrophils* were actually back to normal, and my *LDH* and *AST (SGOT)*[1] test levels were lower than previous readings. In addition, I feared that I might receive another person's cancerous or pre-cancerous cells from this transfused blood and be required to begin my hard work from scratch again. Readers will recall that it takes two to four years for cancer

---

1. *AST (aspartate aminotransferases enzymes); SGOT (serum glutamic-oxalocetic transaminase)* Readers who wish to obtain the precise definitions for, or learn more about these terms would be best served by an Internet search, beginning with www.pennhealth.com.

to become apparent or obvious through most conventional medical tests or visual tumors. So, at that point, I requested ten days to work on raising my blood hemoglobin levels by more natural means.

I returned to my naturopath for advice. I also decided to obtain a comprehensive evaluation of our drinking water. My grandchildren also had low hemoglobin, and although not as low as mine, it seemed to me that we had only one factor in common: the bottled water we all drank.

When the water was tested, it revealed elevated levels of arsenic, albeit within safe limits according to most North American standards. [*Note that most Western European countries have more stringent standards with respect to allowable levels of arsenic.*] Individuals in a weakened condition such as mine are even more susceptible to arsenic contamination, so I immediately stopped drinking that brand of bottled water, and replaced it with water that had been first filtered, then boiled. Later, I purchased a *Nikken Pimag*™ water filtration system. In the meantime, I faithfully juiced with fennel bulb and carrots; beets with greens attached, as well as turnip and alfalfa. By the date of my next blood test, my red blood cell count had increased and I was, for the moment, out of harms way. Since that time, whenever bottled water is required, I choose imported European brands, such as *Evian*™.

WATER

The body consists of approximately seventy-five (75%) percent water, with the brain even higher at eighty-five (85%). As a consequence, water should be ingested on a daily basis equal to at least half of the body's weight, where pounds of body weight are equated to water in fluid ounces. For example, a person weighing 130 pounds (about 59 kilograms) should consume 65 fluid ounces (half of 130) or 1950 milliliters (about two liters) of water daily. Divide those totals by eight ounces (or 240 milliliters) to obtain the number of glasses of water required. For most individuals, that would be about eight to ten glasses of water daily. Remember to increase one's water intake by one-third if disease is present in the body.[1, 2] (See footnotes on the opposite page.) For conversion from Metric to USA or Imperial measures, consult the *Conversion Chart*, page 139, or the footnote at the bottom of page 134.

Water Quality:

In rural areas, all wells must be tested professionally for the presence of bacteria, heavy metals and other potentially toxic substances. Usually a hospital, pharmacy, or local office of the Department of Environment will perform this service for a reasonable fee. In towns or cities the municipal water supply will likely be treated with chlorine. Fluoride may also be present in some municipal systems.

If one has a health problem, it is essential to begin drinking healthier water immediately. Natural spring water is best and glass bottles are preferred. Unfortunately, plastic containers seem to be the only kind available for bottled water in many regions. Plastic containers may be used for short durations, but never for long-term storage of drinking water. Natural minerals in drinking water should also be at least 150 p.p.m. (parts per million) in total; sodium levels should be less than 200 p.p.m.; while fluorides are definitely not recommended for any drinking water.

Much of the information gleaned from the 'alternative' or natural health literature would suggest that it is best not to drink water during a meal, but either after or prior to the meal itself. In fact, it is best to drink water half an hour before meals or one half-hour after meals. In the case of fruit juice or sweetened beverages, two hours is recommended. Drinking water during a meal actually reduces the amount of digestive enzymes available for digestion, placing an increased stress on the body to digest food. Adding a slice of lemon to a glass of water will also aid digestion.

If one's urine is light or clear in color, and not a deeper yellow (unless one is taking a B_{12} or B-complex supplement), that is a good sign that the body has sufficient water. Commonly morning urine will be a bit deeper in color, but it should become lighter during the day if one ingests a sufficient quantity of water. Initially, the body will tend to react to an increase in water consumption with more frequent trips to the bathroom. This is especially true when one increases the consumption to suit their body weight. Once the body becomes balanced, the frequency of urination should decrease within three to four weeks.

---

1. **A few words of caution**: some Japanese researchers have suggested that the excessive consumption of water can actually stress and cause damage to the kidneys, so again balance is important. Stick to the amounts recommended for your body weight.

2. As reported on the CTV National News (Jan. 14, 2007) a woman died after drinking four liters of water (without going to the bathroom) in a media contest. A law suit is pending, as callers to the program warned the show producers that it could be dangerous.

Dehydration produces many health issues that can simply be resolved by drinking more water. One common condition, that increased water intake has been known to resolve is incontinence, often referred to as 'overactive bladder'. So, before one succumbs to the lure of slick television ads promising to 'cure' this condition with prescription medications, try increasing your water intake first. A stiff or sore back may also be the result of dehydration, as spinal discs act like sponges requiring lots of water to function at their best capacity. If possible, give the body the appropriate amount of water for at least a month before attempting to medicate any of these conditions.

"Either you are a water filter or you buy one"

(David Frahm, MD)

Living in a community with a municipal water supply produces its own set of problems, but chlorine intake can be reduced to a minimum by adding water filters to shower heads and taps on sinks. These precautions will prevent many toxins, especially chlorine, from coming in contact with your skin, where absorption rates can be high. Large in-line activated carbon filters on the municipal water intake can be very helpful in reducing toxins, but they can be somewhat expensive, as those filters must be changed annually, often at a cost in excess of $500. Bath water should be filtered as well, especially if one soaks in hot water for therapeutic purposes. Keep a record of when the filters were installed and change them on a regular basis. In communities with a municipal water supply, an automatic dishwasher is also a good choice. If that is not possible, run the hot water into the sink, wait twenty minutes for the chlorine to dissipate, before washing the dishes by hand. Use rubber gloves to avoid skin contact with the heated water and vapors (steam) from the hot water as they may also contain chlorine[1]. It is also important to avoid breathing those vapors as well. Readers can also wear light cotton gloves inside the rubber ones commonly used for washing and cleaning. This procedure will provide protection from chemicals in the gloves themselves. It is very important to protect yourself from additional toxic burdens.

---

1. Chlorine can weaken arteries, as well as reducing or eliminating beneficial bacteria in the colon, which can eventually result in a systemic yeast infection.

Filters:

Reverse osmosis filters remove most contaminants, but they also remove valuable minerals, as well as nutrients the body requires to remain alkaline. The water from such filters may also be used for showers and baths, but is not recommended for drinking water, as it is not sufficiently alkaline. Please note that if non-alkaline water is used as the main source for drinking, the body will eventually become acidic. Reverse osmosis filters are also expensive as they produce only a few gallons (about eight liters) of water per day. During this process a lot of water is also wasted and, therefore, it is not considered an environmentally friendly product. These filters do, however, remove more contaminates or unwanted minerals compared to many other types of filters, including aluminum, radium, uranium, fluoride, lead, pesticides, bacteria and organic matter.

Activated carbon filters, also commonly referred to as charcoal filters, come in three basic types: granular activated, solid block and granular activated with silver. These filters do not remove valuable minerals, but can leave certain unwanted substances such as fluorides and aluminum. Solid, block carbon filters reduce water flow that could potentially create an issue with bacterial contamination, while granular activated carbon filters with silver can, over time, increase the level of toxicity within the liver. Granular activated powder is considered the best of the three carbon filters. Although the water is not in contact with the filtering material long enough to remove all toxins, these filters will certainly reduce the amount of toxins the body receives. A Nikken brand of magnetic energy filter, the *Pimag*™, has several stages of filtration that work naturally via gravity flow, including natural ceramic materials; a carbon-based medium; and an ion exchange resin that reduces water contaminants as well as hardness. It also regulates the acidity/alkalinity (pH) balance and, in the long run, actually costs less than bottled water.

If one lives in an urban area with a fluoridated water supply, one suggestion would be to speak with municipal leaders regarding the removal of fluoride from the community water system; then add filters to remove chlorine and other harmful substances from the home water supply.

Be safe!

Essential Fatty Acids (EFAs)

Essential fatty acids are absolutely necessary for the human body to function properly. The body must have *EFAs*, but, unfortunately, unlike many other mammals, humans cannot manufacture them, and can only obtain them from food. A healthy life without the presence of appropriate levels of *essential fatty acids* in the body is impossible, and, in their absence, one can expect many health problems to develop over time.

Without *EFAs*, cell wall integrity can be compromised, allowing toxins to enter, while the cell itself becomes unable to retain valuable protein and other nutrients. In addition, *EFAs* help the body absorb sunlight and assist in the proper functioning of the brain, sex and adrenal glands. Essential fatty acids are virtually required by all cells in the body. They also maintain chromosomal stability; prevent the development of allergies; buffer excess acidity and burn fats. The body also metabolizes *prostaglandins* from *EFAs*. *Prostaglandins* lower blood pressure; relax coronary arteries; inhibit sticky platelets; affect the tone of muscles within blood vessels, and help keep important membranes flexible. They also carry toxins to the surface of the skin, intestines, kidneys, or lungs, where these harmful substances are discarded. In addition, *prostaglandins* produce life energy from foods and move this energy throughout the body. They also govern cellular growth, vitality and one's overall mental state. Finally, they help to transfer oxygen from air into the lungs and through the lung membranes to the cells where the oxygen is utilized. (See Appendix F, p. 287 for further information on *EFAs* and *prostaglandins*.)

If the body has sufficient quantities of *EFAs*, and if *choline* and sources of phosphate are both present, the body can produce *lecithin*, a substance that keeps cholesterol in a solid state and protects it from oxidation. *Lecithin* also prevents gall and kidney stones from forming, as well as helping to dissolve these stones. It is essential for liver detoxification and the transportation of cholesterol, as well as being a vital component of immune cells, which enables them to kill bacteria. In addition, *EFAs* are membrane builders and are essential for the creation of bile, an important component of the digestive process. *Choline* is found in soybeans, oatmeal, cabbage, cauliflower, egg yolks and other vegetables, while phosphate is derived from many plant sources. It is vital to understand the importance of *Essential Fatty Acids (EFAs)* and the role they play in a balanced and healthy body. Continue to read to gain knowledge and empowerment!!

If I were to recommend one single change in readers' nutritional intake, it would be to incorporate *EFAs* in your diet. If your weekly diet consisted of a minimum of four meals containing wild fish (not farmed), lots of organic nuts and seeds, and fresh cold pressed olive oil then an *EFA* supplement may not be necessary. However, in a modern world of less than perfect foods and living conditions, an *EFA* supplement is a wise choice. And one of the added benefits from a diet that contains sufficient *EFAs* is that the skin will generally be clear and smooth with little need for lotions or creams in dry or cold weather. The skin will also be more supple and give one's skin the appearance of youth. Liquid flax, hemp and fish oils are all readily available in health food stores, as are omega 3-6-9 supplements which supply all three *EFAs*. Capsules are also available in most pharmacies as well.

When a degenerative disease is present in the body, use bottled flax oil rather than capsules. This is a faster and more efficient way to help cells recover. One tablespoon (15 milliliters) of flax oil equals approximately nine to fourteen capsules of flax.[1] Two tablespoons (30 milliliters) of flax oil mixed with a quarter cup of quark (German cottage cheese) has the ability to increase oxygen in the blood, as well as having the potential to restore the body's natural interferon and interluken 2, two essential components of the body's immune system that may have been damaged through illness. Note: about 25% of the population may experience some difficulty digesting flax - symptoms are usually mild indigestion with an oily after-taste. In this situation, hemp oil would be an appropriate substitute. Still other individuals may find that fish/liver oils are very beneficial and may be more easily digested and absorbed than vegetable based oils. It is a very individual choice.

Colleen's Story:

In 2006, I had the good fortune to consult with a client who was seeking ways to reverse her recent diagnosis of *fibro-sarcoma* -a rare form of cancer that is often terminal. Her children were still young, and she was fortunate to have a wonderful husband, with an extended family, and numerous friends who were ready and able to support her through the upcoming battle with this

---

1. Approximately twenty-five percent (25%) of individuals have difficulty with the digestion of flax oil and, therefore, may require hemp oil instead. (See also Appendix F, p.289 for more on *EFAs*)

disease. Colleen had been referred to me through a mutual friend. I supplied her with information about the B.A.L.A.N.C.E. program. She also used cellular detoxification foot baths to help remove environmental toxins, and worked on emotional toxins with *The Way of the Heart*™ program. She also decided to go the allopathic medical route involving rather massive doses of chemotherapy. Her husband, family and friends ensured that her stay in the hospital included nutritional support through organic meals, pure juices, clean water, flax with quark, and an immune builder. Following three days of rigorous chemotherapy, as well as during the seven days following treatment, Colleen removed toxins via cellular detoxification therapy. She had initially been cleared of toxins prior to the chemotherapy, but now had even more toxins in her body than when she began the process. However, what intrigued me most was her story related to the testing of oxygen levels in her blood at the hospital. Her doctors had repeated one test several times, and when she inquired as to why these additional tests were necessary, she was informed that her blood oxygen level readings were at 100% of normal capacity, and the medical staff had assumed the lab had made an error, as cancer patients almost always have lowered blood oxygen levels. Obviously, the detoxification process, as well as the addition of flax and quark to her diet, had made a significant difference.

What are *EFAs* and where are they found today?

There are three *essential fatty acids*, two of which have rather opposing effects on the body, ultimately creating a balance within the body. They are *alpha-linoleic acid (LNA or omega-3), linoleic acid (LA or omega-6), and oleic acid (omega-9)*. Both *alpha-linoleic acid (LNA) and linoleic acid (LA)* are poly-unsaturated, while *oleic acid* is a mono-saturated oil.

Alpha-Linoleic Acid (LNA or omega-3):

Flax oil is the richest source of *alpha-linoleic acid*, while hemp oil is second best. It is also found in walnuts, soy, canola, pumpkin, salmon, sardines, mackerel, fish oils (cod liver oil, halibut liver oil, seal oil), herring, tuna, purslane, black currants, wheat germ oil, and many dark green, leafy vegetables. *Alpha-linoleoic acid* is metabolized to form *eicosapentanoic acid (EPA)* and *docosahexanoic acid (DHA)* when there is an excess of *linoleic acid (LA)* present in the body. *EPA* plays a role in reducing blood vessel constriction, while the latter, *DHA*, has, among other beneficial functions, been associated with optimal brain development in infants. These forms of essential fatty acids are found in pelagic, cold-water fish such as salmon, tuna and mackerel. The layer of fat under the skin of these deep-water fish contains the *EFAs*, so it is crucial to eat this portion of the fish and not cut it away.

Symptoms of an *LNA* deficiency include impaired vision, learning disabilities in children, immune dysfunction, lack of motor coordination, tissue inflammation, behavioral changes, edema, tingling in the arms and legs, a general weakness in the body, and dry skin. *LNA* contributes to a wide range of critical bodily functions. It disperses deposits of saturated fatty acids and cholesterol; produces velvety skin; increases the overall stamina of the body; induces calmness; reduces inflammation and the retention of water; inhibits the development of tumors; as well as reducing the pain and swelling of arthritis. *LNA* can also play a role in the destruction of the malaria virus. It is required for brain development, and will lower *triglycerides (TGs)* by as much as twenty-five percent (25%). The body also requires *triglycerides* to insulate the body, help protect tissues, and to store energy. Unfortunately, excess *TGs* are more common today as a result of the abundance of processed foods containing refined sugars and saturated fats, as well as from the excess consumption of food in many contemporary Western societies. Excessive levels of *triglycerides* can eventually lead to disease.

Daily requirements: It takes one to two teaspoons per day of *LNA* to maintain proper health. If, however, the body is deficient in *EFAs*, it takes approximately twelve (8.5 ounce or 250 milliliter) bottles over a few months to produce a dramatic reversal in the health of the body. The best way to confirm the level of any deficiencies is via *MRT* administered by a qualified practitioner, such as a naturopath or nutritionist. Unfortunately, the long-term exclusive use of *LNA* can also create a *linoleic acid* deficiency, but it would take from one to two years for signs of such a deficiency to occur. Again, B.A.L.A.N.C.E. is crucial

Linoleic Acid (LA or omega-6):

The richest source of *linoleic acid* is found in safflower. Sunflower, corn, soy, free-range poultry, grape seed, cottonseed, black currants, and sesame seeds also contain linoleic acid, while smaller amounts are found in flax, in both the seeds and the oil. Symptoms of a *linoleic acid* deficiency include abnormal hair loss; the retardation of growth, as well as behavioral problems in children; arthritic-like conditions; sterility in males; heart and circulatory problems, as well as miscarriage. Linoleic acid helps produce *hemoglobin*, the essential component of red blood cells, and helps cells to generate electrical impulses that keep the heart rhythm in sequence. A prolonged absence of *linoleic acid* can be fatal!

Daily requirements: The daily requirement for *LA* depends upon levels of stress one encounters in his or her life, the level of physical activity and the body's overall nutritional state. Males also require more than females. Generally one tablespoon per 100 pounds (45 kilograms) of body weight on a daily basis would be sufficient.

Oleic acid or omega-9:

The third *EFA*, *oleic acid* or *omega-9*, can be manufactured by the body, but only if the body has sufficient quantities of *LNA* and *LA* as basic building blocks. *Oleic acid* is mono-unsaturated oil found in olives, almonds, avocados, pecan, cashews, filberts, as well as in macadamia nuts. To convert *LNA* and *LA* to essential fatty acids, the body requires vitamins A, B$_3$, B$_6$, and C, as well as magnesium and zinc. Vitamin E also must be available to prevent *EFAs* within the body from becoming rancid. The body generally metabolizes four times more *LNA* than *LA* to produce essential fatty acids.

As a child, I recall that my mother gave us cod liver oil capsules (an excellent source of *EFAs*) everyday, and if we caught a bad cold, we were given sliced lemon heated with linseed oil. Sometime during my childhood she ceased this practice. It was also common to give children a daily cod-liver oil capsule in public schools until the mid-to-late fifties, but by 1960, that practice was discontinued in most school jurisdictions.

During my recovery, I introduced *EFAs* into my daily regimen and believe that my cells have also healed for that reason. Today, my hair is not brittle or as dry compared to previously. In addition, my nails are stronger, whiter, and my lunula have returned. There is a considerable change in my physical appearance, as well as in the way I feel. I have also introduced these wonderful golden liquids to family, friends, and clients. Each person has been able to identify a noticeable change in his or her body in just a matter of a few months.

To ensure the consumption of appropriate amounts of *EFAs*, it is suggested one schedule an appointment with a naturopath or other health practitioner skilled in *MRT*. Using this approach, the practitioner can assess the body to identify the amount required for optimum health. It is important to remember that too many *EFAs* are just as bad for your body as too little. While waiting for an appointment with a qualified health practitioner, begin taking a basic *omega 3-6-9* supplement or one to two teaspoons of flax oil on a daily basis. Remember to purchase supplements with care to ensure they are free from chemicals, sugars, and preservatives, and develop a habit of eating more wild fish, pure olive oil, organic nuts and seeds.

A Bit More On Flax (Linseed Oil):

Flax is far too important a vital source of nutrition simply to note that it is the richest source of *EFAs* and leave it at that. Flax is also known as linseed oil (*lurium usitatissimun*), but ensure that only food-grade linseed oil is purchased. Do not confuse it with industrial grades of raw and boiled linseed oils that once were commonly used as oil paint thinners and oils for furniture wood. Quality linens are also made from the fiber of the flax plant, albeit the process of making and spinning the fiber is a very labor-intensive one. Flax is also commonly added to livestock feeds.

Flax has all the essential amino acids the body requires, as well as the fat-soluble vitamins A, D, E, and the water-soluble vitamins B_1, B_2 and C. In addition, flax contains important minerals such as potassium, phosphorus, magnesium, calcium, sulfur, iron, zinc, sodium, *choline*, plus manganese, silicon, copper, and fluorine. It also contains valuable trace minerals, including aluminum, nickel, cobalt, iodine, molybdenum and chromium. Selenium and vanadium are also found in flax, however the latter were not listed as ingredients to test for when the original research was conducted. As such, these minerals were not even recognized as substances of specific value to humans at that point in time.

Flax contains valuable fiber for the colon, which both assists in regular bowel eliminations, as well as for cleansing toxins. In addition, this versatile food source also contains mucilage, a type of glue that reduces excess stomach acid, aids in the trouble-free passage of stools through the colon to elimination, reduces cholesterol and regulates blood glucose. As such, it is an excellent choice for diabetics. It also helps to metabolize *prostaglandins,* increases metabolic rate, oxygenates cells, and provides energy for the body.

Liquid flax oil[1]:

As a liquid, flax is golden amber or slightly brown in color. Since liquid flax will lose its quality after three months, unless kept frozen, only purchase sufficient quantities at a time to last for that long. Liquid flax should be of a high quality, expeller-pressed or cold-pressed only, and be bottled in small, opaque glass containers. It should also be stored in the refrigerated section of the supermarket or health food store. *It is highly recommended that one use the above description as a guideline for purchasing this product.*

Ground flax seeds:

Only grind half a cup (125ml.) at a time to ensure freshness and keep it refrigerated. Sprinkle ground flax on baked potatoes, vegetables, cereal or use it in a shake. Two tablespoons of ground flax will add the proper amount of *LNA* to one's diet. Ground flax contains more fiber than liquid forms and, as such, will increase stool bulk and may even act as a laxative for some individuals. Begin with two tablespoons and let the body be the judge. If, after a few days, bowel movements are still loose, decrease the amount, rather than removing it entirely. This is not an allergic reaction. An increase in the amount of feces excreted is a normal response of the body when it is first introduced to ground flax. Ground flax can be added to breads, as well as to other baked products, even if heated above 221 F (105 C). However, if a person is unwell, the crust of these breads should be removed, as the center of the bread will have remained cooler while it cooked, while the outer crust would likely have exceeded the optimum temperature.

Optimally, flax should be taken with a *high quality sulfur protein*[2] in order for it to be properly processed by the body. Organic quark (German cottage cheese)[1] is the best of these proteins, but organic cottage cheese may be substituted if organic quark is not available. Throughout this book it has often been recommended that one not consume dairy if one has a disease process within the body. This recommendation is made on the basis of hormone residues found in many dairy products, as well as the simple fact that dairy products can accelerate the growth of all cells, including cancerous ones. However, one-quarter cup (75 ml.) of organic quark taken on a daily basis, along with liquid *EFAs* is still a good choice, due to the additional oxygen it creates in the blood. While

---

1. As stated earlier in this chapter, approximately twenty-five percent (25%) of individuals have difficulty digesting flax oil and therefore, may require hemp oil instead. (Also read Appendix F, pages 287 - 292 for more detailed information on *EFAs*)

2. See more about *sulfur-based proteins* in Dr. Johanna Budwig's research in Appendix F.)

cancer patients should not consume dairy, with the above noted exception, healthy individuals who wish to retain dairy in their diet, should locate a source of organic or hormone and anti-biotic free dairy products, such as those commonly found in many health food stores.

"Anesthetics and many drugs (i.e., sleeping pills, painkillers; prescriptions and over-the-counter medications) separate highly unsaturated fatty acids from their normal association with sulfur-containing proteins"

PROTEINS

Proteins are the body's structural elements for growth and repair of tissue. Most of one's body mass that does not consist of water is protein. Protein, in proper amounts, is very suitable for the body, as it balances the acidity/alkalinity of the body. There are basically two types of protein: complete and incomplete. Complete proteins contain ample amounts of all the amino acids the body requires, and include foods such as meat, fish, poultry, cheese, eggs and milk. Soybeans, tofu, and soy milk are also complete proteins. Incomplete proteins contain only some of the amino acids the body requires, including grains, legumes, and leafy green vegetables. However, a combination of selected protein-containing foods, such as beans and brown rice, seeds, corn, wheat or nuts, can form complete proteins without the necessity of consuming meat. Plants combine sugar with nitrogen from the air and soil to make amino acids. The body can manufacture many of the necessary amino acids if the body either contains sufficient enzymes or is fed appropriate enzymes.

However, there are certain essential amino acids that the body cannot manufacture itself. Roughly twenty-three different kinds of amino acids are required to make human protein. The body makes fourteen of these, but that leaves humans nine short of the total required for optimum health.

These include:

1. *Tryptophan*: makes *serotonin* that calms the body, stimulates growth hormones, and reduces cholesterol.
2. *Lysine*: builds new body tissue and bone, enhances fertility, and improves concentration.
3. *Methionine*: reduces the fat content of the body and protects the kidneys.
4. *Phenylalanine*: reduces hunger pains, helps produce norepinephrine and collagen, and enhances memory and mental alertness.
5. *Threonine*: assists metabolism and assimilation, prevents fat build-up in the liver, and is a component of collagen.
6. *Valine*: promotes muscle co-ordination and goes directly into the muscle, as it is not processed by the liver.
7. *Leucine*: heals skin and broken bones, as well as promoting mental alertness
8. *Isoleucine*: formulates hemoglobin and is used by the muscle for energy.
9. *Histadine*: dilates blood vessels, alleviates symptoms of arthritis and ulcers, as well as assisting in the production of red and white blood cells.

Can all nine be obtained from plant sources? The answer, of course, is yes. It is also important to note that the body absorbs more amino acids readily from intact protein consumed in regular meals than free-form protein from supplements, unless, of course, an individual cannot absorb the intact protein as a result of allergies to particular foods[1]. A prime source of amino acids is animal protein, or products such as milk or eggs produced by them. Animal's bodies manufacture amino acids from the plants they eat. However, unless these animals are fed organic grains[2] without added hormones, a significant amount of animal-based protein contains excess levels of the hormone, *estrogen*, along with antibiotics and pesticides on animal feeds, the latter which can mimic *estrogen*. These excess *estrogens* and *pseudo-estrogens* can cause fibroid tumors, fibro-cystic breasts, breast cancer, as well as other reproductive system cancers, including cervical and uterine in women and prostate cancer in men.

As suggested above, all the protein required by the body can be obtained through the consumption of vegetables, nuts, seeds and beans. However, if it is difficult to give up meat, poultry, or fish - or if one's system requires animal protein, purchase only organic meats, free-range eggs, and wild game or fish to remain healthy as possible. Check with a naturopath or nutritionist first to ensure that such a diet will work for one's body. It is also important that fish be from 'wild' stocks, not farmed. Unfortunately, farmed fish often consume feeds containing growth hormones or animal by-products. Readers should do some research to ensure they know what they are eating!

---

1. Many of the principal food allergies are specifically allergies to proteins; in fact, allergies are defined medically as involving one kind of protein or another.
2. To locate organic or free-range animal protein, including milk and eggs, consult the Organic Growers Association in your own province or state. In Nova Scotia, check with: *The AEHA Guide to Less Toxic Products* (p. 333) or visit: www.lesstoxicguide.com

This book is about balance, and if one ingests too much protein, the excess goes into the body's metabolic furnace for fuel, which is subsequently stored as fat. Too much protein will cause obesity. Excess protein can leave a residue of ammonia (urea) in the body, which is especially toxic for brain cells. An excessive level of ammonia can also be a burden for the kidneys and liver, and could irritate the immune system, gall bladder, colon, and bones. In addition, there are allergies and auto-immune issues that can occur with the consumption of excessive amounts of protein.[1]

When an individual reviews his or her blood and urine tests with a medical doctor, be sure that the *blood-urea-nitrogen (BUN)* level are checked. High *BUN* readings will eventually lead to a loss of minerals, especially calcium, and result in degenerative conditions such as *osteoporosis*. If kidney disease exists, the blood ammonia will rise and brain function can decline. A high *BUN* reading is one of the first critical signals to immediately begin to lower one's protein intake.

What if there is there too little protein in the body? If protein levels are low, wounds will not heal properly, and hair and nail growth will cease. But how much is too much? Tests should be in the mid-range, not high or low-end results. *The Journal of the American Diabetic Association* states, "A diet adequate to cover hunger, and be satisfied with natural foods, is more than adequate with respect to protein."

Dairy protein:

Dairy as a food for humans is both controversial and political in nature. Since it occupies one major food group on both the Canadian and American food guides, it is natural for most consumers to assume that milk and its derivatives are absolutely essential for good health for everyone. However, there are conflicting messages related to dairy products coming from many health practitioners and consumer advocates. On the one hand, there are the overwhelmingly positive, as well as glamorous and witty, advertisements surrounding milk that are sponsored by the milk producers, dairy associations and milk marketing boards, as well as the generally unquestioning support of the allopathic medical community, especially dietetic associations. But many others,

---

1. *Eat Right F4R Your Type: The Individualized Diet Solution to Staying Healthy and Achieving Your Ideal Weight.* (Peter D'Adamo with Catherine Whitney). The essential thesis of this research is that humans have four major blood types and require four 'personalized' diets for each blood type. Some individuals require meat in their diet to remain healthy, while others do not. Please note: if someone who currently consumes meat protein decides to become a vegetarian as a healthy lifestyle choice, ensure that this topic is very well researched. A visit to a naturopath or nutritionist would be a good place to begin.

including the majority of natural or 'complementary' practitioners, as well as many consumer's groups, raise valid questions about the value and effectiveness of milk-based products for many older adults, very young children (under age two), as well as for most immigrants from countries where herding of dairy cows is not a tradition, especially Africa, the Middle East and many parts of Asia. One notable exception is India, where cow's milk is commonly boiled, not pasteurized prior to consumption. Individuals from many of these areas of the world often are missing the appropriate enzymes to digest milk protein or milk sugar, but now reside in North America, where they are often faced with an endless list of baked, processed and packaged foods containing whole milk or components such as whey, casein, powdered milk, skim milk, lactose and others. Many individuals also develop allergies to dairy products, but these often go undetected or are misdiagnosed due to the pervasive nature of these products in our society, as well as the almost daily consumption of small amounts of milk and milk by-products 'hidden' in so many convenience foods.

While milk and its many by-products may be acceptable, even good nutrition for many individuals, for an increasing number of people that is no longer true. It is difficult to say precisely why so many persons today do not tolerate dairy products well. Some have argued it is a result of modern processing that has altered the structure of the dairy products themselves or has reduced their natural enzyme content, thereby making these products more difficult to digest. It is also suggested that those who belong to specific non-Western cultures, or of an increasing age, may not have the necessary digestive capacity or enzymes to utilize milk products appropriately; while still others argue that it may well be the residues from hormones and pesticides found in most feed grains that are culpable in, and contributors to, many nutritionally-related illnesses found in our modern society.

It is not the intent of this publication to assess blame or argue the positives or negatives of dairy, but rather to alert readers to the growing body of research related to specific types of illnesses and their connection to milk-based products; as well as to suggest viable alternatives in the form of 'other milks', including soy milk, rice milk, nut milks (e.g., almond milk), or goat's milk, which like cow's milk, are commonly fortified with extra calcium and Vitamin D. Indeed hormone and pesticide free (sometimes referred to as 'organic') cow's milk is also readily available in most health food stores. In all cases, readers are urged to do their own research on the efficacy of dairy products or suitable alternatives that can supply the protein and minerals required for optimal nutrition for themselves and their families.

Cow's milk has been linked to eczema or asthma in certain individuals, especially in children less than two years of age. Other research also suggests it may be implicated in cases of early juvenile diabetes. Still other studies have demonstrated that as people age, they may digest certain milk products less completely than before. Lactose is a sugar found in milk. Some children, as well as certain adults, lack the enzyme lactase, which allows them to digest this milk sugar. This condition is commonly referred to as *lactose intolerance*. While *Lacteeze*^{TM} is an option for some, the same issues arise if it is not free of hormone and pesticide residues. It should be noted that butterfat, found in certain cheeses and many ice cream products, is a trans-fatty acid - a product that recent research has demonstrated humans should reduce or eliminate in their diets.

Casein, a protein found in milk, is also believed to be an environmental trigger for cancer in certain individuals. One prime example of a 'hidden' food component is *casein*, commonly used in the manufacture of vegetarian cheeses. Initially, that might not seem to make sense to many readers. How can animal protein be contained in a product labeled as vegetarian? The short answer is that it depends upon the definition of vegetarian or vegan, as certain types of vegetarians eat eggs and milk products, and sometimes fish, but not the flesh of animals. There are, however, soy or tofu-based 'cheeses' that do not contain casein. Again, if any of these products are of concern, readers must learn to **read labels**.

As a person living with cancer, I chose not to eat red meat or dairy products, other than the organic quark mentioned earlier. I was specifically concerned that these substances might contain hormones or antibiotics, both of which can increase estrogen levels, or could mimic them in my body. I did not want the cancer cells to divide and grow more quickly as a result of unwanted or unspecified hormones or related substances. The book that gave me the greatest insights into the potentially negative aspects of many processed dairy products was *Your Life In Your Hands* by Dr. Jane Plant. Her research indicated that one person in 10,000 in China develops cancer compared to one in three in North America. The Chinese have a different diet from North Americans, and foremost among those differences is the absence of dairy products. Dr. Plant was terminally ill, but continued her research until she discovered a solution that included the removal of all dairy products from her diet, which in part, helped cure her breast cancer.

In Dr. Budwig's 'cure', it was necessary to combine sulfur-rich protein with flax. Sulfur-rich proteins contain *cysteine* and *methionine*, two amino acids, which are produced only by plants. Cows and goats, as well as many fish, derive this protein from the plants they eat. As Max Gerson states, "Where does a cow get her protein? The answer is of course, from grass!" So if dairy is a concern, why use cows as filters when these same nutrients can be provided directly by plants?

High protein foods, other than animal products:

Protein should be included in all three daily meals, with the least amount of protein in the last meal of the day. The liver also must be supported when the body is diseased, therefore a reduction of protein after two o'clock in the afternoon will help to ensure the liver has the opportunity to process food properly and to regenerate itself.

Peas, beans, and lentils are high in protein and carbohydrates, as well as fiber, *folic acid (B complex)*, and protective *phyto-chemcials*. One has to be careful though to cook those foods well, as many beans and legumes can be toxic in a raw state. Soybeans are high in protein, are heart healthy, contain *iso-flavones* and *phyto-chemicals* that may also protect humans against cancer. Many nuts, especially walnuts, almonds, hazelnuts and cashews are quite high in protein, as are sesame and sunflower seeds. Try to consume a small handful of seeds daily. A small serving of seeds, added to an oatmeal breakfast, will make that breakfast a more complete protein meal.

In 2004, Jim and I visited my older sister Terry, and her husband Norm, who went out of their way to ensure my diet was not only nutritious, but also chemical free. They baked bread, made veggie burgers and served lots of fresh, organic vegetables grown in their own garden, as well as fresh fish. It was a wonderful stay, the food was delicious, and as their home was located on the shores of a lake, it also fed my spirit. The only issue that arose was with the soy milk, when we subsequently discovered that it contained corn syrup. Unfortunately, corn syrup is often worse than many other refined sugars and is certainly a poor choice for a diseased person. Until I began my research I would not have thought twice about drinking this particular brand of soy milk, and, of course, my sister and her husband had no notion that it could be a problem for me.

Soy products should be researched prior to purchase to ensure they contain no *Genetically Modified Organisms (GMOs)*, as well as any added sugars. When shopping for soy milk, I bought a brand called *Natura*™, one that had won awards, as it did not contain *GMOs*. I also made certain only the unsweetened variety was purchased. Due to difficulty of evaluating many soy products, and especially research into their potential impact upon cancer cells, I now choose rice milk products by the same company. To date, research on soy products produced in North American is quite inconclusive with respect to its benefits, compared to Chinese and Japanese soy, which are fermented varieties, and well-known for their healthy qualities. In fact, there is a growing body of research that suggests soy should be used in its fermented form for optimum health benefits.

CARBOHYDRATES

Carbohydrates and sugars are derived from plants, vegetables and fruit. There are two basic forms of carbohydrates: simple and complex. Simple carbs are composed of one (mono) or two (di) units of sugar (saccharides) linked together in a single molecule; (e.g., fructose, glucose and sucrose) and always taste sweet. *Complex carbohydrates* involve as many as 100 to 1000 units of sugars linked in a single molecule. They are pleasant to taste, but not necessarily sweet, such as potatoes. There are two groups of *complex carbohydrates*: those high in fiber (the healthier choices) such as broccoli and lettuce; and foods low in fiber, such as bananas, tomatoes, squash, many types of bread and most pastas, potatoes, and rice. Cereals and grains may be either high or low in fiber depending upon the degree of processing. Always choose unrefined whole grain cereals and whole grain breads over refined and/or bleached flours. After the body digests carbohydrates, it enters the circulatory system as glucose, en route to the cells where it is burned as energy. They become a threat to humans only if consumed in inappropriately large quantities. Excessive amounts of carbohydrates can cause vascular disease, hyperglycemia (one form of diabetes), obesity, hypertension, heart disease, and can upset the delicate balance of hormones within the human body.

Processed foods are those which commonly have a number of vitamins and minerals removed, and where much of the fiber has been stripped away. The body is not designed to thrive on simple fiber-less carbohydrates. *Complex carbohydrates*, with lots of fiber, should be consumed in appropriate proportions for optimum health, as they are a quality dietary source of many vitamins and minerals. They also contain important digestive enzymes when eaten raw. Eating whole fruit results in the inclusion of abundant natural fiber that assists in the proper absorption of sugar. Fruit juices, which are highly concentrated, should always be diluted with an equal amount of water, as this will maintain the flavor, while the body will be more accepting of it.

Mucus is formed in the body by the linkage of sugar molecules (simple carbohydrates). If one suffers from *mucus-related conditions* such as *asthma* or *emphysema*, it is crucial to eliminate all simple carbohydrates, and to temporarily reduce the intake of complex carbohydrates as well. That includes reducing the intake of sweet fruits (plums, peaches, apples) as well as breads, pastas and pastries, a rather difficult task for many. Check with a nutritionist to ensure that yeast is not the cause of the production of excess mucus and/or allergic symptoms.

Type II Diabetics:
It is believed that Type II diabetics, especially those with adult onset diabetes, may have lost some receptors (molecules that carry information between and within cells), such as insulin receptors, which are found on the surface of most cells. With the proper B.A.L.A.N.C.E. as described within this book, that condition could be reversed.

Starches:
Starches are carbohydrates that contain only four calories per gram, whereas the ingredients used as toppings, are usually made from fats that contain as many as nine calories per gram. Starches are required for quick energy; to help the body lose excess weight; as well as to allow the stomach to feel full more quickly and, therefore, help to lower one's total caloric intake. In many cases it is better to keep the carbohydrates in the diet and throw away the toppings. Too much sugar will eventually become stored as fat, while too little can lead to ill health. Individuals, who switch to diets that reduce fat by cutting out most carbohydrates, such as the *Atkins Diet*[1] advocates, may well cause their systems to become unbalanced. There is that word balance again! But remember that the brain absolutely requires glucose to function properly.

Carbohydrate or 'Carb' Cravings:
Dr. Ariel Dalfen, a well known psychiatrist from Toronto, appeared on a Canadian television program, interestingly also called 'Balance'. Her comments related to low levels of carbohydrates and the negative effect

---

1. The *Atkins Diet* also promotes very high consumption of fats.

they could have on the body, especially if someone is depressed. Research has demonstrated that low levels of carbohydrates reduce the brain's *serotonin* levels, which is essential to create happiness and a sense of well-being in humans. If individuals crave carbohydrates, they may be lacking *tryptophan*, an amino acid. *Tryptophan* is converted to serotonin within the body, and helps keep humans balanced! Two examples cited during this program included *seasonal affective disorder (SAD)* and *PMS*. Dalfen suggested a strong link between the cravings of individuals with these syndromes and low *serotonin* levels. Whole-grains, rice, pasta, cereal and fruit have the potential to raise serotonin levels in the body. *Serotonin* affects one's mood, emotions, sleep and appetite, so eat right to stay healthy and happy.

Before one considers the removal of bread from one's diet, remember that even Old Testament cultures referred to bread as 'Manna' or the 'staff of life'. In fact, bread, whether made from ancient grains or ground seeds, has been an integral part of many civilizations for several millennia. So, rather than remove breads completely from one's diet, ensure that those consumed are made from whole, unbleached grains, non-hydrogenated oils, and are devoid of all refined sugars.

Notes:
1. During fasting, the body tends to conserve energy, which results in a decrease in the body's metabolic rate. Also increased activity levels or exercise will actually decrease one's appetite. To help identify the type of carbohydrate, simple or complex, that will be absorbed by the body when a food is consumed, it is crucial to **read labels**.

2. Beans are complex carbohydrates, and if the body cannot break them down, gas may occur in the stomach or bowel. In such cases, the body may lack a digestive enzyme, *amylase*, found in *Beano*™. This enzyme should be added to the diet, rather than taking an antacid, as the latter may only add to one's toxic burden. In many cases, antacids also decrease the pH of the stomach acid and can actually increase the amount of indigestion. These are more good reasons to consult a nutritionist at this point.

3. Please recall the section on *EFAs* and the importance they play in regulating glucose levels. If someone is a diabetic, now may be the time to return to that section and read it again, to understand why it is crucial that the body have adequate amounts of *EFAs*, and how incorporating them into one's daily diet can make dramatic and positive changes in the body.

FIBER

As previously indicated, there are two major groups of fiber: soluble and insoluble fiber. The body requires both kinds to achieve B.A.L.A.N.C.E. Insoluble fiber includes cellulose and lignin primarily found in whole grains, especially wheat bran. Soluble fiber occurs in other whole grains, nuts, seeds, fruits and vegetables. Fiber protects the health of the intestinal tract by increasing stool bulk and decreasing elimination time. Both of these latter processes protect the colon against disease, including *IBS*. Fiber binds excess bile acids, as well as cholesterol, and prevents their re-absorption into the blood stream, while increased fiber can also help to lower serum cholesterol. Since fiber is slower to digest, it is recommended that it be introduced slowly into one's diet until it reaches appropriate levels. Eating too much fiber, too fast, often causes gas and bloating.

Notes:
Fiber supplements, whether in pill form, powders or straight wheat bran, are not generally recommended. Many of these supplements may interfere with the body's ability to absorb minerals and can cause more gas to form in the bowel.

"Foods that lack life cannot sustain life; are eaten too quickly or in an unsettled state may contribute more to toxicity than to health. It is impossible to be in perfect health with poor digestion".

(David W. Rowland in *Digestion: inner pathway to health.***)**

DIGESTIVE ENZYMES

Digestive Enzymes are required when symptoms, such as gas, bloating, stomach distension, constipation, indigestion, or heartburn occur. One such enzyme, amylase, is normally produced in the pancreas, and was referred to earlier as being essential for the digestion of complex carbohydrates such as beans. *Amylase* converts starch to *maltose*, while a single molecule of *maltase* converts two molecules of *glucose*, which is burned for energy by the body. *Beano*™ or other digestive enzymes should only be taken on a short-term basis, as once the cause has been established and reversed, digestive enzymes should no longer be necessary. Remember balance! In addition, many digestive issues can be causally connected to yeast infections, or adrenal malfunction, the latter which can create domino issues within the pancreas, and more. Other enzymes necessary for digestion that are found in the pancreas include *lipase*, which converts fat to fatty acids; and *protease*, which converts protein to amino acids. Additional enzymes, such as those found in the stomach, are included in the next section of this chapter.

THE DIGESTIVE SYSTEM

Mouth:
Digestion begins in the mouth where bacterial growth is reduced; and the teeth and mouth are cleaned.

Stomach:
Protein and fat stimulate the secretion of the hormone *cholecystokinin (CKK)* into the blood to slow the digestive process. Cells secrete gastric juices containing *hydrochloric acid (HCI)*, *pepsinogen*, *gastric lipase* and an *intrinsic factor* (here intrinsic means that it is both essential and contained within the cell) for the absorption of Vitamin B_{12}.

The role of hydrochloric acid:
HCl converts *pepsinogen* to *pepsin*, which then breaks down proteins; liquefies foods; softens *collagen* in meat; hydrolyzes *sucrose*; and precipitates *casein* from liquid milk protein. It also breaks down inorganic mineral compounds found in food into digestible ionic forms. Two important by-products of HCI in the body are *sodium* and *potassium bicarbonates*, which are released into the bloodstream. These are the alkaline buffers that neutralize acidity in the blood. A quick method to determine whether the body requires HCI would be to dissolve four ounces of water with a half-teaspoon of baking soda on an empty stomach. If burping occurs immediately, the body likely has excessive levels of HCI. One or two small burps in five minutes is normal, but if no burping occurs, that would indicate that the body is likely deficient in HCI, and requires a supplement until the cause has been identified. To confirm via allopathic means whether the stomach pH is or is not at appropriate levels, the gastric contents would have to be sampled and tested in a laboratory situation, which would require a referral from one's family physician.

Small intestine:

Acidified food enters the *duodenum*, stimulating the pancreas to secrete an alkaline fluid containing digestive enzymes (*pancreatin*). *Bile* is released from the gall bladder and insulin from the pancreas is secreted into the bloodstream. All nutrients are absorbed through the intestinal wall. Fat and fat-soluble vitamins are absorbed by the lymphatic system.

Liver:

The liver produces *bile* from *cholesterol*, stores and re-packages nutrients that were absorbed through the intestinal wall for cell distribution.

Large Intestine (colon):

Fiber is critical to the healthy functioning of this organ as it fills out the colon, softens stool, lessens colon wall pressure and eases the secretion of stools. Delayed emptying of the large intestine encourages putrefaction and the formation of carcinogens, which can damage the colon and be re-absorbed by the body.

Chapter Notes:

Emotions and negative thoughts affect the flow of digestive enzymes.

Being overweight could be due to sluggish digestion.

Excess salt and alcohol can destroy stomach cells.

Enzymes regulate the nervous system, as well hormone production and regulation.

Yeast infections can reduce or upset enzyme balance (See more in Chapter Four) and create allergic reactions.

Ginger root (250 mg to 1000 mg) has been an effective digestive aid for over 2000 years.

Gas or belching indicates incomplete digestion and potentially sets up a condition in which toxins could overwhelm the body.

Chronic constipation could be an indication that HCl or bile (or both) are required by the body.

Constipation could also be a thyroid issue.

Potassium is important in the synthesis of most enzymes.

If required, digestive enzymes should be taken after the first bite of food.

CHAPTER TWO SUMMARY

1. Take charge of your body and stay healthy. Develop a baseline for the body's level of health by completing the following four tasks:

a) Visit a medical doctor to arrange blood and urine tests along with a complete physical examination. Ask for a copy of the reports, review them, and compare them with previous readings.
b) Arrange to have a hair analysis or an iridology test; followed by *live blood cell (LBA)* testing.
c) Ask a friend to carefully observe your body's external appearance and record what is observed.
d) Make a list of your own symptoms in relation to the *'seven stages of disease'*.

2. Find a good naturopath and nutritionist. Ask them to confirm any supplements that the body may be lacking or has in excess, as well as any allergies that may be affecting one's immune system. To ensure the best possible evaluation, learn how to tap on the thymus located behind the breastbone for a full minute and ensure your water intake is up to par on that day.

3. Have all household water tested. Use filters for bathing and washing and bottled natural spring (or appropriately filtered) water for drinking as required. Record the date when any new water filters are installed and replace them before they lose their filtering ability.

4. North American standards related to the arsenic content of bottled water are too low, and we must pressure the government to change them. In the meantime, track your blood tests to ensure that arsenic is not affecting you. Purchase European bottled water whenever necessary.

5. Is your water consumption appropriate for the weight of your body? Approximately eight (8) glasses of water is recommended for the average body of 130 pounds to perform all necessary functions, which includes the removal of toxins. Those with higher body weights would require proportionally more water.

6.   Incorporate *essential fatty acids (EFAs)* into your life. A diseased individual who does not receive proper amounts of EFAs through his/her diet will require high-sulfur protein along with a larger quantity of liquid flax to repair damaged cells as soon as possible. Flax is the richest source of *EFAs*. Individuals who may have a difficult time digesting flax oil should switch to hemp oil. Ensure that oils are of high quality, are bottled in opaque glass containers, are refrigerated and dated. Also include nuts and seeds in your diet.

7.   Check your cupboards and refrigerator; read labels and identify products that contain hydrogenated oils, refined sugars, bleached flour or artificial food colorings. Make a point to discard or replace these products with healthier food choices as soon as practical or financially possible.

8. Switch to organic foods whenever possible; eat only free-range meat if animal protein is necessary for your particular diet. Readers should investigate *Eat Right 4 Your Type* (Peter J. D'Adamo) or *Metabolic Typing* (William D. Kelley, M.D.), to determine if animal protein is required for your blood type. In any case, be sure to purchase meat products that have not been injected with antibiotics or growth hormones, or have been raised on feeds grown with pesticides.

9. When your medical reports are reviewed, keep a close watch on your blood-urea-nitrogen (BUN) levels to ensure that a protein imbalance is not being created.

10. Do not eliminate carbohydrates to reduce weight. If the information in this chapter is followed there should be no reason to diet for weight loss, as the body should be receiving a balance of protein, carbohydrate, and 'good fats'(*HDL*), along with pure water to help eliminate 'bad fats' (*LDL*) - and to help organs function properly. Since toxins are stored in body fat, their removal will also facilitate a natural weight loss or gain that is appropriate for each person.

11. It is impossible to be in perfect health with poor digestion. Make an appointment with a nutritionist to ensure you are on the right track.

12. Put the "B" back in BALANCE; become healthy and reverse the disease process.

*"Disease will not grow in a
properly alkalanized body"*

Chapter Three

Alkalinity and pH

An alkaline pH is one of the essential factors for maintaining a proper balance within the body, and ultimately is a key factor in all good health. The body has an amazing ability to regulate itself and first among those is maintaining an appropriately alkaline pH. If the blood is more acidic than alkaline, the body will seek out sources within itself to become more alkaline, often extracting calcium from the bones if is not found in the blood serum. This is called free-floating calcium, which can result in arthritis, cataracts, kidney stones, and can eventually lead to osteoporosis. Low pH is also an indicator of an imbalance within the body that must be corrected immediately to prevent disease processes from becoming established. An excessively high pH is also dangerous and can indicate an acidic condition as well, as the body overcompensates by releasing ammonia into the system in an attempt to regulate the imbalance. Only a moderately alkaline blood pH will maintain good health.

pH: an important concept in understanding this chapter:[1]
pH is a measurement of the relative amount of acidity/alkalinity in any system, including blood. It is a technical, mathematical term used by chemists and medical personnel, who created a simplified scale ranging from 0 (maximum acidity) to 14 (maximum alkalinity) for ease of understanding. A pH of seven (7.0) is the neutral point (e.g., theoretically distilled water has a pH of 7). The pH of blood is extremely important. Normal, healthy blood is slightly alkaline, and occupies a very narrow range of pH between 7.3 and 7.4. Outside this range; i.e., beyond 7.4 or below 7.0, body activity is no longer optimal and one's metabolism is out of balance.

---

1. A more detailed and scientific explanation of pH has been added as Appendix C, pp. 281 - 2.

A relatively small change in pH of 0.2 or more is very significant when it comes to blood. It is also interesting to note that human blood pH is very close to the pH of seawater where all multi-cellular life began. Readers should also note that a blood pH beyond 7.9 could be fatal if it remains that high for more than a short period of time. Similarly a pH that is consistently below 6.7 will also eventually create severe health problems as the blood seeks to regulate itself by finding any sources of calcium within the body. Blood pH is normally regulated through the lungs and the kidneys. Physiological and psychological stress can also play a major role in one's blood pH. Having an acidic pH, and ignoring it, is akin to continuing to drive one's car while the oil pressure light is on!

In late 1998, after only a few months of blurred vision, I was diagnosed with cataracts. This condition was similar to the presence of dirt on a glass lens that could not be removed, and often I would remove my glasses in an attempt to see more clearly. Due to my age at the time, fifty, and the fact I was still working full-time where clear vision was a necessity, my ophthalmologist decided to perform surgery immediately rather than wait for them to become 'riper', an expression that ophthalmologists commonly use related to cataracts. When questioned how cataracts could have developed at such a young age, my ophthalmologist informed me it was the result of genetics, as my mom had just been diagnosed as well. Through research, including sources such as the *Cancer Battle Source Book* by David Frahm, I began to realize that there were nutritional reasons for these occurrences in my body. But as this was several years prior to my research and re-education related to approaches used in natural health, I consented to the surgery.

Many individuals also generally attribute the development of kidney stones to one's genetic makeup. In other words, since their parents or siblings had kidney stones, it seems natural for their offspring to have them as well. While it is true genetics do play a role in one's health, if the body were not pre-disposed to poor health through the ingestion of improper foods and beverages or by breathing poor quality air, then genetics would not have an opportunity to play such a significant role.

An example: If an individual is genetically disposed to kidney stones or cataracts, i.e., if either parents or siblings had them, that would be considered a weak point in the body which free-floating calcium could affect. However, if the body were balanced, with the pH and nutrients at appropriate levels, then the body would not have to 'follow' this genetic thread. Toxins also gravitate to the weakest spot in the body and detoxification plays a significant part in rebalancing one's system. Alkalizing the body is part of that balance, as disease cannot flourish in a properly alkalanized body.

Metabolic sub-products, internal mechanisms involved in food processing, as well as a variety of foods in one's diet can influence the pH level. Additionally, what is considered alkaline or acidic is not so obvious, as certain foods that are acidic in their composition can actually become alkalanized after they are metabolized in the body. Such is the case with lemons, a significant source of citric acid, but eating lemons, which have a low pH, actually alkalanizes the body, thereby raising its pH.

Unfortunately, acidic bodies will become oxidized, and oxidation is synonymous with decay. (Consider iron as it oxidizes and turns to rust.) Excessive acidity causes numerous disturbances such as poor skin and weakened hair, nails, and teeth; deterioration of the digestive tract; excitement of the nervous system; muscular spasms and cramps; and a tendency towards depressive illnesses. It can also create enhanced susceptibility to infections, chronic fatigue, sciatica, as well as an overall inability of the body to function properly.

Hydrogen:

The most abundant element in the universe is hydrogen, with a large amount found in the form of hydrogen ions ($H+$). pH (the hydrogen ion potential) is a key factor in strengthening genes. An alkalanized environment assists the physical and internal body to attract, hold, and stabilize light impulses, which are necessary to communicate harmony for the optimum functioning of humans.

A few simple facts about the importance of life and alkaline pH:

The EGG: the measured pH of a free-range chicken egg is:
the white of the egg = pH of 9.0;
the yolk of the egg = pH of 6.5.

What does that reveal?

The white of the egg, with a pH of 9, acts as a protective cloak that shields the yolk from bacteria, viruses, and fungi, while its internal structure, the yolk, with a much lower pH, is the life giving part of the egg and is involved in the millions of cells that form the body of the new chick. Like the egg, when fluids of the human body are maintained at a 7.4 pH (a slightly alkaline level), they protect the body from attack from bacteria, viruses and fungi.

'*Hydro*' stands for water, while '*gen*' is derived from the Greek for genes meaning to be born, so literally, hydrogen literally means 'born from water'. The body is primarily composed of water (75%), which has the chemical formula, H_2O, containing two atoms of hydrogen and one of oxygen. *Oxy* or *Oxi* means burning and combustion, and when combined with *gen*, oxygen literally means; 'burning of the new born genes'. Accordingly, an acidic pH breaks down normal functions within the body resulting in degenerative conditions, producing an environment for chronic disease. An acidic body requires additional ·oxygen and, therefore, constantly depletes one's internal supply of oxygen.

Factors that influence body pH levels:
Most fast foods, meats, grains, some fruit such as cranberries, prunes, plums, and rhubarb, refined salt, sugar, condiments (i.e., pickles, ketchup), and soda pop, tend to have a pH range from 2.8 to 5.5, which is **highly acidic. Alkaline forming foods** include almonds, all melons, unpasteurized honey, bee pollen, maple syrup, figs, dates, natural yogurt, cheese and dairy, root vegetables (i.e., potatoes, turnip)*;* apricots, avocados, coconut, grapes, molasses, raisins and lemons.

The Role of Emotions:
Joyous, happy, love-filled emotions tend to create alkaline forms of chemical reactions within the body, while anger, fear, jealousy, hate, and sadness, create acid-forming chemical reactions in the body. Read more on this topic in Chapter Seven to see how Norman Cousins laughed his way to wellness.

Balancing the body's pH:
How is it possible to bring the pH of body fluids into an acceptable range between 7 and 7.5, which will then influence the blood to maintain its optimal pH range of 7.35 - 7.4? One of the key factors is the quality of water consumed by the body. Since water accounts for up to seventy-five percent (75%) of body weight (and 85% of the brain) it greatly impacts the pH of the body. Natural spring water is a good choice, as is alkaline water, but both may not be readily or easily available in many communities. Many natural spring wells in rural areas may be fine, but they must be regularly tested for coliform (bacteria), toxic minerals and pH. Unfortunately, far too much of the water consumed by humans is acidic, including distilled water; water produced by reverse osmosis;

and de-ionized water, all of which have had their mineral buffers removed. Most urban water supplies, which use chlorine or fluorine for bacteria control, are acidic as well. Another solution might be to obtain a water filtration system such as a *Nikken Pimag*™ , which alkalanizes the water with pi ceramics made from deep-sea coral.

It is also necessary to add the beneficial properties of unrefined sea salt to one's diet. Sea salt is light gray in color and moist to the touch. If the salt is white and dry, it generally means it has been significantly refined with most, if not all, of the magnesium removed. The presence of moisture usually assures us that the sea salt still contains numerous elements that buffer the sodium chloride portion of table salt and can make up as much as sixteen percent (16%) by weight in valuable trace elements and macro-minerals. On average, natural sea salt contains as many as eighty-two (82) elements, which serve as buffers to protect the body from the negative effects of pure sodium chloride. The gray color of this type of salt comes from the clay (kaolin[1]) beds that line the bottom of most salt ponds. This is pure, edible clay, an essential ingredient that enhances the bioenergetic quality of the salt crystals and assists the ionization process as they form. Sea salt[2] found in health food stores, that is white in color and dry to the touch, only designates its origin not its quality, and can be as detrimental to human health as most other forms of refined salts. When doctors recommend no or low salt intake, they usually are referring to refined salts which can be as high as 99.8% pure sodium chloride. The blood requires salts to function properly. Salts maintain the cells and energize the body, and actually help produce other necessary minerals, as well as re-charging the body's cells, similar to a battery. Salts also aid digestion, including the reduction or elimination of indigestion for many individuals after eating dark green foods.

Unrefined Sea Salt versus pure Sodium Chloride:

All elements found in unrefined salt occur naturally in proportions quite close to those found in the internal human environment, which create a highly synergistic biological system. Minerals work in conjunction with each other and cannot work to heal the body when their relative concentrations are increased or decreased disproportionately, i.e.,

---

1: Kaolin is commonly used in commercial preparations for diarrhea, as well as for the removal of toxins from the bowel, such as toxic ketones that result during the die-off process of Candida Albicans (yeast) cells during anti-fungal treatments.

2: Oven or kiln dried sea salt is heated in excess of 400 F degrees. This particular process removes vital minerals. When purchasing sea salt, ensure that it has been sun and/or wind dried. These latter processes of drying leaves the crystalline structure of salt, along with many important minerals, intact.

beyond the appropriate concentration (in parts per million) for optimal functioning. To deny the body appropriate levels of salts aggravates every problem in which cell repair and rejuvenation must occur to maintain appropriate bodily functions. However, excess salt with low potassium levels can create conditions for disease.

The body both loves and craves salt for a reason: it is absolutely necessary for the body to function properly. But most of the common table salt sold today is not what the body requires, as most of these commercial salts are primarily pure chemicals – simply pure sodium chloride[1].

Unrefined sea salt has countless therapeutic uses, including the correction of excess acidity; the restoration of good digestion; the relief of allergies and skin diseases; the prevention of many forms of cancer; the provision of a steady boost in cellular energy; and for giving the body a heightened resistance to infections and bacterial diseases. It is also valuable as a gargle for a sore throat or as a solution for cuts and bites[2]. It is also recommended that one not only use unrefined sea salt as a food additive, but use it as a bath additive as well. Used in the bath water, the body will absorb minerals via the skin through the process of osmosis. Bathing in unrefined sea salt also assists in the removal of toxins from the body. However, the latter is not recommended for cancer patients who need to reduce sodium and increase potassium levels.

Alkaline-forming foods: (See detailed chart on page 89)
Foods that are alkaline-forming should be introduced into the diet on a regular basis. These include almonds, apricots, molasses, avocados, lemons, coconut, all melons, figs, dates and raisins, natural yogurt, grapes, unpasteurized honey, maple syrup, root vegetables (i.e., potatoes, rutabaga, turnips), alfalfa and other sprouts, cayenne, spirulina (green algae) and lithothamnium (red marine algae). The king of alkaline foods is the organic almond. Eat about fifteen to twenty per day, but eat them earlier in the day to give the body time to digest the almonds before bedtime, i.e., usually not later than two o'clock in the afternoon.

Almonds should also be soaked for twenty-four hours in pure water prior to consumption. This starts the germination process in the seed and activates its life force. The digestive system is then able to assimilate more of the elements contained within the almonds. A daily ritual of preparing almonds in a small bowl in pure water is a great habit to

---

1. To evaluate levels of excess sodium in the body, *Dynamo House Pty. Ltd*, Melbourne Australia, produces copyrighted iridology charts. A solid white circle around the outer edge of the iris indicates excessive intake of salt, a condition commonly associated with high blood pressure, fluid retention and kidney problems. Dark circles can indicate adrenal issues..

2. The publisher of this book commented that he was bitten by fire ants while on vacation in Florida and that the bite marks bothered him for three days, until he took a long a walk in the salt water surf. The bites healed within a few hours.

cultivate. The next day they are ready to eat. This process can also be used to activate the life force in all forms of seeds and nuts prior to consumption. Adding a handful of shelled sunflower seeds is an added bonus. If the body is diseased, with symptoms of common allergies, it is recommended that one use a rotation approach to almond consumption (i.e., one day on - one day off) until the body has begun to heal, so that an allergy is not created. Allergies indicate either a weakened immune system and/or an overload of toxins.

The result of my pH test at the start of this protocol was low, at 6.0. Before breakfast, hydrion strips were used to test my pH using a morning urine stream, as well as saliva on a spoon. Then the saliva was tested again, four minutes after that meal. Even if the saliva pH is low, it should increase after a meal, but mine did not increase. It actually went down and that frightened me. Further research suggested the initial test results were low due to the fact that my body was quite acidic and unable to handle the nutrients I had just ingested. In addition, stress was prevalent in my life at that time. (See also Chapter Seven for more information on relaxation techniques to combat stress.)

Since that time I have increased both the quality and quantity of alkaline foods; drink plenty of pure fresh water, breathe more deeply and even laugh more. Today my pH level is correct and increases after meals are eaten. However, there was a time when my body suddenly became acidic again - within three months of my diagnosis for cancer, during a time when a new tumor appeared in my neck. That was shortly after my mother's illness and death. Fortunately, this situation did not take long to reverse, as my body had become less toxic, and consequently healthier. Most importantly, I now knew how to achieve positive results more quickly.

A large percentage of processed foods are highly acidic, including most baked goods made with commercial flours. One method to raise pH is to add an alkaline substance, such as lithothamnium (red marine algae) to bread dough when baking your own bread. The addition of sprouted grains and seeds to the bread dough, as well as the use of sweeteners that are alkaline forming, such as maple syrup, molasses or unpasteurized honey (instead of refined sugars) is another means to raise the pH of homemade breads.

Lithothamnium Calcareum, a North Atlantic red marine alga, can also be added to many dishes in order to raise the pH. Use approximately one to two milliliters (or one quarter to one half teaspoon) of *lithothamnium* per 250 milliliters (about one cup) of flour for all baking requirements. It can also be added to spaghetti sauces, porridge, soups, or desserts. A general guideline would be to use one milliliter (one-quarter teaspoon) per serving. *Lithothamnium* can also be taken in water or juice. Use one-quarter teaspoon per glass to increase the pH, as well as to mineralize the body. It has a neutral taste and, therefore, will not alter the culinary taste experience.

Cesium Chloride: [1,2]

Another quick method to alkalanize the body is with *cesium chloride*. It is a highly alkaline mineral, discovered in 1860 in an area known for its low cancer rates. It can affect cancer cells in two ways: first, cesium limits cellular uptake of the nutrient glucose, which helps starve the cancer cell; second, *cesium chloride* raises the cell pH to the range of 8.0 which neutralizes weak lactic acid. The ingestion of *cesium chloride* can also help to significantly reduce pain levels in the body, and is known to have done so within twelve to twenty-four hours of consumption.

Monitoring the body's pH:

The body's pH is usually measured with urine or saliva samples[3]. That process is rather simple and requires less than a minute of one's time for each test. Initial tests should be done daily for two consecutive days, then weekly until one's alkaline level stabilizes via lifestyle changes, including appropriate nutrition, clean water, and stress reduction. Individuals should perform both urine and saliva tests to obtain the most accurate evaluation of the body's pH. To maintain good health the body is constantly seeking to get rid of any excess acids that irritate the tissues and deplete them of minerals. The principal organs involved in this purpose are the kidneys (the renal system). A normal rate of acid excretion through the kidneys gives urine a pH that falls between 6.75 and 7.25.

---

1. If one uses *cesium chloride*, it is important that the pH be monitored regularly, as well as the body's potassium levels. Cesium competes with potassium and is known to reduce potassium levels in the body. Too much is just as bad as too little; it should also be monitored by a health care professional. See page 91 for more information on $CeCl_2$.

2. *Cesium chloride* has **not been approved** for human consumption in Canada; it is, however, readily available in the U.S.A.

3. The most accurate test of one's pH is by drawing blood from an artery. This procedure is rather painful and can only be done in a hospital setting. It is not necessary for most situations described in this publication, where the purpose is to alter one's diet and lifestyle to regulate the pH of the body. This procedure is however, necessary in case where patients are admitted for a possible heart attack and blood gases must be obtained from an artery for precise testing.

By testing the acidity of the urine, one can determine whether the body is eliminating a normal amount of acid. If the acid excretion rate is higher than normal, the urinary pH will be more acidic. A lower urinary pH is also an indication that the body is saturated and, therefore, in an acidic state. The ideal time for taking a urine sample pH is the **second urine stream** in the morning, but since people often are forgetful, taking a reading upon rising would be acceptable to ensure that one at least obtains a useful test result.

Another good indicator of the overall pH balance in one's body is the pH of saliva. There is a strong correlation between the pH of the body's internal environment and that of the urine and saliva, as both sources become acidic when the body's internal environment becomes acidic. Perhaps the best way to monitor the body's pH level is to use a digital pH meter as it can monitor the body pH quite precisely between 7.1 and 7.5. Digital pH meters are available in most stores that sell water culture products, such as hydroponics centers. Another option involves hydrion or pH test strips, which are commonly available at many drug stores, health food stores or can be ordered on line. Test strips that have increments of 0.20 to 0.25 pH units, and test a pH range between 4.5 and 9.0 are preferred. Strips that use the double color indicator method allow for a more accurate determination of the pH value of whatever you are testing to properly balance the body pH between 7 and 7.5.

The Salivary pH test:

As stated above, a second indicator of the overall pH balance in one's body is the pH of saliva. When the body has appropriate mineral reserves, those minerals will be indicated by pH readings between 7.0 and 7.5. A low salivary pH reading indicates that mineral reserves in one's body are low, and are being used as buffers elsewhere in the body. The salivary test should be performed before a meal, and then four minutes after that meal. If salivary pH is not in an optimal range, one's diet should focus on fruit and vegetables, (Refer to the chart on page 89 in this chapter). Salivary pH should be approximately 0.5 lower than one's urinary pH. Following a meal, if the pH level increased, that is a correct result; if not, that is a sure sign that one must begin immediately to resolve emotional stress. If your saliva is too alkaline, keeping weight under control could become a problem. Salivary pH is the best indicator of health; it mirrors what is occurring in the blood, liver, lymphatic system and with the pancreatic enzymes. If one uses pH strips, avoid putting strips directly into one's mouth as it contains toxic chemicals. Rather, one should spit into a spoon or directly onto the strip.

The Urinary pH test:

If the urinary pH is below the optimum range, the body has inadequate mineral reserves, and over time, disease can and will set in! The urinary pH indicates the efforts of the body via the kidneys, adrenals, lungs and gonads in keeping the body balanced. **Again, for best test results, test your second urination in the morning**. You will likely see the urinary pH become more alkaline as the day progresses. Test frequently during the day, and determine an average. The greater the spread in the readings between the urine and saliva pH tests, the greater the probability individuals will experience negative symptoms, such as stomach or bowel gas, energy loss, and stress. The acidity/alkalinity chart can also be used as a guide to reduce alkaline levels as well as to increase it.

Excessive alkalinity can cause many significant health related problems such as: indigestion, cramps, drowsiness, itching, sore muscles, and creaky joints. Make sure you monitor pH levels regularly, especially if using *cesium chloride* therapeutically.

In July 2005, I experienced a bout of influenza for the first time in over two years, and wondered, given my current state of health, why that occurred. I checked my pH: the saliva reading was higher reading than my urine test. This situation creates a vacuum where bacteria or a flu virus can enter the body. My next question was: how did this happen? Nothing had changed in my diet. However, I became ill due to elevated levels of arsenic in my bottled water, and the stress on my body created an adrenal issue that I did not recognize or understand until early in 2006, when additional symptoms appeared (See more on *adrenals* in Appendix E, pp. 285- 287.) This, in turn, affected my pH and subsequently my immune system, creating an opportunity for the flu virus to take hold. Although it only lasted for twenty-four hours, this virus was still an unpleasant experience. I then checked with my daughter, who also had the flu and found that her pH levels were also imbalanced. My husband did not catch the flu as his pH was fine; his salivary reading being 0.5 lower than the urine test.

Remember B.A.L.A.N.C.E.!

Indigestion or 'heartburn':

Too much sodium bicarbonate taken for ulcers or heartburn can increase the body's alkalinity beyond safe levels. It can also excite the nervous system, causing hyperventilation, seizures and a calcium buildup within the body. Excess sodium bicarbonate also neutralizes stomach acid, raising the pH from a normal reading of 1.0, which in turn reduces the digestion of food, and ultimately results in undigested food passing from the stomach into the bowel. Since the bowel has a high pH (normally between 9 and 10), many foods cannot be digested in this highly alkaline pH, producing further gas and bloating

For heartburn, try using one to two teaspoons of cider vinegar rather than sodium bicarbonate. If it works within twenty minute, the body requires a digestive enzyme. Consult a naturopath (N.D.) or a registered nutritionist consultant (RNC or RNCP) who can help one obtain appropriate enzymes, as well as the process of monitoring one's pH .

The body does not store protein in the same manner as it stores fat. The liver changes ingested protein that exceeds the body's requirements into fat. If there are too many toxins in the body, or if there is an excessive consumption of protein foods, uric acid may be created. Uric acid is a destructive by-product that can destroy the pH balance.[1]

Added notes:

1. For each tenth of a point change in pH, the oxygen level in the body changes ten fold. Therefore, if the body is acidic, for each tenth of a point (0.1) decrease below an optimal pH of 7.4, the amount of oxygen the body receives is reduced ten fold.

2. It takes thirty glasses of water to neutralize the acid from one can of soda pop.

3. The number one mineral required by the body is calcium; and pH and calcium levels are closely linked. Calcium is the primary alkaline buffer, while coral or calcium-based water neutralizes internal waste products and heavy metals, trapping heavy metals in the gut and flushing them out via the colon along with the feces.

4. Check urine after five o'clock in the morning; ensure that it is a second urine reading. If it falls below 6.4, then the body is stressed. If one consistently forgets to test the second urine, then be sure to at least test a urine stream upon rising to get a basal reading for the day.

---

1. A more detailed and scientific explanation of pH has been added as Appendix C , pp. 281 - 282.

5. Most fruits and greens, when metabolized, become alkaline within the body.

6. Check all past medical reports. What were your alkalinity/acidity levels over the years, especially when you were unwell? Ensure that the family doctor knows that you understand the importance of pH! Medical doctors have test results at their fingertips, but many conventional (allopathic) practitioners have, in the past, not paid close attention to those results. [*I recall that when I asked my doctor why I was so low, and why this was not brought to my attention, his reply was that it is not what doctors normally check, unless it was specifically marked L for low.*]

7. Anyone reading this book should make it a practice of questioning his/her medical doctors about lowered pH readings from this point forward. As a result, more individuals could receive help to alkalanize their body faster to help reduce the onset of disease.

8. Checking the pH of one's saliva and urine should become a priority. Each test represents separate areas of concern, and both are indicators of the overall balance within the body.

9. To maintain a correct pH balance, one should stick to a diet and lifestyle which is eighty (80%) percent alkaline, and twenty (20%) percent acidic. For example, diets that include eighty (80%) percent grains and only twenty (20%) percent fruit and vegetables will eventually create an acidic environment.

10.To alkalanize the body it is recommended to consume fifty (50%) percent of all vegetables raw. This can easily be accomplished through juicing. [See more on this topic in Chapter Four.]

11. Excess vitamin C can also create an acidic body. Purchase non- acidic forming brands of vitamin C, such as the *Ester-C*^{TM} brand.

12. Phosphorus and sulfur also act as buffers to help maintain one's pH.

13. pH levels have a profound effect on enzyme activity and stability.

14. Other signs of an acidic body include: excessive sighing, insomnia, water retention, recessed eyes, low blood pressure, bumps on the tongue or in the mouth.

15. Other products/foods that can help an acidic body become more alkaline include: Tri-salts, Kelp, *Coezyme A, Oxy Caps* or *Oxymax* as well as Umeboshi plums (eat one plum every four hours for three days then reduce to one per day).

To maintain the correct pH balance stick to a diet and lifestyle which is 80% alkaline and 20% acidic. Examples are listed in chart below:

ACIDIC	ALKALINE
lack of sleep/overwork	deep breathing/exercise
worry/negative emotions	laughter/love
dried peas & beans/meat	meditation/relaxation
caffeine/alcohol	Umeboshi plums
tobacco	ginger
meats	kelp
cranberries	soybean products
dried fruit, berries	carob (chocolate subs.)
mayonnaise	buckwheat
drugs/aspirin	pure honey
rhubarb	sprouts
mushrooms	agar agar (gelatin made
prunes	from seaweed)
apple cider	molasses
cakes/donuts, etc.	all ripe fruits (except prunes,
pickles/dressings	cranberries, and rhubarb)
pasta	corn
poultry/eggs	dates and figs
soft drinks	root vegetables -
prunes	(e.g., onions,potatoes,turnip)
fish	lima beans
oatmeal	vinegar
catsup	maple syrup
cocoa	almonds[1]
refined sugar	lemons[2]
_____	_____
_____	_____
_____	_____

1. The king of alkaline foods is the almond. However, if a person has cancer it is not recommended that one eat more than five almonds per day. They should also be eaten before two o'clock in the afternoon in order for the body to digest them prior to bedtime. Almonds should be germinated: put them in pure water for 24 hours as this will create a more alkaline enriched product. Note: If a person does not have cancer then the total can be increased from 15 to 20 nuts per day.

2. Lemons, although acidic themselves, actually help the body become more alkaline when eaten.

It is time to take control of your own health!!

CHAPTER THREE SUMMARY

1. Test the body's alkalinity/acidity levels in the morning, just before a meal, as well as four minutes after the meal, for two consecutive days for a proper basal reading.

2. If the body is acidic, re-adjust one's food intake, including the addition of clean water. Clean water could include properly tested well water, natural spring water, or the installation of a *Nikken Pimag*™ or similar quality water filtration system.

3. A drop in pH after ingestion of a meal indicates stress, causing higher acidic levels. Consult a naturopath, and practice coping and relaxation skills as outlined in Chapter Seven. Work on your inner child; find out what may be affecting you emotionally.

4. Change from white refined salt to gray, unrefined salt or sea salt. (Only use one-third the amount suggested in most recipes.)

5. Individuals with cancer must reduce sodium and increase potassium levels.

6. Remember, it takes thirty glasses of water to balance the body after just one can of soda pop (carbonated beverages) is consumed.

7. An acidic condition means less oxygen uptake and more disease.

8. Take charge, talk to a medical doctor about your pH and review past reports with him or her.

Cesium Chloride[1]

A highly alkaline mineral, cesium was discovered in 1860. Low cancer rates are found in areas of the world where it is abundant. Cesium occurs naturally in the form of a salt, and the most common isotope is not radioactive. It is a water-soluble compound, and it is the most electropositive and least abundant of the five naturally occurring alkaline[2] elements

This compound affects cancer cells in two ways. First, cesium chloride ($CeCl_2$) limits the cellular uptake of the nutrient glucose, ultimately starving the cancer cell. Second, cesium raises the cell pH to 8.0, neutralizing the weak lactic acid, and eliminating pain within twelve to twenty-four hours. As a result the cancer cell dies, and within a few days these cells are absorbed and eliminated from the body.

Always take cesium therapeutically with food: one gram at breakfast, one gram at lunch and one gram at supper. This particular supplement must be taken in conjunction with vitamins C, A, as well as the minerals zinc, selenium and potassium.

---

1. This product is not approved for use in Canada, but can be readily obtained in the USA.

2. The terms alkalanize and alkanalize are synonymous, and although the former is the standard scientific spelling, the latter has come into more common usage due to the ease of pronunciation However, alkalanize has been generally used throughout this publication.

The Lymphatic System[1]

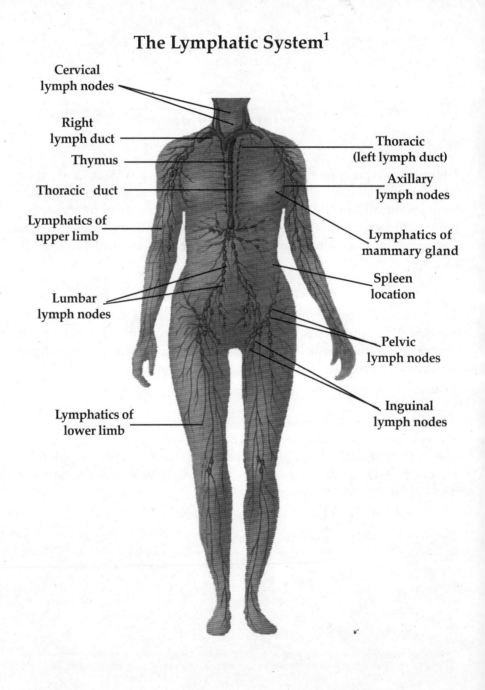

Cervical lymph nodes

Right lymph duct

Thymus

Thoracic duct

Lymphatics of upper limb

Lumbar lymph nodes

Lymphatics of lower limb

Thoracic (left lymph duct)

Axillary lymph nodes

Lymphatics of mammary gland

Spleen location

Pelvic lymph nodes

Inguinal lymph nodes

1. Adapted from medical text with permission; labelling added.

Chapter Four

The Lymphatic System[1]

What is the lymphatic system?

The lymphatic system is the natural garbage collector that continuously and aggressively cleans waste from all cells, breaks it down, and arranges for its elimination from the body. The lymphatic system is an integral part of the body's defense system, which involves the production of white blood cells (*lymphocytes*) that seek out, capture and destroy foreign invaders such as bacteria and fungi. Two years before being diagnosed with cancer, my *lymphocytes* were listed at twenty-seven percent (27.6%), well within the normal or healthy range, but after that initial report, they continued to drop. Unfortunately, unless the standard blood analysis report specifically indicates 'L' for low beside the specific reading, most medical doctors would likely not take special note of that reading.

I only know the latter today as copies of my blood test reports over the past five years were provided upon request, which has allowed me to make appropriate comparisons. A month after the diagnosis of cancer, my lymphocytes were a mere thirteen percent (13.5%), but only after four months of following the B.A.L.A.N.C.E. program they were up to sixteen (16.3%) percent, still not normal, but certainly headed in the right direction. And only nine months after beginning B.A.L.A.N.C.E., my lymphocytes were up to nineteen (19.3%) percent, within the normal

---

1. The lymphatic system is composed of nodes, fluid, organs, nodules, ducts, glands and vessels.

or expected range. In addition, one's 'absolute lymph' value should range from 0.90 to 5.2, but mine had been as low as 0.84. Again, after four months on this program., my 'absolute lymph' readings had returned to a normal range (about 1.00), and within nine months, they were safely up to 1.11. Thus, in a short period of less than one year, the six test results that originally had been dangerously low, were back at appropriate levels.

Given the right tools, your body can heal!!

The body contains three times as much lymphatic fluid as blood. Except for hair, cartilage and nails, the entire body is bathed in lymphatic fluid. Lymph nodes are easy to locate, especially in the neck, under arms and groin, even in healthy individuals. Tonsils are also a part of the lymphatic system, and when they become enlarged tonsils make it difficult for large particles of food to pass, creating the necessity for food to be pureed or juiced. This latter process facilitates a shorter period for digestion - in as little as fifteen minutes - rather than the normal two hours for whole foods, especially those that are cooked. Juicing allows a more efficient absorption of nutrients and permits the body time to work on any viruses that may be present. Unfortunately, and far too often, decisions are made to remove tonsils, rather than listening to what the body is 'saying'. Rather than removing tonsils, one should begin a process of *detoxification*, including juicing and re-building the body's immune system through nutrition until it returns to a normal state. Tonsils are a vital part of the body's defense mechanism and should only be removed as a last resort, not as a first choice.

The lymphatic system also absorbs fat from the digestive tract. The greater the volume of food digested, the greater the workload of the lymphatic system. Lymph nodes fill and empty on a continuous cycle, in all areas of the body, including women's breasts. This is a normal process, but when waste in the body accumulates at a greater pace than it can be eliminated, the lymph nodes become overburdened and enlarged. Removal of a node will not eliminate a problem; nor does it create positive changes within the body. The influx of excess waste must cease, and the removal of waste that has accumulated from years of 'abuse' must begin.

There are approximately twenty-nine types of lymphatic cancer, and the diagnosis I received was for *non-Hodgkin's Lymphoma*, the low, indolent follicular kind. Until then, I not only ate as most North Americans did, consuming far too much refined and processed food, but for twenty years, I had also worked in a factory that used toxic chemicals during various stages of production. *Non-Hodgkin's Lymphoma*, once a relatively rare disease, has increased at an accelerated pace due to increased levels of environmental toxins found in the workplace and in the home. Toxic signs were certainly evident early in my illness, but I had insufficient knowledge to understand that it was these toxins that were primarily responsible for my poor state of health.

In 1998, I developed cataracts, followed quickly by a giant leap into menopause, soon followed by symptoms of depression, anxiety and aggressive behavior. I easily became poisoned by foods, developed colds and influenza that required antibiotics and eventual hospitalization. Without the knowledge I have today, I was unable to recognize what was wrong, and neither could my medical doctors. Test after test came back with negative results, but I was unable to act.

The diagnosis: terminal cancer!

It was not until 2001, when an enlarged node appeared just below my right jaw line, did I suspect something more serious. But even that was insufficient to raise the alarm, as two medical specialists (an *ENT* specialist and a surgeon) also missed these early signs of cancer. In late 2002, the bell rang even louder with the appearance of another enlarged node, this time in my groin. Then doctors immediately arranged for its removal and biopsy.

Two other medical specialists informed me that if the disease had been discovered and diagnosed based on those earlier signs in 2001 – such as a tumor located in a single location (i.e., a stage one or two lymphoma) - the cancer might have been treatable by conventional chemotherapy, with a reasonable chance for survival. Today, I accept the lateness of the diagnosis as a gift, not only for me personally, but also for each reader of this book. If not for the late diagnosis, I would never have worked so diligently to find answers for myself, and this book might have never been written or published. And I also know now that chemotherapy would not have cured me. The toxins would have remained in my body and the cancer would have eventually returned in a more virulent form. Without very significant lifestyle changes and extensive detoxification[1], this story would likely have never been told.

Lymph nodes are warriors within the body and humans cannot live without them. Cancer cells do not work their way into a lymph node; cancer cells are 'trapped' by the node. It is a significant part of the body's defense system. Lymph nodes contain *phagocystic*[1] cells. Their job is to gobble up and break down foreign substances in order for the body to expel them. As described above, the toxins and cancer cells became trapped, but due to the extraordinary levels of toxins in my body, there was no place for them to be expelled. So they remained and ultimately became *non-Hodgkin's Lymphoma*.

When the enlarged node was discovered, I assumed it was necessary to have it removed from my groin for biopsy, both to detect the presence of cancer, as well as the type and stage of the cancer I had developed. Since then I have learned that a simple needle biopsy would have been sufficient. When a node is removed, swelling near the extraction site may be experienced, and it might continue to swell from that point forward. In my case, the removal of the node left my leg with a tingling sensation, while the back of my left knee remained swollen. My naturopath then outlined the proper way to massage the leg to obtain relief: begin by pulling the muscle towards the heart, keeping the leg elevated. This process moves trapped lymphatic fluid, and in my case, eventually resolved the problem.

Unfortunately, one young mother I met during the presentation of my program on BALANCE was not so lucky. Surgeons had removed numerous lymph nodes in her leg in hopes of halting the spread of cancer, which had been originally discovered as a melanoma on her ankle. Her leg swelled, she was in constant pain, and in a fairly short period of time, she died.

Question: Would a person have a lung or colon removed for simply doing the job they were supposed to do?

1 **Note**: there is a more radical detoxification method employed by some medical practitioners known as *chelation*. Primarily used for heavy metal toxicity, but some jurisdictions also permit its use for arterial plaque removal.

2. Phago means "to eat" and cystic means "cell".

However, some surgeons do remove lymph nodes, especially in cases of breast cancer. It has become a standard practice, but is not a medical necessity. Lymph nodes do not spread cancer; they are merely there to inform the patient and his/her medical advisors that the cancer has already spread. The main pathway for the drainage of lymphatic fluid is found in the right armpit; damage to this area of the lymphatic system via surgery can reduce the body's ability to remove toxins on an on-going basis. Protection and preservation of the lymph nodes are vital to one's health as they have an important function, as do all parts of one's body.

Re-bounders (also known as mini trampolines):

Lymphatic fluid does not move throughout the body by way of a pumping action, such as the blood does with the help of the heart. It takes a minimum amount of daily exercise to move lymphatic fluid through the body. One of the best ways to move lymphatic fluid is with the use of a re-bounder which requires one to work out for at least fifteen minutes a day. This will help move the lymphatic fluid filled with waste products, such as cancer cells, infectious viruses or heavy metals, towards its dump site (the bloodstream) for removal from the body. As an individual bounces on the trampoline the effects of gravitational forces on the body changes, opening and closing valves, thereby forcing the lymphatic fluid to flow throughout the body.

Re-bounders also:

a. strengthen the body's muscles, including the heart;
b. double the strength of body tissues;
c. equal and surpass the aerobic effect of running, without the wear and tear on the ankles, knees or lower back;
d. strengthen and stimulate bowel function; and
e. stimulate every cell within the body.

If one uses a rebounder, the following list is recommended as a guide:

1) If illness is present, consult a health care advisor before beginning its use.
2) If one is too weak to bounce, then sit on the mini-trampoline and have another person do the bouncing.
3) With both feet planted squarely on the re-bounder, begin to bounce slowly and continue in a gentle fashion.
4) In the beginning, try five minutes, three times a day, or fifteen minutes all at once, or even as little as one minute per session, fifteen times a day. All combinations are beneficial to one's health.
5) Keep the body straight, and tuck in the pelvic area as this will help prevent back strain.

Standard re-bounder (mini-trampoline)

By 1998, I was constantly ill with colds and viral flus that required antibiotics and cough medicines, as well as significant amounts of rest and care. On one occasion, I was even admitted to hospital. Between 1998 and 2000, I also experienced a great deal of pressure in my chest and was naturally concerned about the possibility of a heart condition. The pressure felt as if someone was sitting on my chest, and since it was extremely difficult to breathe properly, a heart condition was at first suspected. My family doctor arranged a visit with a specialist in internal medicine who ordered an *EKG*, treadmill test, and thorough physical examination, But as in previous situations, my test results were negative!

In late 2000, I began to see a naturopath who helped me to understand that my immune system was compromised. He taught me how to relieve the symptoms of the chest pressure with gentle taps on the breastbone, which stimulated the thymus gland that lies behind it. This procedure should be done for approximately one minute, five to six times a day. It worked immediately, relieving the pressure on my chest. Unfortunately, by this time, my immune system was in serious trouble. Although we had immediately begun to work on my situation, I now realize that it was a poor decision to schedule fewer visits with the naturopath, as with the latter course of action my health may well have been improved more quickly.

Early in 2003, when I finally began to focus my attention on natural medicine, each of the above actions helped to improve my immune system dramatically. During the year that followed, my husband, children and grandchildren had several colds, as well as the flu, while I had fewer viruses for much shorter periods of time. Even when I contracted a flu virus, it lasted only a few hours, while other family members illnesses lasted for three or more days. As a result of my stronger immune system, I did not succumb to colds or flus for nearly a year. The naturopath reviewed my research and, with his guidance, the following regimen was determined:

1. Tapping my breastbone to stimulate the thymus.
2. The introduction of an immune builder, *Tahitian Noni Juice*, as a daily supplement, along with *Aerobic Oxygen*™ drops. [Other immune builders include *Moducare*™, *Essiac*™, *echinacea*, *Goji juice* and GoldenSeal]
3. A reduction in my sugar intake, including the elimination of soda pop and refined sugars in any and all forms.
4. The addition of breathing techniques for stress reduction.

The Immune System:
Immune cells are produced by the thymus and in the spleen, both of which are part of the lymphatic system, as well as in the bone marrow. They are carried through the body via the lymphatic vessels to the nodes, where they are stored, creating a barrier against infection. A balance of vitamins, minerals, deep breathing and exercise help the immune system to function properly. Free radicals can also damage the immune system.

Impairment of the immune system:
1. *Mercury fillings* can impair the immune system. (See more in Chapter Five)
2. Dry air in the home can cause the membranes of the nose to become excessively dry, increasing the ability of bacteria to penetrate the body, thereby reducing the capabilities of the immune system. Maintaining the humidity in the home between thirty and fifty percent humidity should prevent this from happening.
3. Eating garlic, onions and/or horseradish can help to fight harmful bacteria.
4. Smoking is definitely not part of a wellness program, as it tends to deplete the body's store of vitamin C. However, if one is unable to stop smoking or if one finds oneself in a smoking environment, it is important to take extra doses of vitamin C as a precautionary measure.

5. Antioxidants such as vitamin C, E and A also stimulate and support the immune system.

6. The *thymus* gland acts as a nursery for the development of immune cells that help fight infection. Unfortunately this gland shrinks somewhat with age, but the simple tapping exercise suggested earlier could help to boost the immune system. Five minutes per day should be sufficient. [Another symptom of a compromised thymus is experiencing pain where the neck and shoulders meet.]

7. One minute of anger has the ability to suppress the immune system for up to six hours, whereas one minute of unrestrained laughter can boost the immune system for as much as twenty-four hours.

8. Food allergies develop as a hyperactive response of the immune system.

A question?

How could the lymphatic system destroy and transport diseased cells to the liver to be expelled if lymph nodes were no longer present and if their elimination pathways had been removed via surgery? Lymph node tumors are markers and removal damages the ability of the body to heal - they are the body's warriors – a primary line of defense against invaders. A B.A.L.A.N.C.E. program works to reduce toxins from the liver and kidneys, and gives the body sufficient energy to work on the destruction and removal of tumors from the lymphatic system as was intended.

Non-Hodgkin's lymphoma is a cancer that involves numerous tumors throughout the lymphatic system. Prior to the reduction in size of those tumors, whenever I swept the floor or simply attempted to carry a handbag, the pressure on my shoulders actually threw my joints out of alignment, causing pain throughout the entire length of my arms. This condition was painful enough to require assistance from a chiropractor. In **late 2005**, two tumors were still visible on the right side of my neck, near my jugular vein. If you touched my neck, more tumors could be detected, including one next to my right ear. I wondered how a weakened immune system could get rid of these tumors. Although my immune system had improved somewhat, I believed the volume and size of the tumors were simply too much for my body to dissipate without more assistance.

That situation led me to search further, eventually locating an enzyme, *Wobenzyme N*, that appeared to be potentially beneficial in reducing tumors. After consulting with my naturopath, he tested this product using *MRT* to determine if it were compatible with my body. *Wobenzyme N (Wobe-Mugo)* has been used in Germany for more than forty years. It contains pancreatin, papain, bromelain, trypsin, chymotrypsin, lipase, amylase enzymes and the flavonoid rutin. This particular combination of enzymes is known to remove the fibrin coating from cancer cells, making them more susceptible to destruction, and for this reason should be taken one hour before meals, otherwise it could interact with the digestive process, reducing its beneficial ability to remove the fibrin coating on the tumors. It also reduces adhesion to other cells and cellular walls; and it reduces *circulating immune complexes (CIC)*, that can weaken the immune system. NOTE: Caution must be taken in the use of *Wobenzyme N* for organ transplant patients, diabetics, pregnant or nursing women, or immediately prior to surgery. *Wobenzyme N* is also recommended for acute and chronic inflammation from injury, disease or surgery.

After one month, the initial results included a reduction in size of one tumor by seventy-five percent and several others by approximately twenty-five percent. However, after a few months, my body required a break from those treatments. Again we used *MRT* to probe the body for answers. A few months later I resumed the use of this product with even more success. The tumors located near the jugular vein that felt as if they were one large lump several months ago, had now separated into two smaller tumors. One of the beneficial results of this process was that several tumors were reduced with this approach, while a rejuvenated and strengthened immune system took care of the rest.

The primary reason the seventh stage of disease (cancer) is given such prominence in this book is based on the fact that one in three persons in North America now develop cancer. Cleaning the lymphatic system to help it function properly can prevent advancement to a higher stage. It can also begin to reverse the process through the stages of disease - towards good health again. *Cardiovascular disease* is also a significant issue in North America as one in two now experience heart or vascular disease in one form or another. As such, moving lymphatic fluid and strengthening the heart muscle is a vital part of any journey toward wellness.

THE LIVER

Where is the liver located in the body?

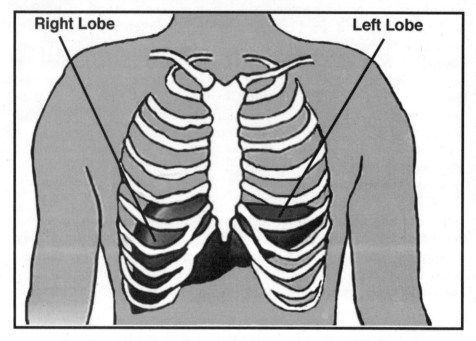

Hand drawn sketch based on Internet medical diagrams.

The liver is the second largest organ in the body, the first being the skin. It performs over five hundred (500) functions. A small sampling of the functions performed by the liver include the conversion of food to energy, the digestion of fats, cleansing the blood, controlling blood sugar levels, as well as controlling hormone levels in the body at specific times. If the liver does not function properly, many of the following conditions can occur: poor digestion, poor elimination (constipation or diarrhea), blood sugar issues (diabetes/hypoglycemia), intolerance to fatty foods, and more. Individuals with any form of degenerative disease also exhibit a degree of liver damage.

It is essential the liver have less trash (toxins) than it is commonly required to process. What is required is more raw vegetables, fruit and fresh water, both to sustain the liver and give it a rest. A reduction in medication, reduced intake of alcohol, less sugar and caffeine, consuming fewer refined and processed foods; as well as eating more alkaline foods are a few of the ways to decrease the toxic effects on the liver. The addition of *essential fatty acids (EFAs)* are also very important to help carry toxins to the surface of the skin, and to the intestines, kidneys and lungs where they are expelled. Symptoms of liver congestion include cysts such as *fibroids, benign tumors* or *endometriomas* (blood filled tumors) - all signs that the body is having difficulty ridding itself of toxins. Drinking freshly squeezed lemon juice in a glass of water in the morning can help to prevent liver congestion and maintain proper hormonal balance.

When the body fills with toxins, it affects the liver in several ways. The best way to describe this phenomenon is through the following chronology, which traces my health from **1994 to 2002:**

1994 - 1997:

I had never experienced anxiety attacks until 1994 following surgery for a benign lump on my thyroid, a sixth stage disease state. My first anxiety attack came just three days after that surgery. My body was telling me it was stressed from the accumulation of toxins and in desperate need of cleansing. However, at that time I did not know how to listen to my body - and I was frightened. After that initial event, the periodic episodes of anxiety continued, and at times became full-blown panic attacks. This seemed to occur with yeast infections, or if unwanted bacteria were present in a recently ingested meal. These reactions were all due to the extremely high levels of toxins in my body.

Physiologically, I had learned to handle these attacks until late in **1998**. This breakdown was a sure sign that my body had really begun to deteriorate. On one occasion, I experienced food poisoning on two successive days, yet my husband had eaten the same foods and was fine. From then on, I had to be very careful of what and where we ate. We eliminated all take-out foods and any products that contained *monosodium glutamate (MSG)*. This was difficult as most soups and canned goods, as well as a large variety of frozen foods contained *MSG*.

1998 - 1999:

The year began with depression, not the '*stay in bed - I am sad*' kind, but actual suicidal thoughts that would come and go. Yet I loved life, my family and wished to live. I could not understand what was happening and it scared me. I would also become anxious, angry and, at times, felt as if bugs were crawling up and down my arms. My chest also felt as if a weight had been placed upon it. The family doctor sent me to specialists who arranged an *electrocardiogram (EKG)* and other tests, but none of these tests revealed anything new that would help to explain these feelings or symptoms. Medication was prescribed for depression, and although the prescription was filled, I decided not to take it. Rather, I chose to conduct more research, eventually discovering Dr. Andrew Weil's publications: *Spontaneous Healing* and *Eating Well for Optimum Health*. Reading these books prompted me to begin a regimen of exercise. Initially the exercise lasted for twenty minutes, either performing 'jumping jacks' at home, or riding a stationary bike at the YMCA. I also ate plenty of tomatoes and took Vitamin B complex. While this regimen helped reduce the level of depression temporarily, I still had not recognized that those symptoms might be caused by an extreme overload of toxins – and that I was in a **virtual fight for my life.**

Late 2000-2002:
Then I discovered a new direction, one that gave me courage and hope: a naturopathic doctor, Bruce Hayhoe. Today I attribute one-third of the improvement in my health to my own determination and thirst for knowledge; one-third to Dr. Hayhoe; while the final third is a result of a combination of my family's unconditional love, my immune builder (*Tahitian Noni juice*), and the advice of a nutritionist. Without any one of the above, I might not have had the energy or courage to keep going - to find the answers recommended in this publication. And without God's guidance - what some believe is an innate belief in a power beyond the self or a basic survival instinct - I would not have found what was required to make me well again. Throughout my life I had always credited hard work for most of the positive factors in my life, but now believe that had I listened to God more and to my ego less, my path in life may have been much smoother.

Since 2002, I have talked with many people who appeared to have symptoms similar to mine and who were also unable to receive the answers they required to resolve their issues. Unfortunately, far too many allopathic practitioners either lack training or are unable to identify problems associated with a stressed liver resulting from being saturated with toxins for many years. If the body is overloaded with toxins, the liver cannot function properly. Hormones created in the body naturally are then 'dumped back into the system', wreaking havoc, including the 'crawly' feelings, anxieties and depression.

Bowel Elimination:
Elimination on a regular basis is of vital importance, as it is one of the best ways to rid the body of toxins. However, the colon must be healthy

to function properly. Normal, healthy persons should have at least two good bowel eliminations daily. The approximate amount should be about two feet of fecal matter, should float and not be too dark, but not too light in color either. The perfect elimination should be approximately one inch in diameter and be in one piece, with a curved shape such as a comma or an 's'. If feces sink, stink or appear undigested, it often indicates a problem that must be addressed, as well as one which may require the assistance of a nutritionist or naturopath. A good practitioner will identify problems, and recommend appropriate enzymes and specific nutrients that will help to heal and revitalize the colon so it can function properly. It is also important to reduce the toxic load on the body by reducing anti-diarrheal medication or stool softeners. Toxins can also destroy good bacteria in the colon and lead to a variety of bowel diseases including *IBS* and *Crohn's Disease*

Again, far too many in the allopathic medical and health professions suggest it is normal to have fewer bowel eliminations per day, or may even suggest that eliminating every other day is normal. Unfortunately, the yardstick they use to ascertain normality often is to compare one patient's elimination pattern or volume to other patients, who may, themselves, be unwell. Be sure to seek the advice of a professional who can properly investigate why these problems occurred in the first place.

Tammy and Stacy, my daughter and daughter-in-law respectively, were both diagnosed with *Irritable Bowel Syndrome (IBS)*, and both had suffered with this rather undefined condition for a number of years. Stacy made the choice to visit a naturopath, one who was able to help balance her system. With a change of diet and added nutrients, she is now free of this disease. On numerous occasions, my daughter had been admitted to hospital in severe pain, was subsequently prescribed various medications, but none helped her condition. Medical specialists had wanted to remove several parts of Tammy's body, including segments of her colon, her ovaries and uterus in hopes of eliminating the pain and discomfort. Toxins can also destroy good bacteria in the colon thereby creating disease conditions such as *IBS, Crohn's Disease,* or a *chronic overgrowth of yeast (Candida Albicans)*. Like me, Tammy had worked around chemicals in a factory for a number of years. Her IBS had been quite severe, but after following the B.A.L.A.N.C.E. program, along with advice from her naturopath and nutritionist, the addition of powdered vegetable greens, revitalizing powder[1] and appropriate enzymes her *IBS* has disappeared.

---

1. Revitalizing powder was created for people with food allergies, poor digestion and 'Leaky Gut Syndrome.' Formulated by Dr. Michael R. Lyon, M.D. and Dr. Michael T. Murray, N.D. to provide gastrointestinal healing and complete nutritional support.

For most individuals, the liver's peak functioning period occurs between one and three o'clock in the early morning hours. This is based on the *Meridian Clock* or 'sun time' rather than standard time zones, and, therefore, must be adjusted for one's location within the time zone, as well as for daylight saving time. For more information on the *Meridian Organ Clock*, please consult Appendix G. As such, working night shifts or simply too many late nights can lead to liver distress. The latter can induce bouts of anger, frustration, fatigue, and reduced creativity. To enable the liver to work more efficiently, especially if the body is already in a diseased state, it is important to warm it. This should be done just before bedtime by placing a hot water bottle (not an electric heating pad) on the body covering the area above the liver.

If food is consumed after seven p.m., it may also add to the liver's burden. If the body is diseased, the liver must remove more toxins, including work on removing cancer cells, cancer-causing agents or other toxic conditions. It is also necessary to relieve some of the burden on the liver, such as occurs with the daily processing of the foods we eat. A good choice might be to have a larger meal of the day at noon and a smaller meal in the later afternoon (a light supper) for this same reason. This is a common practice in the sun-belt regions of the world. If this is not possible, then ensure that the larger meal is eaten as early as possible in the evening. Consuming heavy meals after seven o'clock in the evening is not the best practice.

At the time, my liver was slightly enlarged, causing much discomfort - and I assumed my body was reacting to the food ingested. The solution was to massage my liver with three or four gentle pushes, three times a day. This not only relieved the discomfort, but also any agitation or anxiety experienced at the time. Often, within twenty minutes following this procedure, I felt the need to eliminate. That was quite consistent with what many others had experienced.

Other practices followed that gave my liver much needed support included the following: twice a day my husband pressed on the edge of my diaphragm just below my rib cage. He also massaged my liver at the right edge of my diaphragm, as well as the pancreas on the left, and, using *MRT*, checked to see if my body was functioning properly. The liver's position should only gently nudge the diaphragm, but not be tight against it. This particular exercise relieved any tightness I was experiencing. I also applied an organic castor oil compress, consisting of two tablespoons of oil on a cotton cloth, to the area over my liver for five days. A hot water bottle was then placed on top of this compress and remained in place for two hours. For readers who wish to follow this practice, it is recommended they take two days off after the first five days on the cycle, then repeat the entire procedure for a total of three times. This process also helps with bowel elimination. If required, the entire process can be repeated every few weeks.

To provide the liver with opportunities to function at its full capacity, as well as help protect the immune system, it is important to have proper sleep. Research suggests that most women require seven hours of sleep a night, while men require eight. An earlier bedtime is one way to ensure the liver, as well as other organs, complete their appropriate functions while one sleeps. Some research even suggests that a bedtime between nine and ten p.m. would be quite beneficial for many, if not most individuals. The body works on a cycle to regenerate and rejuvenate.

Clean water (without fluorides, chlorides, excess sodium or bacteria) is also important for proper liver functioning, as it helps to flush out toxins. Remember the body requires sufficient water on a daily basis to maintain good organ functioning equal to half of its weight (in pounds), expressed as fluid ounces of water; even more if caffeinated beverages are consumed. Another excellent way to increase liver functioning and improve the detoxification process is through juicing.

Juicing:

The body digests raw juices more easily, as it only requires about fifteen minutes to digest raw juice compared to two or three hours for cooked meals. Juicing also gives the liver a break to allow it to concentrate on the removal of toxins that may have accumulated in the body. Fruits and vegetables (both raw and natural, not canned or processed) are natural sources of valuable nutrients and are essential for health and the body's well-being. Juicing breaks down the fiber in the plant and extracts the nutrients. This is much easier than chewing, especially for the elderly. Juices are for everyone, not just for those who are ill.

It is important to find a juicer that strips the fiber, but leaves enzymes in place. A centrifugal juicer may be less expensive, but it does not leave enzymes intact in the same manner as a two-stage juicer. The very best juicers are ones that grind and press, such as *Champion*™ or *K&K* ™ brand juicers. They are more costly, at between three to five hundred Canadian dollars each (or about 250 - 450 USD). The ultra juicer is the *Norwalk* ™, which, unfortunately, costs approximately two thousand dollars. The body requires all of the available enzymes from vegetables and fruit if it is to heal properly. If individuals are unable, due to financial limitations, to purchase a juicer that leaves enzymes intact, another suggestion would be to partner up with a friend or even two. Still another idea would be to arrange a juicing date at a friend's home, and bring your own fruit and vegetables. If one has no other reasonable option, a centrifugal juicer is better than processed juice or not juicing at all.

Juice fasting:

Fasting (from solid food) is commonly believed to be solely a religious practice, but the origins of fasting can be traced to many ancient societies, which understood that the body required a break to rejuvenate the body and the spirit - to remain healthy. Since fasting often coincided with periods of rest, including light exercise and / or with meditation, it took on a religious connotation related to abstinence in several ancient civilizations, especially in the Far and Middle East. Fasting placed an emphasis on control over the habits of the population, and in later societies also became a political tool of dissent against governments or to foster institutional change.

Those fasting practices eventually became part of their respective religious codes and traditions. Today, nutritionists and others have re-discovered some of those ancient 'truths' and practices, believing that the body indeed does need time to rejuvenate. It is now almost a given that the body's detoxification pathways must be strengthened to improve the immune system. Juice fasting is simply one of the modern ways to accomplish those ancient goals.

The average length of time for fasting with juices only would be from one to three days in succession. During this fasting period, no other food is consumed other than juices. Juices should be consumed within four hours of the time it is processed to ensure that the enzymes remain intact. [*My personal preference for juice fasting would be once every three months.*] Begin a juice fast on a weekend in case a reaction occurs Preparation of the fruit and vegetables takes up a lot of time as the juice is consumed every two hours. Drink a glass of fruit juice first, then vegetable, and continue to rotate in this manner throughout the day. That amount of juice is sufficient for most individuals, and most persons will be surprised that they do not experience hunger. The addition of apples to vegetable juices acts as a sweetener and makes them more acceptable to drink. The only negative impact one might experience could be slight amount of diarrhea, which is understandable as the body adjusts to the changes brought about by raw foods in liquid form. The liver will not only benefit greatly from this process, but those on the fast will feel much better when the liver is no longer stressed, or indeed, has healed. **Caution must be taken if one is diabetic. Carrot juice has a high glycemic index that is not beneficial for diabetics. Diabetics can fast, but not with carrot juice. Cancer patients who may be weak or have lost too much weight should not fast at all. If fasting is being contemplated, please consult a nutritionist.**

Many juicers do not require that fruit and vegetables be peeled prior to juicing. Purchase organic fruits and vegetables whenever possible, but ensure they have not aged or have begun to sprout. All produce should be washed prior to use, and if organic produce is not available, ensure they are thoroughly washed, scrubbed or peeled prior to juicing. Apples, carrots and pears do not need to be peeled and actually provide higher levels of nutrients juiced that way. Peelings also add to the amount of beneficial fiber in the juice. It is also a good practice to add pure water to juices to dilute them. This is especially true for carrot juice, a drink high in sugar. As with all juices, take a mouthful, hold it for a few seconds until the digestive enzymes kick in, and then swallow it slowly. Too much taken too quickly, especially carrot juice, is very stressful on the pancreas. As stated above, caution must be exercised due to the high glycemic index of many juices, especially for diabetics. Natural juice will detoxify the system, clear away a considerable amount of metabolic waste, and, as a diuretic, will help the kidneys to expel urine. Approximately 2.3 kilograms (about 5 pounds) of fruit or vegetables produce a little more than a liter (nearly a quart) of pure juice. This is also a wonderful way to change the body from acidic to more alkaline while, at the same time, giving the liver much needed support.

My grandchildren, Katie, (thirteen years old) and Ben (eighteen) were diagnosed (labeled) with *Attention Deficit Hyperactivity Disorder (ADHD)*. For a number of years they had been on rather heavy doses of medication under the supervision of specialists, including a psychologist and a psychiatrist. There appeared to be no other solution at that time. Even while they were on medication, this condition produced other significant health and social issues that had to be overcome on a daily basis. That included a lack of concentration, depression, growth retardation, insomnia, loss of appetite and difficulty with transference of material from the blackboard to their notebooks. However, knowing what I now know – and have described throughout this publication – there were, and are, better solutions available to combat *ADHD* without drugs.

With the help of *NAET*[1] or *NMT*[2], the addition of essential fatty acids and natural vitamins to their diet, the removal of added sugars, dairy products, food colorings, processed foods, and red meats, there was a significant improvement in a few months. Their physical appearance - a more natural color and the absence of dark circles around their eyes - was also appreciably better.

We also learned through this process that when Katie was quite aggressive (and sometimes downright nasty), her liver was hard. After a gentle liver massage and elimination, a gentler little girl re-appeared. Over time, the *ADHD* medications, a rotation of *Ritalin*[TM], *Dexedrine* and *Cylert*[TM], had added an additional toxic burden on her body. Katie's liver also appeared to have difficulty processing these toxins and produced symptoms we assumed at the time were also associated with *ADHD*.

Six months into B.A.L.A.N.C.E., as well as a visit to a nutritionist, who recommended additional nutrients for her daily regimen, my daughter was able to gradually reduce[3] the children's medications, and, in 2004, eventually discontinued them entirely. The results have been phenomenal: Katie is now able to fall asleep quickly and sleep through the night. Both children have put on weight, as previously they were quite thin; they also laugh more and socialize better; both have grown in height an unusual amount during that particular time span; and today, everything is fine at school. Earlier, when my daughter, Tammy, tried to reduce the medication[4] without the B.A.L.A.N.C.E. program, the children's behavior always worsened. This caused difficulty for them, their parents, and their teachers.

---

1. NAET is an acronym that stands for Nambudripad Allergy Elimination Technique developed by Dr Devi Nambudripad (DC, L.Ac., RN, Ph.D) For a brief description of this treatment procedure, see page 141 in Free to Fly (2nd Edition) or consult www.naet.com

2. NMT stands for Neuro-Modulation Technique developed by Leslie S. Feinburg, DC,. A brief description can be found in Free to Fly (2nd Edition), p.115 or visit the following website: www.neuromodsulationtechnique.com

3, 4. **Caution: Removing medications without the aid of a health practitioner could result in withdrawal symptoms, including suicidal tendencies or even death. Always consult your family doctor or prescribing physician, as well as a naturopath for advice before modifying or reducing prescribed medications.**

Take care of the liver; you only have one. Rejuvenate it, give it a break and feel healthy again!

DETOXIFICATION

What is detoxification and why is it required?

Many individuals who don't smoke, consume modest amounts of alcohol, and who exercise regularly believe that it is unnecessary to detoxify the body. However, it is important to remember that the author of this book also matched that description at one point in her life, and was ultimately diagnosed with terminal cancer! In today's world, it is necessary to do some form of detoxification, especially if one is on medication, whether prescription or over-the-counter, or if one is constantly assaulted with chemicals in the workplace or in the home. Individuals who work as hairdressers, mechanics, farmers, factory workers or those who have had surgery or any number of routine x-rays, should make it a habit to detoxify. This is especially true if one consumes a significant amount of processed and packaged foods, which can leave toxic residues within the body.

One of the primary messages in this chapter involves the necessity to clean out the toxic buildup in the body that has accumulated over time. Another is to empower the reader with the knowledge to restore and strengthen the body's powers of healing. Having dealt with support for the lymphatic system and the liver, it is now time to begin a major cleaning of the body. Think of it as the annual spring-cleaning, or being somewhat akin to cleaning out useless temporary Internet files and 'cookies' on one's computer or 'defragging' the hard drive.

If one begins a detoxification process with an excessive amount of accumulated toxins in the body, many individuals may experience symptoms similar to the flu during the detoxification process. This is normal and will pass. During this time, avoid medications for headache, diarrhea, or stomachache, as these medications will only add to one's toxic burden.

Drinking more water will also help if a headache should occur as a result of the detoxification process. In those situations the body is likely dehydrated. Make sure lots of pure water is consumed and refrain from caffeinated beverages such as coffee, colas and many darker teas. Fever and diarrhea also occur for a reason; it is the body's response to the removal of toxins, or when a virus is present in the body. It is recommended that one only take medication for fever if the temperature exceeds 38.9 Celsius (102 °F). In the case of diarrhea, take anti-diarrhea medication only if the symptoms last for more than twenty-four hours.

> *Never detoxify while pregnant. The best situation would be to choose a detoxification regimen prior to becoming pregnant.*

I experienced both nausea and diarrhea with my anxiety attacks, but the realization that I would be fine once the toxins were eliminated certainly made a big difference in my attitude. Within five months all anxiety attacks, which were really toxin attacks, disappeared altogether. That was after suffering for eight years! It was absolutely wonderful to feel healthy again. The worst attack occurred just before I began the detoxification process, when the cancer was still in stage four. When this occurred, I could not eat or drink. My body seemed to be in shock: first diarrhea, then vomiting, followed by cold chills, shakes and hot flashes. I lost my independence and could not be left alone.

One night in particular, about two months after my initial diagnosis, my husband and I were at home while a major snowstorm raged outside. The roads were packed with snow, and being both ill and frightened, I contacted the local hospital. The outpatient nurse on duty assured me that a medical doctor would be able to see me should that become necessary. My thoughts at the time: "What could medical doctors or nurses do for me? Perhaps, no more than I was doing myself, other than supply a sense of security." My husband wished to go outside to clear the driveway in case it became necessary to leave for the hospital. I desperately wanted him to do that, but fear and anxiety prevented me from being left alone. We finally called my daughter, Charlene, who talked with me on the phone while Jim went outside to shovel. This was the only way I could let him go. Although still feeling ill, when Jim returned I began to search the Internet for a faster or better way to stop this insanity. The episode frightened my family and I was determined that no one would ever see me so vulnerable again.

Three months after that incident, while writing this chapter, my husband was at work on the graveyard shift. No longer did I fear being left alone. My children were secure that mom was back to her old self. But most of all, so was I!

The skin is the *'largest organ of the body'*: what does that mean?
The skin is the best place to begin eliminating waste from the body - to keep it clean from clutter – and to permit it to do its job properly. To do that it is necessary to learn about the use of soaks, saunas and how to dry brush on a regular basis to keep the skin cells open and active.

Soaks:
These are among the easiest procedures to accomplish at home. Soaks are also reasonably inexpensive ways to detoxify, as only a bathtub and a few simple supplies are required. Shop around for Epsom salts, as they tend to vary greatly in price. Make sure that fragrances, colors and preservatives have not been added to the salts, as the additives will only increase the body's toxic burden.

One common procedure for preparing an Epsom Salt soak:
1) Fill the tub with water as hot as the body can tolerate.
2) Add one and one-half to two cups (or about 500 ml.) of Epsom Salts.
3) Soak your body in this mixture until the water becomes cool.
4) Rub the skin gently with a natural sponge or white cotton face cloth.
5) If the body contains larger amounts of toxins, a scum may appear on the water's surface from the removal of heavy metals, paint and other chemicals stored in the body. Do not be alarmed. It is necessary if toxins are to be removed from the body.
6) While the tub empties, quickly shower to remove any scum that may be on the surface of one's body. If no shower is available, use a clean, wet white cotton face cloth and wipe the skin with clean water.
7) Dry with a little vigor; again use a white cotton towel. Colored towels and face cloths have dyes that might increase the burden on an already weakened body. (Remember that the skin is an organ and absorbs what comes in contact with it).
8) For added pleasure, as well as to stimulate and enhance the immune system, try three to five drops of essence of lemon, rosemary, thyme, peppermint or jasmine in the bath water. Make sure it is a natural essence, with no added chemicals to enhance the scent. If the latter are present, they can subsequently pollute the body as well.
9) To reduce tension and relax the nervous system while soaking in the tub, try an essence of chamomile, geranium, lavender, pine, birch, sandalwood or ylang ylang.

Notes: When a drop of essence is added to the bath, be careful not to allow the drops to come in contact with the skin until they are diluted with the bath water. These drops are very condensed and potent. [*Once, I made a mistake and forgot to put lemon essence in first; then added several drops after I was in the bath water. It burned the skin on my knee.*] The addition of essential oils to an Epsom salt bath increases moisture in the skin. Essential oils such as lemon or frankincense are beneficial as an immune builder without the necessity for Epsom salts. While soaking in an Epsom salt bath, refrain from sharing one's bath with that special someone. Remember that the skin is highly absorbent, and can easily absorb any toxins eliminated by another person.

Saunas:
Dry saunas are preferred over steam rooms, although a steam room is fine if purified water is used. Most municipal tap water contains chlorine, which can easily be inhaled or absorbed into the body in a steam room. Many commercial steam rooms do not use 'pure' water.

A good procedure for saunas:
1) Drink two to four glasses of water (one to two bottles) before beginning any sauna.
2) Spend fifteen to twenty minutes in the sauna; longer is not better as the body starts to deplete valuable minerals and nutrients after this time. Remember B.A.L.A.N.C.E.!
3) Invite a friend to share the experience if it is difficult to manage the process alone, especially if illness is present.
4) If one is receiving chemotherapy treatments, spend a shorter period of time in the sauna – five to ten minutes would be appropriate.
5) Shower immediately after the sauna to wash the toxins from the skin; a thirty-second cool shower will likely be sufficient.

> **WARNING: Anyone with high blood pressure, should first check with a medical doctor before using a sauna.**

Performing aerobic exercise (e.g., rowing, walking while the arms swing, step aerobics, rebounding) for approximately fifteen minutes prior to taking a sauna will produce far better detoxification results. Aerobics bring toxins closer to the surface of the skin and allow them to be more easily eliminated from the cells.

Can one afford to go to a sauna?

YMCA/YWCA's in North America have a policy to help people acquire memberships if they do not have the financial ability to do so - and most 'Y's have a sauna. If one is financially burdened, contact the nearest 'Y' to inquire and, if possible, apply for a sponsored membership. In some cases it may be necessary to contribute some volunteer time in exchange for a membership. If one's income is moderate, but not quite enough to manage a full membership, then a small fee might be requested rather than the full price. (See page 319 (*Resource List V*) for YMCA/YWCA contact information or consult the yellow pages in the local telephone directory.)

If a YMCA or YWCA does not exist locally, but there is a sauna at a fitness club, contact them and see what can be done in exchange for use of their sauna. Contact an employer, either past or present, and ask if they might agree to become a sponsor, or ask a friend or family member. If one is diagnosed with a disease, or have symptoms such as those described throughout this book, it is too important not to ask for help. You have only one life!

Dry Brushing:

To dry brush, a natural fiber brush is necessary; any other type will damage the skin. Make sure it has a long handle to ensure that the brush can easily reach all areas of the body. Dry brushes are usually reasonably priced, and can be found in most natural food stores. Check local department stores first, but remember they can call the brush 'natural' by name, but the bristles may, in fact, not be natural at all. Ask questions before purchasing a brush, or go on-line to research the company to get confirmation that their product is exactly what is advertised or what is required. (See Resource List II for contact information)

Dry Brushing has a number of valuable benefits:

1) Healthy skin eliminates up to almost half a kilogram (one pound) of toxic waste every day via sweating.
2) Dry brushing helps to keep the skin healthy and free of dead skin cells that contain toxins.
3) Dry brushing helps to stimulate and invigorate the body's 'electrical' system.
4) Brushing also massages lymphatic fluid and moves it throughout the body.
5) It helps to break down cellulite. It is of interest that one seldom sees an oriental woman with cellulite on her hips or thighs, as dry brushing is an intricate part of the oriental way of life.

6) Twenty-five (25) per cent of the body's detoxification is accomplished daily via the skin.
7) Dry brushing increases cell renewal.
8) Most individuals will find that lotions are no longer required as the skin will become as soft as that of a baby.

A good procedure to follow would be to apply the natural bristle brush, starting with the bottom of the feet where nerve ends affect the entire body. Move the brush in circular motions in a counter-clock wise pattern. As each area of the skin is finished, keep the brush's path moving in the direction of the heart. Do not scrub the genital area or nipples as they are too sensitive. Brush the face, neck and head, remembering to proceed in circular, counter-clockwise motions towards the heart. Some individuals may prefer to purchase two brushes; a softer brush for the facial area, although a stiff brush will greatly invigorate the entire body. When the process has been completed, it is suggested that one take a cool shower to rinse off dead cells and 'seal' the skin. Every few weeks it is necessary to wash the brush thoroughly and let it air-dry. Each person in the family must have his or her own brush to keep the transfer of toxins to a minimum. Dry brushing can be done seven days a week.

Other Methods of Detoxification:

Green tea:
The Japanese custom of drinking green tea came from China about 800 AD. The use of tea for medicinal purposes began in AD 1191 when Buddhist monks, who had traveled to China to study, returned to Japan with tea as a medicinal beverage. Eisai was one of these monks and he stressed the beneficial effects of tea in his book *Drink Tea to Improve Health and Prolong Life* (1214 AD). Green tea is a miraculous medicine for the maintenance of health. The benefits of green tea include fortifying the immune system to prevent cancer as well as other diseases. It helps to prevent disease by controlling blood pressure and blood sugar levels. Green tea also reduces low-density lipids (*LDL* or 'bad' cholesterol); kills bacteria; reduces food poisoning; and is an antioxidant.

Some individuals may be concerned about the amount of caffeine in green tea. Caffeine that is contained in normal servings of green tea can stimulate the nervous system, the muscles and the brain. Green tea also contains lower amounts of caffeine than most other caffeinated drinks, and utilizes caffeine and catechin (the main component of green tea) to benefit health rather than inhibit it, as do many coffees and soft drinks. Try decaffeinated green tea, but be aware that many of decaffeinated beverages may well be processed with chemicals (e.g., ethanol), and unless they are processed with pure water, they are actually less safe to drink. Again balance is important; one should not have more than four cups of green tea per day. To prevent excess stimulation at bedtime, ensure the fourth cup is no later than six PM or about four hours or less before one's bedtime.

> I was not a tea or coffee consumer prior to beginning this research, but now relax with a fragrant cup of green tea. Occasionally I add a slice of lemon to enhance the flavor, which not only aids digestion, but also increases the alkalinity of my body. *Rooibos tea* was later introduced to me by one of my naturopath's patients. Her suggestions prompted me to do additional research for the next section of this chapter.

Rooibos Teas:

Rooibos (pronounced roy-boos) means 'red bush', an African slang word of Dutch origin, is a member of the legume family. It is originally green, but turns red when fermented. *Rooibos teas* have been consumed in South Africa for over 300 years, contain natural healing properties, are naturally caffeine free, low in tannin, and high in vitamin C, calcium and iron. These teas can help to reduce the effects of aging; prevent damage to the circulatory system; blocking carcinogens and inhibit allergies. These teas also contain three valuable flavonoids (antioxidants): *Quercetin, Luteolin,* and *Aspalathin.* The latter, *Aspalathin*, is found only in Rooibos tea. This is the best type of tea for most adults and children. It is also commonly used for stomach cramps, colic and nausea, and can be applied to cradle cap or skin rash. Remember that it is always best to consult with one's health provider before changing dietary habits.

Coffee Enemas:

Coffee enemas rapidly help to remove toxins from the liver. In this process, the liver produces more bile, opens the bile ducts and causes the bile to flow, thereby ridding itself of a considerable amount of toxins in merely a few minutes. In addition, coffee contains two other chemicals, theophylline and theobromine. These substances dilate blood vessels and counter inflammation in the gut. They also enhance the enzyme system responsible for the removal of toxic free radicals from blood serum. It also permits the fluid portion of the enema to stimulate the visceral nervous system to promote smooth muscle contractions and accelerate the movement of diluted toxic bile from the duodenum and out the rectum.

Since an enema lasts for about fifteen minutes, and since all the blood in the body passes through the liver every three minutes, *"these enemas represent a form of dialysis of the blood across the gut wall"*. Coffee enemas often provide quick relief when one is fatigued, sleepy, suffers with headaches, or just feeling 'poorly'. They also protect against spasms, pericardial (heart, throat, chest) pain and symptoms that result from the withdrawal from certain medications. Coffee enemas are also effective in the relief of pain. Patients with cancer, for example, can, at times, achieve relief from pain with this process even when standard pain-killers fail. For individuals with cancer, it is suggested that coffee enemas be administered daily, or at least four times a week - for three to four month's duration for the maximum benefit for the colon and liver. This regimen should not be begun unless the body has first been given proper nutrition. Again, first consult a health care provider as the misuse of coffee enemas could affect the adrenals.

Initially, I had resisted trying coffee enemas as I assumed that this would not be a positive experience; as well as the potentially negative effects of high levels of caffeine found in most coffees. Additional research alleviated that initial response. Reading several good books, such as *Cancer Therapy* by Max Gerson, *One Answer to Cancer* by William D. Kelley, and the *Healthexcel Newsletter* helped me to better understand the process. Further research suggested that the human body does not break down the caffeine contained in coffee enemas in the same manner as if it were consumed as a drink. The veins of the anus are close to the surface of the bowel and, therefore, the caffeine is absorbed quickly and efficiently through the hemorrhoidal veins, then directly into the portal veins and on into the liver. Armed with the above information, and after a consultation with a naturopath, as well as conversations with a number of former patients of the *Gerson Institute*, I garnered the strength to embark on a ritual of one enema per day for four months, using ground organic caffeinated coffee. Later I reduced that to one enema three times per week. Since the adrenals affect blood pressure, allergies, emotions, hair loss and more, the above practice was carried out in consultation with my naturopath. Again caution and balance are important watchwords when significant health changes are being made or contemplated.

A coffee-enema procedure:

I used a flannel sheet and rotated four old towels for my enema regimen. Accidents can occur and coffee does stain fabrics. That is why I choose to perform the enema close to the toilet on the bathroom floor. During enemas, some cramping can occur and it may be necessary to carry out a hasty manoeuvre. If that is necessary, pinch the enema tube, remove it and make a quick transition to the toilet. If there is still plenty of coffee in the bag or pail, then reposition yourself, re-insert the tube, release the pinch and continue. Removal of socks and / or wearing old clothes during this process may be wise as they can become stained if an accident occurs. I also placed two pillows under my head for comfort as well.

One personal issue I had to deal with was overcoming the embarrassment that occurred with my first enema. I now realize that just thinking about the process involved, likely brought this on. There is also a lot of work involved with the setup for this process of detoxification, including making the coffee, performing the enema itself, making fresh juice and then the cleanup – pots, towel, dishes, and so on. Despite any initial concerns, the results were worthwhile, but readers who wish to undertake this detoxification regimen may require some assistance with this procedure. For alternatives, please read more on cellular detoxification on pages 123 - 124 of this publication.)

It would be best to stay at home as much as possible during this time, but when I traveled for more than a couple of days, I used an old kit bag for my towels, flannel sheet, enema equipment, and an alarm clock; adding a hot plate, tablespoon, coffee, strainer, and a small bottle of olive oil when a hotel stay was necessary. In large cities fresh juice can easily be purchased, but for some trips, you may have to bring your own juicer as well.

While the preceding paragraphs may seem a bit much for many readers, if all the toxins have not been removed and positive signs of health have not completely returned, it may well be the right decision to make. My naturopath was quite surprised that I was able to stick to my regimen while away from home and that my body showed no negative reactions after that two-week trip. For me, the results were well worth the effort.

It takes many years for one's body to become diseased, with the liver assuming most of that burden. When you learn to recognize when your liver is toxic and under stress during the rejuvenation process, you will understand the importance of enemas and the positive feeling that you have taken the right path toward wellness. For a detailed procedure related to the preparation of a coffee enema, please refer to Appendix K, p. 307.

More on enemas:
During an enema, the bile, which contains poisons, can produce spasms in the duodenum and small intestine, and cause some overflow into the stomach. This may produce nausea, which could result in the vomiting

of bile. If this happens, drink a strong peppermint tea to help wash out the bile from the stomach. This, however, is not a common occurrence. Enemas can be performed in the morning or evening, as well as before, after, or between meals. The morning is preferred as this process could affect one's sleep patterns. Choose a time that will accommodate one's schedule best. As a general rule of thumb after each coffee enema, drink three glasses of fresh juice, such as carrot, apple, or other vegetables. (See specific recipes in Appendix J, pp. 304 - 5)

According to the *Gerson Institute*, the best protocol in advanced cases of disease is to rapidly remove toxins with three to four enemas a day, followed by juicing and a specific regimen of organic food. The institute also recommends centers where professionals can monitor the enemas, or in other situations they may be carried out at home under the guidance of professionals who have been trained in this protocol. Coffee enemas are designed to enable the liver to expel the dead cancer cells at a more accelerated rate. This also prevents a build-up of toxins in the liver, as the retention of toxins by the liver can create liver disease. (See Resource List II, p.316 for contact information for the Gerson Institute.)

After a few months, my adrenals began to malfunction due to the impact of the coffee enemas. I became depressed and 'weepy' for no apparent reason, so it was necessary to make changes to continue with this procedure. The amount of coffee was reduced to two tablespoons, while the detailed procedure outlined in Appendix K (p. 307) was changed somewhat. I used boiled water instead, added the coffee and let it sit for eight (8) hours. I then strained the solution. This reduced the effect of the coffee on my adrenals and provided me with a better balance during the detoxification process. That is another reason why it is so important to be under the care of a naturopath or other experienced health professional during this or any other detoxification process.

Coffee as a beverage: not just a male problem:

It is important to remember that many coffees contain high levels of caffeine, as well as other highly-caffeinated beverages, and can impact negatively on the male *prostate* gland. Caffeine is implicated in over fifty percent (50%) of all cases of *benign hyperplasia* in men. In North America prostatitis and benign hyperplasia now affect about half of the adult male population. Swelling of the prostate often begins by age 40, and is quite common in men over 50, but can occur at a much younger age. Much of this is **not simply due to the aging process** as is commonly assumed. At least one drug manufacturer advertises this condition as a 'growing problem', which their drugs will help to alleviate. While the latter may be true, given the known side effects of many medications, why would one choose to start with that choice as a 'solution', rather than asking what is causing the swelling or growth in size? In many cases, clinical research has clearly demonstrated that the swelling in large percentage of males can be directly attributed to the excess intake of caffeine and refined sugar in diets, as well as to sedentary lifestyles.

While there is little evidence that benign forms of hyperplasia are precursors to cancer, it is logical to assume that repeated stress on any part of the body can ultimately lead to weakened organs and further disease. In any case, the pain, bladder pressure (including bladder and urinary tract infections) and incontinence, as well as the negative sexual side effects associated with repeated or chronic bouts of *prostatitis* and / or *benign hyperplasia* should be enough to prompt sufferers to reduce their caffeine and sugar intake. Excess levels of caffeine are not good for women either as it has been implicated in fibro-cystic breast disease.

The most recent research reported in the *American Medical Association* suggests that drinking smaller (i.e., four to five fluid ounce) cups of caffeinated coffee, have no appreciable negative effect on most humans, and can be beneficial in promoting activity within the brain and muscles. However, ten to sixteen ounce cups of coffee can be very problematic, especially if consumed with sugar. The 'double-double' or 'triple-triple' orders commonly heard in many popular coffee shop line-ups will, in time, catch up with most people. Drinking extra-large cups of caffeinated coffee, causes the adrenal system (and one's energy levels) to bounce around like a yo-yo. One relatively simple solution to this dilemma is either to brew coffee at home or order a medium (10 fluid ounce) cup of coffee in a restaurant or kiosk that is a half and half mixture of regular coffee and decaf. The taste is the same, but drinking coffee this way provides the recommended maximum serving of five ounces of caffeinated coffee in a ten (10) ounce drink that many people enjoy. Several major coffee importers now offer packaged half- and half coffee (i.e., with half the caffeine) mixtures for sale in selected supermarkets. It can be made at home by either grinding a mixture of caffeinated and decaffeinated coffee beans from the local supermarket or coffee specialty store - or by mixing decaf and regular ground coffee in one's kitchen. Or simply order it that way in any coffee shop. It's a great way to reduce caffeine intake or be weaned from those huge jolts to the adrenals provided by extra-large size cups of caffeinated coffee laced with sugar. To remove caffeine altogether, first try half and half (or less decaf to begin more gradually), then graduate to one-quarter regular and three-quarters decaf and so on until the caffeine has been eliminated. This process of adjustment will help with the transition to a better balance, which is the main purpose of this publication. It is also important to reduce one's refined sugar intake from all sources - and a good place to start for heavy coffee drinkers would be to eliminate the sugared donut, as well as any added sugar in the coffee itself! After some practice, most good quality coffees actually taste better without sweeteners. If however, coffee drinkers cannot live without some form of sweetener, choose liquid or powdered *stevia* over other sugar substitutes. One or two drops of *stevia* is sufficient for most individuals. Small bottles of stevia can be kept in one's pocket or purse, or purchase powdered form (packets) for travel.

An added concern: Certain personalities, known as *sympathetic dominant* - the 'race horse' type - should refrain from drinking caffeinated coffee at all, while placid or lethargic personalities - *parasympathetic dominant* types - may comfortably consume two cups a day prior to two o'clock in the afternoon. Other medical research indicates that while coffee is a good stimulant for the brain and can be comfortably consumed throughout most of the working day, moderation is the key. Adhere to a level that can be comfortably tolerated by each person. Be careful, as caffeine is one of the more addictive drugs in our modern world!

More recent research from the *AMA* (June, 2006), reported on by the *CTV Evening News*, suggests that two chemicals that occur naturally in coffee have beneficial health effects that are preventative in nature, providing protection against free radical damage, which is implicated in a wide range of disease processes. This protection is found in all coffees, including decaffeinated, so one does not have to consume additional caffeine to achieve the latter benefits. Readers are reminded of the recommendation in the section on dehydration (Chapter Two), that if one feels tired, replace that afternoon coffee break with a water break.

Other highly caffeinated drinks:

Manufactures have developed a new rave in caffeine beverages designed for the younger set. One such beverage is *Jolt*^{TM} which contains natural ingredients and flavors with no preservatives, but it does contain 150 milligrams of caffeine. In comparison, an eight fluid ounce cup of coffee contains approximately 85 - 100 milligrams of caffeine, with most colas and black teas listed at 30 - 50 milligrams. Other energy drinks that contain caffeine, glucose and other fast metabolizing sugars include *Red Bull, CRUNK Juice, AMP, Full Throttle, Go Fast, Effect* ®, *Monster, EAS Piranha, Defcon3, Liquid Ice, Energy 69* [N.B.- most are trademarked products], with more coming on the market every day. These drinks commonly also contain herbal ingredients, vitamins and amino acids designed to produce even higher levels of energy from fats, carbohydrates and protein in your body. Beer and caffeine combos are also available and have approximately three times the caffeine than colas. Another more recent 'rave' involves the ingestion of caffeine pills containing 200 - 400 milligrams of caffeine and washed down with a pint of beer. Young party-goers have been known to ingest this combination several times throughout a night while literally dancing the night away - then 'crashing' (collapsing) for more than twelve hours. Unfortunately a few deaths have also been reported as a result of this practice, as the pancreas and adrenals can become very stressed during the process. Research also suggests that caffeine may be linked to infertility as well as being connected to miscarriages if one's intake exceeds 300 milligrams a day. As stated above, it also can have a negative impact on the adrenal system, especially when consumed in large amounts in a cyclical pattern, leading to extreme highs and lows. It is important that parents monitor the level of caffeine and sugar intake of teens or even younger children.

Again remember that caffeine is a very addictive drug and it is common for heavy coffee drinkers (or even some individuals with a more moderate caffeine intake) to experience symptoms of withdrawal such as headaches, restlessness or anxiety if they try to quit or reduce their caffeine intake abruptly. During withdrawal, which accompanies most attempts to quit or reduce caffeine intake, it is recommended that drinkers first wean themselves by reducing the amount of caffeine in the manner suggested in the proceeding section on coffee. Always remember to use organic Swiss water-processed decaffeinated coffee to reduce your intake of toxic substances. Another alternative is a product called Caf-Lib™, found in many supermarkets today, which is a chickory-based coffee substitute that contains no caffeine at all.

Energy Balance Cellular Detoxification Therapy:

Cellular detoxification therapy is based on bioenergetic technology, which creates an energy field similar to the energy produced within the human body. The principal is similar to how magnets work through opposing polarities - attraction and repulsion. This therapy utilizes water and sea salt with an ionic array as a conduit for exchanging negative and positive ions in a foot bath. This process helps cancel out ionic charges, producing neutrally charged elements which come out of solution, thereby eliminating harmful free radicals and other toxins from the body. It also restores the body's energy: balances and facilitates the natural detoxification processes; balances and restores the body's pH and electromagnetic energy; and aids the removal of toxins to strengthen the immune and digestive systems, as well as enhance liver function.

Samples of Cellular Detox:

29 year old smoker

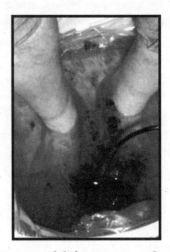

50 year old factory worker

In April 2005, my naturopath changed the method by which my body was detoxified when he purchased one of these cellular detoxification devices. He had researched this particular process for over three years and I became one of his first patients to use this machine. It removes toxins at a high rate in a very comfortable manner, without the normal thirty days of flu-like symptoms and nausea commonly associated with heavy metal cleansing supplements. **And I also said goodbye to lying on the floor during coffee enemas.** The relationship established between teacher and mentor grew even stronger as Dr. Hayhoe taught me how to operate this piece of equipment. Eventually, I purchased a machine in July, 2005 for my own use, and subsequently opened a counselling clinic to help others move forward in their pursuit of wellness utilizing natural medicine and electronic detoxification methods. A second machine was obtained in 2006.

Wheat Grass:

Wheat grass is the richest source of chlorophyll of all foods consumed by humans. Only two ounces of wheat grass juice is equivalent to one kilogram (about two pounds) of raw broccoli. The benefits of *wheat grass* are as follows: it is a live food, full of vitamins and enzymes; it cleanses and re-builds the blood; and improves skin and hair, including the return of hair pigment. It also helps one look younger, especially since there is less sagging of the skin. *Wheat grass* also builds muscle and endurance; helps to fight infections; lowers blood pressure; dissolves tumors and scar tissue; and it regenerates the liver through detoxification. Author Ann Wigmore, was the first person to investigate and promote *wheat grass juice* in North America. In *The Wheat Grass Book* she includes evidence for blood cleansing; the body repair capabilities of *chlorophyll*; its effect on the circulatory system and oxygen supply; and its role in detoxification, including the regeneration of the liver.

Wheat grass juice is a potent source of enzymes. Young people have a natural abundance of enzymes in their cells, as well as an abundance of friendly bacteria in the bowel. Over time, a combination of eating too many cooked foods, excess toxins and viruses deplete the body's store of enzymes - as much as fifty percent by the age of sixty-five. Due to this reduction in enzymes, the pancreas becomes less efficient with age. This can cause digestive problems, which further reduces the absorption of nutrients. Therefore, even if the body is well fed, it may not be able to utilize the nutrients ingested. *Wheat grass* is also an energizer that increases vitality, which is maintained throughout the day. As a blood builder, *wheat grass* and *hemoglobin* are molecularly similar. The only difference is that the central element in *chlorophyll* is magnesium, whereas in *hemoglobin* it is iron. *Chlorophyll* also breaks down carbon dioxide and releases more oxygen into the blood stream in the process. Other research suggests that most, if not all, individuals with cancer or heart disease have low levels of magnesium. *Wheat grass* helps to alleviate that problem.

Wheat grass also builds red blood cells quickly. In fact, red blood cell counts can double within days with a *wheat grass soak* or juicing. According to Dr. Hagiwara, a Japanese scientist, researcher and educator: "When the 'blood' of plants is absorbed in humans it is quickly transformed into human blood". Wheat grass also normalizes high blood pressure by dilating the blood pathways, while it stimulates healthy tissue-cell growth.

There are many reasons to cleanse the body with wheat grass, including drainage of the lymphatic system and the subsequent removal of large quantities of toxins from all cells within the body. When an injury occurs, such as strained tendons or joints, or if a degenerative disease process is present, there is a natural build-up of mucous in the lymphatic system in that particular area. This natural mucous helps ensure that moisture is present, and assists with the proper flow of lymphatic fluid. *Wheat grass* helps to break down the mucous, which allows it to drain, relieving pressure as well as promoting healing.

In *Survival into the 21st Century*, Victoras Kalvinskas states: "In therapeutic amounts, wheat grass will detoxify the body with the elimination of hardened mucous, crystallized acids and solidified, decaying fecal matter." The high enzyme content helps to dissolve tumors and it is the fastest, surest way to eliminate internal waste and provide an optimum nutritional environment. It may also be used as a poultice, wash, douche or bath, to stimulate healthy new cells and fight infections. Chlorophyll increases functioning of the heart, improves the vascular system, uterus, intestines and lungs.

Wheat grass can be used as a sterilizer for water and to clean vegetables of toxic residues. Toxic metals stored in the body such as lead, cadmium, mercury, aluminum, and excess copper, can be successfully removed using small, incremental dosages of wheat grass. It is one of the richest natural sources of vitamin A and vitamin C, as well as an excellent source of calcium, iron, magnesium, phosphorus, potassium, sodium, sulfur, cobalt, zinc, and protein. Bundles of *wheat grass* suspended in an aquarium can both purify and disinfect the water.

Barley Grass:

*Barley grass i*s another of the green grasses - the only vegetation on earth that can supply sole nutritional support from birth to old age. Barley has served as a food staple in most cultures. The use of barley for food and medicinal purposes dates as early as 7000 BC. Roman gladiators ate barley for strength and stamina.

Extremely high quantities of vitamins and minerals are found in green barley leaves. The leaves have a special ability to absorb nutrients from the soil. When barley leaves are twelve to fourteen inches high, they contain very high concentrations of vitamins, minerals, and proteins essential for the human diet, including chlorophyll. These concentrations are easily assimilated throughout the digestive tract and give the body instant access to vital nutrients, including potassium, calcium, magnesium, iron, copper, phosphorus, manganese, zinc, beta- carotene, B_1, B_2, B_6, C, *folic acid*, as well as *d-pantothenic acid* (*calcium d-pantothenate*). Indeed, *green barley juice* contains **eleven times the amount of calcium in cows' milk, nearly five times the iron in spinach, seven times the amount of vitamin C in oranges,** as well as 80 milligrams of vitamin B_{12} per hundred grams of barley green extract or powder.

Barley also contains *glucan,* a fiber also found in oat bran that is reported to reduce cholesterol levels. The roots also contain the alkaloid *hordenine,* which stimulates peripheral blood circulation and has been used as a *broncho-dilator* for *bronchitis.* Barley bran, like wheat bran, may also be effective in reducing the risk of cancer.

Candida Albicans

Ordinarily *Candida Albicans* is a helpful, common fungus that works in conjunction with a range of friendly bacteria in the bowel to digest food, yet its overgrowth in the bowel has been linked to many common yeast 'infections' or infestations within the body, as well as being the most common cause of chronic fatigue. *Candida Albicans* has the ability to change from fungal to pathogenic (disease causing) when the body's pH has become acidic or if the immune system has become impaired due to excess toxins, including antibiotics. This in turn suppresses the immune system even more, and disrupts the *endocrine (glandular) system: pineal, thymus, pituitary, parathyroid, thyroid, pancreas, adrenals and gonads (ovaries and testicles)*. It is important to note that a thyroid issue may well be a symptom of stressed adrenals caused by an overload of toxins in the body. Through the secretion of hormones, the *endocrine system* regulates critical bodily processes such as growth, reproduction and nutrient uptake (metabolism) by the body's cells.

Several ground-breaking books that encouraged the addition of this topic, *Candida Albicans* and other common yeast infections, in this program on B.A.L.A.N.C.E. included *Free to Fly, a journey towards wellness* by Judit Rajhathy, as well as *The Yeast Connection* (an older edition) and *The Yeast Connection and The Woman* (a newer publication) by Dr. William G. Crook. This topic is very important and could well have been included in Chapter Two (**B** for Body), immediately after the section on carbohydrates, as refined sugars play such a major role in yeast overgrowth, as well as in Chapter Three (**A** for Additives and Chemicals). However, since the lymphatic system is such an important component of the body's immune system, and since yeast infections help disable that system, the decision to include *Candida* here in this chapter became much easier.

Wide-spectrum antibiotics can kill off all five major groups of 'friendly' bacteria in the gut[1]. These bacteria are often quickly replaced by a *Candida* overgrowth. When *Candida* cells die they can emit toxins into the gut and bloodstream, which sets up the conditions for increasing the levels of yeast cells within the body, and can contribute to diseases such as *autism, ADHD, asthma, M.S.* and *chronic fatigue.*

---

1. *Birth control pills*, as well as chlorinated water, can also bring about a reduction of beneficial bacteria in the colon which in turn can help to precipitate a yeast infection.

Candidiasis is far reaching in scope, indeed numerous books have been written on this single topic alone. If readers suspect a *Candida overgrowth*, they should immediately contact a naturopath or medical doctor trained in dealing with systemic yeast infections. Reading one of the numerous books available on the subject would also be helpful. Yeast infections often occur after individuals have been treated with wide-spectrum antibiotics, especially when that course of antibiotics is repeated. When that happens, *Candida* grows more rapidly in the body, which creates a continuous and vicious cycle of events. When the following cycle occurs: from infection to antibiotics, to more yeast overgrowth, to re-infection and back to antibiotics again, the body becomes susceptible to a wide range of allergies and disease. It is critical that this cycle be broken and repairs take place in what has been termed a 'leaky gut', where toxins migrate into the blood stream through the bowel wall. For more information on this topic read the author's personal story in Chapter Seven, related to Spirit, Mind and Body, as well as in chapters three to five of *Free to Fly*.

Candidiasis:

1. creates pathogens that inhibit nutritional uptake;
2. permits *rhizoids* (long stringy structures to penetrate the upper layer of the intestinal wall) that cause conditions such as *IBS* (see facing page 129);
3. penetrates the gut wall, which can become inflamed and porous;
4. allows toxins to penetrate the bloodstream and spread throughout the organs of the body, which, in turn, creates food and environmental sensitivities; and
5. creates conditions for auto-immune disorders as the result of:
    - mal-absorption of minerals / vitamins;
    - the deterioration of enzyme functions;
    - a reduction in levels of copper and zinc,
      which are associated with *autism* in children
    - reduced magnesium levels (such as in fibromyalgia);
    - impairment of the nervous system (toxins affect the brain, and can cause paralysis and death);
    - the onset of *chronic fatigue*, depression, toxicity, including the buildup of excess *tartaric* and *malic acids*; and
    - *hyperglycemia* and protein dysfunction.

Wheat and dairy products are a large part of life in North America and unfortunately, these foods can create negative responses to an overgrowth of yeast. The ingestion of these two common foods can cause the overgrowth to enter the nervous system (brain) and produce a morphine-like interaction with the secretion of *endorphins* and *natural opiates* that impact negatively upon the body's response to pain, cognition, memory, perception, blood pressure, as well as sexual activity and immune system responses. If the liver's detoxification ability is impaired from inadequate nutrition and toxic overload, then these toxins are stored in the body's tissues, and can eventually lead to chronic disease.

Symptoms displayed in the initial stages of *Candidiasis* include: bloating and gas, joint and muscle pain, vaginal yeast infections, food sensitivities and allergies, bladder infections, fatigue, sugar cravings, brain fog, bad breath, blurred vision, chemical sensitivity, depression, sinus problems and insomnia. Night sweats may also be linked to *Candidiasis*.

Definition of *rhizoids*:
Rhizoids are finger-like protrusions that fungal yeast cells produce to gather food, such as sugars for their own sustenance. They attach themselves to the intestinal wall and, over time, burrow directly through the intestinal wall causing a condition commonly referred to as a *'leaky gut'*.

Saliva test for excess levels of *Candida* (as a yeast infection):
Put a clear glass of water by the bedside. When you wake in the morning, and before clearing your throat or brushing your teeth, spit into the glass of water. It may be necessary to repeat this process three to four times to cover the entire surface of the water. If within thirty minutes, string-like strands (somewhat like a jellyfish) appear, or if one observes suspended cloudy specks, or cloudy saliva at the bottom of the glass, it is quite possible that one has a *Candida* issue. The more strings, cloudiness, or the faster it develops, the greater the overgrowth. If the water remains clear for one hour, with the original saliva still floating on the surface or if it has dissipated altogether, there is likely no *Candida* problem.

SALIVA TEST

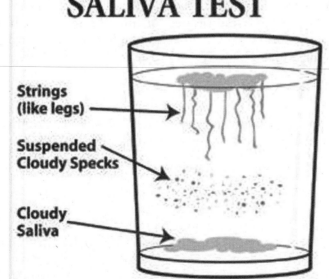

Strings (like legs)

Suspended Cloudy Specks

Cloudy Saliva

Another way to determine whether a *Candida overgrowth* is an issue for you would be to take the self-test for *Candidiasis* inside the front cover of *The Yeast Connection*. If you fail the latter self-test or the saliva test, you should consult a RNCP, RNC, naturopath or MD trained in such protocols for confirmation and treatment.

Common characteristics of a yeast over-growth include:

1. constant cravings for grains, dairy and sugar;
2. poor attention span/memory;
3. hyperactivity;
4. anger, mood swings;
5. depression/anxiety;
6. heartburn/indigestion;
7. jock itch, athletes foot, acne or canker sores;
8. thrush, vaginal infections;
9. dry-itchy-flaky skin;
10. severe diaper rash;
11. food and environmental sensitivities; and
12. difficulty falling asleep.

Treatment of Candida overgrowth:
Eliminating the *Candida* over-growth is crucial, but remember that the process of elimination can take four to six months with most natural anti-fungal products, such as *Caprylic Acid,* or even an older, but highly tolerated drug, *Nystatin*; and while an appropriate diet only keeps the over-growth at bay, that diet must be strictly followed for at least thirty-days or longer. There are also more powerful drugs on the marketplace (e.g., *Diflucan*TM), but they are quite expensive and can be rather toxic to the liver. Great care, research and proper consultation with health care providers are crucial before making any decision to use such powerful modern anti-fungal drugs. The two latter drugs can only be prescribed by a licensed medical doctor.

Probioics:
The use of *probiotics* can help to eliminate excess yeast by re-populating the gastrointestinal tract with friendly bacteria. It is best to use a probiotic that does not contain *lactobacillus acidophilus* or *bacillus bifidus*, as these friendly bacteria may be too sensitive to temperature changes. *Lactobacillus sporogenes* is a higher quality probiotic. A commercial product, *ThreeLac*TM, developed in Japan in the 1990s, and promoted as a fast, effective *probiotic*, is now available in North America (See *Resource List II*, page 316). Many common probiotics have difficulty surviving in stomach acid, and only as little as two to five percent active cells may remain if they dissolve in the stomach, while *ThreeLac*TM is estimated at

eighty to eight-five percent. This latter product is known to help cure ninety-five percent of *Candidiasis* issues. If one is unable to purchase *ThreeLac*™ powder, it is important to choose *Lactobacillus sporogenes* in enteric-coated capsules that dissolve in the bowel, rather than in the stomach. It is also suggested that one take *ThreeLac*™ or other appropriate pro-biotic along with pure dissolved forms of electrolytic oxygen such as *Aerobic Oxygen*™ or *Oxygen Elements Plus*™. These brands contain non-toxic, stabilized electrolytes of oxygen in molecular form and are virtually tasteless products that kill harmful bacteria without affecting the body's beneficial bacteria. It is not hydrogen peroxide, but rather is a dissolved oxygen product sold in health food stores in small plastic bottles. Prepare a solution by adding two to twenty (2 - 20) drops of this product to eight (8) fluid ounces of water. The amount will depend upon the body's requirements as determined via *MRT*. Ingesting too much, too quickly can often cause a headache similar to what breathing pure oxygen too quickly would. It is also very energizing. The oxygen helps to kill any systemic yeast cells in the bloodstream or other areas of the body, and aids *ThreeLac*™ in a system-wide cleansing routine. Use these dissolved oxygen drops one half hour before a meal for best results. It is also best to have the body's requirements checked with *MRT* before embarking on this protocol. A naturopath or appropriate qualified health practitioner will be able to help in this regard.

In addition to the use of natural *anti-fungals* and *probiotics*, vitamins and mineral supplements are also important additions, as one must ensure that any deficiencies that were caused by the overgrowth have been remedied. Then add *glyco-nutrients*, which are simple sugars, such as *mannose, galactose, fructose, xylose, sialic acids*[1], *N-acetyl-glucosamine, and N-acetyl-galactosamine* to one's diet to replace the more common processed, crystalline sugars such as *sucrose*. One should also eat more phyto-nutrients: (raw fruits and vegetables); digestive enzymes and/or sweet bitters; and natural herbs which have anti-fungal properties such as raw garlic (four to six cloves a day) or garlic capsules; grape-seed extract; olive leaf extract, or a product known as '*cats claw*'.

Visits to a *naturopath (N.D.)* will help an individual to balance his or her body, but this usually takes quite a few visits and without a health plan may be somewhat costly. A nutritionist (or *registered nutritional consultant - RNC/RNCP*) can help guide individuals through a month or more of elimination of yeast, sugar, dairy, wheat, as well as fungus bearing foods such as grapes, mushrooms and peanuts. After that process, one may wish to consult a naturopath to ensure that the body is completely balanced

---

1. Sialic acids (N-acetylneuraminic acid) refer to the groups of sugars, including neuramic acid and its derivatives. It is an amino sugar, an essential substance for the body.

The answer to the question of what to eat may seem rather daunting at first, but after a period of time to locate alternate foods, it can become relatively simple. Instead of wheat flour, buy or bake products that use *spelt, rye, kamut,* or *quinoa* flours. Having a European bakery in the area would be a plus as they generally bake with much less yeast and sugar, as well as using alternatives to wheat. If you choose to purchase baked products, always read the labels carefully to know what ingredients are included. Also read *Free to Fly: a journey toward wellness* or *The Yeast Connection and the Woman* for more detailed information on this topic.

Check foods such as spaghetti sauce, cereals, salad dressings, as these are products that also contain added sugars. Dairy products, such as milk, cream and cheese, are foods commonly used on a daily basis by many people. It is important, initially, to replace these items with suitable non-dairy alternatives (such as soy, rice or nut milks) that can supply important nutrients such as calcium. It is also important to remember that even greater amounts of calcium can be obtained from eating green leafy, cruciferous vegetables or sea vegetables. Preparing menus in advance, perhaps for a month, can help to avoid the anguish of realizing just before mealtime that certain foods cannot be eaten today, especially if one is to maintain a proper diet to support your health regimen.

My granddaughter, Katie, age eleven at the time, completed a thirty-day *Candida* diet. I purchased *'walking bread'* from a European bakery – it was made with potatoes and spelt flour without yeast, sugar, hydrogenated oil or wheat. That particular type of bread is quite soft, similar to the bread we have become accustomed to in North America. The replacement of peanut butter with almond butter (or hazelnut or cashew butters), and the exchange of commercial packaged cereals for oatmeal or puffed cereal were not a problem for her. Katie's mom purchased all natural fruit bars available through local health food stores or WalMart. Currently, she takes carrot sticks and bottled water to school for a snack.

As mentioned in an earlier chapter, Katie had *ADHD*, in addition to, or exacerbated by, the *Candida* overgrowth. Ever since the appearance of her first teeth, she had experienced infections followed by frequent courses of antibiotics. In the summer of 2004, it seemed as if Katie had begun her normal hormonal changes related to puberty rather early. In addition, her behavior was out of control, especially in the mornings. It not only scared us, but Katie as well. Her mother, Tammy, had already gone through an elimination process after reading Judit Rajhathy's *Free to Fly,* and had followed that with a nutritional consultation. Her immune system is now much stronger as a result of these changes.

To help Katie remove processed sugar from her diet, I agreed to purchase a *Groovy Girl Dolphin*™ for her as a reward. Katie wrote and signed a personal contract to seal the deal. The formalization of contracts between a child and an adult is often a useful tactic. I was extremely proud that Katie stuck to the contract without a lot of fuss. There was a noticeable change in her behavior and, when asked, she agreed there has been a significant difference in her life. Changes in her eating habits have remained constant, and still includes the consumption of 'walking bread.

Infections

Children with ear infections or tonsillitis:

Before a child begins a course of antibiotics for an infection, consider other less invasive options. It is doubly important before a child's tonsils are removed, to remember that tonsils are a part of the lymphatic system and are required to protect one's health. When tonsils become enlarged that is the body's early warning system speaking out. If at all possible, and without jeopardy to the child's health, consider alternatives other than a direct progression to antibiotic treatments. First, eliminate all dairy and added sugar from their diet. Give them ample amounts of water (half of their body weight in pounds, expressed as fluid ounces[1]) daily, as well as unsweetened fruit juices. Also include extra vitamin C to strengthen the immune system, along with the addition of liquid zinc sulfate. A stronger immune system will benefit the child for more than just this moment in time.

What do pain and swelling tell us?

Pain might indicate that the immune system has begun to experience difficulty. Take note of the amount of sugar that children have ingested in their short life span to date. Include artificial and refined sugars found in cereals, juices, sweets, medications, baked goods, sauces, condiments and, especially, soda pop. Did this attack occur around Halloween, just after a birthday, or perhaps at Christmas, Chanukah, Ramadan or other special holiday when extra sweets may have been more abundant?

When it is necessary to take an antibiotic, have the medical doctor also prescribe an oral anti-fungal such as *nystatin* powder or *enteric-coated* capsules, as the liquid form contains far too much sugar. In addition to

---

1. <u>Conversion Chart: Imperial/US to metric equivalents:</u>

2.2 Pounds = 1 Kilogram; 1 fluid ounce = 30 milliliters; 8 fluid ounces = 1 glass

the antibiotic, purchase a *probiotic* powder (e.g., *Lactobacillus sporogenes* or *ThreeLac*^{TM}) or other high quality enteric-coated probiotic capsules available from health food stores. The inclusion of an anti-fungal should also help prevent repeated ear infections or bouts of tonsillitis - and very possibly prevent the development of a systemic yeast infection in the bowel, which, as stated earlier, appears to be a pre-cursor for many negative health conditions, including *ADHD* or *autism*.

> **Make sure to always check with a medical doctor, naturopath, or nutritionist first before contemplating any major intervention in a child's health or changes in one's own diet or lifestyle.**

My daughter, Charlene, always had problems with enlarged tonsils, but has never had them removed. Recently, she telephoned me about a throat infection. She was quite concerned, as the antibiotics prescribed for her throat infection had not resolved the infection (or the tonsillitis) and more than fourteen days had passed. Charlene was afraid that if it was not resolved, she might require surgery, something she did not want to occur. After her call, and based on some earlier research, she eliminated all sugar-containing products to give her immune system a break; increased her vitamin C; added *Tahitian Noni juice* as an immune booster; drank plenty of pure water; and sucked on fresh cut pieces of organic garlic, an antibacterial agent, every 20 - 30 minutes or so. Natural raw garlic has a strong odor, but works quickly to draw out infection. The white spots on her tonsils disappeared shortly after she began using the garlic, while her tonsils reduced in size. She has not had another bout of tonsillitis since that event.

Care of colds and viruses:

When symptoms of a cold or flu appear, it is generally in response to a weakened immune system, and a time when the body requires help to fight those viruses. When the body's immune system is strong it is able to fight most colds, influenza and other infectious diseases, including *SARS* or the *West Nile Virus*. Flu bugs and other viruses will occur when the body is out of balance, a time when urine pH readings become lower than one's salivary pH. Again these are symptoms that should be addressed by a nutritionist, naturopath or other experienced naturo-therapist.

To prevent such infections, it is necessary to re-build the immune system starting with one of the following products: *Tahitian Noni juice, Goji juice, Moducare*[TM], Essiac[TM], or *GoldenSeal*, along with *Aerobic Oxygen*[TM], or a similar quality source of dissolved oxygen. Have a medical doctor, naturopath, or nutritionist perform a *Muscle Response Test (MRT)* to ensure which of these products is best suited for one's body.

When cold or flu symptoms appear, the first response should be to increase fluid intake and decrease the ingestion of food. Always listen to the body. Keep nourished with juices, preferably home-made ones, such as cold-pressed or juiced carrot and apple; and drink green or Rooibos tea. Use sugar free 'popsicles' if it becomes difficult to drink liquids, but be sure they are made from organic juices without added sugars. Pour boiled water over any toothbrush after each use to prevent re-infection and the return of symptoms associated with the flu. Make sure that each person in the house uses his or her own clean, personal hand towels. Do not share towels or face cloths at this time. Sheets and comforters should also be changed on the bed a few hours after rising. Just toss them in a warm dryer for a short time to eliminate bacteria as a precaution to get over the flu as quickly as possible, as well as prevent the transfer of viruses to a spouse or other members of the household. Toss any robes in the dryer as well, and if the day is spent in pajamas, put on a fresh pair upon rising. Sunshine will also work to reduce pathogens from the flu on blankets or robes, so if preferred, hang them outdoors on the line.

Eliminate sugar, especially refined sugars, from the diet when someone is ill, as it reduces the efficiency of the immune system. Brewing sliced lemon in water can make a good healing drink. If a sweetener is required, use a little organic, unpasteurized honey.

Garlic:

1. Garlic contains vitamin A, B_1, B_2, and C, as well as several minerals, including selenium, zinc, calcium, potassium, magnesium and iodine.

2. For the greatest benefit, garlic must be crushed, cut or cooked so that its natural essential oil, *allicin* is released.

3. Garlic has natural healing properties, lowers cholesterol, disinfects and thins the blood. Garlic has blood-thinning properties so persons with bleeding disorders, such as *hemophilia* or *platelet disorders*, should not use garlic supplements or medicinal doses of garlic. It is also important not to consume garlic two weeks prior to surgery or before one's due date (to deliver a baby), as too much garlic can increase one's risk of additional bleeding during or after such procedures.

4. Garlic is an antibacterial as well, and sucking on a broken garlic piece can reduce tonsil and lymph node inflammation. It is also helpful for staphylococci infections. Remember to use a new piece of garlic several times a day.

5. It is also helpful for vertigo when the imbalance is caused by a middle ear infection. Place a piece of freshly cut garlic wrapped in gauze in the ear canal. One can also use warm garlic oil drops available from most health food stores, which is suitable for both middle ear and external ear canal infections.

> In January 2004, I awoke one morning with vertigo and a blocked middle ear canal. The vertigo was so extreme that Jim had to help me to the bathroom. This particular episode produced severe nausea, with considerable vomiting. My family practitioner wrote me a prescription that I took out of desperation, but it was not effective. Then I visited my naturopath who helped me find more relief. He also loaned me a book, written in 1940, on garlic: *Raw Food Treatment of Cancer* by Humlegaarden and Nolfi. The book recommended a fresh piece of garlic be placed in gauze and inserted into the ear canal. Within five minutes my vertigo was gone. Garlic has known antibiotic properties and the active ingredients are absorbed through the skin/ eardrum into the middle ear.

6. Garlic also can regulate *Candida Albicans*, kill ringworm, increase one's *white blood cell* counts, and is helpful in the treatment of *rabies, scarlet fever, tuberculosis* and more. Three cloves a day is recommended, but start with one clove to get used to it - either chew it, chop it up in salad, or juice it for many applications. One to two drops of peppermint oil on the tongue will counteract the taste and smell of the raw garlic. *Kyolic* garlic (aged garlic extract) can be consumed without the pungent odor of garlic that can emulate from one's sweat glands and is not as harsh on the stomach. Remember, supplements should be organic, contain no preservatives and be checked by a naturopath or nutritionist to ensure they are in balance with the body.

I had a wonderful experience, related to the birth of my granddaughter, Gia. She was the first child of my son, Dan and his wife, Stacy. Gia took a while to come into this world, and her parents and grandparents were pretty frazzled when the decision was finally made to perform a cesarean section to deliver her. The night she was born was an entire story in itself, including a bomb scare, which kept us all trapped in the hospital for hours after her birth. Gia's early life brought back memories of my own children: gripe water, oral drops and, eventually teething gel, so I decided to research these products, as well as others, to ensure that they were both natural and healthy for my grand-daughter.

Choose brands of gripe water that contain natural fennel, dill and ginger, and are made without preservatives, dyes and sugar. However, be cautious, as some brands can also contain alcohol and artificial preservatives. Always read labels or ask a pharmacist!

Stomach upset: choose chamomile tea:
While researching healthy natural products for a newborn affected by gas, a story in *The Tale of Peter Rabbit* by Beatrix Potter came to mind. Peter was not feeling well one night, so his mother made him some chamomile tea before she put him to bed. This particular recipe was available on the Internet, from Rodale Books, in *Herbs for Health and Healing*. It satisfied me that there was something natural available to use with Gia, if need be. Babies should not have sugar added to medicines or juices, except those that occur naturally in the juice itself (Refer to this recipe in Appendix J, p. 296). Remember that refined sugar depletes a baby's immune system. As always, read labels.

Ginger as an alternative to Gravol™ and dramamine:
Gravol™ and dramamine, the generic form, commonly used for nausea, can cause many individuals to become drowsy or fall asleep. These substances often make people feel uncomfortable when they must be fully awake to enjoy a trip and especially to drive safely. So to avoid taking Gravol, alternatives were sought. Taking a ginger pill is a good alternative for travel sickness with few or no side effects for most individuals. Research suggested that 750 or 1000 milligrams of ginger over a twenty-four hour period could work well as an anti-nausea product for most persons. Take one 750 mg ginger pill twenty minutes prior to departure to obtain relief from nausea. Read the label or check with a medical doctor if you are unsure about the use of ginger. Drinking a little ginger tea before strapping on that seat belt is also helpful for many individuals.

Merely setting foot on a boat that floats on water, results in nausea for me. In July 2000, I had been invited to the wedding of one of my mentors in Newfoundland, and the most economical way was to travel by car, for four hours, then take a ferry for six more. Five friends from the YMCA decided to pool their resources and travel to Newfoundland together. Ginger was a real savior for me that weekend. The return trip by ferry was via the Newfoundland CAT, nicknamed the 'vomit comet', an extremely fast vessel that saved two hours of travel time, but also created a lot more motion, especially when the strait was choppy. Marine Atlantic staff actually handed out wet towels and sick bags for each passenger. But the ginger pill taken that day before boarding the CAT, worked like a charm - I was able to stand, walk around and even eat a meal. Ginger was also helpful in another case. My friend's daughter, with *Type I Diabetes*, experienced extreme nausea during her chemotherapy treatments, a very common reaction for most persons. The normal prescribed medication for nausea caused her diabetes to go out of control and she had to be hospitalized. The use of ginger, in consultation with her medical doctor, was the only solution necessary. Another time, offering a ginger pill to a bridegroom, who was a little under the weather from his bachelor party the night before, also worked like a charm. Within twenty minutes the groom's head was clear and his upset stomach had evaporated.

Notes:

If a particular type of cancer spreads to other parts of the body, the cellular makeup is the same. In other words, it is not liver cancer if it initially began in the colon; it is colon cancer in the liver. If a cancer spreads to another part of the body, people often become more frightened if they think they have two different types of cancer. This makes it more difficult to envision a return to a state of wellness.

One possible contributor to breast cancer is the use of deodorants and other cosmetic products which contain a preservative called *paraben*.[1] (*para-hydroxybenzoic acid*). These preservatives are used in many cosmetics and some foods to increase their shelf-life. As such, these deodorants can compromise (clog) the pores of the underarm lymphatic glands, thereby preventing the body from releasing toxic accumulations that are in turn dumped back into the lymphatic system. Some *parabens* can also mimic the hormone estrogen, confusing the body into thinking it has excess levels of that hormone, which in turn, has been linked to the development of certain breast cancers. A detailed discussion on *parabens* can be found in Chapter Five under additives.

1. See discussion in the *Journal of Applied Toxicology* (Vol. 24, p. 5) and page 168 of this book

Deep breathing through the diaphragm stimulates and cleanses the lymphatic system. Deep breathing can increase the body's toxic elimination rate by as much as fifteen times the normal amount compared to situations where breathing techniques were not used.

Conversion Chart and Glossary

2.2 Pounds = 1 Kilogram.	1 fluid ounce = 30 milliliters
1 cup = 240 milliliters (ml)	1 tablespoon = 15 milliliters
1 teaspoon = 5 milliliters (ml)	1 ounce (weight) = 28 grams
g = grams	mg = milligrams (0.001g)
ug = micrograms (0.000001g)	iu = International Unit
re = retinal E	AI = Adequate Intake
Normal body temperature:	98.6 F = 37 C

SUMMARY OF CHAPTER FOUR

1. Lympth glands are the body's warriors; they are essential for life. Learn to keep them clean and toxic free.

2. Rebounding on a mini-trampoline can help to ensure the exchange of lymphatic fluid in the body; can help tighten essential muscles; as well as provide daily exercise, especially for those who find other forms of exercise difficult.

3. Take care of the liver. Massage it and use a hot water bottle at night to warm the liver and assist it to produce extra energy. It is best to not eat after seven at night, get plenty of rest, and drink lots of pure water.

4. Juicing foods helps to relieve stress on the liver. It adds important enzymes that the body requires and helps to alkalanize the system.

5. The skin is the largest organ in the body; help it to work better through the removal of toxins with the use of Epsom soaks, saunas and dry brushing.

6. Drink green tea or Rooibos tea to detoxify. Both add vital anti-oxidants, fortify the immune system, and help to lower blood sugar, cholesterol and blood pressure.

7. Consider a coffee enema to eliminate toxins rapidly. Use only organic ground coffee and follow each enema with three glasses of recently processed juice.

8. Add wheat grass to a daily routine, as a tea or juice. It is the richest source of chlorophyll for the body. Try barley grass as well. Always remember to have a naturopath or nutritionist test one's body for acceptance of theses substances, as well as for the optimum quantity required for the body. Remember that too much may be just as harmful as too little.

9. Think twice before a child is put on antibiotics. If it is necessary, take steps to prevent an overgrowth of *Candida Albicans* and potentially related immune disorders. These may occur after treatment with antibiotics if preventative steps are not taken.

10. Look for all natural alternative 'medicines' before choosing a chemical one, especially for children.

11. Check the web site: *www.4ebr.com* for an energy balance detoxification clinic near you. Also check the August 2006 issue (p. 105) of *Alive: Triangle Healing Products*.

Get Healthy – Stay Healthy
– Make Today Count!

*The majority of people in
North America
do not realize that most
fluorides are poisons!*

*In many countries of the
world, mercury amalgam
fillings are banned!*

Chapter Five

Additives, Chemicals . . . and more!

In the preceding chapter, readers learned about the removal of toxins; this chapter will deal with how to keep additional toxins from entering the body. Having reduced the level of toxins, it is now time to learn how to prevent them from continuing to accumulate in one's tissues. That process is somewhat akin to fixing a leaky boat. It is of little value to continue to bail water from a sinking ship, without also plugging the holes though which water continues to pass. As such, the primary purpose behind this chapter is to increase the reader's knowledge of chemical additives found in common foods, additives hidden in preserved or packaged foods, as well as those contained in common household and personal care products. It is also hoped that the information in this segment will provide the reader with some insight regarding the impact environmental pollutants and radiation can have on one's health.

It is critical to one's survival to understand how additives in foods and personal care products, as well as environmental factors, can negatively affect the human body, ultimately creating disease. Readers will learn how to use that knowledge to protect their bodies, and ultimately create a healthier lifestyle for themselves and their families.

While it is not possible to cover all chemicals and food additives in a single chapter in this or any other book, readers should gain at least a reasonable insight into the chemical laden world in which they live. Research on significant toxins should also leave individuals with the ability to carry out their own research on specific substances that may be negatively affecting their life, or the lives of family and friends. Finally, it is hoped that the information presented will raise sufficient cautions to prompt readers to

read labels on foods before they are eaten, as well as on products purchased for household cleaning and personal grooming, before they are used.

To enable the body to begin to heal itself, readers must obtain knowledge about toxins contained in the foods we eat, the water we drink, and the air we breathe, as well as in the personal care and cleaning products used on a daily basis. With that knowledge comes empowerment and the ability to take action to protect themselves and their loved ones from harm. Today, in North America, as toxins continue to accumulate in humans, the negative consequences of that process has become rather self-evident, especially with near epidemic levels of cancer and heart disease, as well as significant increases in *Crohns' disease, IBS, Fibromyalgia, MS* and more. The lymphatic system, skin, liver, and kidneys are places where toxins accumulate, and these organs may well need assistance to enable them to function properly after years of toxic buildup. Research suggests that everyone is vulnerable or may be at risk until they become educated about toxins, learn to read labels, ask questions, and make appropriate changes in their lifestyle.

Teeth

How many readers have mercury amalgam fillings in their teeth? Mercury is extremely poisonous and many individuals are highly allergic to this type of dental filling. Mercury is not easily eliminated from the body, which becomes a storage container for excess mercury over time. The body can absorb mercury from amalgam fillings through the mucous membranes in the mouth; or in some cases, ingestion of trace amounts from contaminated foods. This can result in mercury poisoning. In other words, virtually anyone with amalgam fillings has been poisoned to some degree, especially if they ground their teeth while sleeping. That may also explain why mercury fillings often cause major sinus problems.

Symptoms of mercury poisoning range from depression, moodiness, nervousness, and insomnia, to fine tremors, convulsions, and kidney inflammation. The most important effects of mercury toxicity are observed in the brain and nervous system. Mercury poisoning can also mimic symptoms of *Multiple Sclerosis* and is linked to cancer in infants. After plutonium, mercury is the most toxic element known to man. The character of the *Mad Hatter* in *Alice in Wonderland* by Lewis Carroll comes from the period in history when *mercury nitrate* was introduced into the hat industry. The constant exposure to mercury vapors eventually caused neurological and behavioral changes in people who worked in the hat industry, hence the term *Mad Hatter*.

Alice and the *Mad Hatter* at the tea party.

It has been documented that people with poisoning from amalgam fillings often exhibited pre-*Alzheimer's* symptoms of depression, anxiety, poor memory and other signs associated with mental deterioration.

Case Study One: The first study, found in *Beating Alzheimer's* by Tom Warren is of special interest. He was an American diagnosed with *Alzheimer's*, but who refused to give in to the diagnosis. He had his amalgam fillings removed, and began a process of detoxification to remove the excess mercury from his system. Amazingly, in 1987, after his body was cleared of the mercury along with appropriate nutritional support, he demonstrated no evidence of his previous 'disease".

Case Study Two: This case is from the early 1990s, and involves a man in his late forties who traveled some 6,000 kilometers (4000 miles) in search of a dentist who specialized in the removal and replacement of amalgam fillings. After replacing his amalgam fillings with high quality gold at considerable cost, everyone commented that it seemed as if he had a 'personality transplant', as his previous symptoms of depression, anger, suspicion, blaming and confrontation had all but disappeared. It was a complete transformation and he was able to live a happy and productive life from that point on. It had been the mercury in what were commonly known as 'silver fillings' where the mercury content was as high as 52%. Today this type of filling can still contain as much as 47% mercury - and there is very little real silver in these amalgams.

There are many dentists who know the proper techniques [1] for removing such fillings safely, but if one is contemplating such a procedure, it is important to first do some research to find an appropriately trained dentist[2]. Today there are also a variety of acrylic and ceramic-like fillings which are safer and less expensive than gold[3]. As always, have a naturopath or another experienced practitioner test these products for acceptance by the body and/or be de-sensitized to them. Of course, each individual is different. The reaction one person may have to mercury amalgams may not be the same as another. It depends on the level of sensitivity to mercury, the number of fillings, the amount of mercury absorbed into the system, and one's state of health at the time[4].

Case Study Three: Sandra's Story

A number of years ago while reviewing applicants for a job, one resume came across my desk that was of particular interest. However, with a high volume of choice candidates for the same position, the ability to interview all of them was not possible, so Sandra's file was set aside. Almost a year later, we had an opportunity to meet. It was about six-thirty one morning when we struck up a conversation. Sandra was the new aquatics director at the "Y" and I was working on my detoxification protocol in the YMCA sauna. After hearing her story, I felt that meeting was no accident, but indeed was meant to be! At that precise moment, I also happened to have the precise information Sandra required to complete her healing.

---

1. The safety precautions associated with amalgam removal are outlined in a later section of this chapter, as well as in Appendix L, pp.308-9. Readers may also wish to check out the following: www.mercola.com/article/mercury/detox protocol/htm or consult www.toxicteeth.org

2. To locate a dentist trained in proper removal techniques, consult the following web site: http://www.talkinternational.com

3. While gold as a dental filling was always preferred over amalgams, recent research would suggest that metals of any kind in the mouth should be avoided as much as possible, including those used in root canals. Please refer to Appendix L on pages 308 .-309 for additional information on mercury amalgams.

4. For more detailed information on the scientific evidence related to the dangers of amalgams, check the Internet for articles, testimony and web sites related to Dr. Boyd Haley, primary researcher for the World Health Organization's investigation into amalgam fillings. A rather poignant discussion of mercury amalgams can be found in Dr. Haley's testimony before the House Government Reform Committee (US Congress) hearings into this subject (Nov.14, 2002) Refer to: http//:whale.to/v/haley.htm. Dr Mark Richardson, Environment Canada, was also a prominent world voice on the dangers of mercury poisoning, especially with respect to amalgam fillings.

Sandra's mother had been diagnosed with *non-Hodgkin's Lymphoma*, so Sandra and her husband put their lives on hold and moved to a small community to be near her mother. The conversation that morning had begun with a discussion of the potential benefits of a wellness program, offered through the 'Y', might have for her mother. However, the most compelling part of the ensuing conversation related to Sandra's agonizing nightmare that had begun so innocently with a piece of chewing gum.

While chewing the gum, Sandra cracked a tooth with a portion of the amalgam filling becoming imbedded in the gum. However, as she was in the process of drinking water at the time, Sandra accidentally swallowed the gum along with some portion of the broken amalgam filling. Unfortunately, her immune system was low at the time due to a variety of factors in her life. Her father had just recently passed away and she was in the initial stages of a new relationship, both rather stressful situations. Added to those stressors was her demanding work as a fashion model. While it brought her independence and a lifestyle she loved, it was a very demanding career. In some respects, she was on top of the world, but too many changes, too fast had created a high level of stress for her.

Approximately one month after Sandra ingested the filling, she began to experience excruciating pain in her joints. As a former university athlete, she had suffered many serious injuries, including broken limbs, so she both knew, and could withstand, a lot of pain. But this pain was unbearable. Unfortunately, her family doctor diagnosed her condition as arthritis, and although her tests had come back negative, he prescribed arthritic medication. This medication had a profound effect on her body: her feet and hands swelled; mood swings appeared out of nowhere; and the pain was unrelenting. At this point, *Percodan*TM was prescribed for the pain, along with muscle relaxants. She also was self-medicated with more than a dozen *Advil*TM (generically known as *ibuprofen*) daily - to little avail. Sandra could not even walk by herself - her husband even had to carry her to the bathroom to assist her with any personal care. The burden of the medication, as well as the pain and loss of mobility, also precipitated a weight gain of over one hundred pounds. This was a woman who commonly swam up to a mile and played tennis for two hours - on a daily basis! Sandra never consumed alcohol and rarely took medication before this incident, but was prepared, if necessary, to try street drugs to find some relief.

Then her situation took a turn for the better. Based on her own research and intuition, Sandra ceased her medications and began to juice three times a day, with every possible mixture of fruits and vegetables, along with added spices. She added garlic, kava kava, and shark cartilage to her diet along with large quantities of multi-vitamins. A combination of circumstances also led her to a medical doctor who specialized in pain and environmental issues. Most of his patients were wealthy, and although Sandra could not really afford his services, her story intrigued him. He ordered blood tests and conducted three hours of pain testing. The conclusion: Sandra had a high threshold for pain. After a multitude of questions, and reviewing past circumstances, the incident with the gum and the cracked tooth surfaced. Sandra and her doctor agreed she should continue with the juicing protocol and maintain appropriate nutrition.

Sandra's protocol had returned some independence to her life, but not much relief from the pain. One day while shaving her leg, she noted a lump on the back of her calf; moments later a large piece of mercury amalgam came off in her hand. Sandra called her husband who removed another piece with tweezers. Since that day the physical pain has ceased! While this portion of Sandra' story may seem far-fetched or incredulous to some - and although there is no obvious explanation as to how the amalgam ended up in her leg - the story is none-the-less true!

However this story is incomplete! There was more pain attached to Sandra's ordeal, but this time it was emotional pain. Although some two years had passed since the removal of the *mercury amalgam* from her leg, the physical activity Sandra always enjoyed in the past, such as endurance swimming, could not be tolerated due to what she believes are toxic levels of residual mercury in her body that continues to affect her joints. And then the most difficult stressor in her life - two subsequent miscarriages, the most painful involving the loss of twins at four months.

Instinct and intuition are powerful vehicles for learning. Or perhaps it was simply God's way of speaking to Sandra, and this meeting was not by chance, but simply one positive juncture on Sandra's personal journey in life. With the help of a nutritionist and naturopath, her body could return to normal, and detoxification of heavy metals would be one part of that process. The knowledge she required to become well again was readily available, but she had to contact a qualified nutritionist to help her continue that journey.

This story illustrates an important point: amalgam fillings are potentially hazardous and caution must be an important watchword when they are present in anyone's mouth. Readers of this book with similar health issues may not immediately recognize the reasons for their illnesses, but it is important to understand that many health issues may be related to one's teeth. In such cases, it is important to evaluate that potential with the help of a naturopath, nutritionist and dentist.

If anyone is considering the removal of amalgam fillings, as suggested earlier in this chapter, it is essential that only dentists with experience in appropriate mercury amalgam removal perform this procedure. Protective equipment and special procedures are necessary to ensure that both patient and dentist do not inhale mercury vapor, as well as to shield the patient from particles that could easily be swallowed. Mercury amalgam removal has improved the health of many, including the strengthening of the immune system, the reduction or elimination of symptoms of *MS*, *sinusitis*, and other disease processes. There are many potential benefits from amalgam removal, but it must be done safely.

In my own situation, I was afraid to proceed with the removal process (only two amalgam fillings) until I had spent more time on the detoxification of my body. I was already in a weakened state and did not believe my body could handle additional toxins should an error occur. Before beginning the removal procedure, a naturopath neutralized my body's sensitivity to accept the original fillings. Following that procedure, my immune system became stronger.

However, the time came to remove those mercury-based fillings and give my immune system a further boost. First, samples of the porcelain and adhesive to be used as replacement fillings, as well as a sample of the anesthetic, were taken to a naturopath. He evaluated them for any potentially adverse reactions and to ensure my body could tolerate these products, especially with respect to any allergies or additional toxins that may be present. Secondly, we ensured that the dentist took all the necessary precautions, including the placement of a rubber dam in my mouth, as well as the use of a face mask, to reduce the mercury amalgam dust from coming in contact with my body. My vitamin C intake was also increased the day before, the day of, and the day following - for a total of three days. I also decided against a local anesthetic as my body was not receptive to anesthetics. The procedure went well, followed by a measurable increase in my level of energy.

Once my amalgams had been removed, Jim decided that it was time for him to have this procedure done as well. He had a greater number of amalgams, as well as constant sinus problems. His family dentist refused to perform this procedure, stating it was unnecessary as there was no danger to his health. However, Jim believed otherwise and made an appointment with my dentist for removal. Before he left for his first appointment, Jim still had some uncertainty as to whether he could have the amalgam removed without freezing. However, upon his return, it was obvious that Jim had opted not to take the anesthetic, with no difficulties or complications. We are both happy with our decision to remove this toxic substance from our bodies.

For those requiring a local anesthetic, especially if illness or disease is present, it is recommended that one limit the strength of the anesthetic from the normal 20 mg to 6 or 7 mg (i.e., about one third of a normal dose) to prevent a more severe toxic reaction. If a person has an alkaline pH, a lower dose of anesthetic is often sufficient compared to those with an acidic pH. It should be noted that infections in the mouth can reduce one's pH level from the normal 7.4 to between 5.5 and 6.0.

In many countries of the world, mercury amalgam fillings are banned!

Thimerasal:

Thimerasal, a crystalline, organic mercurial compound, well known for its anti-fungal and anti-bacteriostatic properties, was commonly added to many vaccines as a preservative. The debate over this substance raged throughout the 1990s and is still debated today. It was withdrawn from all children's vaccines in most jurisdictions throughout the world, while both Canada and Sweden banned this substance from all vaccines in 1995. It is still permitted in selected vaccines for adults in the USA. For more information on this debate, please search the Internet using *Google*™ or your favorite search engine.

Fluorides:

Brushing teeth or drinking tap water has always been such a normal thing to do, and while many people understand that most common toothpastes contain fluoride; how many readers understand that many municipal water supplies, as well as some bottled water, may also contain fluorides? These compounds are known to cause cancer, ulcers, inhibit enzymes, and weaken bones, muscles, skin and certain organ systems. Fluorides are toxic by-products of the aluminum industry processing and are commonly used as insecticides to kill roaches and ants. Most of the developed world rejects the use of fluoride, yet, in North America, it is still used daily in many communities.

Many children receive fluoride treatments annually at school or through state or provincially sponsored health programs. Many parents are also unaware that if a child should eat a family sized tube of toothpaste containing fluoride, it could, and has, caused death in the past. **Caution**: parents who do not change their toothpaste to a brand without fluoride should ensure that all young children never have access to it. **Note**: Newer toothpastes made specifically for children usually do not contain fluoride, but may contain *parabens*, *SLS* and other chemical compounds containing the prefix, *'propyl'*, such as *propylene glycol* or *iso-propyl alcohol*. (See additional information on chemical additives later in this chapter.)

Australian research has shown that as little as one part per million (one ppm) of fluoride can slow down the repair of the body's DNA, as well as inhibiting enzyme activity within the immune system. One should also remember that the immune systems of many senior citizens are already in decline, and the ingestion of added fluoride could increase that rate of decline. Japanese research indicates that similar amounts cause chromosomal damage, while research from Poland discovered that as few as 0.6 parts per million of fluoride could damage blood cells.

When research on this topic was begun, it was a shock to read the back of the family tube of toothpaste. It read "Do not swallow; children under six years of age should use only a pea-sized amount and be supervised while brushing." But perhaps the next and more important question to ask is: "What about absorption?" This is especially important given the highly absorbent membranes of the mouth, where fluoride is readily absorbed upon contact. It is also impossible not to swallow some fluoride when teeth are brushed. Toothpaste with silica, an essential mineral, would be a better option as it helps to prevent cavities by hardening the teeth.

Another fluoride study was conducted in a poison control centre of a major North American city. It cited a total of over 11,000 cases in a single year of children being poisoned by fluoridated toothpaste alone, including three deaths. **The better recommendation would be to purchase children's toothpastes that contain NO fluorides.**

Fluoride in water:

And then fluoride is added to the drinking water! If the local municipal water facility adds fluoride to the water, the best course of action is to drink and cook with bottled 'spring' water. Unfortunately, none of the carbon filters remove fluoride, and while the process of reverse osmosis does, it is expensive and reduces local water pressure, as well as the alkalinity - it lowers the pH of the water. It is also important to avoid the use of fluoridated water in humidifiers as well. Many non-organic juices can contain unusually larger amounts of fluoride from pesticide residues left on the fruit itself. This is often true for oranges. As suggested several times in a previous chapter, the best kind of juice is made at home with organic vegetables and fruits.

Since the 1940s, the percentage of individuals who consume fluoridated water in North America has steadily increased, yet ninety-nine percent of western continental Europe restricts or bans fluoride! The increase in the number of communities with fluoridated water has not only resulted in an increase in the amount of fluoride found in soft drinks and fruit juices, but it has also increased in canned goods (notably soups), which unfortunately leads to increased fluoride levels in individuals who live in communities with non-fluoridated water systems. Even baby formulae can contain this toxin. Fluoride can also lead to hip fractures, and although it promotes new bone formation, those bones are of a poorer quality.

To find answers to wellness issues, illness prevention and natural cures, my journey took me to Ottawa and Winnipeg in Canada, as well as through a portion of the U.S.A. The generosity of relatives along the way gave me time to reconnect with family members and helped to reduce costs. However, at my sister Cathy's home in Ottawa, I soon discovered a situation that created an obstacle for me – the local municipal water contained fluoride! This meant no normal showers or baths if I were to keep moving forward in search of wellness. The solution was to purchase bottled water in which to bathe and to wash my hair. Even after my sauna at the YMCA, I had to resort to pouring bottled water over my body to rinse off and seal my pores. On a more positive note, larger cities with more diverse populations have the luxury of many organic restaurants and foods, as well as many more products from which to choose. Other than the fluoridated water, it felt as if I were at a virtual feast in these larger cities.

On the second leg of my trip by car to Winnipeg, we ran into the same issue with water at hotels and motels. In most cases, hotel management, upon request, contacted local municipal government offices to ascertain whether the local water supply contained fluoride or not, as staff at each of these hotels did not know the answer before calling. It was safe to shower at my older sister's (Terry's) home, as they had a reverse osmosis filtration system, but again I was forced to continue to drink bottled water, as the water produced through reverse osmosis was not alkaline enough for me. In fact, anyone in a diseased state should not drink water produced by a reverse osmosis process as it does not promote an appropriate acid/alkaline balance within the body, and is certainly not alkaline enough to assist someone to return to a state of wellness.

The very same situation existed with many hotels in the U.S.A. Fluoride was present in many of these water systems, and hotel staff were usually unsure, and, therefore, had to obtain confirmation from the local municipal office. In one place in which we stayed, my luck improved – the motel was located in a small community that used water from wells that were regularly tested for bacteria and other contaminants. It was wonderful to have a normal bath. Sticking with this regimen, the results were positive. No negative symptoms were found during the next appointment with my naturopath and none from observations of my own body.

Then my daughter decided to change her brand of toothpaste prior to completing her research on that topic. She purchased toothpaste that was advertised as being both herbal and all natural, and while that particular brand did not contain fluoride, it did contain *propyl glycol,* another chemical that should be avoided. [See more on *propyl glycol* later in this chapter.] The telling point of this particular example is the importance of reading labels carefully, something which cannot be overstated, so you will hear it often as you continue to read this publication.

Topical fluoride treatments are used to help minimize cavities and reduce costs for governments and business in the administration of health care. A healthy diet, proper dental hygiene and healthy saliva from proper nutrition can have a similar effect – and the reduction of refined sugar in cereals would be a wonderful way to begin. The best recommendation would be to eliminate fluorides altogether as their use (and the implied need for them) only masks the real problem in our overly processed food supply - far too much sugar!

Unfortunately, most citizens living in North American communities do not realize that most fluorides are poisons!

Teeth Whitening:

Hydrogen peroxide can also cause cancer of the tongue; and peroxide is the principal active ingredient in whiteners. Baking soda, even the aluminum-free kind, is abrasive and, over time, can cause damage to tooth enamel. *Silica*, an essential mineral, removes stains caused by coffee, dark teas, colas, red wine and more, and may be a better product to seek out for cleaning teeth. Inclusion of silica in one's diet also helps to prevent cavities by hardening the teeth, and also prevents bleeding gums, gum recession, inflammation and bone loss. (See more in Chapter Six on minerals.)

Root Canals:

A root canal is a procedure to allow a tooth that is painful or no longer viable, due to nerve damage or a dead nerve in the tooth, to remain in the mouth. However, root canals can suppress the immune system, and can include toxins from those substances used to sterilize the interior of the tooth during the procedure. In many cases, it is simply a solution of sodium hypochlorite (the same active ingredient as in Javex™ or Chlorox™) or a mixture of Javex and *EDTA*. In addition, toxins generated by the root canal can combine with mercury leached from amalgam fillings, creating even higher levels of toxicity. It is also possible for dangerous bacteria to develop in the cavity left by the removal of damaged tissue from the center of the tooth. This can cause, or contribute to, a rather long list of illnesses and degenerative disease processes. If a root canal is necessary, ensure that a highly qualified dental specialist minimizes any of those possibilities.

According to traditional Chinese medicine, upon which acupuncture is based, each tooth is linked to a specific organ in the body and can affect the functioning of that organ if the tooth is diseased or in distress.

The importance of preserving teeth:

In Chapter Four, *vertigo* was discussed with respect to garlic placed in the ear canal to eliminate dizziness, nausea and vomiting. That vertigo was a symptom of what modern Western medicine assumed to be a virus in the middle ear. Subsequent research in Eastern (Chinese) medicine, however, suggests that when back teeth are removed, they not only weaken the organ that they are associated with, but also weaken the muscles and other structures on that side of the face. Then, when a virus attacks the body, it gravitates to that weakened area. Viewed in this way, teeth are living organs and it is vital that they be protected as much as possible. If teeth were removed earlier in life, it is essential that a bridge or partial plate is installed to help strengthen the face muscles to help prevent middle or inner ear issues in the future.

Pesticide residues and chemicals are found in or on many foods eaten today.

Pesticide and chemical residues:

Chemicals may be intentionally added to processed and packaged foods for a specific function, such as to preserve shelf life; sweeten or color a product; or to assist in the processing itself. Unintentionally, or by design, chemical additives can remain in or on the foods consumed or become trapped in the packaging, or in the packaging itself, such as chemicals found in bread bags made from plastics, or in certain dyes used for advertising on the package. Hormones or antibiotics in dairy and meat products, as well as pesticide residues on fruits and vegetables are some of the more common contaminants found in foods.

To continue one's own research, it is recommended that the following books be read: *Free to Fly: a journey toward wellness*, by Judit Rajhathy, *Additive Alert: A guide to Food Additives for the Canadian Public* by Linda R. Pim, and *What Have They Done To Our Food? A Consumer's Action Guide* by Pollution Probe. See also **Resource Listings I** and **II** (pp. 310 - 316) for a list of useful web sites and publications related to chemical additives.

Approximately eighty percent of all farming operations use pesticides, either to protect the seeds they use to grow crops, to prevent spoilage of those crops, or to improve their appearance! These toxins are also regularly applied to feed grains for animals, which are subsequently consumed by humans. Antibiotics may also be administered to farm animals to combat parasites or as a prevention against disease. Residues from these products accumulate in the fatty tissue of the animals that are eaten by humans, adding to the toxic burden of many individuals.

Hormone and antibiotic residues:

Meat and dairy also contain hormones and antibiotics that have been included to enhance growth and prevent infections in the herds. Due to added hormones from many sources, far too many young girls begin puberty as early as age nine, instead of age fourteen to fifteen, as in the past. One of the best descriptions of this phenomenon is contained in David Steinman's 1990 publication, *Diet for a Poisoned Planet*.[1]

If meat is a necessity to enjoy life or for your body type, one should read *Eat Right F4R Your Type* by Peter D'Adamo and/or *Metabolic Type* by Dr. William Kelly. It is also recommended that one purchase animals/chickens that are free-range; are free from pesticides and hormones; and have been raised on organic grains. Unfortunately, many individuals drink milk and eat meats that contain both natural and chemical hormones. But hormones increase cellular growth and why would individuals with cancer want cancer cells to grow faster? It is particularly important that women with *estrogen-dependent breast cancer* follow a diet that is strictly free of added hormone and/or pesticide residues.

Remember that many pesticides mimic the structure and activity of natural hormones, especially *estrogen*, increasing the overall burden for many women. Perhaps the best reference for this phenomenon was broadcast on a full segment of the CBC's *The Nature of Things* with Dr. David Suzuki, which dealt with substances that mimic estrogen in the body, including certain degraded plastics and pesticides.

Coloring in foods: [2, 3]

Coloring is used in the food industry for appearance. The three basic dyes used to color food products include:

---

1. A condensed outline and discussion of the 1980 Puerto Rican study is also found on page fifty-three (53) of *Free to Fly: a journey toward wellness*.

2. While Canadian regulations on chemical additives may generally be somewhat stricter than those in the U.S.A., Canada still has nearly 300 chemicals registered for use in food production and food handling, including twenty-three used as starch modifiers alone·

3. Regulations in many western European countries are generally much more stringent than those in North America. Most Scandinavian countries, for example, ban the use of all artificial colors in foods, as well as the addition of fluoride compunds to drinking water.

1.) *Cochineal*, made from the dried bodies of insects, which have been used for centuries.

2.) Natural dyes, made from plants, animals and minerals. However, even naturally colored products can contain chemicals and preservatives, unless they are organic. One common substance is paprika (a sweet pepper) used to color cheese, jams, bread, butter, fruit juice, pickles, ketchup, and ice cream.

3.) Synthetic dyes, commonly made from coal tars and petroleum, are among those found in the majority of today's food production. Tartrazine (yellow dye #5), for example, is fed to chickens and is commonly found in tinned fruit, mushrooms, ice cream, desserts and flavored soft drinks.

Synthetic colorings can cause learning difficulties in children, and are linked to specific forms of cancers, asthma, allergies, and more. Synthetic dyes are used because they are cheap and easy to manufacture, as well as for the intense colors they produce. For example, citrus red #2 is still used to color the skins of oranges, yet as early as 1973 it had been judged to be toxic and was withdrawn from the edible portions of food. Many Florida oranges are still sprayed with ethylene gas and red dye #2 to enhance their appearance. In contrast, Norway banned the use of all synthetic colors in foods in 1979.

Preservatives:
Twenty percent (20%) of the world's food loss is due to spoilage. To counter that loss, manufacturers and food producers preserve food a number of ways:

a. chemical additives	b. drying
c. freezing	d. canning
e. refrigeration	f. salting
g. added sweeteners	h. curing (usually with smoke)
i. added spices	j. pickling
k. fermentation.	

There are basically two types of preservatives: anti-microbial, to prevent the growth of micro-organisms, such as molds, yeasts, and bacteria, as well as anti-oxidants to protect food from spoilage and discoloration. Anti-microbial preservatives allow products to have a longer shelf life and are commonly used by many manufacturers. A healthier way would be to dry, freeze or keep food in cold storage. Unfortunately these are not used as much as they should be as processors search for less expensive ways of preserving food.

Readers should also be aware that family-sized packages are among the worst culprits as they often contain higher levels of preservatives to maintain a longer shelf life during shipment, as well as while on display in stores; and/or in the cupboard at home.

Sulfites (sulphites):

Sulfites (sulphites) are commonly allergenic or hypersensitive substances for many humans, but are routinely used as preservatives in dried fruit, (e.g., grapes, most raisins, figs, dried apricots, many fruit snacks), pickles, canned vegetables, ketchup, and many beverages. If one drinks an occasional beer, to lessen the intake of sulfites always choose draft beer (without additives) or bottled imported varieties from Mexico, Europe, or made by *Sleeman's*™ in Canada. No sulfites are used in these bottled products. Consumers should know that the largest majority of wines produced in North America, South America and Australia also contain sulfites. One notable exception in Canada is the *Jost Winery*™ located in Nova Scotia. Again one should choose Western European wines, such as those from France or Germany where additives are either prohibited or severely restricted, or read labels on bottles from other countries diligently. **NOTE:** Most asthma sufferers are sensitive to sulfites.

Typical reactions to sulfites range from mild to very severe. Milder allergic responses can range from simple hives, to a general weakness in the body to some degree of difficulty in breathing, while moderate reaction include vomiting, diarrhea and abdominal pain (cramping). More severe reactions could result in the development of tumors, or produce *anaphylactic shock* resulting in a loss of consciousness or even death.

Nitrates and Nitrites:

Nitrates and nitrites are used to prevent botulism and enhance the flavor of foods, as well as to retain the bright red color, which is commonly assumed to be the 'fresh' appearance of unprocessed meats. They are also found in most processed meats such as luncheon meats and hot dogs. The latter contain especially high concentrations of nitrates. In the past, many of these substances were extremely volatile, and were found in products as diverse as bacon and beer. Nitrates/nitrites are also contained in cigarette smoke, some prescription medications, as well as in tap water from many municipal water supplies. In addition, nitrates/nitrites are often by-products of food spoilage; and are commonly used by food processors to extend the shelf life of many foods. These additives are strongly linked to cancer and birth defects.

BHA/BHT:

Butylated hydroxy-anisole and *butylated hydroxy-tolene*, commonly knows as *BHA/BHT*, are used to prevent oils from going rancid, as well as in the production of powdered drinks and chewing gum. They are also found in some meats and cereals. Both are carcinogens and both are strongly linked to birth defects. *Propyl Gallate*[1] adds a green tinge to food and is commonly used in combination with BHA/BHT. In 1981, several studies demonstrated that this combination produced cancers in rats.

Vitamins C and E:

These vitamins are antioxidants that can safely be used to preserve food, but are regarded as too expensive by many manufacturers. Alternatively, putting packaged items in dark glass containers would eliminate the requirement for an anti-oxidant. Note that the best quality oils are cold-pressed oils, such as pure virgin olive oil, hemp, or flaxseed oils, which are bottled in opaque brown or green glass containers. Vitamin C is also valuable in preventing harmful by-products formed in the body by nitrates.

Flavors:

There are two types of flavorings: natural and artificial. Natural is much preferred over synthetic, but readers should be aware that even natural flavors can be suspect unless their origin is known. For example, artificial vanillin is made from wood fiber, whereas real vanilla is made from pure vanilla beans (from the vanilla orchid), but the latter is usually much more expensive. And natural strawberry flavorings may not have come from strawberries. In fact, to artificially create the strawberry flavor requires one hundred different ingredients; whereas many other flavors may contain at least five such ingredients. So be wary of flavorings – and if unsure, research any items of concern. Artificial flavors can also cause allergies such as heartburn, headaches, asthma, hives, as well as hyperactivity in children.

Enhancers:

Brominated vegetable oil (BVO) is commonly added to many fruit beverages. It can cause fatty deposits in the heart, liver and kidneys, which can accumulate over time. *BVO* is banned in Sweden and Britain. *Quinine* is toxic, but is still used to flavor beverages, such as tonic water. *Quinine* is also known to cause birth defects and it can induce premature labor. Symptoms include difficulty breathing; closing of the throat; swelling of the lips, tongue, or face; or hives; vision problems; headache; diarrhea; nausea or vomiting; restlessness or confusion; fever or stomach pain.

---

1. Reference: World Health Organization, the State of California and the United Kingdom.

Caffeine:

Caffeine is not only found in coffees and many darker teas, but is commonly added to colas, as well as many other drinks. As always, be sure to read labels. Excess levels of caffeine can cause or exacerbate ulcers, heart disease, benign breast lumps, benign *prostatitis*, birth defects, including miscarriage, as well as infertility. It can also affect bone growth. If it is necessary to use decaffeinated products, look for those that have been processed with water, as all other types of decaffeination use chemicals that leave residual deposits on the coffee beans. *Caffeine* and other substances found in coffee, consumed in moderation, also appear to have beneficial effects on humans, so be sure to read the major discussion on caffeine found on pages 121 - 124 of this publication.

Monosodium Glutamate (MSG):

There are no limitations to the list of products or foods in which *MSG* may be found. Common symptoms or reactions to *MSG* include tightness of the chest, a flushed face, headaches, tingling sensations, asthma, depression, and diarrhea. *MSG* also stimulates brain cells; and as an excito-toxin, could aggravate or even precipitate brain disease such as *Parkinson's, Huntington's, ALS* and *Alzheimer's*. In higher concentrations, *MSG* can even excite cells to the point of death. It also has been scientifically proven to be a contributor to obesity. Unfortunately, on many labels, MSG may be disguised as glutamate, spices, natural flavoring, and so on. Some food processors may even refer to *MSG* as hydrolyzed vegetable protein. Therefore, it is vitally important to become a literate consumer and constantly ask questions about additives in foods. On a more positive note, many Chinese restaurants and take-outs, that once routinely added *MSG* as a flavor-enhancer have stopped this practice or will leave it out upon request. Since only processed or prepared foods contain *MSG*, try to purchase fresh foods wherever possible. In short, since the ingestion of *MSG* only appears to be negative for most humans, it would be wise to avoid all sources of this flavor enhancer as is realistically possible.

By 1998 my body had become very sensitive to foods that contained *MSG*. Eating foods that contained *MSG* would cause anxiety, often followed by diarrhea. Unable to sleep; my mind raced and I would become fearful. My husband, Jim, also had reactions to this chemical additive. As a result, we stopped purchasing most canned soups, except minestrone or tomato. We had noted that all soups containing meat, almost always also contained *MSG*. We also eliminated most frozen entrées, battered fish, bacon, luncheon meats, and fast foods from our shopping list. Even many of the packaged fresh meats were found to contain *MSG*, as did many of the fore-mentioned prepared Chinese foods.

When I visited Vancouver, B.C., I noticed that most oriental and other ethnic restaurants had signs that indicated there was no *MSG* contained in their food. Approximately one year later, this was also the trend on the Canadian east coast as well, as most Halifax restaurants had menus that stated they used no *MSG* in preparing foods. I questioned a few restaurant owners who acknowledged that more and more of their patrons had become sensitive to *MSG*, including members of their own families. Unfortunately, many food processors do not, as yet, understand the problem with *MSG* or simply choose to ignore it, as a vast amount of canned or packaged products still contain this sensitizing chemical.

Sweeteners:

Aspartame™:

Aspartame™ is 200 times sweeter than sugar, and contains two amino acids: phenylalanine and aspartic acid. *Phenylketonuria (PKU)* is a metabolic disorder related to excess levels of phenylalanine in the body (or *hyperphenylalanemia*). It can be deadly, causing mental retardation and brain damage in newborns. Even in moderate quantities, *Aspartame*™ can cause headaches, seizures, confusion, and depression. It is also highly addictive. Recent studies, involving some 10,000 people in Florida, reported many negative side effects from *Aspartame*. For more information on this artificial sweetener, as well as the function of the amino acids listed above, please conduct an Internet search.

Sucralose:

Sucralose is a naturally occurring isomer of common table sugar (sucrose). It is extracted and concentrated from sugar and is primarily marketed as *Splenda*™. It is 600 times sweeter than sugar, but since sucralose cannot be digested by humans, it is calorie free. However, when consumed in larger amounts, tests on laboratory rats revealed shrunken thymus glands, as well as enlarged livers and kidneys. The latter may be related to the inability of humans and rats to digest this substance. Sucralose often contains chlorine derivatives, likely from the extraction and/or concentrating processes.

Pure cane sugar, honey and maple syrup:

Pure cane sugar can be found in many larger food stores, as well as most stores that sell natural foods. However, some individuals may have allergies to this member of the grass family. Unpasteurized organic honey and organic maple syrup are excellent sweeteners. Note that honey or cane sugar, in larger amounts, are not recommended for anyone, especially diabetics.

Stevia:

Stevia, a plant based sweetener, has been available for many years and does not affect the pancreas as other sugar products do. Although it may seem to be rather expensive, when one considers the fact that a single teaspoon of stevia equals approximately one cup (500 milliliters) of regular sugar, a container of stevia certainly goes a long way. It is also available in small convenient dropper bottles. Merely one or two drops are sufficient to sweeten a cup of coffee or tea. Some individuals prefer to mix it with chicklin or chicory root powder to improve the taste, but many others are satisfied with the taste as is.

> Originally, when baking for my children and grandchildren, my preference was for smaller amounts of organic cane sugar or applesauce, but stevia, in my view, is the best replacement for sugar, and I now use this product in most of my baking.

If one has an ongoing disease process, the best recommendation would be to refrain from consuming foods with added sugar, in order to allow the immune system time to repair itself, as sugar inhibits the proper functioning of the immune system. As stated earlier in this publication, just one bottle of soda pop can negatively influence the immune system for up to six hours.

Texturizing Agents (i.e., *carrageenan, sucro-glycerides and gums*):

Many texturizing agents can cause allergies, and generally are not digestible by humans. They are commonly used as emulsifiers to prevent liquids from separating; or in the production of gels (such as in desserts); as humectants for moisture (i.e., shredded coconut and marshmallows); or as sequestrants, which combine with metals to affect color and texture (i.e., beverages, dressings, canned meats); and as thickeners for puddings and pie fillings.

Food Processing Agents:

These agents are used to hasten what manufacturers consider the 'natural' processing of food. These include the bleaching of flour; the use of ethyl alcohol for decaffeination; or alcohols in aerosol cans, and so on. Unfortunately most agents used to process foods are chemically based, as it is more cost effective for manufacturers to use them to speed up many forms of processing food.

The following are common examples of processing agents used in foods:

a. acids to prevent batter bubble, i.e., bread and butter spoilage;
b. alkalis to counteract acidity, i.e., chocolate and baking powder;
c. anti-caking agents to prevent the occurrence of moisture, i.e., in table salt;
d. anti-foaming agents to prevent a film from forming on jams and oils;
e. bleach to whiten, and hasten the ageing process, i.e., flour;
f. clarifying agents to remove particles such as iron and copper;
g. dough conditioners make it easier to handle, as well as reducing the preparation time;
h. chemical agents used to extract caffeine;
i. firming agents to keep canned goods and cheeses "firm";
j. enzymes are used to create a desired reaction i.e., cheese curds;
k. glazing creates a polished or shiny appearance;
l. pressurized dispensers create aerosol sprays;
m. releasing agents prevent sticking;
n. starch modifiers;
o. agents for whipping creams, etc.;
p. yeast fermentation, such as alcoholic beverages and breads;
q. surface coatings found on cheeses, fruit and vegetables;
r. dusting agents, i.e., gum; and as
s. 'wetting agents' to produce a dry beverage mix.

Notes: There are significant discrepancies in what is approved or not approved for human consumption in many jurisdictions. Europe and North America have significant differences, but even within North America many anomalies can be found. Many are political, based on food industry lobbies and not scientific evidence. Some examples: Canada permits *red dye #2* and *carbon black*, but the United States does not, while Canada bans *saccharin* and the USA does not. Another example includes *sodium carboyl methylcellulose*, used in processing milk, mustard, pickles, dressings, ice cream and cheeses. The latter chemical is a known cancer-inducing agent.

Both prescription and over-the-counter drugs contain additives and preservatives such as sulfites and *tartrazine* (yellow dye #5). In many cases, it is the additives and not the active ingredients that cause many of the negative reactions attributed to medications. The body often reacts to the coatings, colorings or preservatives used to render the medication into pill form. Many of these allergic reactions may be incorrectly interpreted as negative responses to the drugs themselves. And, if a medication contains several additives, it may be very difficult to determine the offending substance. For example, one common pain medication, *ibuprofen*, often marketed under the brand name, *Advil*™, was found to contain as many as fifteen additives. It is also possible to put the same amount of *ibuprofen* in a capsule with no additives whatsoever. Unfortunately only a small number of pharmacies in Canada or the USA use this technology to package medications in this manner. Many common medications are often enclosed in gelatin capsules, which are manufactured from animal by-products. It is better to seek out clear vegetable coatings that are free from dyes from any source, just to be sure. Again it is important to read labels, or ask the pharmacist.

Estrogen-progesterone pills can actually cause an aggressive form of breast cancer, or could make it more difficult to detect tumors until they have grown to a less curable stage. These medications also elevate the risk of heart attack and stroke. There are alternatives: consult a naturopath, nutritionist or medical practitioner, especially an endocrinologist, who is knowledgeable about more natural products or approaches that could help in these situations.

Acetaminophen **(e.g.,** *Excedrin*^TM **or** *Tylenol* ^TM**) or** *acetylsalicylic acid (ASA)*
ASA tablets (e.g., *Aspirin* ^TM) and *acetaminophen* belong to a class of chemicals known as analgesics and are commonly used for pain relief or the reduction of fever. They are used in preventative therapies as well. In such cases, they are always advertised as low-level or 'correct' doses for individuals. For example a children's aspirin-a-day (or two per day by some practitioners) regimen is promoted as being appropriate for people with certain types of heart conditions , or indeed as a preventive measure for protection of the arteries. Caution is suggested as recent tests have shown that higher levels of these medications, in certain circumstances, can lead to acute liver failure. Manufacturers have also commonly added acetaminophen to a variety of cough medicines, which again adds to the possibility of receiving an over-dose of this medication, especially for individuals who are not careful in measuring their total intake of such drugs from all sources. One should not drink alcohol with *ASA* or *acetaminophen*; and these medications should always be taken with food, and never on an empty stomach.

The Canadian Press (April, 2004)
reported that 10,000 individuals
die each year from
prescription drug use alone!

Remember, B.A.L.A.N.C.E. is critical to good health!

When diagnosed with cancer in 2002 (medical doctors estimated the cancer was active at least two years earlier, in 2000), I had been on *estrogen replacement therapy* (*ERT* or *HRT*) for approximately four years. When the B.A.L.A.N.C.E. protocol was begun, I had attempted to cease all hormone medications, but, at the time, my body was not ready for that. Ten months into the new protocol, I had cut the medication in half; and two weeks later, eliminated it completely. Due to the fact that toxins had been reduced by a variety of detoxification protocols, my body did not experience symptoms of depression or anxiety, especially compared to the withdrawal experienced earlier.

I had, however, begun to experience hot flashes. Actually, they were quite numerous, with as many as four per hour. Herbal remedies seemed like a good idea, but muscle response testing indicated that not all herbal remedies that could be used to reduce symptoms were acceptable to my body. Once again my naturopath came to the rescue by teaching me a method of Chinese acupressure that reduced the hot flashes by over fifty percent. Pinching the top of both ears hard (at the same time) while counting to thirty helped to reduce the severity and duration of the hot flashes.

Personal Care Products and the chemical additives in them.[1]

Propylene glycol:
Propylene glycol is a cosmetic form of mineral oil found in automatic brake and other hydraulic fluids, as well as in industrial antifreeze. It is found in many skin and hair care products and works to retain the moisture content of their products. *Material Safety Data Sheets (MSDS)* for this chemical warns users to avoid skin contact as it is a strong irritant, and that it can also cause liver abnormalities and kidney damage. In general, any additive with the prefix '*propyl*' in any product used for personal hygiene should be avoided.

---

1. References: World Health Organization, the State of California and the United Kingdom.

Sodium lauryl (or laurel) sulfate (SLS):

SLS is the active ingredient in many harsh detergents and wetting agents used in garage floor cleaners, engine de-greasers, and automobile cleansing products. SLS is a well known skin irritant; is rapidly absorbed and retained in the eyes, brain, heart and liver, all of which may result in long-term harmful consequences. SLS compounds can retard the natural healing process; can increase the risk of breast and endometrial cancers; could speed the onset of cataracts in adults; lower sperm counts; and can retard the proper growth and development of children's eyes. The MSD sheet for this compound recommends the use of self-contained breathing apparatus, along with rubber boots, chemical resistant gloves, and safety goggles. It also advises that all operations be performed in a chemical fume hood for added protection. Yet, it is commonly found in make-up cosmetics, shampoos, conditioners, toothpaste, and more!

Sodium laureth sulfate (SLES):

SLES is the alcohol form (ethoxylated form) of SLS. While it is slightly less of an irritant than SLS, use of this product may cause increased dryness of the skin. Both SLS and SLES may cause potentially carcinogenic forms of nitrates and dioxins to develop in shampoos and cleansers by reacting with other ingredients within these products. These reactions can even cause relatively large amounts of nitrates to enter the blood stream during a single shampoo. They also irritate the scalp and can increase hair loss.

Deodorants:

Deodorants are usually processed with aluminum. Use natural crystal deodorants[1] instead, which are available at most natural food, health food and several department stores. Ensure that no chemicals have been added to enhance the deodorant, including fragrances other than essential oils. Always remember to read labels.

Mouthwash:

Mouthwash made with ethyl alcohol has been implicated in oral, tongue and throat cancers, so it is important that readers conduct research to find acceptable alternatives to commercial mouthwashes. A variety of safer commercial mouthwashes, as well as some options for making your own are listed in the AEHA Guide to less toxic products (see pp.333 of this publication)

---

1. Visit www.nonscentedtoxicfree.com for more information on natural crystal deodorants, as well as other toxic free personal care products.

Hair dyes:

Research suggests that several dark or black hair dyes can cause cancer and are also known to effect bone marrow development. Approximately twenty percent (20%) of all cases on *non-Hodgkin's Lymphoma* are linked to hair dyes. There have even been cases of people with bone marrow cancer who went into remission once they stopped dying their hair. Again caution is the important watchword!

Diethanolamine (DEA):

DEA is a colorless liquid used as a solvent, emulsifier or detergent (wetting agent). It works as an emollient in skin softeners, lotions or as a moisturizer in other personal care products. When DEA is found in products that contain nitrates, it often reacts chemically with those nitrates to form potentially *carcinogenic nitrosamines*. While earlier studies seemed to indicate that *DEA* was not a carcinogen, more recent research has demonstrated its carcinogenic potential, even in formulations that exclude nitrates. *DEA* may also irritate the skin and mucous membranes.

Other additives to avoid:

One should also avoid products that contain *triethanolamine (TEA)* and *mono-ethanolamine (MEA)*. The best way to be protected is to recognize those ingredients that are most likely to cause contamination. These include ingredients that contain prefixes or inclusions such as *PEG, polyethylene, polyethylene glycol, poly-oxyethylene*, as well as those with suffix 'eth', as in *sodium laureth sulfate*. The latter may also be referred to on the labels as *SLES* or *oxynol*.

Polysorbate 60 and polysorbate 80 ™:

Polysorbates are typical ingredients in de-greasers and detergents, but are also commonly found in cosmetics, hair restorative products, as well as bath and body products. These products can also contain contaminants. They are also found in several trade name brands of artificial ice cream bars savored by teens. Teachers report that after eating these products that those kids became "wired, unable to concentrate or learn". Many schools in Nova Scotia and other jurisdictions have banned synthetic ice cream bars from cafeterias and canteens.

Sodium poly-acrylate:

Disposable diapers contain *sodium poly-acrylate*, which absorbs water and urine, draws moisture from the skin and, in the past, has caused toxic shock syndrome in tampon users, and while it has been removed from the latter, it is still permitted in the manufacture of diapers.

Methyl parabens (methyl para-hydroxybenzoic acid [1,2]):
UK scientists have claimed that preservative chemicals found in samples of breast tumors probably came from underarm deodorants. Their analysis of 20 breast tumors found high concentrations of *para-hydroxybenzoic acid* (*parabens* is the shorthand name for this class of chemicals) in 18 out of 20 samples tested. *Parabens* can mimic the hormone *estrogen*, which is known to play a role in the development of breast cancers. These preservatives are used in many cosmetics and some foods to increase shelf life.

"From this research it is not possible to say whether parabens actually caused these tumors, but they may certainly be associated with the overall rise in breast cancer cases," says Philip Harvey, an editor of the *Journal of Applied Toxicology*, which published the research, "Given that breast cancer is the largest killer of women and a very high percentage of young women use underarm deodorants, I think we should be carrying out properly funded, further investigations into parabens and where they are found in the body," Harvey told the *New Scientist*.

Chemical cousins of *parabens*: a discussion
The new research was led by molecular biologist Philippe Darbre, at the University of Reading. She says that the ester-bearing form of *parabens* found in the tumors indicates it came from something applied to the skin, such as an underarm deodorant, cream or body spray. When parabens are eaten, they are metabolized and lose the ester group, making them less strongly *estrogen-mimicking*. One would expect tumours to occur evenly, with 20 percent arising in each of the five areas of the breast," Darbre told the *New Scientist*. "But these results help explain why up to 60 per cent of all breast tumours are found in just one-fifth of the breast – the upper-outer quadrant, nearest the underarm."

However, Chris Flower, director general of the *Cosmetic, Toiletry and Perfumery Association*, challenged the studies findings. "There are almost no deodorants and body sprays that contain *parabens*," he says. "Although they are in most other creams and cosmetics, the safety margin is huge and they would not have any effect on enhancing growth of new tumours." Darbre replies that deodorants and antiperspirants have only stopped containing *parabens* in the last few months and that the tumours she studied occurred prior to this time - and that many products containing *parabens* can still be found in the marketplace.

---

1. If readers are interested in learning more about parabens, try an Internet search on Google[TM] where dozens of articles on this substance can be found.

2. To obtain information or purchase products that are guaranteed chemically free of parabens and other toxins, and are scent free as well, contact www.nonscentedtoxicfree.com

A small survey by *New Scientist* of three British High Street shops and one supermarket found deodorants in each location that contained *parabens*, although many of the other products did not. However, many other products used under the arm commonly contained parabens, such as body sprays, hair removal creams and shaving gels. Body lotions, face creams, cleansers and shampoos also frequently contained *parabens* .

Lead Poisoning:

Individuals with lead poisoning may become hyperactive, agitated, or experience temper tantrums. Even short-term exposure to high doses of lead can cause an individual to vomit; experience diarrhea or convulsions; slip into a coma; or even die. Long-term exposure can result in anemia; can cause damage to the nervous system; as well as fatigue, sleeplessness, headaches, and more. Cataracts can be caused, in part, by heavy metal poisoning within the body.

More recently, lead has been discovered in low-cost jewelry worn by children, yet no level of lead is deemed safe for a child. Note that as little as the amount of pure lead that can fit on the head of a pin can cause damage to a child's health. Fortunately, lead has been removed from paints and gasoline, which were the largest contributors to lead poisoning in the past. Although lead has not been used in household plumbing for two generations, some older types of solder used in copper pipes[1] did contain lead. As a consequence, older homes should be checked for the presence of lead in the plumbing or in the soil around the perimeter of the home that was a result of old, flaking, lead-based paints. Remember that the body can store lead in the bones, soft tissues and organs for decades adding to the toxic burden on the body. In the USA, children are routinely screened for lead, while in Canada, this does not occur. Home testing kits available include the *Lead Inspector* ® manufactured by Abotex.

A few heating and cooking issues:
Candles (paraffin):

When a paraffin candle burns, particles are released that can go directly into the lungs. Beeswax or plant-based candles are best as they actually clean the air around them in a room. Unfortunately, a variety of imported wicks used for candles can contain lead. To test for lead in a wick, rub the metal core of the wick against paper to see if a grayish black smudge appears. If it smudges, that is usually due to lead in the wick. To ensure safety, it is best to avoid wicks with shiny metallic wire cores.

---

1 When re-soldering copper pipes used for drinking water or bathing/showers, ensure that the solder used contains no lead. It is only marginally more expensive than the type that contains lead. If advice is required, ask a reputable plumber or qualified hardware store representative.

Barbecues and Carbon Monoxide:

Charcoal barbecues can give off dangerous gases, especially, carbon monoxide. The better choice for barbecues is propane, with ceramic bricks, rather than charcoal. Remember to heat up the bricks prior to cooking with them for the first time. This will drive off any unwanted residual contaminants that may be present from the manufacturing process or from the packaging.

"Teflon", PFOS and/or PFOA Cookware:

Teflon is a man-made substance that will never break down in the environment. It contains *perfluororo-octanic acid (PFOA) or perfluororo-octanic sulfonate (PFOS)* and has been linked to birth defects in humans, as well as the deaths of pet birds. Individuals can even experience 'teflon flu' symptoms from heating this product found in a wide range of commercial cookware. These chemicals are also commonly used in the photographic and aviation industries, chromium plating, and more. In June 2006, the Canadian government announced regulatory changes that would soon ban these coatings on the cooking surfaces of pots, frying pans, WOKS and other cooking utensils. They are already banned in many countries in the European Union and it is expected that many other countries will soon follow their lead.

Microwaves and Plastics:

Plastics often contain dioxin-based carcinogens that can cause cancer, especially breast cancer. Plastic containers, including plastic wrap, should **NEVER** be used in a microwave. Use glass, *Corning Ware*™, or ceramic containers for heating food in a microwave. Instant foods such as TV dinners, instant soups, and the like should be removed from their original packaging and heated in one of the safer containers mentioned above. Do not freeze your plastic water bottle as this also releases dioxins from the plastic.

Microwaves can distort the molecular structure of food and, as a result, the body may be unable to absorb the nutrients properly. A microwave oven can change the molecular structure of food through the process of radiation. In 1989 a research article by Dr. Lita Lee entitled *Health Effects of Microwave Radiations - Microwave Ovens*, observed an increase in the rate of cancer cell formation in the blood of subjects tested related to food cooked in a microwave. A 1992 publication, prepared for forty-three (43) American states by Raum & Zelt, stated that naturally occurring amino acids had undergone isomeric changes, as well as a transformation into toxic forms. Several Russian studies in the 1990s revealed negative chemical transformations within foods and, as such, microwaves were banned from sale or use in the old Soviet Union.

A test that readers could perform for themselves might help to illustrate the information in the preceding paragraph: take two plants of the same height, variety and apparent health; then water each - one with water from a microwave (cooled to room temperature) and one from your drinking water. It has been demonstrated that over a six-week period, the one fed with microwave-heated water slowly died while the other continued to flourish.

> During one period of recovery, I removed the microwave from my home. After that occurred, my grandson arrived one day and wanted to re-heat food from the refrigerator. He noticed the microwave was missing and could not understand how he could re-heat food without it. Unfortunately, it is the only way children of my grandson's generation know how to re-heat food. Now he is quite capable of putting a stainless steel pot on the stove to steam the food or pop a slice of leftover pizza in the oven.

Prions:[1]

Sometimes a scientific discovery shakes the confidence of scientists, making them question whether they truly understand nature's 'ground rules'. That's exactly what *prions* (pronounced pree-ahns) have done to scientists' understanding of the ground rules for infectious diseases. Prions cause diseases, but they are not viruses or bacteria or fungi or parasites. They are simply proteins, and proteins were never thought to be infectious on their own. Organisms are considered infectious, but proteins were not, or, at least, they never used to be. Now researchers are coming around, albeit reluctantly, to accepting the somewhat shocking fact that naked protein can become infectious. *Prions* entered the public's conscious and vocabulary during the *mad cow epidemic* that hit England in 1986. This disease is technically known as *spongiform encephalopathy*, which refers to the ravaged brain looking somewhat like Swiss cheese. More recently, it has been the subject of heated debate between Canada and the United States related to the importation of beef cattle and beef products. Sheep and goats also can contract a form of this disease called *scrapie*, while the human equivalent is referred to as *Creutzfeld-Jakob disease (CJD)*. The latter can be fatal, and although once considered rare, there have been an increasing number of deaths in the past twenty years. Since *prions* are linked to these devastating diseases, bone meal and blood meal should not be used in the garden as contaminated dust could permit *prions* to enter one's system.

---

1. To learn more about this topic, read *Prions: Puzzling Infectious Proteins,* by Ruth Levy Goyer, Ph.D.

These additives and chemicals are only but a few of the many that are present every day in our food supply and in our environment.

So what can be done to reduce additives entering the body?

Begin by reading labels and purchasing fewer processed foods. Whether a person buys organic or not, all produce should be washed and rinsed thoroughly. Toxin-free soaks and washes for produce are available in most health-food stores, as well as in some supermarkets. One can also peel away the skin as much as possible if organic produce is not available, but remember, in some cases, the fruit or vegetable may have absorbed chemicals (such as excess pesticides or enhancers) through the skin and, therefore, it is not possible to completely remove these contaminants. The more one buys fresh local products, the less likely that an enhancer is required to keep the product fresh for market.

Buy organic:
It may cost more to buy organic produce, as it is a more labor-intensive process to farm organically, but as more people buy organic the more the price could be reduced, albeit it will always remain somewhat more expensive due to the increased labor costs. Although such a price reduction may be in the future, a healthier life is worth the extra cost today. In addition, some organic farmers sell directly to the pubic through weekend or farmers' markets, thereby eliminating the middleman. In these situations, organic produce or free-range meats often cost only slightly more than those containing pesticides or hormones commonly sold in most grocery stores. And try out one's green thumb: grow produce in the garden and put the excess in cold storage for the winter. Ensure the soil has been tested for proper nutrients and that no pesticide residues exist before planting an organic garden.

Certified organic:
Certified organic products are individually labeled. Hand written signs on or near the product does not prove the product is organic; ensure that appropriate stickers are attached. Organic farms must undergo a

yearly inspection to ensure that no pesticides or chemicals have been used. There must be no pesticides or chemicals in the ground for three years previous to new plant growth to become certified as an organic grower. Unfortunately, neighboring farms that still use pesticides can contaminate crops on organic farms either due to water run off or wind-borne particles that can be carried to adjacent fields. In these situations, those fields cannot qualify as being 'certified organic'. However, since crops from these fields have incidental residues that are generally lower than foods grown with pesticides, they can be sold as *"not grown with pesticides"*, and these crops are certainly better than pesticide-sprayed produce. Still, 'certified organic' is the only way consumers can know for sure.

Readers should reference available information for sources for pesticide-free or free-range and organic food products. They are readily available from most provincial and state organic growers' organizations, or consult The *AEHA Guide to Less Toxic Products* produced by the *Nova Scotia Division of Allergy and Environmental Health Association*. In the Atlantic Canadian region, a pamphlet entitled *What on Earth is ORGANIC ?*, sponsored by the *Maritime Certified Organic Growers* and *Speerville Flour Mills of New Brunswick* contains a very clear, but simplified explanation of this often misused and overused term.

Reduce the consumption of farmed fish or larger fish species:

If one consumes animal products, it is important to buy anti-biotic free and hormone-free (free range) as much as possible. Low fat salmon, containing high levels of omega-3 fatty acids, is among the best fish choice as long as it is not 'farmed' salmon. Wild salmon is the best choice, although it is not easily available due to the depletion and contamination of many of the wild stocks. Most Pacific canned salmon is made from overrun wild stocks and is a good source of *omega-3 fatty acids*. Unfortunately, farmed salmon almost always contains hormones or antibiotics. In addition, larger pelagic (deep ocean) tuna often contains higher levels of mercury compared to smaller fish such as cod or haddock. Albacore tuna, a smaller variety of tuna, often used for canning, should contain less mercury, although new warnings were issued in January, 2007 related to the amount of this particular fish that should be consumed, especially for children. A general rule of thumb to remember is the following: if one fish consumes another fish, it not only includes its own quantity of mercury, but that of other fishes as well.

Pesticide use on lawns:[1]

Discontinuing the use of pesticides on lawns and ensuring that neighbors do not promote this practice as well is the only way to go in the 21st Century. Re-think what is considered a weed. In Europe, as well as in

---

1. One of the easiest-to-comprehend discussions related to the cosmetic use of pesticides is found in *The Garden of Eden, Revisited* (Chapter 15) of *Free to Fly: a journey toward wellness.*

rural communities in times past, dandelions were commonly accepted (and even used for food) rather than obliterated with pesticides. If you wish to eliminate dandelions, the mind set should be to dig and pull rather than spray and choke. The exercise will be beneficial as well. Replace weeds with a piece of sod to ensure another weed does not take its place. If the soil is too wet, too dry or lacks nutrients, weeds may spring up. Carry out an inspection (visual check) to determine what the lawn requires and fix it organically. In Canada, there are over 142 communities that ban pesticides for cosmetic use, such as on flower beds, lawns and gardens. The largest urban municipality (>400,000 pop.) to do so in Canada to date is the *Halifax Regional Municipality*. They used a four-year-phased-in program to accomplish this feat, but not without considerable political lobbying by environmental, health and citizen's groups, and opposition from vested interests such as the chemical/pesticide manufacturers and commercial applicators. Readers should try promoting this approach in their town, city or rural community.

Companion planting:
If you have rose bushes, plant radishes, garlic or chives to protect them from unwanted pests. This approach also works to protect other plants as well. Like weeds, pests indicate a problem with soil conditions in the garden, so remedy the cause, not the symptom.

'Natural' pesticides:
Common herbs such as paprika, red chili powder, or lemon peel all help to ward off ant infestations. Other natural pesticides for plants can easily be made at home. One example is to put garlic and green onion tops into a blender, strain this puree, mix with soapy water and spray on the leaves and stems of plants. Make sure the container is labeled before storing it away. Also check the *Canadian Green Consumer Guide Directory* for further tips.

Use natural products such as organic vinegar to soak the shower nozzle or clean scum from shower doors and walls rather than commercial products that commonly contain chlorine or ammonia. A more appropriate commercial choice would be *DownEast* ™ or *Nature Clean*™ brands of home cleaning products. A very inexpensive booklet, entitled *AEHA Guide to Less Toxic Products* also lists a wide range of cleaning and home care products that one can make on their own. Updated information is also available at www.lesstoxicguide.ca.

Notes: Although a few processed foods indicate they are natural or organic, this does not mean they are necessarily healthy to eat. They may contain *propylene* or other chemicals with a *'propyl'* prefix, which are commonly used in industrial products such as *propylene glycol,* a commercial grade antifreeze. Although they can cause kidney damage and inhibit skin growth, manufacturers commonly use these substances to obtain smoother textures in makeup, hair and skin care products, as well as in some toothpaste. It is a buyer beware situation!

The bedroom:

The most beneficial time for healing is while the body sleeps. This is a time when the body energizes itself and when the liver does its best work. It is also a time when other organs are rejuvenated. For that reason, the bedroom should be a safe, serene and healthy place. There are hundreds of suggestions to ensure that happens. Many are found in Environmental Health Centers in many states and provinces, or in an extensive chapter entitled *Sleeping with the Enemy* in *Free to Fly: a journey towards wellness* by Judit Rajhathy.

Make one's bedroom an oasis!

For detailed information on safer building materials as well as those toxins commonly found in homes, contact *Canadian Mortgage and Housing Corporation (CHMC)* and ask for a free copy of their latest catalogue, *All About Housing. CHMC* produces a large list of inexpensive books for sale related to healthy homes, including *This Clean House, The Clean Air Guide,* and *Building Materials for the Environmentally Hypersensitive.* In the United States, contact *HUD* for similar product guides and information booklets. In the Atlantic Provinces of Canada, contact Robin Barrett at *Healthy Homes Consulting,* for detailed environmental testing and advice on environmentally safe building construction.

Some basics for maintaining the bedroom as a safe haven include:

• Keep pets such as cats, dogs and gerbils out of the bedroom.

• Plants create mold, but if they are desired in the bedroom it is important to leave a two inch head space in the container; use only clean soil; cover the top with marbles or stones; and water from the bottom, rather than the top.

• Bookshelves; remove them from the bedroom and tuck any book being read at night in the drawer; that will ensure that dust does not have a place to collect.

• Do not make the bed until after it has been 'aired out' for a few hours.

• Vacuum the mattress when the bedding is changed, preferably in the morning.

• Ventilate the bedroom while asleep. If necessary, shut the door, then open a window.

• Reduce clutter.

• Floor covering: choose hard surfaces such as wood or tile rather than softer ones, as hard surfaces absorb less and are more easily cleaned.

• Walls: use paint rather than wallpaper, as most wallpaper not only out-gases chemicals initially, but it can re-absorb those gases and continue to out-gas chemicals for years.

• Windows should be low emission (low-E with argon gas) to reduce ultra-violet and infrared rays. It also saves money on energy bills and will prevent sun fading of fabrics. Be sure to use cotton curtains to ensure that dry cleaning is not required.

• Furniture: Avoid the use of *MDF* board, interior plywood or particleboard; or seal any exposed edges that are made from above materials, including the backs and bottoms; use low emission paints - those with no *VOCs* are recommended; use aluminum tape and vapor barrier or foil to seal any products that might emit toxic fumes. The refurbishing of furniture must also take place outside of the home during the months of May to September (in Canada especially) to ensure that toxins from varnishes and stains are reduced or eliminated.

• Closets: Clothes should have room to move, especially if the closet is on an outside wall; closets that are too full, limit air circulation, which in turn can create mold. Closet doors should fit loosely and not too tightly in the frame;

• Beds: Use a densely woven barrier cloth cover (300 threads) cotton or 100% nylon over the mattress; and ensure it is lined with cotton. Beware of dark colors, and choose unbleached cotton wherever possible. Pillows should be 100% white cotton and newly purchased annually. Wash all products, before using them, at least two to three times to remove the chemically based sizing added by the manufacturer. Change the bed linens weekly; and vacuum the mattress at this time.

Notes: It takes approximately two months to one year to air out a newly manufactured mattress. If one has sensitivities or has a disease, it is best to purchase a display model or switch mattresses with the guest room for a few months until the new one has been fully aired.

It is also possible to order beds for environmentally hypersensitive persons that are made entirely out of cotton and wood. A *Google*™ search will usually locate sources/manufacturers of such beds close to where a reader may live.

Around the House:

● Laundry: it takes a heat of 140 °F (60 °C) to kill dust mites, although freezing temperatures for several hours will also destroy dust mites. Stuffed toys can be placed in the freezer or thrown in the dryer on low with a clean tennis ball.

● Mats: use one outside the main entrance and one inside the door. Ask people to remove their shoes when they enter the home. Residues such as cadmium from tires, pesticides and other toxins can be carried in on one's shoes.

● Squeegee the shower dry to prevent mold.

● Dust furniture with a damp cloth.

● Do not steam-clean in the summer; perform this operation between October and April, especially in more northern climates.

● In more northern latitudes, purchase new furnishings between May and September so that proper outdoor ventilation and out-gassing can occur.

● Dry-cleaning: Try to purchase clothes that do not require cleaning with chemicals, but if it is necessary, ventilate the vehicle on the way home and hang the articles outside without the plastic wrap for a few hours before storing them in a closet.

● Dyes used in clothes can have an affect on the body's health, especially darker colors, i.e., dark blue or black jeans and the like. The color applied to blue jeans is fixed within the fabric by adding a mordant, which is an aluminum-based product.

● Anti-bacterial products, such as *Javex*™ and tile cleaners that contain chlorine, can weaken the immune system.

Avoid the following chemicals commonly found in cleaning products:

1. *Phosphates* accelerate algae growth and reduce aquatic oxygen supply.

2. *Nitrilotriacetic acid (NTA)*, and *ethylene-diamine-tetra acetic acid (EDTA)* release heavy metals into the food chain.

3. *Nonylphenol ethaxylates (NPEs)* are toxic to marine life and may have disruptive effects on wildlife. *Nonylphenol*, a by-product of *NPE*, can have an immediate negative impact on aquatic life.

4. *Halogenated organic solvents* biodegrade very slowly and can have carcinogenic effects when they accumulate in human organ systems.

5. *Butoxyethanol* is one of many *volatile organic compounds (VOCs)* that react with oxygen to create ozone.

My personal cleaning tips:

• Use organic vinegar to clean windows, wood and ceramic floors, counter tops, stoves, and walls. It is also effective for eliminating mold spores. For scouring sinks, toilets, tubs, or the shower, use aluminum-free baking soda and water. Both baking soda and vinegar are chemically safer to use and are cheaper to purchase.

• For a natural mosquito repellent, use a quarter of a cup of olive oil with five drops of lemon essence. Employing this protocol, we had no problem this past summer with mosquitoes. This mixture not only smells great, but also leaves the skin and hair shiny and moist. Remember that essences are concentrated and can burn your skin, so be careful to dilute them properly.

• I recently discovered a wonderful national award-winning soap shop, *Oliver*, located in Bouctouche; they also sell these products at the Farmer's Markets in Dieppe and Moncton, in New Brunswick (Canada). They carry soaps, shampoos, and conditioners in a range of wonderful essences, made from all natural ingredients. (See *Resource List II*, p.316).

• There are literally hundreds of suggestions available through the *AEHA Guide*, health books, environmental health centers, and more. Be sure to read labels, as natural does not always mean safe. *Nature Clean* ^{TM} and *DownEast* ^{TM} products, including dish washing powders, laundry detergents and shampoos, are available in many supermarkets and appear to pass the test environmentally as well.

Diagnostic x-rays:

X-rays are inherently dangerous to human health. Avoid x-rays if at all possible, and certainly minimize the number required for diagnostic purposes. Mammograms are also controversial, as these tests also involve x-rays, but do have the potential to detect the early stages of breast cancer. Individuals without a high risk for breast cancer should, at least, read a 1995 study, published by the *British Medical Journal*, before deciding to have a mammogram. That particular study verified a 200 percent increase in inductal carcinomas attributed to mammograms. As the *American Cancer Society* states: "X-ray is radiation, there is no safe level of exposure." If one must have an x-ray, a few precautions should be taken after the procedure to eradicate the negative effect on the body. Those include eating eggs (in moderation), Iceland Kelp or Dulse, and adding garlic, onions, chives or leeks to soup or vegetable dishes on the day of the x-ray, as well as for a few days after. Additionally, one should increase or add vitamin C to your diet the day before, the day of, and the day after the x-ray to help enable toxins to dissipate. It is also recommended that one could also soak for twenty minutes in a bath containing one cup of natural sea salt and one cup of organic baking soda.

More on X-Radiation Treatments and Bone Scans:

As noted above, after any treatment with radiation, one should eat one free-range egg per day, as well as lots of garlic to help the body to repair damaged *DNA*. Also drink only natural spring water that has been boiled to eliminate all possible toxins in any form. In addition, one should only wash with pure water while undergoing such treatments; do not use soaps of any kind, including herbal soaps. NOTE: Lungs lose fifteen percent (15%) of their capacity as a result of chemotherapy or radiation treatments. After bone scans, drink carbonated beverages containing phosphoric acid, such as colas. The phosphoric acid will help to flush the radioactive agent from the body as quickly as possible.

In modern medicine, it is sometimes difficult to avoid having x-rays. It seems to be the one test that many doctors order automatically. For example, I felt it was necessary at the time to have a larger number of x-rays to determine the precise location of the cancer. I accepted that. What I could not accept was the 'logical necessity' on the part of my oncologist to have an x-ray prior to each and every visit to his clinic. This was expected of all patients! His reasoning: if the examination at the clinic revealed that you were ready for chemo, the x-ray that ensured your heart and lungs were fine, had already been completed. Prior to completing my own research, I accepted this and dutifully had the x-ray.

After that appointment I was informed, "All's well and we'll see you again in three months."

Since that time, I have refused routine chest x-rays. The clinic is informed via e-mail each time a requisition for blood and urine tests, x-ray and clinic appointment is received. One appointment included a request for a stomach x-ray to inspect the tumor that had been documented in 2002. My bowel elimination was regular; I had no eating issues, bloating, pain or cramps, so why would I need an x-ray? The oncologist advised me that it was necessary in order to begin chemotherapy on time - before an issue got out of hand. He would know when chemo was required by the size and location of the tumor.

My response was that radiation could increase the size of a tumor, so I declined the x-ray. He hoped that I would change my mind before the next visit, but unless I was in distress with symptoms that related to my stomach, that would not happen. It takes a lot of courage to say no, and I found it a difficult, but necessary decision for my own wellbeing. Unfortunately, patients should not be forced into a situation where they must respond in this manner or, indeed, suffer feelings of guilt.

The appointments with my first oncologist were extremely stressful due to his lack of faith in my utilization of complementary (natural) approaches to healing and my feelings of losing control during each appointment. I was very positive in my beliefs, yet always had a feeling of trepidation prior to each appointment and a loss of personal power following it. I acknowledged that in an e-mail to him, and we subsequently spoke about it, but in the end little changed.

In 2005, I wrote the oncologist a letter ending our relationship as patient and doctor. Before the letter was able to reach him, he called concerned about my low blood test results. The blood work indicated to him that I had *disease-induced anemia* (meaning caused by cancer) and his recommendation included a blood transfusion, followed by chemotherapy. My research indicated otherwise and I refused both the transfusion and the chemotherapy. I then informed him that I no longer wished him to continue as my cancer specialist and a letter to that effect was in the mail. I explained that my decision was based on the negative way he interacted with me during each visit. During each and every appointment, he persisted in stating: "You are going to die from this disease". On the phone, however, he agreed that he "had overstepped his bounds in the hopes of changing my mind about natural medicine". My response included a rather blunt statement that he "was not God, and did not have the right to take away my hope, indeed anyone's hope. Doctors are supposed to be teachers!" He replied: "He only wanted me to have a better quality of life and felt that chemotherapy would achieve that". We agreed to disagree and parted company. I have since sent him brochures of my work in the off chance that he might indeed give hope to others when modern medicine is unable to help them or when it is appropriate to complement conventional medical treatments with natural health protocols.

I was eating healthy, sleeping seven hours a night, eliminating twice daily, breathing deeper, exercising regularly, and having more fun than I had for years. Why would I want to add toxins, throw-up, lose my hair, breakout in sores, sustain possible nerve damage and ultimately create an even more aggressive cancer? The tumors were shrinking, and blood tests were beginning to return to normal.

Chemotherapy:

Chemotherapy treatments can cause many adverse reactions in the body. The suggestions listed below may help to alleviate many of the negative side effects of chemotherapy. Therefore, after each chemotherapy treatment, consider some or all of the following:

a. Cold sores can be treated with a piece of raw garlic rubbed directly on the sore.

b. Infections at the base of the nails should be bathed in warm salty water. Use the unrefined sea salt as outlined in the second chapter of this publication.

c. Hemorrhoids are unfortunate, but none-the-less common side-effects of chemotherapy. Organic flaxseed consumption will help; and *Kyolic garlic* can be taken as a supplement or, alternatively insert a fresh cut piece of organic garlic into the rectum (like a suppository). Witch hazel is also a wonderful product to help reduce hemorrhoids, but ensure that it is chemical free. Carving a piece of ice into the shape of a suppository and inserting it into the rectal canal is also helpful.

d. As soon after each chemotherapy treatment as possible, drink freshly made juices that are high in folic acid, such as bean sprouts or leafy green vegetables.

e. Avoid fruits that contain strong acids (e.g., lemons, oranges, limes, berries, rhubarb and grapefruit) to prevent cystitis or painful joints; eat apples, pears, melons, peaches, apricots and bananas instead. Purchase fresh, ripe and organic fruit, if available.

f. Increase the intake of fruits and vegetables, but limit the amount of spinach, beets and tomatoes. Use at least three times as many vegetables as fruit, as the latter are generally more acidic and contain more sugar.

g. Drink green tea to inhibit infection.

h. Take additional supplements of selenium, vitamins A, B, and E to enhance the immune system following chemotherapy. The immune system must be kicked into high gear quickly - as much as up to thirty times its normal strength - following chemotherapy. The appropriate amount of supplements required for one's body can be verified using *MRT*. Be sure to select a qualified practitioner who is skilled in this procedure.

i. Try ginseng (whole root or pieces) to help overcome tiredness and lack of mobility;

j. Consume light miso soup, kombu and nori.

k. Boil all water, including bottled water.

l. Add Ginger (750 to 1000 mg) - one pill per day will help to prevent nausea whether traveling, fighting a flu or during chemotherapy treatments. (Please consult a qualified health care practitioner.)

m. Chemotherapy destroys the immune system. Try *Noni Juice, Essiac, Moducare, Goji juice* or other immune supplements to increase one's immune response.

n. Juice one half-pint (one quarter of a liter) of Granny Smith (green) apples with fennel; then add one half-pint of carrot juice. Also include melons, beans, nuts, seeds and green leafy vegetables in a daily diet.

o. Detoxification should be undertaken prior to beginning chemotherapy; between treatments (usually 1-7 days depending upon the strength of the chemo); as well as after the treatments have been completed. It is critical to support the liver and the immune function (Read more in Chapter Two).

Tamoxifen ™:

Tamoxifen™ is administered to breast cancer survivors, but has been linked with endometrial cancer of the uterus and cervix. It also has several unpleasant side effects. In 2001, the Journal for the National Cancer Institute stated: "Not only does *Tamoxifen*™ fail to reduce breast cancer, but it can also increase the incidence of this disease". Look for alternatives that benefit the body and discuss them with a health care provider. Pomegranate juice is one such alternative, as it has been found to inhibit the enzyme aromatase by up to eighty-percent without the side effects of drugs. Aromatase inhibitors prevent androgen from being converted to estrogen, as excess amounts of this hormone, as well as chemicals that mimic estrogen, such as many pesticides and some plastic by-products, are strongly linked to cancer. For a discussion of the critical side effects (e.g., other cancers and pulmonary embolism) as well as less serious side-effects of *Tamoxifen* and *aromatase inhibitors*, please go to www.breastcancer.org.

> *If someone with cancer goes back to the same lifestyle after chemotherapy, radiation or surgery, "the cancer will return". It would be akin to thinking that no more apples would grow because they all were picked off the tree.*

Electromagnetic fields (EMFs) **and** *electromagnetic radiation (EMRs)*:

1. The human body is a complex electrical system (ranging from 2 to 20 Hz, which is the basis for all cell division, vision or movement by or within the body.

2. Electricity is all around us in the workplace, in our home or at play, and includes appliances, computers, heating pads, curling irons, hair dryers, fax machines, and more.

3. Mutant cells in the body are produced by long periods of exposure to *EMFs* through electrical fields used by the gadgets and gizmos that are a part of everyday life - and indeed, make the world fast, fun and efficient. Even a watch battery up against one's wrist could cause cellular changes.

4. Recommended safe levels for *EMF* near the body is less than 0.2 milligauss - the scientific measure of electromagnetic frequency and wavelength. A new computer monitor's *EMF* levels should be at zero milligauss at 10 inches (25 cm) from the screen or lower if possible. And remember that the *EMF* emission levels are highest at the back of the monitor, so one should not sit opposite the back of any terminal or PC. Beginning with what was termed the '*Swedish II standard*' in the mid-eighties, rigorous standards for monitor emissions have been adopted for computer monitors and televisions. Today, most new monitors have very low *EMF* or *EMR* emissions. If you have an older monitor or are concerned about possible *EMR* emissions, purchase a grounded *EMR* screen filter for your computer monitor. Also make sure that you sit a comfortable distance away from the screen, and ensure that the back of the monitor does not point towards another user. Better still, if you can afford it, replace your old tube-type monitor with a new flat *LCD* screen.

5. As a rule of thumb, the smaller and cheaper the motor, the higher its *EMF* output. One notable exception occurs when the motor's rpm level is very high. Electric hand drills and saws fall into the latter category. Both drills and skill saws emit high levels of *EMFs* but, in addition, these motors are in close proximity to the user - in his or her hand. It is also recommended that small appliances be unplugged when not in use, as they still can continue to emit *EMFs*.

6. Have a naturopath test your body for *EMF* endurance with MRT utilizing a hair dryer as the test object. If your body reacts to this appliance, then it may be necessary to carry a magnet to minimize *EMFs*. *MRT* may also be used to also check magnetic field strength, as not all magnets have the same strength or capacity.

In 1998, when I became seriously ill, my body had begun to let me down. A medical doctor suggested that one of the problems could be that my electrolytes were out of balance, but again the tests came back negative. Then, in 2000, a naturopath asked me if I slept close to any electric apparatus such as a clock, night light, electric heat register, or if I used an electric blanket or heating pad. I answered yes; I was quite close to an electric heat register in bed. He suggested we turn the heat off at night. I did so and my body felt better almost immediately, and to such a degree, that I no longer trembled anymore. Today, I warm my bedroom up a half an hour before bedtime, and shut the heat off completely while I sleep. I now feel far more refreshed each morning as well.

There are many sources for electrical fields and the resultant *EMFs* they produce. It is important to search for alternatives to reduce levels of *EMFs* that humans come into contact with on a daily basis. For example, when I warm my liver, I use a hot water bottle instead of a heating pad. I even stopped using a microwave, as I personally felt that the food's chemical make-up was distorted in the process of heating. Today I use an air popper, or expeller-pressed canola to make popcorn. Hair rollers that use steam would also be a wonderful replacement for an electric curling iron. Fortunately, my hairstyle is short and easy to air dry. Even my husband had a bad experience while using an electric drill, actually experiencing feelings of anger and depression when in use. Until this topic was researched, we never understood the reason for his behavior.

Try this change tonight: move the phone, clock, or any plugged-in electric appliance to at least five feet or more away from the bed. Buy or borrow a gauss meter and test all electrical appliances at home and in the office, including faxes, photocopiers, shredders, computers and monitors.

With the writing of this book, came many new sources of information, as well as the refining of my instincts, which leads me to a personal story about my home and *EMFs*. I had lived in my home for slightly less than five years before my body began to break down. The elderly couple that lived here before me had both died of cancer; the home next door also had cancer related deaths involving a husband and a son. Cancer has also affected people who lived in three other houses in a circular area around my home. At the time I had suspected chemicals may have been implicated, although I was unaware that any had been used in this section of the town. Later, the name of an elderly gentleman that performed dowsing came up, (i.e., he checked homes for *EMFs*), and I telephoned him late one evening. Fifteen minutes later, seated in my kitchen, we began a long discussion related to *electromagnetic fields*, including his knowledge of some electrical wiring that had been placed underground a number of years ago, just a short distance from my home.

The discussion that followed included information on the *Hartman Grid*, a checkerboard twelve-foot square of negative electrical energy found under every home. It was named for its discoverer, a German physician, who investigated the lines of negative energy the grid created with regard to its impact on his cancer patients. After this meeting, I went on-line and learned about the *Curry Net*: sets of positive and negative energy lines about twenty-five to fifty feet apart that have been implicated in a range of illnesses, including cancer. Although these energy lines are not found under every home, it is suspected that they can cause sleep disturbances, depression, inflammations and rheumatic diseases. Larger cells and cancerous cells can be created where the *Hartman* and *Curry Net* lines intersect.

CHAPTER FIVE SUMMARY

1. Fix those mercury amalgam fillings!! There are two choices: replace the fillings, ensuring that the removal or filling replacements are done safely, or see a naturopath to de-sensitize the impact that mercury has on the body. While removal is an option, especially if teeth and gums are diseased, but since each tooth is connected to other organs in the body, it can weaken that organ, as well as the underlying structures from which they are removed.

2. Remove fluoride from your life. If fluoride is in your municipal tap water, purchase natural spring water for cooking and drinking. Lobby the local government for change. (Refer to the section on water filters in Chapter Three.)

3. One should assume that pesticides are found on all produce, unless it is certified organic. Be sure to wash and/or peel all vegetables and fruit. Buy organic as much as possible - ask the grocer to keep the organic department well stocked. Grow produce yourself or have a friend or relative with a green thumb help with the gardening.

4. Meat and dairy: pesticides collect in the fatty tissue of animals; hormones and antibiotics are fed to those animals as well. If it is necessary to consume meat as a part of one's diet, then make sure it is free-range, that the animals were fed with organic grains, and that they have not been fed hormones or antibiotics.

5. Artificial sweeteners only add to the toxic burden in one's body. Use natural cane sugar, unpasteurized honey, maple syrup and stevia as sweeteners. Reduce the amount of sweetener recipes call for, and in appropriate situations, substitute applesauce or fruit juice for sugar. (See recipes in Appendix J, pp.296-307.)

6. Do not purchase products that contain artificial colorings.

7. To reduce the amount of preservatives on fruit and vegetables, purchase local produce as much as possible, and eat what is in season. Make sauces, pickles, and jams, and bottle or freeze them.

8. Eliminate products with monosodium glutamate. Most oriental restaurants now cook many dishes without MSG. More and more people today have adverse reactions when they consume products containing *MSG*. Comparison shop, read labels and ask questions.

9. Check with a pharmacist before purchasing medications to ensure their safety, including negative side effects and additives. Read labels on over-the-counter supplements to ensure that preservatives, coloring, additives, coatings have not been added to these products.

10. Avoid low-cost jewelry and keep it away from children, unless the jewelry has been guaranteed to be lead-free.

11. Create an oasis in the bedroom; make sleep a healthy experience.

12. Read labels carefully and replace all personal care and cleaning products if they are unsafe. Use vinegar or baking soda for as many cleaning projects as possible.

13.Chemotherapy and x-radiation involve heavy metals and poisons. The body must flush any toxins produced during these procedures as quickly as possible. It is your life that is at stake, so follow the guidelines on pages 179-183.

14. Test for *EMFs* and ensure that all appliances in the home and office work efficiently. Protect your body.

15. Consider removing your microwave, as well as all pots and pans covered with "teflon", PFOS and/or PFOA coatings.

"Everyone has the ability to be the best one can be. Each person is unique and no one is inherently better than anyone else; it is simply that each person chooses to use opportunities in different ways."

Eating twelve-grain bread alone is not sufficient to create a state of health!!

Chapter Six

Nutrition[1]

In the past, much of our food was not cooked; vegetables were eaten raw; fruit was not processed; and nuts were consumed directly from the shell. There were no pesticides, no chemical additives and no requirements to transport food vast distances as most food was locally grown. There was also no need for large warehouses or grocery stores, as populations were smaller and consumers purchased what they required on a daily basis. In many areas of the world, including most of Europe, fresh food is still purchased daily, but that practice is a rare occurrence within most regions of Canada or the USA.

Today, most of our food is cooked, while chemicals are added to preserve canned and packaged foods, as well as to protect fruits and vegetables. Refined sugars[2] and hydrogenated oils are found throughout the food supply; raw fruits, vegetables, nuts and seeds are eaten less often; and bodies generally do not get the nutrition they require for a level of functioning essential for maintaining good health. Toxins, such as pesticides, or those that emanate from x-rays, have caused declining sperm counts in males, while the addition of hormones in meat and dairy has resulted in the early onset of puberty in females, ultimately

---

1. Editor's note: The information in this chapter is presented somewhat differently than previous chapters in the hope that the large quantity of complex information contained within will be easier to read and process, thereby allowing it to be utilized effectively and efficiently by the reader.

2. If readers feel unsure about the impact of sugar on one's health, read *Lick the Sugar Habit* by Nancy Appeleton. Her *136 Reasons Why Sugar is Ruining Your Health* is also quoted by Carolyn Dean MD, ND in a chapter entitled *Death By Sugar* in her latest book, *Death By Modern Medicine*, Matrix Verite Publishing ©2005

leading to earlier menopause and fewer child-bearing years. In addition, recent research suggests that high levels of caffeine intake may be linked to *infertility* and *miscarriage*, especially if one's intake exceeds 300 milligrams a day. At this rate, future generations may well be destroyed, especially if conception cannot occur to produce more children. While the latter statement may seem somewhat radical, remember that in North America one in three persons now get cancer, and many more of them are children. In addition, one in two individuals have one form of heart disease or another, and humans are experiencing increasing levels of *MS, Parkinson's, Alzheimer's, Celiac Disease, IBS, Crohns, Fibromyalgia,* as well as viruses such as *Epstein-Barr*.

In my first year following the B.A.L.A.N.C.E program, there were dramatic changes in my body. I no longer craved chocolate, but sought out more vegetables instead - and actually shook my head, wondering how these changes were possible? I was literally destroying my body, the receptacle of life, but today that has all changed.

I could have simply accepted the diagnosis of terminal cancer, and carried on as in the past: eating poorly, without regard for the consequences; continuing to consume refined sugars and hydrogenated oils; drinking water containing chlorides and fluorides; as well as using chemicals to spotlessly 'clean and enhance' my home. That was what was done for most of my life, ultimately creating an ever-increasing toxic burden within my body. I could have continued on that path, but my choice was to read and research to find solutions that would allow my body to heal.

While I did not look like a malnourished person, my body was unable to function properly and lacked appropriate nutrition. The negative signs experienced prior to implementing these changes included:
   a. eliminating only once a day; and expelling feces that did not float;
   b. transparent nails that broke and split easily
   c. placque on my teeth, requiring a thorough dental cleaning every three to four months;
   d. allergies to cats, dogs, smoke, perfume, detergent, certain plants, grasses and more;
   e. heartburn after eating cucumbers, or certain spicy foods;
   f. developing a hernia, such that the consumption of any hot food or drink caused discomfort in my chest;

g. dry skin;

h. dry and brittle hair;

i. aches and restriction of finger joints and knees (at the time, considered to be a form of arthritis);

j. kidney stones;

k. sweating (in the summer) to the point I had to change my top during the day;

l. being overweight by 18 kilograms (forty pounds);

m. constant colds and influenza that courses of antibiotics for up to four weeks would not relieve;

n. surgeries for a fibroid tumor, two benign thyroid tumors, a thyroid cyst, cataracts, toxins, tumors, extreme thirst, burning in the middle of my back, reduced energy levels, and finally . . .

p. cancer; today my body no longer has any symptoms related to this disease!!

At the time, I was only 53 years of age, exercised three times a week, and ate what was assumed to be a healthy diet !!!

One year into B.A.L.A.N.C.E.:

a. I eliminated two to three times a day and the excretions floated.

b. My nails were thicker and my half moons (lunula) had returned.

c. Dental placque had been eradicated for for over ten months.

d. The allergies with which I had suffered since 1980 were gone - no itch, headaches, or sniffles.

e. The heartburn had ceased.

f. Spicy foods and hot beverages could be consumed - without discomfort or reaction.

g. My skin was smooth, soft and without blemishes.

h. My hair was thicker than in fifteen years; it was also shiny and healthy in appearance.

i. The aches or pains in both knees and hands had disappeared.

j. All kidney stones had dissipated.

k. The body's thermostat was back on track; as a result, it was no longer necessary to wear deodorant in the summer.

l. My body weight was forty-pounds less, with a body mass appropriate for my height.

m. In the past year, each of my grandchildren and children, as well as my husband had contracted colds and influenza at least twice, and while I had a few sniffles in the morning and/or an upset stomach, those symptoms lasted for only a few hours compared to the many days during which the other family members were ill.

n. My last six blood tests, all previously recorded as low (L), have now returned within a normal range.

o. Cancer: reduced toxins, reduced size of tumors, no excessive thirst, no burning pain in my back, and my energy has increased to a level that was only experienced many years prior to the beginning of this illness.

The first year after the diagnosis for cancer, I continued to work full time as I enjoyed my job, and once the toxins were under control, I felt great. I exercised at the YMCA three times a week. If it were not for the lumps that remained in my nodes, I would not have even known that I had cancer. Previously, I could not even perform normal housework due to the enlarged nodes that would crowd my neck, but a year later, I could accomplish all of those tasks again.

A year later, I made a decision to cease working, as my health had taken a step backwards, while aspects of my personal psychological past[1] had begun to haunt me. This setback, as well as my ongoing research into my illness, helped me to understand that in order to heal properly and completely, it was necessary to get adequate rest, plenty of fresh air, sunlight, and proper nutrition. Therefore, a work environment was not the best place to complete the healing process.

As stated earlier in this publication, had the information been easier to locate in a single source after my initial diagnosis, I truly believe my body would have been functioning at its peak efficiency much sooner. My active cancer was gone, and only the pathways needed to be strengthened to a point where no negative symptoms remained. My immune system was strong enough to resist colds or influenza, but was not, as yet, strong enough to completely dissolve benign tumors that remained in the lymphatic system. The original tumors in my right jaw no longer existed, while the former egg-sized tumors in my left groin had now shrunk to the size of small marbles. My liver was stronger and free from distress, and strong enough to withstand the onslaught of massive quantities of dead cancer cells released as the immune system completed its job. Later, when the parasites had been cleared from my system, the process of healing continued naturally. There was proof of that every day.

---

1. Read more on this subject in the personal story segment in Chapter Seven related to *Coping Skills*.

So where does that leave you, the reader?

Perhaps a review of what has transpired thus far will help readers assess their own personal situation.

Chapter Two:
a) Have you looked at your body and determined what health issues exist?

b) Have you begun to include *Essential Fatty Acids (EFAs)* in your diet?

c) Have you determined the correct balance of protein and carbohydrates for your body and begun to make changes?

d) Have you begun to drink and cook with clean water, either by using pure spring water or by adding filters to your taps?

Chapter Three:
a) Have you measured the alkalinity/acidity of your body through saliva and urine pH testing?

b) If your body was acidic, have you begun to alkalanize it yet?

Chapter Four:
a) What detoxification protocols have you attempted?

b) Which of those do you like best, or which work best for you?

Chapter Five:
a) Have you begun to read labels?

b) Have you made any changes in the brands of food you now buy?

c) Have you stopped purchasing foods that contain additives and chemicals?

d) What about that bedroom oasis? Have you begun to make seven to eight hours of sleep each night a priority - a habit that is beneficial to your health?

Now that this brief review has been completed, it is time to learn about the foods that should be eaten and why!

Vitamin C:

Vitamin C is an essential nutrient for the body and warrants additional discussion in this chapter. A fascinating read related to this important vitamin is: *Why Animals Don't Get Heart Attacks, But People Do!* by Dr. Matthias Rath. It outlines research on the natural prevention of *heart attacks, strokes, high blood pressure, diabetes, high levels of cholesterol (HDL)* and many other cardiovascular conditions. Lack of vitamin C is a primary factor in each of these conditions. The body produces *lipoprotein (Lp-a)* to compensate for a lack of natural vitamin C, and as such, increased levels of *Lp-a* constitute a marker that suggests cardiovascular disease is present or occurring within the body. Dr. Rath's research negates the more commonly held view that cardiovascular disease is simply the result of elevated levels of cholesterol or high fat diets. As with genetic attributes, these factors can only become a risk if the walls of the arteries are weakened by a *vitamin C deficiency*, a common disease, known as *scurvy* that afflicted many sailors in times past. Unfortunately, chlorine and bromine, which are commonly added to municipal water systems and swimming pools, are today's equivalent of scurvy, as they also weaken the walls of the arteries. Fortunately, the addition of additional vitamin C can help the body overcome this man-made affliction.

Animals, on the other hand, are able to produce their own vitamin C, enabling their bodies to protect blood vessel walls and eliminate cardiovascular disease. A combination of magnesium and vitamin C relax the blood vessel walls and normalize *high blood pressure*. Cardiovascular cells consume vitamins and other essential nutrients at a high rate, and if the body does not receive proper nutrition, disease can set in. It is interesting to note that both cancer and heart disease patients always have low levels of magnesium. Vitamin C is a *water-soluble*[1] vitamin and, therefore, is not stored in the body, but rather must be replenished up to three times each day.

Dr. Rath's book is definitely recommended reading. The local nutrition center I usually frequent sold their copies at cost, which is indicative of just how much the center's holistic professionals believe this is information that everyone should read. I was in the center to purchase products for my daughter, when I noticed the book on the counter with a very low sticker price. When I asked about it, I was informed how crucial the information in it was for everyone's health. Since it was their last copy, it was my lucky day, as perhaps a day or even one hour later, this book might not have been available to me.

---

1. For purposes of this publication, stating that something is *water-soluble* simply means the body cannot store these vitamins, so they must to be consumed on a daily basis. On the other hand, *fat-soluble* means that the body stores those vitamins in the fatty tissues for use at a later time. A fat-soluble vitamin or mineral should be taken with the daily meal that contains the greatest amount of fat, as that will promote the proper absorption of fat-soluble nutrients within the body.

Five years ago, my former brother-in-law, Len, was diagnosed with significant heart disease, and his condition was inoperable. Since that time, medical doctors had not given him much hope as his body continued to fail him. Most days, he was unable to walk even a short distance or work in his garden. When I informed he and his wife, my sister Marg, what I had learned about Dr. Rath's work, they immediately began a regimen that included additional vitamin C and *essential fatty acids* on a daily basis. They also increased their water intake and reduced the quantity of refined foods, as well as the amount of hydrogenated oils in their diets. Only time would tell what impact those changes might have on either or both of them.

Serving sizes:

A single serving is roughly equal to the following examples:

<u>Fruit</u> - One full slice of melon; one half a cup of berries; one -half a cup of canned fruit; one-quarter cup of dried fruit; or three-quarters of a cup of juice.

<u>Vegetables</u> - One half cup of vegetables chopped raw; one half cup of cooked dried beans or lentils; one cup of raw, leafy greens; one medium potato; eight carrot sticks; or six ounces of juice

(For Metric conversions, consult the footnote on page 134 or the chart in Chapter Four of this publication, p. 139)

If it fits easily in one's hand, it is a serving!

Vitamin and Mineral Charts

The next five pages list the most common and important vitamins and minerals for providing optimum health. *Permission is granted to readers to photocopy these five pages to keep them handy for easy reference.*

Vitamin	Required for . . .	Source
A (retinal is the most usable form) - fat-soluble - 700 mcg daily (equal to one carrot or sweet potato, or two thirds of a cup oatmeal).	Supports bone, cellular and immune functioning, improves the healing of wounds, the development of one's teeth, reproduction, mucous membranes, as well as being an anti-cancer agent. It also helps promotes healthy skin and eyes. (Helps one see in dim light.)	Egg yolks, cod liver and halibut oil, fish, dulse, kelp, asparagus, oatmeal, green leafy vegetables, carrots, and fennel.
Beta-carotene (pro-vitamin A) [as in **A** above]	Infection fighter, thyroid activity, immune functions, respiratory and blood glucose health, night vision, and enhances the skin. (Note: Diabetics cannot convert beta-carotene into Vitamin A efficiently, due to poor functioning livers. They need to get all of their vitamin A from fish liver oil.)	Dark green, red and deep yellow-orange vegetables, especially carrots. Fish liver oil.
B$_1$ (thiamine) - water-soluble - 12 mg daily	Energy and vitality, mental & heart function, important for proper digestion, promotes growth and is a light diuretic. Facilitates removal of lead from tissues.	Brown rice, brewer's yeast, broccoli, whole grains, egg yolks, soybean.
B$_2$ (riboflavin) - water-soluble - 1.3 mg daily - activates B6 (should require same amount) - helps body absorb iron	Enhances metabolism, improves vision, required for cellular health and growth; also can prevent cataracts.	Green leafy vegetables, soybeans, whole grains, almonds, poultry, fish and egg yolks.
B$_3$ (niacin) - water-soluble - 15 mg daily - destroyed when food is cooked - consumption of alcohol and insufficient protein will increase the body's requirement.	Heart and circulation, lowers cholesterol, aids adrenal and hormone production, calms nervous system, helps natural secretion of bile and stomach acids, boosts energy, memory enhancer, reduces mental disorders, i.e., dementia, schizophrenia.	Avocados, whole grains, legumes, broccoli, carrots, nuts, seeds, brewer's yeast, eggs, fish and poultry.

Vitamin	Required for . . .	Source
B6 (pyridoxine) - water-soluble - 1.3 mg. daily (a large banana or a baked potato with its skin)	Supports immune and nervous systems, reduces heart disease, mental clarity as well as heart function; also helps with *PMS* and *menopause.*	Cantaloupe, bananas, potatoes, cruciferous vegetables, eggs, whole grains, salt water fish, brewer's yeast, carrots, peas and spinach.
B12 (cobalamine) - water soluble	Metabolism (carbohydrate, fat, protein), blood cell formation, appetite, and a healthy nervous system	Fish, eggs, dairy, and organ meats
B15 (dimethylglycine or pangamic acid) - water soluble - relies on vitamin A and E - more effective with vit. B	Decreases pain severity and morning stiffness in rheumatoid arthritis and osteoarthritis sufferers. It also protects against hardening of the arteries; stabilizes emotional and mental problems (anxiety and panic attacks); acts as a detoxifying agent; and neutralizes alcohol cravings.	Whole grain cereals, brown rice, brewer's yeast, eggs, pumpkin, and sesame seeds.
B17 (amygdalin or laetrile) - abundant in untamed nature (has bitter taste) - zinc helps transport to the cells	Releases cyanide only at cancer sites, thus destroying cells while nourishing non-cancer tissues and building the immune system.	Apricot pits (caution is required as they contain cyanide) elderberry, chokecherry, fava, wild blackberry, millet, buckwheat, macadamia nuts, and alfalfa sprouts.
Biotin (H) - water-soluble - member of B complex group - 30 u.g. daily	For energy production, healthy hair and skin (limits and repairs baldness), metabolism, growth; reduces muscle pain, depression, nausea and vomiting.	Wheat bran, whole grains, egg yolks, nuts, legumes, soy flour, yeast, cauliflower, sardines and salmon
C (ascorbic acid) 75 to 100 mg twice daily - water-soluble - diarrhea can occur if the body has excess; reduce the amount slowly - most tolerate 3000 mg/day (1000/eight hours) More can acidify the urine and lead to kidney stones. (if deficient a greater quantity may be required)	Antioxidant, antiviral & antibacterial; enhances glutathione, which is required for detoxification; improves cardiovascular and immune functions.	Vine-ripened fruits and vegetables, cruciferous vegetables, black currants, raisins, citrus fruits, sweet red and green peppers.

Vitamin	Required for ...	Source
D - fat-soluble - 200 i.u. daily (two ounces of mackerel) to 400 i.u. (four ounces cooked salmon).	Improves level of calcium absorption; reduces muscle cramps; essential for thyroid function and improves skin condition.	Egg yolks, cod liver oil, fatty fish, or 15 to 60 minutes of sunshine daily.
E (Alpha-tocopherol) It is the only form of E that human blood can transfer to cells as required. - d-alpha-tocopherol is natural (use it rather than dl-alpha-tocopherol, which is a synthetic) - fat-soluble - 400 i.u. to 800 i.u. daily	Improves blood circulation and brain and heart function, reduces effects of stress, improves skin and hair, reduces cramps and *PMS* symptoms, protects against free radicals, arthritis, macular degeneration and diabetes, as well as preserving *DNA*.	Dark green leafy vegetables, cold-pressed organic nuts and seeds, as well as their oils, (especially almonds, walnuts and cashews) wheat germ, egg yolks, avocados, salmon, tuna, shrimp, lobster and soy.
Folic Acid (folate or un-numbered B or B_9 vitamin) - water soluble - 400 mcg daily (one and a half cups chickpeas or two cups black beans or asparagus) - Pregnant women need a higher dose. It loses potency when cooked or stored.	Crucial for attempting to conceive or when pregnant - for development of fetus; reduces birth defects; enhances digestion; helps to prevent anemia if taken with B_{12}; elevates serotonin from the brain, strengthens the immune system, and is required for cellular repair.	Asparagus, citrus fruit, lentils, oranges, root vegetables(potatoes, turnip, etc.) legumes, whole grains, salmon, dates, beets and green leafy vegetables.
K (phylloquinone) - fat-soluble - 70 to 80 u.g. daily - dihydrophlloquinone is an unhealthy version of vitamin K.	Controls blood clotting; also required for bone formation and repair, as well as for healthy liver functioning.	Green leafy vegetables, asparagus, cruciferous vegetables (brussels sprouts broccoli, cabbage), whole grains, and egg yolks.
P (hesperatin) - water soluble - bioflavinoid - to work at its best it requires vitamin C and other bioflavinoids [i.e.,rutin, hesperatin, eriodictyol, quercetin, and quercetrin].	Prevents and reverses varicose veins with an improvement of the capillary linings. Corrects the tendency for bruising, bleeding gums, night cramps, and the reduction of pain.	Citrus fruit (membranes and white part of the skin), blueberries, blackberries, peppers and plums, plus buckwheat, black currants, apricots, cherries, grapes, and rosehips.

Mineral	Required for ...	Source
Boron	Necessary for brain function, healthy bones, the metabolism of other minerals, as well as helping to prevent osteoporosis.	Apples, carrots, grapes, green leafy vegetables, whole grains, and nuts.
Calcium	Prevents bone loss, improves nerve function, energy production and healthy heart function. *(Excess calcium can decrease levels of magnesium in the body.)*	Sea vegetables, kale, green leafy vegetables, cruciferous vegetables, sesame and sunflower seeds, plus brazil nuts, almonds and tofu.
Chromium	Stabilizes glucose levels, enhances energy and metabolism. It is also important for weight loss; lowers cholesterol and triglycerides.	Whole grains, brewer's yeast, eggs, brown rice, pumpkin & sesame seeds.
Copper	Important for nerves, cellular respiration, helps to treat anemia.	Shellfish, legumes, almonds, avocados, and dark green leafy vegetables.
Germanium	Improves oxygenation of cells, assists detoxification, and supports immunity.	Shitake mushrooms, garlic, onions, ginseng, and aloe vera.
Iodine	Critical for thyroid; regulates estrogen in breast tissues,; protects against fibrocystic breasts; and is important for reproductive functions.	Salt water seafood, kelp, dulse, asparagus, lima beans, sesame seeds, and soy beans.
Iron	Crucial for hemoglobin production, enzyme activity and growth; also supports immune function and energy production. - Molybdenum is essential for the metabolism of iron.	Eggs, fish, poultry, green leafy vegetables, brewer's yeast, dulse, kelp, lentils, pumpkin, sesame seeds, watercress, oats, raisins, black strap molasses. Limit intake of red meats.
Magnesium[1] - 400 to 600 mcg daily - 1 oz. of pumpkin seeds (150 mcg) - 3 oz. salmon (30 mcg) - half a cup of spinach (75 mcg)	Promotes nerve health, prevents bone loss and diabetes, supports muscle and enzyme function, as well as cardio health. (Magnesium is noticeably low in persons with heart problems and cancer.)	Tofu, whole grains, green leafy vegetables, nuts, seeds, legumes, salmon, bananas. <hr> *1. Neck, shoulder and back pain can indicate lowered magnesium levels.*

Mineral	Required for ...	Source
Manganese	Critical for blood sugar control, thyroid activity, energy metabolism; important for skin, hair and nails. It also can bring up iron levels if deficient.	Whole grains, nuts, green leafy vegetables, avocados, seaweed.
Molybdenum	Crucial for detoxification; anti-cancer agent, essential for iron metabolism.	Whole grains, dark green leafy vegetables, legumes.
Phosphorus	Vital for healthy bones and teeth, cell growth, heart and kidney function.	Asparagus, brewer's yeast bran, eggs, fish, legumes, nuts, whole grains, seeds (e.g., sesame, sunflower and pumpkin).
Potassium - 3,000 to 6,000 mg. - one banana (465 mg) - 8 oz.fresh orange juice (495 mg) - apples and potatoes contain more potassium than bananas.	Necessary for nerves and heart, prevents stroke; aids in muscle contraction; regulates blood pressure, and transports nutrients. *Cancer patients require more potassium and less sodium.*	Whole grains, apricots, bananas, oranges, avocados, brewer's yeast, potatoes, figs, dates, raisins, brown rice, dulse, carrots, yams, apples, nuts, legumes, poultry and apples.
Selenium [a synergist for Vitamin C - works together with a greater effect on both]	Anti-cancer agent, that improves one's immunity; important for the repair of cells; and inhibits the oxidation of fat.	Brazil nuts, walnuts, oatmeal, whole grains, broccoli, brown rice and eggs.
Silica or Silicon	Essential for strong bones teeth, nails plus mineral absorption & hair growth.	Beets, brown rice, bell peppers, whole grains.
Sulphur	Disinfects blood, helps to fight harmful bacteria, protects cells against radiation & pollution; stimulates bile.	Brussels sprouts, onions, cabbage, soybeans, eggs, fish, kale and garlic
Vandium	Important for blood-sugar control, cellular metabolism, bone and tooth formation.	Radishes, eggs, organic nut and seed oils, olives, snap beans, buckwheat and oats..
Zinc [*Poor appetite results from low zinc levels. Chemotherapy reduces zinc in the body.*]	Supports thymus function; helps to resist infection and repair wounds; protects against hair loss, improves skin and nails, and supports joints and tissues.	Oysters, nuts, wheat bran and germ, pumpkin seeds, beans, lentils, egg yolks, whole grain cereals.

Cesium Chloride is a valuable mineral for fighting cancer. For details, see page 91.

Balance is also required when vitamins and minerals are added to one's diet. For example, too much B_3 can create a disturbance in liver functioning, while excess B_6 could result in damage to peripheral nerves, which in turn, cause progressive numbness in the limbs. Since the intake of vitamins and minerals should be in as natural form as possible, choose five to ten servings of organic fruits and vegetables per day.

Non-organic strawberries are often full of *methyl bromide* from pesticides, a known carcinogen. Unfortunately, it is not very easy to scrub strawberries! Unless a person purchases pesticide-free berries, they are not recommended, whether one is healthy or ill. There are many organic/pesticide-free U-PICK farms in many regions of both Canada and the USA, so always ask first! Other than those certified organic, most grapes have been sprayed with sulfites. Balsamic vinegar often contains sulfites; as do many North American wines. Head lettuce is commonly full of heavy metals that it draws from the soil. Leaf lettuce or other field greens are preferred.

Always read labels, and if produce is not labeled, ask the grocer what (s)he knows about additives or sprays on these foodstuffs.

The role of potassium in the body:
Too much sodium and too little potassium can create an imbalance in the body that can contribute to hypertension, high blood pressure and cancer. Cancer patients almost always require more potassium than sodium to survive, as all disease begins in the liver, especially when potassium is deficient. The Gerson Institute recommends a formula comprised of equal parts of potassium acetate, potassium gluconate and mono potassium phosphate (KH_2PO_4) in powder form, available from *The Key Company*), as a good solution for rebalancing the liver.

Remember to consult a health care practitioner before beginning any form of potassium supplementation.

Organic apples, potatoes and bananas, which are available in many farmers' markets, as well as in organic produce sections of selected supermarkets, are good natural sources of potassium. Also check with provincial or state

Organic Grower's Association for locations of markets or producers who sell organic fruit and vegetables directly to the public. Specially tagged organic bananas are also often found in the regular produce section of many supermarkets; however it is important to note that apples and potatoes both supply more potassium than bananas.

In Chapter Seven, descriptions of events that often occurred on a daily basis and were extremely debilitating to me emotionally will be outlined. During those episodes my body would go into a shock, a condition known as the *Raynaud Phenomenom*, in which the blood supply to the fingers and toes was interrupted; they felt frozen. Subsequent research into this condition suggested the importance and role of potassium in its treatment. I discovered that adding one-quarter teaspoon of potassium bicarbonate powder to a glass of water helped alleviate the problem. **Again caution is urged, so be sure to consult with a health care practitioner first before beginning such a regimen**.

As with all vitamin and mineral supplements, it is important to know how they were produced, or what additives were included to make them into pill form. Some cheaper brands can actually contain toxins, including traces of lead (likely from the manufacturing process itself), so be sure that one's research is thorough. If information on labels is missing or insufficient, contact manufacturers via e-mail (or regular mail) to obtain information on products. If the information is not forthcoming, do not purchase that product. Even if they eventually reply, remain cautious and double-check the information with other sources. Most manufacturers do not deliberately intend to do harm, and, at times, actually take the lead by removing toxic additives, such as was found with fluorides in several personal products.

Phyto-chemicals:
Phyto-chemicals boost the body's defenses against disease. They are not essential as nutrients, but they are very important to the body. Many plants contain these powerful antioxidants.

1.i. *Poly-phenols* are contained in every member of the plant family: and are powerful cancer inhibitors. They also protect against coronary heart disease. The *polyphenols* found in olive-oil protect it from oxidation; they are also found in green teas.

ii. *EGCG (epigallocatechin gallate)* is found in green tea and apples. It protects the heart and arteries from oxidative damage; provides protection against cancer; and protects the skin from ultraviolet radiation when applied to the skin. It is commonly referred to as *catechin*, or condensed *tannin*.

iii. *Anthocyanins* and *proanthocyanidins* are red and purple in color, and supply the color for berries, cherries, red grapes, plums, pomegranates, red cabbage , as well as some beans and grains. They supply protection for the heart, lungs and blood vessels.

2. *Carotenoids* are found in vegetables such as carrots, pumpkins, squash, sweet potatoes, tomatoes, cantaloupes, peaches, mangos, as well as dark, leafy greens. They provide strong cancer protection: *lutein* and *zeaxanthin* protect vision, while *lycopene* (from tomatoes) is known to reduce the risk of *prostrate cancer*.

3. *Phyto-estrogens* interact with estrogen receptors on cells within the body. *Iso-flavones* in soy help prevent hot flashes in menopause, and provide protection against toxins. Lignans are found in flax and other seeds that produce oil.

4. *Polysaccharides* are the structural components of many cells. They are found in mushrooms, specifically *shiitake, oyster, enokidake,* and *maitake*. They exhibit a powerful enhancing effect upon the immune system. Please note that common button mushrooms are not included in this group

5. *Ellagic acid* is a cancer inhibitor found in raspberries and blueberries.

6. *D-limonene* is found in citrus peels, and inhibits cancer.

7. *Sulforaphane* is another cancer fighter commonly found in broccoli.

8. *Isothiocyanates* are found in members of the cabbage family. They are also cancer-inhibiting agents.

9. *Allicin*, contained in garlic, is responsible for lowering blood pressure and is a natural antibiotic.

10. *Shogaols*, found in ginger, reduce inflammation.

Other important supplements:

Wheat grass juice contains vitamins A, B, C, E and beta-carotene; alkaline minerals: calcium and magnesium; iron and potassium; twenty amino acids; many essential minerals, including zinc, selenium, manganese, copper, phosphorus, as well as proteins and enzymes. *Spirulina* (a micro-algae) is good for all body types. It supplies all essential amino acids, *EFAs*, and reduces *hypoglycemia*, as well as cooling and detoxifying the body. The powdered form is recommended.

Silica (another essential mineral) is a vital element for good health. It helps with the absorption of other minerals; prevents cavities by hardening the teeth; helps to prevent skeletal deformities; slows the degeneration of connective tissue, which is responsible for youthful, elastic skin, and it stimulates the immune system. *Silica* also prevents pain from *osteoarthritis*; maintains and restores the body's processes of self-repair; prevents the bleeding and recession of gums; and inhibits aluminum absorption. Silica also prevents *tuberculosis*; restores hormonal balance within the body that is caused by an imbalance of calcium and magnesium; hardens nails; inhibits baldness, stimulates hair growth; and inhibits coronary heart disease. Again, speak to a health care provider first, and use only *organic vegetable-based silica*, not a synthetic kind. *Silica* may also be found in supplemental form in *springtime horsetail*. The mineral charts on pages 196-200 list the best food sources for this important mineral.

Lipotropic Factors (biological sources):

1. *Choline* is required for proper brain and nerve functioning, optimum liver activity, and gall bladder regulation. *Choline* is listed as a constituent of B-complex although it is not a vitamin itself. Egg yolks, *lecithin*, legumes, soybeans and whole grains are good sources of *choline*.

2. *Inositol* is vital for the nervous system, cell functioning and healthy hair growth. It reduces cholesterol levels and is also identified as one of the B-complex members. *Inositol* is found in egg yolks, brewer's yeast, fruits, raisins, legumes and whole grains.

3. *Coenzyme Q10* is an anti-aging antioxidant, important in energy production, aids circulation, and is required for cardiovascular health. The body can make this ortho-molecule, yet many people with heart problems exhibit a functional deficiency. It is also believed that certain kinds of cholesterol medications (*statins*) block the synthesis of this valuable substance. If one is deficient in *Co-Q10*, the addition of one

hundred mg or higher supplement would likely be appropriate, but check with a health care practitioner (medical doctor, naturopath and nutritionist) first. Supplements of *Co-Q10* are also somewhat expensive. Elderly diabetics who take a lot of medications for viral infections, may also be unable to manufacture this antioxidant in their bodies. Natural sources of *Coenzyme Q10* are found.in mackerel, salmon, sardines and spinach.

Essential Fatty Acids (EFAs)

Essential Fatty Acids (EFAs) reduce inflammation; are important for cell function and protection; as well as for heart and skin health. The immune function is also quite dependent upon adequate levels of *EFAs*. Cold-water fishes, fish and fish liver oils, flax seeds, hemp, pumpkin seeds, many cold-pressed organic nuts and seeds and their oils, as well as the purslane herb are good sources of *EFAs*. *Tocotrienols* (alpha, beta, gamma, and delta) protect against macular degeneration (a form of eye disease), diabetes, arthritis, *PMS* and menstrual cramps; help improve heart function; and reduce the effects of stress. Other good sources of *essential fatty acids* include dark green leafy vegetables, egg yolks, avocados, soy, tuna, halibut, shrimp, lobster, flax and flax oil, olive oil and wheat germ.

Flours, breads and baking:

Prior to 1860, all flour was stone ground. About that time, steel roller mills were introduced to make the processed flours that are used today. The steel-roller process removes the wheat germ and fiber. Manufacturers preferred the latter as the bread made from fiber-less grains stays fresher longer. Unfortunately, over eighty percent (80%) of all essential minerals are lost in the manufacture of flour employing this type of processing. Manufacturers commonly add synthetic vitamins B_1 and B_3, as well as inorganic iron to flours, but unfortunately, inorganic iron supplements are not well absorbed by the body. So ensure that all iron enrichment comes from organic sources. 'Stone ground' flours are still the preferred choice for breads, as they maintain the fiber as well as the essential vitamins and minerals.

Hydrogenated oils and refined sugars are also used in most commercially baked goods. These baked products do not provide the body with the essential minerals it requires to function properly. In most cases the body only obtains chemicals, preservatives and trans-fats each and every time a loaf of poor quality commercial bread is consumed. It is an unfortunate situation, but many consumers are often fooled by the words 'diet', 'enriched' or 'twelve grain' labels on wrappers. One must research those terms carefully.

The most important question to ask is: was non-hydrogenated oil used to make the bread? If the answer is no, then it contains trans-fats. Has it been enriched with synthetic vitamins and minerals? If that answer is yes, that would likely mean fewer nutrients, chemical additives, and reduced or minimal fiber, resulting in a poor quality food that would be insufficient to support and maintain good health. If the expiration date is for more than a few days, the bread almost surely contains preservatives.

The first problem encountered as I began a search for healthy breads was that almost all breads found in grocery stores or supermarkets contained hydrogenated oils, as well as bleached flours and refined sugars. Fortunately today, some supermarkets and almost all health food stores carry specialty breads, but the textures of most of those breads were difficult for me to deal with. As a result, I began to bake my own bread, rolls and pizza dough using a bread machine. Although one hundred percent whole wheat caused me some difficulty, buckwheat, rye, or a combination of whole wheat and unbleached flours allowed me to enjoy the texture and taste as in the past. Currently, I bake with *spelt*, *kamut* and *quinoa* flours more often, utilizing whole wheat much less.

Try a bread machine. They are easy to use and the instruction booklets provided often contain a variety of recipes that utilize alternate flours. Additional books can be purchased from book or health food stores. Use virgin olive oil in place of shortening or margarine (cup for cup), and replace powdered cow's milk with powered soy milk if dairy is a problem. Replace refined sugar with non-pasteurized honey, and use only un-refined sea salt when required. Experiment and enjoy healthier baking.

Corn tortillas are easy to make if you enjoy fajitas or enchiladas for a meal. (Note the tortillas recipe in Appendix J.) European bakeries have wonderful breads that contain virgin olive oil; are made with a variety of different flours (*kamut, spelt, rye, quinoa*); as well as breads made without sugar. Specialty breads, such as "*Historic*" or "*Walking*" breads from a bakery, can be frozen to ensure freshness, otherwise breads without preservatives become rancid or moldy in two to three days. Organic flour does not contain preservatives and is sold in smaller bags for that reason. Farmers' markets or health food stores are also places that usually sell healthier breads. And always make sure the bread is made with non-hydrogenated oil, unbleached flours and does not contain refined sugars.

Achieving Balance!

Six months after beginning *B.A.L.A.N.C.E.*, I made an appointment with a nutritionist. It was absolutely necessary for me to ensure my body had actually achieved a proper balance. The main concern was whether I could ingest and digest sufficient amounts of protein. Red meat and dairy were eliminated from my diet, although that was contrary to what I had been taught - both at home and in school. The important question was: would my body be able to receive the proper levels of vitamins and minerals required to function properly and to perform the body's vital jobs without these foods?

A few months earlier, I went to a nutrition center to purchase an immune builder, *Tahitian Noni juice*. While visiting the center, a staff consultant spent twenty minutes with me and reviewed my health background and history at no cost - and this was on a Saturday. It was easy to recognize the love she had for her work. She commented that a nutritionist worked out of the center and booked an appointment for me, as well as for my daughter. Before the appointment, a completed questionnaire was required - it contained fifty-five sections. Each section was related to bodily functions, such as bad breath, mucous in stools, indigestion, and the like. This was not intended as a diagnosis of disease, but rather to assess the body for signs of underlying imbalances. Six months earlier my responses to this questionnaire would be significantly different. After the questions were reviewed and an interview completed, she commented on how much healthier I was compared to many others she had counseled. It confirmed I was on the right path. One valuable suggestion she made was to switch from organic cane sugar to stevia with chicklin for baking.

I had been worried about my daughter's health for quite some time and was glad she agreed to follow this process as well. Her score on the questionnaire was actually higher than mine would have been six months earlier. The nutritionist began with a revitalizer[1] for her colon, which added beneficial digestive enzymes; plus powdered green vegetables; *Udo's Oil*[TM], containing *EFAs* and *lecithin;* and *acidophilus* capsules that contained beneficial bacteria that occur naturally in the digestive tract. Positive results became evident in only thirty days. Her bowel finally functioned properly, after years spent with medical specialists who were unable to determine what was wrong with it. At

---

1. Revitalizing powder was created for people with food allergies, poor digestion and a *'Leaky Gut Syndrome'*. It was formulated by Dr. Michael R. Lyon, M.D. and Dr. Michael T. Murray, N.D. to provide gastrointestinal healing and complete nutritional support.

one point, medical specialists even suggested removal of a portion of her colon, as well as her uterus, in hopes of alleviating the pain and discomfort she had experienced for so many months.

We were empowered after this appointment with the nutritionist! That session allowed the next visit to my daughter's family doctor to be an even more productive meeting. We were able to stress the importance of a consultation with a medical specialist to determine if heavy metal poisoning was a possibility. Subsequent blood tests determined that she had three times the level of arsenic that humans can tolerate, as well as excess amounts of other heavy metals in her tissues. We believe this was due to working in a metal processing plant for many years. I highly recommend anyone who feels unwell to seek the services of a nutritionist and naturopath, in addition to regular medical checkups.

Supplements:

While there is likely little harm taking a multi-vitamin, do not take daily supplements until you are sure what is appropriate for you. Too many supplements may be just as difficult on the body as too little. Rather one should research a product, purchase it, and before the product is opened, have a naturopath or other qualified practitioner compare that product with your body for compatibility. This is usually done through *NAET* [1] and/or *MRT*. Return the product for a refund if it is not compatible. Readers should be aware that it is not possible to pack all daily requirements for vitamins and nutrients into a single one-a-day supplement. It would have to be as large as a golf ball to accomplish that. Additionally, tablets do not dissolve properly to ensure that enough of the nutrients are available for absorption by the body. Remember too, that fat and water-soluble vitamins should be taken on a different schedule, due to the manner in which the body processes them. This is just not possible with a one-a-day supplement.

Side-effects can occur with some vitamin and mineral supplements, but it is usually due to the method used in processing the product, especially if synthetic dyes, artificial colors, or coating agents are added to the supplement itself. To ensure that products are of a high quality, read

---

1. The *Nambudripad Allergy Elimination Technique (N.A.E.T.)* developed by Dr. Devi Nambudripad uses methods adapted from the disciplines of *Applied Kinesiology* or *muscle response testing (MRT)*, *Chiropractic* and *Acupuncture*. It is natural, drug-free, painless and non-invasive - and can be used safely from infants to elderly. (For more information, visit www.naet.com)

labels carefully. Both citrates and maleates are better than oxides or carbonates for absorption. In addition, always check the expiration date on the label.

Also check for the *recommended daily allowance* (*RDA*) of nutrients on the label. Vitamins and minerals should at least meet that daily allowance, although in many cases, individuals may require a therapeutic dose that is higher than the *RDA* value. Remember that *EFAs* are also essential nutrients. Their discussion is located in a separate section in Chapter Two due to their importance for the body.

Stress:

Stress increases the need for additional nutrients; including physical stressors such as excessively cold temperatures, high heat or noise. Nutritional stresses are created by the consumption of excess amounts of junk food or alcohol, while mental stresses are caused by anger, depression, or anxiety. Stress can also be created or increased by bacteria, viruses, or parasites that have taken up residence in the body, as well as from toxins in cigarette smoke, over-the-counter or prescribed medications and more. Each person is unique and requires different levels, or different combinations, of nutrients.

In the beginning, my body seemed to prefer the following: B-complex; 3000 milligrams of vitamin C; calcium with vitamin D, vitamin E, kelp and *kyolic garlic*. I had been on B-complex since 1998, after reading Dr. Andrew Weil's publications. Calcium and D were added earlier with the onset of joint pain, while the remaining B vitamins were included in my diet when diagnosed with cancer. To use all of these supplements required considerable research and review of my nutritional intake, as well as the help of a naturopath before they were included in my daily regimen. After a year, the nutrients supplied via supplements required by my body had diminished. Currently I only supplement with vitamin C, flax and *Tahitian Noni juice*. These changes were determined during monthly assessments utilizing *MRT*, and were later confirmed by my naturopath. A natural diet now provides virtually all my essential nutrients. With the consumption of organic foods, more nutrients are available for absorption. In addition, appropriate methods of cooking ensure that vitamins and minerals have not been removed or destroyed.

Some readers may find it rather strange that the appropriate kind and quantity of supplements required by one's body can be determined without conventional blood or urine tests. [*As a long time believer in, and adherent to allopathic medicine, I was skeptical as well.*] However, the body is composed of a complex electrical system that is powered by the sun, fresh air, water and the nutrients it ingests. When it is out of balance, the body displays correspondingly negative symptoms. Naturopathic doctors understand the body, and know that when a weakness exists in the body, precisely how that weakness may be revealed via specific symptoms. *Muscle response testing (MRT)* can also help to identify weaknesses; it is a process somewhat akin to asking the body a question and having it respond with an answer. Once positive results have been experienced, many individuals usually become more supportive of natural ways of healing the body.

> One example: my granddaughter went for an appointment with a nutritionist, and through the examination of her symptoms, the nutritionist suggested Katie was likely anemic. She then was taken to the family doctor, where her mother requested a copy of the results of her latest blood test. It was then that an error was uncovered - Katie was indeed anemic according to conventional allopathic medical standards. The nutritionist recommended a chlorophyll drink, from which organic iron is more easily absorbed by the body than standard supplements often suggested by most medical practitioners. Katie's red blood cell count returned to normal in a short period of time.

Notes:

1. *Kyolic garlic* is properly aged garlic, which does not cause the body to exude the smell of garlic from its pores after consumption. It also does not have a negative effect on the stomach. This type of garlic also inhibits tumor growth, such as fibroids.

2. Calcium should always be taken in combination with vitamin D for proper absorption, as well as with the mineral magnesium in a 1:1 or 2:1 ratio. Choose more highly absorbable citrates or maleates, or ionic coral calcium, rather than less expensive carbonates.

3. When the body requires zinc, lozenges containing this mineral will taste sweet, but once the body becomes balanced and no longer requires this supplement, those lozenges will have a bitter taste.

4. Smoking 'burns up' vitamin C in the body, as do other chemical pollutants.

5. Iron supplements should not be used if cancer is present in the body as it interferes with lymphocyte production. Rather than taking an iron supplement, additional manganese can help the body with the absorption of iron found in food.

National Food Guides:

People have generally followed the Canadian or American Food Guides or other specific diets in hopes of losing weight and/or to stay healthy. While the intent of these guides is useful for the 'average' person as a guideline and would benefit many who eat poorly, it has been argued that there is no such thing as an 'average' person - each individual is unique biochemically, genetically and in terms of his or her life circumstances. As such, all diets should be individualized based on a range of factors with food guides being but one of the tools considered in that process. Remember, too much of a particular nutrient is just as problematic for the body as too little. When either an excess or deficiency occurs, the body responds by exhibiting a range of negative symptoms. An appropriate diet would take such circumstances and symptoms into account.

Registered Dieticians, working in hospitals across the nation, generally compare one's diet to the national food guide to ensure that the proper portion sizes and quantity of servings from each food group have been included. Using this approach, it would be common to recommend that two to three servings of milk per day are required for everyone, yet some individuals cannot digest milk or absorb nutrients from this source. A different approach is required for those persons, indeed all persons should be considered as unique in order to heal the entire body, not just to allay one or more symptoms exhibited at any one point in time. *Nutritionists*, on the other hand, seek to evaluate the whole person, utilizing symptoms to identify health issues, designing an individualized diet for each person based on their assessments. It should be noted that some *Registered Dieticians*, especially those working **outside** of institutional confines (or in private practice) often take this more personalized approach to nutrition. Some of them are also certified as *Registered Nutritional Consultants (RNCs or RNCPs)*.

Canada's Food Guide (see more on pp. 213-216):

Eating Well with Canada's Food Guide is a four-banded rainbow where each band or color represents one of the four major food groups. The rainbow indicates that all food groups are important, but that different amounts are required from each group. The larger outer arcs of the rainbow include grain products, fruits and vegetables. Canada's dietary guidelines suggests that these foods should make up a larger part of a healthy food plan. Similarly, the smaller inner arcs, including milk products, meat and meat alternatives, should comprise a smaller proportion of a healthy food plan. The primary role of a food guide is to communicate an optimal diet for the overall health of an entire population. Whether a star, pagoda or square is used, all are meant to improve one's quality of life and nutritional wellbeing in a simple and understandable way. However, all food guides must be adjusted to meet individual needs. Each person is unique and must consume a diet tailored to his/her specific requirements. With one in three persons in North America ultimately being diagnosed with cancer; with fifty percent having some form of heart disease, along with the excessive levels of immune diseases on this continent, it is time for a change.

Please note that the *Canada's Food Guide* illustrated on the following pages (pp. 213-215) is no longer considered a draft guide by Health Canada. The revised English version was officially released on February 5, 2007. The French and aboriginal language versions will be released during the summer of 2007. For detailed information on the most recent release, as well as to obtain a more individualized assessment based on one's age, sex, weight and more, please go to *http://www. healthcanada.gc.ca/foodguide*

USA Pyramid Food Guide (see pages 216 - 217):

The pyramid shape is perhaps one of the better-known food guides. It conveys the concept of variety and the relative amounts one should eat from various food groups. The food pyramid concept has been used widely in Australia, United States, Malaysia, Vietnam and Singapore. However, due to differences in the communication of symbolism and other cultural differences, the pyramid is not necessarily the graphic of choice for food guides worldwide. But always remember, food guides are just that - GUIDES! If nutrients are removed through processing of any kind, simply following a food guide may not allow the body to gain the valuable essentials from food that are necessary for life and the body can become diseased. Similarly, if dairy products or meats are consumed that contain residues from hormone supplements or antibiotics, either fed or administered to cattle, it is not possible to ensure a healthy body would result from that quality of food. Unfortunately the food guide does not speak directly to the quality of foods required, or about contaminants found in meats, eggs, dairy, or chemical residues on vegetables and fruit. What if a body is diseased and required more magnesium or more alkaline foods to reduce acidity within the body? How should one adjust a diet to account for these factors? Therefore, it is recommended that readers consider these food guides as a general or broad guides for that 'average person' mentioned above - and adjust accordingly.

Canada's Food Guide

Please note that these newer guides also recommend that a portion of one's diet include fresh, **uncooked** vegetables and fruit, as well as better ways of cooking foods such as baking, broiling or grilling, rather than frying, especially if the latter exceeds the optimum temperature for cooking foods. This is especially true if those items are fried in inappropriate oils, such as saturated oils, trans-fats or those which exceed their 'smoke' point.

Canada Food Guide: Page 2

What is a single serving according to the Food Guide? See examples below:

Fresh, frozen or canned vegetables
125 mL (1/2 cup)

Leafy vegetables
Cooked:125 mL (1/2 cup)
Raw: 250 mL (1 cup)

Fresh, frozen or canned fruit
1 fruit or 125 mL (1/2 cup)

100% Juice
125 mL (1/2 cup)

Bread
1 slice (35 g)

Bagel
1 bagel (45g)

Flat Breads
1/2 pita or 1/2 tortilla (35g)

Cooked rice, bulgar or quinoa 125 mL
(1/2 cup)

Cooked Pasta
or couscous
125 mL (1/2 cup)

Cereal
Cold: 30 g
Hot: 175 mL(2/3 cup)

Milk or powdered milk (reconstituted)
150 mL (1 cup)

Condensed milk (evaporated)
125 mL (1/2 cup)

Fortified Soy beverage
250 mL (1 cup)

Yogurt
175 g
(2/3 cup)

Kefir
175 g
(2/3 cup)

Cheese
50 g
(1 1/2 oz.)

Cooked fish, shellfish poultry, lean meat
75 g (2 1/2 oz.) 125mL (1/2 cup)

Cooked legumes
175 mL (2/3 cup)

Tofu
150 g or
175 mL (2/3 cup)

Eggs (2)

Peanut or nut butters
30 mL (2 tsp.)

Shelled nuts
and seeds
60 mL (1/4 cup)

Oils and Fats

. Include a small amount-30-45 ml(2-3 tsp.)-of unstaurated fat each day. This includes oils used for cooking, salad dressings, margarine and mayonaise.

. Use vegetable oils such as canola, olive or soybean.

.Choose soft margarines low in suturated and trans-fats.

.Limit butter, hard margarine, lard and shortening.

Canada Food Guide: Page 3

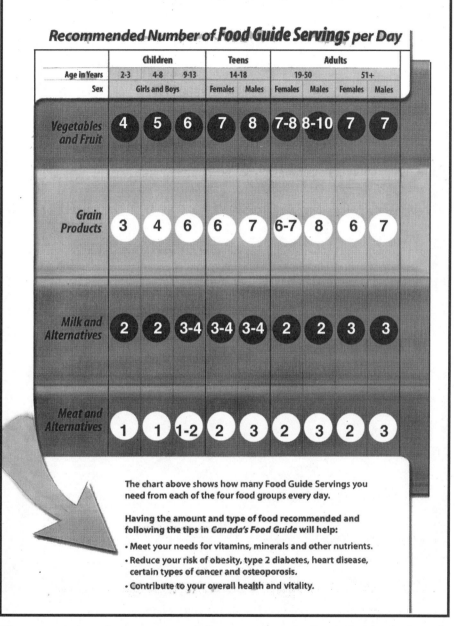

Recommended Number of *Food Guide Servings* per Day

Age in Years / Sex	Children			Teens		Adults			
	2-3	4-8	9-13	14-18		19-50		51+	
	Girls and Boys			Females	Males	Females	Males	Females	Males
Vegetables and Fruit	4	5	6	7	8	7-8	8-10	7	7
Grain Products	3	4	6	6	7	6-7	8	6	7
Milk and Alternatives	2	2	3-4	3-4	3-4	2	2	3	3
Meat and Alternatives	1	1	1-2	2	3	2	3	2	3

The chart above shows how many Food Guide Servings you need from each of the four food groups every day.

Having the amount and type of food recommended and following the tips in *Canada's Food Guide* will help:

- Meet your needs for vitamins, minerals and other nutrients.
- Reduce your risk of obesity, type 2 diabetes, heart disease, certain types of cancer and osteoporosis.
- Contribute to your overall health and vitality.

The remaining three pages of the *new Canada Food Guide* deal with important concepts such as activity/exercise, reading labels, serving sizes, substitutions and alternatives, as well as portion sizes/servings based on sex, age, size/weight and level of activity. Please consult the following website that can offer help to individualize the guide for each person: *www.http://www.healthcanada.gc.ca/foodguide*

USA Food Pyramid

The food guide developed by the US Department of Agriculture features a five-banded pyramid, which places more empahasis on servings of **fruits and vegetables**, which have their own category in the new guide. This is a commendable change. It also speaks to those who cannot or do not consume milk reason or another, an issue referred to many times in this publication. Another improvement is the issue of serving sizes - these sizes are very clear as suggestions are based on standard cup measures for many categories.

USA Food Pyramid: page 2

GRAINS Make half your grains whole	VEGETABLES Vary your veggies	FRUITS Focus on fruits	MILK Get your calcium-rich foods	MEAT & BEANS Go lean with protein
Eat at least 3 oz. of whole-grain cereals, breads, crackers, rice or pasta every day.	Eat more dark-green veggies like brocolli, spinach, and other dark leafy greens.	Eat a variety of fruit. Choose fresh, frozen canned, or dried fruit.	Go low-fat or fat-free when you choose milk or yogurt and other milk products.	Choose low-fat or lean meats or poultry. Bake, broil, or grill it!
1 oz. is about 1 slice of bread/about 1 cup of breakfast cereal, or 1/2 of cooked rice, cereal or pasta.	Eat more orange vegetables such as carrots, sweet potatoes and yams. Eat more dry beans and peas, such as pinto beans, kidney beans, and lentils	Go easy on fruit juices.	If one cannot or do not drink milk, choose lactose-free products or other calcium sources such as fortified foods and beverages.	Vary your protein source - choose more fish, beans, peas, nuts and seeds.

For a 2000-calorie diet, you need the amounts below from each food group.   To find the amounts that are right for you, go to MyPyramid.gov

| Eat 6 oz. every day. | Eat 2 1/2 cups every day. | Eat 2 cups every day. | Get 3 cups every day - kids (aged 2-8) need 2. | Eat 5 1/2 oz. every day. |

Find your balance between food and physical activity:

Be sure to stay within your daily calorie needs.

Be physically active for at least 30 minutes most days of the week.

About 60 minutes a day of physical activity may be required to prevent weight gain.

To sustaining weight loss, at least 60-90 minutes a day of physical activity may be required.

Children and teenagers should be physically active for 60 minutes every or most days

* Know the limits on fats, sugars and salt (sodium):

Make most of your fat choices from fish, nuts, and vegetable oils

Limit solid fats such as butter, stick margarine, shortening and lard, as well as foods that contain these fats.

Check the Nutrition Facts label to keep saturated fats, trans-fats and sodium low.

Choose food and beverages low in added sugars. Added sugars contribute calories with little, if any, nutrition.

USDA
U.S. Department of Agriculture
Center for Nutrition Policy and Promotion
April 2005
CNPP-15

MyPyramid.gov
STEPS TO A HEALTHIER YOU

Newer food guides, such as those produced in recent years by the United States (USDA) and Canada (Health Canada), are definite improvements over recommendations promoted over the past several decades. However, while they have included some food alternatives, little is said about food quality, chemical additives, or alternatives for those who are ill or suffer from allergies. It is a good place from which to start, but more research is required to find what is optimum for each reader and members of their families.

Parasites:

No amount of information on nutrition would be complete without some mention of parasitic infestations as they can have such an impact on one's nutritional status by robbing the body of essential nutrients. There are over 100 different types of parasites known to inhabit the bodies of humans. Some are microscopic in size, while others can be seen quite easily with the naked eye. They can be found in the water we drink, the air we breathe, or the food we eat. *Parasites* are responsible for exacerbating many health issues, as well as creating health problems of their own. They can burrow holes in organs, lump together to create clusters or tumors, which can often be mistaken for cancer.

Once established in the body, parasites will eat the same foods you eat - and they will eat you!

Parasites rob the body of vital vitamin and mineral nutrients, as well as amino acids required for digestion. A strong immune system often will keep them at bay, but once the immune system has been compromised, parasites can take over and further suppress the immune system. They can also destroy cells faster than they can be regenerated. Poisons emitted by parasites as they are being eliminated can cause a skin rash. Symptoms and the damage they cause vary a great deal, depending on the type of parasitic infection.

Symptoms of parasitic infestation include:
Itchy ears, nose and anus – bed wetting – gas and bloating – yellow skin – pain in the navel – eating too much, but still feeling hungry – drooling while sleeping – grinding teeth while sleeping – pain in the back region, thighs, shoulders or heart – foggy thinking – loss of appetite and so on. Parasitic infestation can create devastating symptoms, are often misdiagnosed, and can damage organs, possibly resulting in death.

Many people consider parasites to be a third world problem, but many common parasites are found in humans in developed countries as well. In fact, ninety per cent (90%) of all North Americans have had some form of parasites at one time or other in their lives. As suggested above, a strong immune system will usually limit the degree to which parasites affect the body, however, severe illness and / or immune deficiencies can permit parasites to multiply, devouring vital nutrients as they increase in number and tenacity. Parasites also have the ability to hide in many organs, even in lymph nodes. As they grow out of control, they can literally destroy the organs they inhabit, and of course, the body itself!

Treatments:
Parasite kits are available at health food stores, but please ensure you consult with a pharmacist first if you are taking any prescription medications, as there may be a conflict between these prescribed medications and the herbal ingredients in the parasitic cleanses. Such a conflict can result in a corresponding negative reaction, which could be dangerous to one's health. An effective cleanse must include active ingredients to neutralize parasites so they will release their hold on the body. Cleanses must also contain herbs that can flush the parasites (and the toxins released as a result of 'die-off') out of the body, as well as nutrients/herbs to cleanse the blood. In addition, probiotics are required to strengthen, balance and repopulate the intestinal flora of the body. Think 'bitter foods' while spending the one to three months to cleanse the body, and eliminate all refined sugars and natural sugars, as well as greasy or refined foods from your diet. Use raw garlic to supplement the process and drink plenty of water to flush out the toxins.

A few natural parasitic remedies:
   a. Pumpkin seeds and onions mixed with soy milk;
   b. One or two teaspoons of apple cider vinegar in a glass of water;
   c. Cloves, goldenrod and golden seal root for liver flukes;
   d. Milkweed, pennyroyal and black walnut for blood fluke;
   e. Bitter melon for pinworms;
   f. Sugar should be avoided as parasites thrive on it;
   g. A healthy immune system;
   h. Hydrogen peroxide [three (3) per cent maximum] on a swab for the inside of the nose.

It was not until much later into my journey that the potential devastation that could result from parasitic infestations was understood by me. Until specific symptoms arose, this issue was certainly not apparent or considered to be an issue. During my recovery, my fingernails had changed from being quite transparent to a solid color, and while they were much stronger than before, they were not as strong as they could be. At that point, I simply assumed it would take more time for that to occur. The longitudinal striations were still on my nails, which indicated mal-absorption issues, but it did not concern me until new symptoms appeared. Those included excessive drooling while sleeping, grinding my teeth, feeling hungry and a need to eat constantly, even after a heavy meal. It was somewhat like being pregnant and eating for two. But I certainly was not pregnant, so what was happening to me?

Then I recalled my childhood! As children we were regularly de-wormed (usually for pinworms) at home, and our parents occasionally giving us something extra to prevent or kill tapeworms. However, those practices had been abandoned many years ago. Then I reviewed David Rowland's book, *Listen to Your Body*, and completed a 'lifestyle assessment' that my daughter Tammy had been using while studying to become a nutritionist. After that assessment, it was abundantly clear that I likely had parasites[1].

It would be less than honest if I implied that I was unaffected by the notion of parasites, including worms, inhabiting my body. I felt revulsion at the very thought of tapeworms as long as twenty-five feet in my intestinal tract. Then it struck me: perhaps parasites had infested my lymphatic nodes and that could be why they had only reduced in size by seventy-five percent. A friend later confirmed that suspicion, as a program on the *Discovery Channel* had recently dealt with that very issue.

From a nutritional standpoint, I had been eating quite well for the past three years, and especially so since the diagnosis for cancer, but sharing my body with 'extra appetites' explained volumes related to the final stages of wellness, as well as my current nutritional status. I also wondered if there might have been a connection between a probable infestation and my higher *LDH* and liver *AST/SGOT* readings - the only remaining tests that had not returned to normal. At the time, those high readings still puzzled me.

A naturopath agreed with those suspicions, and began to work to find a way to detach, destroy, and flush any parasites from my body. During this process, the lymph nodes reduced in size by another fifteen percent. This process took two months, but the parasites were gone, although my body had not fully recovered as yet. Who would have ever anticipated such a connection?

---

1. For additional information on parasites read *God Helps Those Who Help Themselves* and *Parasites: The Enemy Within* by Rev. Hanna Kroeger, MsD and *Parasites are a Serious Health Concern*, a booklet by Brenda Watson, N.D., C.T. The following web sites are also quite informative: www.trilightherbs.com/merchant/antiparasite.htm and www. appliedozone.com/parasites.html

Bypass Surgery:

David W. Rowland wrote a wonderful handbook called *The Nutritional Bypass*. In it he describes how to reverse *atherosclerosis* without surgery. This booklet is a must for anyone interested in complete nutritional programs that successfully reverse and prevent hardening of the arteries. There is a time tested, safe, non-surgical method of removing arterial blockages without negative side effects. By-pass surgery only provides a temporary extension of life, as it does not address what produced the problem in the first place. Surgical methods can usually only treat symptoms, not causes, unless it repairs, for example, a genetic defect from birth. In addition, blood clots from an operation itself often migrate to other locations, causing strokes or other complications. The *New England Journal of Medicine* (Sept. 22, 1988) suggests that from twenty-five to forty-nine percent of coronary angioplasty cases become blocked again, often within six months. For long-term survival, surgical interventions often also require quite drastic changes in nutritional habits, as well as exercise levels.

The human body was designed to repair itself. Readers can take charge of their own health with respect to preventing and reversing health problems. David Rowland's book gives you another choice. Again consult one's health care provider. B.A.L.A.N.C.E. is the key. Use all of the health professionals available; seek guidance not only from medical doctors and pharmacists, but also from a naturopath and nutritionist.

Chapter Notes:

1. Vitamins A, D, E and K do not work well with mineral oil. These vitamins dissolve in the oil and are lost as nutrients.

2. Alcohol destroys vitamin B_1. Individuals who regularly consume moderate to larger quantities of alcohol require supplements to sustain the central nervous system. Smaller amounts, such as a glass of wine taken with a meal, according to most research, seems to be beneficial, but it is still important to support the body with food or supplements that contain vitamin B_1.

3. Non-hydrogenated potato chips with sea salt constitute a much better snack than cereal, that contain sugars, chemicals and hydrogenated oils

4. There are nutritional, as well as social, emotional and academic advantages that occur in children when families share meals together. They generally have a better sense of stability and belonging, have fewer behavior problems and attain higher grades in school. Children are also less likely to be depressed, drink, smoke or do drugs within this kind of family atmosphere.

CHAPTER SIX SUMMARY

1. Begin with a review of chapters two to five, and set personal health goals for yourself.

2. List those foods the body does not receive and, therefore, cannot benefit from.

3. Make a list of the vitamins and minerals that the body is not obtaining from food. Establish a goal to add them to your body.

4. Choose to eat healthier. Buy or make healthier breads or sauces that contain non-hydrogenated oils. Use only unbleached, whole wheat, or alternative flours such as kamut, quinoa, spelt, or rye. Make sure these flours are organically grown and are properly ground.

5. Learn to read labels.

6. Locate a qualified nutritionist or nutritional consultant (RNC or RNCP), one that does not simply sell products, but is interested in the assessment of the whole person and in the body's overall balance. Note that many nutritional consultants had been ill themselves and their direction in assisting others comes from their personal experiences, as well as their training.

7. If you are unable to afford the service of a nutritionist, then check the library to see if they have David Rowland's book, *Listen to Your Body*, or order one on-line.

8. Do not use one's genetic heritage as an excuse for being unhealthy. Poor genes may account for the weaker parts of the body, but only if toxins, improper nutrition, and/or poor quality water make up a major portion of what the body ingests, will genetics become a self-fulfilling prophecy.

9. Surgery is serious; it alters the body forever. Nutrition can play a significant role in reversing many health conditions where surgery is indicated. This is especially important before considering heart surgery, so if you are contemplating such an operation read more from authors such as Dr. David Rowland and Dr. Matthias Rath. Other conditions that may be helped include gall bladder, fibroids, tonsillitis, blockages in the colon (*IBS, Crohn's*) and more. In many cases, you may have other choices.

"When the food one ingests is of a higher quality, the body discards lower quality tissues to make healthier ones."

"The great error of our day of modern treatment of the human body is that physicians separate the soul from the body."

(Plato)

Chapter Seven

Coping Skills

Coping skills: what are they? The simple answer is that coping skills are strategies and behaviors used by humans to solve problems.

Why? While the mind can create a plan of recovery or produce a level of despair that emotionally and physically affects the body, emotions can also alter one's ability to cope.

How to problem-solve: a) identify the problem; b) take ownership; c) keep cool; d) look for alternate solutions; e) resolve the problem, being accountable for both the problem and the solution; and f) evaluate the outcome and the solution used to resolve the problem.

The following exercise will clearly illustrate how the mind can literally affect a physical end result.
Find a metal washer (a needle will work as well) and a piece of thread about six inches (15 cm) long and tie it to the washer. Hold the thread attached to the washer with the thumb, fore and middle fingers. Keep it in front of one's body, and ensure that the washer does not move. Then focus your thoughts on it, and use your mind to imagine that the washer on the string is moving back and forth in a straight line. Concentrate while this is being done.

What happened? Did it move back and forth with one's thoughts only?
Now, imagine the washer on the string can move in a circle, clockwise motion – going round and round. Concentrate and remember that the hands must not move. How was that experience? Was it not amazing, yet a bit fearful at the same time? Changing from being fearful to a moment

of opportunity is one significant outcome that can result from the application of visualization techniques.

Walt Disney used imagery to create his dream. A variety of sport and film stars, as well as many business people, also envision success and then set out to accomplish just that. However, other individuals often allow negative thoughts to creep in to their conscious mind which may well lead to negative actions or consequences. Thoughts of illness and death deep within the sub-conscious could well become one's destiny, as the body is ultimately directed by both the conscious and sub-conscious mind.

Negative and positive life experiences, contribute to the development of coping skills and may be relatively easier for some individuals. Negative experiences can drive some individuals to their knees, but acquiring knowledge along with positive attitudes can also enable them to recover and move forward in life. Disease can be a significant lesson in one's life. It can negatively impact upon individuals and their families, and change them forever. However, it is important to view life's challenges in more positive ways. The greatest challenge for most individuals is to eliminate negative thoughts, as they often negate positive changes within the body.

> Ultimately, I accepted my diagnosis of terminal cancer as a gift, not just for me, but also for anyone who reads this book. Past life experiences, as well as the skills required for coping under pressure, have provided me with the ability to relate to people at every level of society, and has enabled me to help others in my professional and volunteer roles. My instincts and intuition guided much of the research for this book and the associated development of a workshop program I now deliver for others. Life's experiences seem to ebb and flow like the tide; I have learned to simply go with the flow. My recovery has, in a very short time, directed me to many new resources, and it has already begun to touch the lives of others.

Just imagine, if prior to prescribing medication for a mental health diagnosis, medical practitioners were first able to ascertain the level of toxins and the nutritional intake of patients. How many individuals with anxieties, creepy-crawly feelings and depression could be found with elevated levels of toxins in their bodies, are lacking in B vitamins, or perhaps manifest a 'leaky gut' caused by a Candida overgrowth? Unfortunately, in the world of the 21st Century, toxins are often added to already stressed bodies through medications, including anti-depressants.

The latter substances often compound an already depressive situation by increasing, rather than decreasing, the toxic burden on one's body. Imagine seniors in nursing homes receiving wheat grass, and other freshly pressed juices daily - and being taught methods of detoxification! Is that just a pipe dream or a real possibility someday?

For several years, I have known that the symptoms my mother exhibited were related to elevated levels of toxins in her body. Subsequently, her medical history confirmed that was precisely what was wrong with her. It is very possible that Mom may not have been confined to a nursing home if the information discovered during my own research had been more accessible to our family at that time.

My purpose in writing this book was to give hope to those who have had their hopes diminished. Books have helped me cope during my most desperate times, and that journey with books began long before my diagnosis. Two books that influenced and expanded my coping skills, as well as the direction of my life over the past ten years, included Stephen Covey's *Seven Habits of Highly Effective People* and *First Things First*.

I was unemployed at the time and my employment insurance had ended. That was after twenty years of working in a single factory. However, economics had changed and the plant closed. It was a significant low point in my life; my tears were a mute testimony to that! But I persevered, and when a new business opened in town, I introduced myself to the owners. At the time I could not afford to purchase a daily newspaper, but would walk to the library to read it. Later I joined a group of unemployed persons who met weekly to brainstorm for job ideas, review one another's resumes, compare skills, and meet with local employers to find out what was valued in an employee within their companies.

Colleen, a volunteer facilitator at one of these sessions, introduced us to Stephen Covey's *Seven Habits of Highly Effective People*. Although I could not really afford to buy this publication, intuition prompted me to purchase it anyway. Covey's books teach us to look at the end of one's life when setting goals, as well as at more difficult situations, but always to take a 'win-win' approach to each. Remember that each individual looks at his/her life from the perspective of the many different paths that person has traveled. I often use Covey's 'circle of concern/circle of influence' as a quick brainstorming technique - the inner circle outlining the issue at hand, while the outer circle represents the ways in which the issue might be resolved, In fact, I often carry a double circle in my handbag or briefcase, should a situation arise where these tools could be useful.

James Redfield's *The Celestine Prophecy* and *The Tenth Insight* were two other important books that came my way through a close friend, Ruth Ann, who had loaned me the latter title. Enrolment in an evening credit course in Sociology gave me an opportunity to read Redfield's first book with an open mind, and it, subsequently became a source of revelation for me. It taught me how to visualize, and the importance of the connections among one's spirit, mind and body. Reading that book also helped when I applied for a job at the local YMCA, where I met Clare, who would eventually became a mentor in my life. She saw things in me that I had not seen in myself, gave me wings, and let me soar. At the YMCA I also met Bill and his friend Richard, who eventually offered me more guidance on my journey. Meeting these people at just the right time is one of life's unique mysteries.

Information and knowledge decrease emotional turmoil!

The third author whose work helped me to expand my coping skills was Dr. Phil McGraw. His books included *Self Matters* (including the companion workbook), and *Life Strategies*. At that time in my life, my behaviors in public were not always the same as my responses in more private situations. I still had issues to deal with from my past. Many of us do, but I had to let go of specific issues and find ways to forgive myself. I had to feel more positive, not only in what I did, but about who I was; Dr. Phil's books helped me with both. I had finished *Self Matters* a month prior to my diagnosis, and was presented with the companion workbook as a Christmas gift. This ultimately helped me to visualize better and to gain a better insight about who I was in this life. The responses from an e-mailed questionnaire from the *Self Matter's* workbook to several friends and family members were terrific. One reply from a friend especially inspired me: "I couldn't answer this for you Susan, as there is no need to; you already know the answers, just look inside yourself." Dr. Phil's books also enabled me to find the courage within myself to help my mother through her fears on her deathbed. Just before slipping away to join my dad in the hereafter, mom uttered the words I had longed to hear all of my life: "I love you Susie".

Books, especially those in the self-help and psychology sections, helped me cope with life's ups and downs. In the late sixties and early seventies, self-help information was not as readily available as it is today. Programs such as *Oprah* had not aired as yet, so other kinds of writing, including romance and mystery novels, were my books of choice.

I have been married twice; the second for over twenty-five years to a fantastic man. In contrast, my first marriage could only be described as a disaster. I spent eight years with a man, the father of my eldest daughter, who abused drugs, was jailed several times, cheated on me, and was physically and mentally abusive. One never knew if there would be money for food or a roof over our heads, although I continued to work outside the home during most of that period. He was also very controlling. I coped by figuratively climbing inside a book to live another's life, which helped me to repress the heartache in mine.

In North America, the typical response to many problems is to treat everything as a crisis. Contrast that with most of the people in China, where the symbol of crisis is regarded as opportunity, where negative situations are actually viewed as opportunities to develop and grow. It is not the good times that challenge us, rather it is overcoming adversity that helps us become thoughtful and caring humans.

Crisis ⟶ Balance ⟶ Recovery

Unfortunately, many individuals in crisis attempt to cope via obsessive-compulsive behaviors. Addictive personalities try to numb the crisis through a range of compulsive behaviors, including excessive shopping, drugs, alcohol or sex. Still others try to cope by suppressing their real feelings or by withholding information. They ignore, ridicule, or place blame on others rather than themselves. Behaviors are often shame-based and are related to physical, emotional or sexual abuse, addictive backgrounds; disabilities or handicaps; mental illnesses; or restrictive and radicalized religious beliefs - the latter, a situation commonly referred to as 'all law and no grace'.

Some Guidelines for Learning to Cope:

1. Do not panic, stay calm and think issues through.
2. Try not to be too dramatic about a problem, but be reminded that this is a situation which can be dealt with by most individuals. Look for the best solution, not the easiest fix, or a subsequent situation could result that will have to be dealt later in life.
3. Clarify the problem and look for answers; Stephen Covey's circles of concern and influence may be helpful here.
4. Try the breathing technique in Chapter Two; learn to be quiet and listen to one's inner voice and intuition.
5. Talk a problem through with a friend, co-worker or relative, but remember that it is not following advice that is important, but rather simply talking through situations out loud, so to speak, that is crucial. Often the question is resolved simply through the process of questioning itself.

Change comes about with the attainment of life goals through skills developed in the process of learning, coping and growing as a person. Some individuals are fortunate enough to have learned many of those skills and behaviors in the context of a supportive family, while others may have learned it through life's more difficult experiences, or perhaps, simply through reading. Those with friends or family members who have lost all hope, may find it again through the information contained in this or other books.

After one of my presentations on B.A.L.A.N.C.E., one group of four sisters came forward. They had already lost three siblings to cancer, and were simply waiting their turn to contract the disease and die! They did not know there were ways to potentially reverse that situation. A combination of their belief in genetic pre-disposition, as well as a lack of knowledge of other possibilities, had unwittingly condemned them to a pre-determined sentence of death. However, B.A.L.A.N.C.E. ultimately gave them renewed hope, which is a central theme of this publication. Those who made important changes based on what they had learned through the B.A.L.A.N.C.E. program also noticed signs of a physically healthier body with in a few short months.

A story of the thistle:

I once read an article about how a common thistle plant could assist individuals to attain a firmer grasp of their problems in life. This resonated with me, as my mom had often mentioned thistles from her early life in the U.K. The article asked readers to consider the thistle as a problem in their life and how to take hold of that problem, deal with it quickly, thereby allowing one to feel much better about the situation. The example cited in the article suggested that one grab a thorny thistle and squeeze it firmly and quickly. Surprisingly, it did not hurt, nor did this action crush the thistle. Only when the grasp was indecisive, did injury occur to the person's hand or the plant itself. This is a good analogy related to the use of visualization to deal confidently with an issue that must be resolved and tackling the problem head on to rid oneself of the issue, quickly and decisively.

Thistle

Laughter as a coping skill:

Norman Cousins had an irreversible disease (*ankylosing spondylitis*) that had crippled him for many years. With only a few months left to live, he checked out of the hospital, and with the help of high doses of vitamin C and humor, literally laughed himself to wellness. He then shared his experiences through his book, *Anatomy of an Illness*. Fifteen years later, after a near fatal heart attack, he wrote *The Healing Heart*. Modern medical science discovers more everyday about how laughter can be utilized to help heal patients. The film, *Patch Adams*, was a humorous but true story about the power of laughter to heal. Even more recently, numerous articles have been written in prestigious national newspapers and magazines that stress the importance of the role of laughter in the process of healing. A hearty belly laugh releases *endorphins* (*serotonin*) into the bloodstream, thereby strengthening the immune system. Vibrations from laughter actually shake up and release stress caused by pent up emotions that negatively affect human organ systems.

Most healing humor arises spontaneously out of situations, but it is often helpful to keep items that are particularly funny on hand - a toolbox of comedy, so to speak. This can include a favorite cartoon, video, joke, album, CD or cassette, greeting card, bumper sticker, book, toy, or even a hand mirror with which to practice one's smile. Learning to laugh at oneself in such a way allows life to become a bit less serious. Indeed, the old saying that laughter is the best medicine definitely appears to be true when it comes to the protection of the heart, said Michael Miller, director of the *Center of Preventive Cardiology* at the *University of Maryland Medical Center*. The healthful benefits of laughter are cause for celebration among psychologists. They now recognize the therapeutic value of humor in the workplace and have begun to recommend it for their patients. Daniel Coleman, writing in *The New York Times*, commented that humor can also aid problem-solving, as well as contribute to creativity in the business environment.

There can be an overly serious side to my nature. Even in my teens, I had issues with humor, often unable to find many situations humorous, while others around me figuratively cracked up. When I facilitated a course on life skills a few years ago, I gave participants a task in which they had to present an unfamiliar subject to their peers. We, of course, had a typical 'class clown', a great guy named Bob, who kept us all in stitches. Bob felt that I didn't laugh enough and the group assigned me a task in which I had to make a presentation on laughter. I accepted the challenge and came dressed for the occasion: blonde pigtail wig, flower power pants and top, and more. I learned to laugh at myself and, in turn, the group laughed along with me. This process also built a better environment for teaching the remainder of the course.

Some basic techniques that could help with the introduction of humor in one's life:

1. Set the stage: place cartoons or funny sayings around the room most often used for discussion groups. Place post-it notes on mirrors in the bedroom, bathroom, on the computer screen, and so on. Short jokes are great, as are photos that have been hidden away for years, especially those with period clothing, dated eyeglasses or hairdos.

2. Use a journal to write down humorous anecdotes from the past. Everyone has something in their past that can precipitate gales of laughter with friends or family. It might begin an entirely new way of

communicating. Others will often share humorous information from their pasts as well, giving everyone even more to laugh about, or perhaps, to write in their journal for those times when one is depressed.

3. Make a list of funny people and note what it is about their brand of humor that is attractive. [*My all-time favorites were Lucille Ball and Red Skelton.*]

4. Organize a humor party. Ask guests to bring a humorous item to share at the party. That could include jokes, cartoons, photos, or simply ask them to dress in costume for the event. One game that might be played at the party to create laughter involves charades. Take aside two close friends and have them cued to act in an exaggerated manner during the presentation, including obviously not listening, boredom, being rude and so on. Make sure it is an individual who would be totally out of character in these circumstances. This will certainly add to the hilarity of the situation.

5. An interesting game that is sure to make everyone laugh (humor is contagious) involves these simple rules based on a variation of musical chairs. Begin with everyone seated; anyone can stand up whenever they wish; but cannot remain standing for more than five seconds at a time. They can, however, sit down and stand right back up again. Only four people can be standing at one time. (Weinstein and Goodman, 1980)

6. Another exercise for evoking humor and honing problem-solving skills includes the following. Ask participants to think of humorous situations for problem solving, such as different ways a rubber band can be used, or ways to send love messages over long distances. Remember to laugh with others. Let someone choose to be the butt of the joke, but do not make that choice for them.

Some points to remember:
1) Humor must be experienced; begin today to add humor to one's life.

2) Give oneself permission to laugh. Let go and enjoy the experience.

3) Take a child-like attitude to regain one's spirit of humor. Find out where the spirit went, locate it and help restore it to one's daily life.

4) Put ideas together, but remember that humor is more than just connecting the dots. Try doing something funny today; it is all about attitude, not whether one gets it right or not.

Volunteering:

Many individuals can handle two problems or difficulties at the same time - their own and another's - and often better than they can handle their own problem by itself. Life is magic, but at any moment life could end. Each day the magic begins again - all eighty-six thousand, four hundred seconds of it. One of most beautiful aspects of life is the one thing that makes us truly human: the joy of sharing. Everyone has something within himself or herself to share with others, whether through community organizations or just being a friend to someone else. Spending time with relatives or friends can also bring joy to one's life, as well as to help others take their minds off current problems.

> *"It is one of the most beautiful compensations of this life that no man can sincerely try to help another without helping himself ... serve and thou shall be served."*
>
> (Ralph Waldo Emerson)

The YMCA/YWCA:

The local YMCA is a good place to begin. The YMCA originally was conceived as a place where Christian teachings inspired young men to be the best that they could be, but today it serves all people regardless of age, sex, faith, background or abilities. At the 'Y' a person can become involved in health, fitness, membership, childcare, camping, education, leadership, international development, or philanthropy. Early in the last century, the YMCA taught survival swimming to soldiers in the Great War. By the Second World War, they visited prisoner-of-war camps to ensure the humane treatment of those incarcerated. Today the Y's have expanded their role and worldwide are located in over 130 countries.

For me, the YMCA provided a wonderful place to volunteer in many capacities over the years: from chaperoning teen dances, teaching life-skills, or as a facilitator for a wellness program for prisoners, including goal setting, life-skills, crafts, cooking, and fitness. Other activities included fund-raising activities, creative advertising and marketing, as well as serving as a board member and chair of a committee.

I believe the reason I am able to deal with adversity better today is my ability to cope, which includes expanded problem solving skills, reading and research, volunteering opportunities, as well as helping others to cope every day through my work and volunteer positions. When I was diagnosed with cancer I was working full-time and remained in that position while the process of detoxifying my body began. Working enabled me to help others cope with their problems, while somewhat distracting me from mine. However, in 2004, I chose to stay home to ensure that I received plenty of fresh air, sunshine and rest. That process continued until 2006. Today I assist others to remove toxins from their bodies using cellular detoxification therapy, present lectures and workshops, as well as personalized consultations to guide individuals through the natural wellness process. I still exercise at the 'Y' several times a week, use the sauna, and continue my volunteer work.

Before I began the process of detoxifying my body, I would arrive home exhausted, unable to cook supper or perform everyday chores. However, I was fortunate to have a husband who understood my situation and was more than willing to take over those duties for me. Now that significant amounts of toxins have been removed, and my former diet has been replaced with healthy, nutritious foods and pure water, my energy has returned. We now share the cooking and housework, and Jim's help enables me time to work on this book, give talks and spend time with clients of my new business venture.

Relaxation Techniques:
There are many relaxation techniques with which to experiment and enjoy. Breathing is only one such technique. What follows is a stress-relieving exercise that works well to relax every muscle in the body. Try it and see what happens.

1) Loosen any uncomfortable clothing, choose soothing music and relax. This can be done while seated, standing or in a horizontal position.

2) Tighten the muscles in the toes and hold for a count of ten. Relax and enjoy the sensation of the release from tension.

3) Flex the muscles of the feet. Then hold them tightly for a count of ten and then relax again.

4) Move slowly up through the body: legs, buttocks, abdomen, back, and neck (try to raise your shoulders to touch your ears); then contract the muscles of the face - even stick out your tongue to stretch it.

5) Breathe deeply and slowly. Remember to breathe deeply not only from the lungs, but also through the nose and out through the mouth. Let the body reach a deeper level of relaxation, calmness and serenity while one moves through this exercise. This breathing exercise is also beneficial by breathing through the nose only (as in yoga), concentrating on the breath coming from your heart and filling one's soul.

6) Then minimally tense every muscle in the body, until that tension is felt throughout the rest of the body: in the face . . . eyes . . . shoulders . . . arms . . . chest . . . back . . . legs . . . stomach. Do them all at once and be sure to continue to breathe normally. Feel the tension in every part of the body. Let the entire body relax. Experience the waves of calmness as the tension in the muscles is released?

7) With eyes closed, take a deep breath and hold it. Take note of the tension . . . exhale and feel a relaxation and calmness develop in one's body.

Hydrotherapy:
For centuries, people have used warm water as a way to calm moods and relax muscles. A 'spa' environment at home can simply be achieved with the addition of relaxation ingredients to the bath water. Epsom salts not only work to detoxify, but also help to relax the muscles. It can, however, dry the skin, but the addition of essential oils, such as lavender, or lemon should help keep the skin moist. Ensure that the oils are natural and contain no additives or preservatives. Dr. Richard Schulze (ND, MH) advocates a fifteen-minute program of alternating hot and cold water therapy (always ending with cold) as a great immune builder. The latter can aid in the prevention of colds or influenza, as well as stimulate the body's regenerative processes.

Yoga[1]:
The word *yoga* comes from the ancient and classical language (Sanskrit) of the Hindus and is a term that literally means 'yoke' (to join or unite) and implies the harnessing of oneself to God. *Yoga* utilizes stretching postures, breathing, and meditation techniques to calm the emotions and the mind, as well as to tone the body. It was derived from a melting pot of dozens of religious and quasi-religious systems and methods, most of which were health-oriented. The actual physiological/mental techniques themselves are included in the practical and contemporary definitions

---

1. An excellent reference guide for yoga exercises for beginners or intermediate participants is: *Creative Yoga Companion: A WORKBOOK* by Jodie Myers (Glen Margaret Publishing).

of yoga. These techniques concentrate on posture and alignment, as well as creating a higher consciousness of self and God. In Yoga, the body and mind are linked to create a state of internal peacefulness, integration and to bring the individual from a state of separation to self-unity and acceptance. Ill health is a state where the body and mind are out of balance.

Tai Chi (also known as *Tai Chi Ch'uan*):

Tai Chi, a part of the *Tai Chi Ch'uan* system, was originally a form of martial arts that operates on several levels of awareness. It embodies Taoist philosophy and is extremely beneficial for good health. *Tai Chi* is a comprehensive series of gentle physical movements and breathing techniques, with mental and spiritual intent, which allows the self to experience a meditative state. It calms and rejuvenates, assisting the body and mind to maintain balance. It exercises the body, mind and spirit together with the internal organs, and includes both inner and outer expressions of the body and mind. *Tai Chi* balances the *Yin* and *Yang* life force energy of Chi. In this way it develops an ability to balance the 'yield and attack' aspects of martial art combat and is still a major influence in all modern forms of martial arts today.

Just prior to my diagnosis with cancer, intuition came into play once again, but this time it was not me, but rather my husband who made a seemingly out-of-character decision that both surprised and pleased me. He decided to join a *Tai Chi* Club; later becoming president of the local chapter. His knowledge helped immensely during my toxic attacks. Before detoxification began to help me, I had assumed these were anxiety attacks. Jim would gently guide me through the *Tai Chi* exercises that decreased the stress I was experiencing at the time. Even in the sauna my mind would race, jumping from one thought to the next, resulting in more stress. *Tai Chi* hand movements helped me to relax and remain calm. Jim's decision to enroll in this course certainly paid dividends for both of us. The person with an illness is not the only member of the family that is affected emotionally; Jim had to de-stress and re-focus as well.

Qi Gong (pronounced che-gong):

Qi Gong is a system of practices for rejuvenation and health that can be loosely translated to mean: "Life force gained through the merit of practice." *Qi Gong* improves flexibility, strength, mental focus, and physical and emotional balance through visualization, meditation, stretching, movement, and self-massage. This practice has been known to help hypertension, asthma, diabetes, immune functioning, the reduction of negative energy, as well as frozen shoulder or neck, chronic back pain, knee and ankle pain plus fatigue, insomnia and infection. There are even cases of heroin addiction that have been helped by *Qi gong*

Support systems/affirmations:

Social support and self-reflection are required to help recover from trauma or disease. One must remove negative thoughts and feelings from the past and to let go of one's ego. It is important to restore and expand one's consciousness so the past can heal, and to deal with it directly so that old triggers do not continue to affect life in the present. Be meaningfully busy, not just busy for the sake of being busy, and move ahead in life. Find an affirmation that will move you forward such as, "I will move forward in wellness and in life." Repeat one's chosen phrase three to five times a day. An affirmation should be repeated daily for at least thirty days for the subconscious to accept and retain it.

"If you are willing to do the mental work of releasing and forgiving, almost anything can be healed.

(Louise Hay, *Heal your Body*)[1]

When diagnosed with an illness or disease it is important to look for emotional connections and perform the necessary work to remove them. Ask *what* does this disease give one permission to do: to leave a job or one's partner, to stop enabling others (doing their work instead of giving them knowledge and letting them grow) or something else. Then ask yourself *why* the conscious self did not have the strength to do this? Look for *where* this learned behavior began in childhood, including one's parents, siblings, baby sitters, teachers, friends, or others who may have negatively affected you. This internal work must be accomplished first in order to fix the external problem.

---

1. Louise Hay's book, *Heal Your Body* is also a great way to pin-point emotional patterns, and along with the use of affirmations, can help to release the sub-conscious.

My own answer came when I finally realized that I was constantly enabling others and had done so for many years. Those included my husband, daughter, sister, friends - even some of my clients at work. The load had become far too heavy, but my conscious self could not say no. A diagnosis of terminal cancer ultimately became my opportunity to say no! This enabling pattern was learned as a child through my mother who taught us to do her bidding to enable her - there were even times we had to carry her purse. In the end, I was able to do inner work by writing my deceased mother a letter, thereby releasing my deep-seated anger and following through with forgiveness. I then burned the letter in the fireplace. This helped resolve the conflict within me. I now have the ability to say no and have ended my enabling behaviors with others, including my own family. Everyone has grown positively from this experience, especially me.

Spirituality:

Each person has a unique perspective on spirituality. It is very personal and is rooted in one's culture, family, and community. For some the belief in God and involvement in church helps to create and maintain those feelings. For others it is found through volunteer work, leisure activities such as carpentry or art; or just finding a quiet space to observe nature or listen to music. Still others find it through meditation, time to enjoy a good book or quite simply, through quality downtime. Do whatever it takes to give guidance to one's self and to re-energize the spirit. The body requires balance and harmony to bring zest and pleasure to life.

After my diagnosis for cancer, I returned to church for the first time in thirty years. Although baptized a Roman Catholic, I was not even sure if that would be the religion I would feel most comfortable with at this stage of my life. My husband and I spent a few Sundays in different churches throughout our town, and in the end we chose the Nativity Catholic Church. We let our instincts guide our search for a sense of belonging and comfort. A few months later, my husband, who was not baptized, decided to become a Roman Catholic and began to attend classes to become a member of the congregation. I joined him as sponsor. The process continued over a number of months, with Jim eventually receiving the sacraments of Baptism and the Eucharist.

The journey has been enlightening and the people we met on our spiritual path have been marvelous. Not only did Jim learn what was necessary for his commitment to the faith, but I was able to refresh my knowledge as well. The sense of belonging to a spiritual community was the deepest part of that journey. Our faith deepened even more when Raymond, who also was on a similar spiritual path as my husband, was diagnosed with cancer and entered the hospital for surgery. We knew he required support, so within hours of his admission to the hospital, the religious community, including a priest, deacon, a nun, two leaders of the musical community, Jim, myself, and Raymond's sponsor assembled in the small hospital chapel. Raymond was brought to the chapel and the sacraments of the Eucharist and for the sick were performed. Raymond had been fearful of missing an opportunity to receive these sacraments, but those gathered made sure that his spiritual needs were met. Spirituality filled that small chapel and was felt by each of us, and Raymond attained a sense of family as well. My intuition was spot on! I had found my path and was finally home again, thanks to my husband whose love and commitment had helped to create this very special moment in time!

Raymond in the chapel with sponsors and friends

An aside: During Jim's journey to convert to Roman Catholicism, we had an emotional talk one evening. Jim understood that the body was a host for one's spirit, but wanted to know if I died from cancer and left this world, how would he recognize my spirit when we met again in another place? My reply: "If I were brain dead in the hospital on life support would that body lying there be who I really am?" He then understood that I am my spirit and that he would always be able to find me anywhere . . . in the afterlife . . . in heaven.

"I am the master of my fate;
I am the captain of my soul"
(William Ernest Henley.)

Gardens:

Garden's have been healing places for thousands of years. Spending time in a garden, either resting in or tending it, helps people attain a sense of peace, serenity and wellbeing. When was the last time joy was found - for a day, a week, a month, or a year? There are only so many special moments in one lifetime; is now not the time to make today count? Keep a journal of the things that provide inner peace and uplift one's spirit. Then take time out of a busy life to carry out what had been written - just do it!

The Spirit, Mind, and Body Connection:

The mind can affect the disease process as well. Two people might work in the same toxic environment; one might get a disease, while another may not. Negative past life experiences linger in the sub-conscious and can effect both the present and future. A naturopath or life coach can help to uncover subconscious issues affecting one's health. Cranial sacral therapy is one tool that could be used. Or one may prefer reading books, including *Life Strategies, Self Matters,* or *Legacy of the Heart.* The latter discusses the issues and spiritual advantages of a painful childhood. Other helpful books include John Bradshaw's *Home Coming,* a story about reclaiming and championing your inner child, or *Not All in the Mind* by Dr. Richard Mackarness.

At the beginning of my journey I was quite ill, but over time many of my negative symptoms became more positive, and by 2005 I had felt quite healthy for nearly two years. However, something had changed. Unfortunately, I had not noticed it until a significant issue surfaced with respect to my digestive processes. That occurred while I was busy with my research, and I was unable to detect the early warning signs as both muscles and body tissues had begun to deteriorate again. (Read more on *catchexia* in Chapter Eight.) Dropping at least one half pound per day, within four days I had become terrified. The more I ate, the less I weighed. My spirit was crushed and I was unsure where to turn for help. In all likelihood, my family physician would have suggested another visit to the oncologist, who, in turn, would have wanted me to begin chemotherapy immediately. But the latter was not a viable option for me. Dropping to my knees, I prayed for guidance; with tears flowing down my face, I wrote a letter to my husband and children. I wanted them to know how much they were loved and how much life here with them on this planet meant to me. I also wanted them to understand that my belief and reliance upon natural therapies had not let me down.

Writing that letter gave me time to pause and reflect. I re-read my own letter, and by the time the second page had been reached, I was ready to begin to work again - to seek help at a more accelerated pace. Research led me to *spirulina*, a micro-algae, that could, perhaps, help my body absorb nutrients. The liver was also stressed and required more support, subsequently I located a new product, *desiccated liver*, which helped. With the aid of these two natural products, I was able to avert a crisis and regained the two pounds within a week. I had been given the strength to overcome this difficulty, and to succeed in my quest for a more complete solution.

Still, it was not a satisfactory solution. These products only addressed symptoms, not the underlying issues, as the latter were still unknown to me at the time. So I returned to the B.A.L.A.N.C.E. approach described in Chapter Two. I listened to my body, re-checked my most recent blood tests, and searched for additional information on pH, eventually discovering that my emotions were playing a significant role in the larger picture of my health. My salivary pH dropped shortly after I ate, which was another clear indication of underlying emotional issues requiring substantial work on my part.

Later a web site on systemic *Candidiasis* was located. It described a *pathogenic yeast overgrowth*, a condition that may well have been contributing to these digestive and mal-absorption issues. A thyroid imbalance was another possibility. Additional tests indicated that my carbon dioxide and bicarbonate levels, as well as pH, were still out of balance. Again emotional issues were implicated as potentially contributing factors. The acidic climate created by those emotions was the perfect place for a systemic *Candidiasis infestation* to grow out of control.

More symptoms arose. My extremities, especially my fingertips and toes, became extremely cold and my nails turned blue. Those symptoms suggested that I had developed what was known as *Raynaud's Phenomenon*, obvious signs of emotional and environmental stress. Compounding this problem was the onset of significant food sensitivities: first to oatmeal and raisins, then dates, wheat, buckwheat, corn, and more. It seemed each time I ate, something new affected me. My naturopath worked on my emotions and attempted to desensitize me, but to no avail. It was a vicious circle, as my mind was still sabotaging me.

To tackle stress, one must first accept the issue, such as the diagnosis of terminal illness or significant weight loss, and then learn to deal with it, so I began to keep a log of each time my hands or feet turned blue. A pattern emerged immediately - the *Raynaud's symptoms* occurred at two very specific times: while writing this book and while working on my diploma in adult education. After comparing my previous attempts to obtain a university diploma with past medical information, it became abundantly clear that the stress of writing in each of these situations actually increased the level of illness in my body.

First, there were benign tumors in the thyroid (1977 and 1994); fibroids in the uterus (1996), which required surgery; then a broken bone in my writing hand during university exams; followed by toxin attacks, and finally, cancer. The next steps were to locate any possible or probable environmental triggers and to determine any past connections with these illnesses/injuries. Reading and research were constant companions in the attempt to resolve this problem, as earlier learning had suggested that disease was not only created by these toxins, but was also influenced by previous emotional trauma.

A few months following the diagnosis for cancer, I had to deal with a personal need to hear my mother say that she loved me, automatically assuming there would be a total connection when that occurred. Since that time I had worked on other stored and repressed guilt, including a situation whereby a former male friend had molested my daughter. In that particular situation, the guilt stemmed from not having him charged with a criminal offence at the time. It was a poor decision based on all the wrong reasons, and one that eventually returned to haunt us both.

What else?
Upon further reflection, I came to recognize connections between dropping out of school in grade eleven and the marriage to my first husband, Fred. That fateful decision was taken on New Years Eve. I had left home to baby-sit for friends, subsequently informing my family that I would

not be returning home. I was only sixteen at the time. My father was furious, but he realized that neither emotional nor physical force would bring me home. He even asked the local police to take me to the station for a chat, but legally little could be done to change the situation. My father and the police officer warned me that by leaving home at that age I would likely never complete my high school education, let alone earn a post-secondary degree. They reminded me that I had been an excellent student and had the ability to make something of myself, if only I returned home to complete my schooling. It is clear to me today, that my subconscious had held onto those words for all those intervening years, especially the guilt associated with hurting my family, as every time I attempted to further my education, my mind sabotaged me with health-related issues, time and time again.

Once I made that connection, all symptoms of *Raynaud's Phenomenon* ceased. To ensure the diagnosis of terminal cancer did not become a self-fulfilling prophecy, further searching was required to ensure that nothing else lay hidden in my past. A spiritualist helped. A friend had given me her name earlier, and Hazel, another friend, had reminded me of it again. It was perfect timing. The last set of issues had to do with my father. What would cause a sixteen year old to leave home? It just did not make sense for someone not into drugs, who did well in school, was the captain of athletic teams, and an entrepreneur. But this was not a rational or intellectual decision - it went much deeper!

My assumption all along had been that I left home because I felt unwanted. Mom never told me she loved me. Today, I understand that she was likely incapable at the time of doing so. At the age of twelve, after my mother's own bout with cancer, my older sister and I were left with much of the responsibility for the household. Mom was placed on tranquilizers, unable to cope. But the real issue was my alcoholic father. He had dropped out of school at sixteen (another connection to me) to join the armed forces. Patsy, my eldest sister, died at age five from meningitis; after that my father's life with the bottle became the norm. We just accepted it. He worked full-time and took several part-time jobs in the evening and on weekends to support the family and his habit. At the time, I had rationalized his behavior: we always had a roof over our heads and food in our stomachs, so the drinking was acceptable.

At Christmas, due to a shortage of money, the eldest children usually received second-hand gifts. The last Christmas I lived at home it seemed as if that situation might be different, as I had received a new pair of black cocktail boots that year. But two days later that illusion ended as well, as my father returned them to the store in order to pay a bill. That was the final straw, the reason I chose for leaving home!

Before entering my teens, I worked part-time, with half of my income going towards household expenses and half for clothes. Then there was the work in the home doing my mother's work, followed by work outside the home - at age eleven - without receiving much in the way of monetary value or compensation for my labor. It began with typing addresses on envelopes; by age twelve, a newspaper route; at thirteen I had begun to baby-sit for neighbors, picked fruit and made soap decorations that were sold door to door. By fifteen, in addition to baby-sitting outside the home, as well as within the home, I became a hat check girl at many air force functions. Thus I earned the money that would have been spent on me by my family for clothing and bus-fare, and, consequently felt that my labor was of little value to me.

Today, I realize that for many individuals, under the right set of conditions at home, those events might have been very positive learning experiences. However, given the atmosphere in my home at the time, it only spawned resentment, and consequently created subconscious reasons for me to leave home at age sixteen. Although these events ultimately helped me to develop responsibility and independence, they also created an imbalance within me. I was taught to work and give to others, but not how to receive the same in return. According to natural medicine, the right side of the body is connected with giving, while the left side is responsible for receiving - the *yin* and *yang* - and both need to be in balance for good health. To be fully human, and to be balanced in life, we must learn both - to give and to receive. It was, therefore, critical to determine whether the old patterns were still affecting me in my current situation. Was that the reason why I worked so diligently at issues today? At that point, I only had more questions than answers, but at least this kind of hard work had its own reward - my health and my life!

Even with these previously hidden patterns now exposed, I could not be angry with my dad, and continued to make excuses for his actions. So where did that leave me? I had discovered the saboteurs of my health, but was still stuck in the past. Intuition pointed the way. Stephanie, my yoga instructor, helped people move forward through a program entitled *The Way of the Heart*™. Stephanie and Connie, co-founders of *Dream Field Consulting Group,* taught me wonderful stress reduction techniques to create space and energy and helped me to move forward toward my heart's intention. That was not without some difficulty, however, as toxins had begun to re-enter my body, drastically affecting my life again.

My *LDH* had increased. Disease is indicated when *LDH* readings rise above 139 U/L; mine was as high as 235. My liver enzymes, *AST/SGOT,* were also high. High levels of *LDH* also indicate the presence of *lactic enzymes*. As these *lactic enzymes* increase, the liver must work harder to convert them to glucose, and a vicious cycle can continue until death by wasting (*cachexia*) is the final result. In this state, the body continues to waste even if one is eating properly, as the nutrients are used in the disease process itself to grow unwanted cells.

In 1980, my father died at age fifty-six, following surgery for a blocked colon. His liver had finally failed! It had degenerated from years of alcohol abuse, as he had only quit drinking mere months before his death. To resolve my issues with my father it was also necessary to write him a letter, then burn it completely, leaving no unburned fragments. Resolving past issues in this manner also works when someone is alive, but where direct contact is not possible. I was the same age as my father when I became seriously ill. Was that merely a coincidence or was it somehow linked to past traumatic events, or was it the mind linking the guilt of leaving home with dad's controlling ways? Most importantly, were these unresolved issues also pre-disposing me to a sentence of death?

The issue of control was also linked to my oncologist, to my ex-husband, and to the cancer itself. During each visit to his office, my oncologist would inform me that I was going to die from this disease. To help regain my power, my sense of control, I also wrote him a letter and explained that his approach was extremely negative and it was becoming more difficult for me to overcome that negativity. We talked about it, but before leaving the room, he repeated it again. It is reasonable to tell someone they are terminally ill; to give them time to research, to leave a legacy and/or to say their good-byes, but no one has the right to take away anyone's hope for a day or even an hour, let alone for a year and more.

Later, when we spoke on the phone regarding this matter, he admitted that he had attempted to control my decisions with fear, especially with respect to choosing natural approaches to fight my cancer. With that conversation, I regained my personal power by standing up for my beliefs, especially those related to natural medicine, and subsequently dropped him as my specialist. Today, I have a wonderful quality of life as a consequence of those decisions.

As for my first husband, the connection relates back to the night I asked him to leave the family home. He left, but returned an hour later. Since I was young and inexperienced at the time, I did not realize that this could happen, as he re-entered the house, put a gun to my head and pulled the trigger, but the shell jammed. I now believe I was meant to live! He then raped and beat me, breaking his knuckles on my cheekbone and upper teeth, causing both to break and my ear to swell. I also lost great chunks of my hair. The original tumors that appeared several years ago were on that same side of my face, and more recently I became deaf in my right ear. Were these merely coincidences or were they also linked to past events? However, I chose life. With God's help working through my intuition, as well as with an ongoing research of appropriate allopathic and natural medical literature, I continue to move forward in wellness and in life. B.A.L.A.N.C.E. has given me the nutritional and environmental base that has permitted me to tackle these latest hurdles. When we use intellect alone to make important decisions, rather than including one's intuition, it is possible to err in judgment.

The Way of the Heart™ is a program that teaches participants to listen to their heart and be guided by it and their own intuition, thereby creating more value in their life. The program integrates art, science and spirituality to empower one's life purpose and Divine self-awareness. It uses shadow and archetypal work, breath work, and field of work utilizing a digital, numeric, geometric language. The latter speaks directly to the information or memory fields that hold the records, both past and present, of who each person is and what her/his potential in life could be. It is your personal blueprint. Individuals can change memory fields that hold negative imprints from the past, much like over-writing a CD-RW, and helps to set one on a more positive path for the future. In this way, people choose to live the life of their deepest imagination, to live a truer destiny, rather than merely relying upon fate. The *Way of the Heart* ™ is a process that requires the best from each of us. Everyone is on this earth for a purpose. Each person has the ability to shine like the brightest of stars, but, unfortunately, many do not position themselves to do so. More often individuals simply accept their fate.

One example of not accepting one's 'fate', but rather positioning oneself to succeed may best be illustrated by the following example from my own life. In 1990, from among 20,000 applicants, I was selected to participate in a mission to visit 'ideal companies' and determine how they had excelled at customer service. One of those companies was *Disney World* ™. The one thing I did not understand then, but certainly do today, is that *Disney* positions itself in every possible way to succeed. They do this in every small detail of their operation, even down to the directions for use of their garbage cans, which are strategically placed to foster use, rather than simply becoming more clutter on the ground. We must do that to succeed with our health and in our life. When we store negative experiences in our sub-conscious, those hidden thoughts tend to take on a power or life of their own. Examine one's life; analyze it in a manner similar to the examination of the physical body in Chapter Two. It is now time to look deep within again. Once the past has been uncovered, begin to focus on the present using programs such as *Yoga, Tai Chi* or *Qi Gong*; then move into the future with *The Way of the Heart* ™ or other forms of affirmations. And always remember B.A.L.A.N.C.E.!

Approximately eighteen months ago, I assumed that I was home free, that the cancer was in recession. My tumors were shrinking; my platelets had returned to normal, and my *LDH* and *AST* levels were lower. I had survived systemic yeast infection, anemia from arsenic poisoning, even catchexia, and although everything seemed to be back on track, there was more to come. A new problem appeared: a red spot on my neck/chest region developed into an even larger patch of red as the result of trapped cell debris and bacteria, causing my skin to stretch until the blotch became quite large and hideous. I subsequently discovered that it was caused by a lymphatic capillary that had become blocked. My naturopath agreed, and a surgeon later confirmed that diagnosis. This caused a lack of re-absorption of blood protein, creating an osmotic imbalance between blood and tissue fluids. In this situation, the blood cannot re-absorb the water it released into the tissues, and without help from the lymphatic capillaries, these tissues can become quite swollen. The lymphatic capillaries also absorb most of the fat digested in the intestine, and this capillary blockage also prevented the left side of my lymphatic duct from emptying completely. Eventually this condition could have been as devastating as the cancer itself, as the toxins that build in the body could not find pathways through which they could be expelled.

Lymphatic capillaries:
The lymph capillaries are tiny, blind-end vessels, which are located in the inter-cellular spaces. Tissue fluid, containing proteins and other materials, is absorbed into the lymph capillaries and slowly flows through these capillaries which converge to form small lymph veins, which then unite to form larger and larger veins. At that point, two very large lymph ducts empty into the large veins of the blood circulatory system in the upper portion of the thorax, near the heart. Those lymphatic capillaries are highly permeable to protein, and any blood protein that leaks out of them can diffuse into the lymph vessels, which then returns it to

the blood. This process is very important in maintaining the normal osmotic balance between the blood and the tissue fluid. Under certain conditions major lymph vessels can become blocked; the protein concentration in the tissue fluid steadily rises to a point where the difference in osmotic concentration between it and the blood steadily diminishes, resulting in progressively smaller amounts of fluid being reabsorbed by the blood capillaries. (Check out the series of photos in Appendix H, pp. 294 -5)

Again, more research was required. My family doctor wanted me to visit an oncologist, but I asked for time to resolve this latest development on my own. Sea salt was added to my diet to raise blood pressure, as increased blood pressure helps, in part, to open and close valves in the lymphatic capillaries. I also increased my rebounding, which improved the action of the valves as well. In addition, my naturopath guided me through my emotional responses using *MRT*. He also unblocked energy fields in my body, using *NAET*. The patch stopped growing, but did not immediately reduce in size.

The next step was a process of elimination related to repressed thoughts and feelings. At first, I realized that trusting in my decisions with respect to my body was playing an important part in my recovery. I had worked on that through *The Way of the Heart*. It was apparent that my husband and daughter's dependence on me were also key factors in my recovery. When my illness was at its peak, they had assumed many of the household and family responsibilities, but now that I was nearly back to normal, those responsibilities had reverted to me again. My husband had assumed that I wanted all this responsibility, so left me to decide on virtually everything of significance. My daughter was so used to me taking charge of her life, and was unaware that she had slipped back into her old ways, into her old *modus operandi*. I had just accepted these changes, without realizing their impact on my psyche and physical body; I had regressed into my old 'MO' as well. Several discussions later, they both realized I wanted to participate in, but not be in charge of, their lives. My younger children had managed to stand their ground; they had not let me control their lives, yet still wanted me to share in them.

My childhood was still affecting my life. My mother had delegated her responsibility for household chores to my older sister and me. We were only ten and twelve respectively when this happened - a time when Mom seemed to stop living in the present. For the next six years, we assumed responsibilities that rightly belonged to her, and when I eventually left home, the next eldest sister in line took over the housework, including the care of a younger sibling, cooking and more. Those experiences taught us a lot, but they also deprived us of a normal childhood. Next I had to work on the anger towards my mother. Life includes many serendipitous events, unexpected twists and turns, both positive and negative, which can affect each of us in very different ways. I loved my father and mother in spite of the mistakes they made, but today understand that I harbored deep-seated anger with respect to those decisions that had adversely affected my life. But there were also many special moments, traditions and warmth as a family. As a result, I dearly love each of my siblings. The past affects the present, and eventually the future. It is incumbent upon each of us to seek out those hidden family treasures that ultimately allow us to shine and grow as adults.

Today I realize that my ability to live in the present had been lost after my father passed away. After he died, my mother moved to be physically closer to my family. She had difficulty coping and expected me to assume my childhood role - to take on her responsibilities, such as making hair or medical appointments, tasks she was perfectly capable of performing herself. But again I did not deal with this issue directly, but rather chose to opt out of the present to live in the past and/or the future, consequently missing out on many valuable times with my own children and family. However, thanks to my diagnosis with cancer in 2002, I now work hard to remain in the present through *Yoga, Qi gong* and meditation. As always, B.A.L.A.N.C.E. is essential in every aspect of one's life. Today, this story is being told to help others understand how stress and emotional imbalances can negatively affect one's health. It is abundantly clear to me that both chemical and emotional toxins are detrimental to one's health.

Meditation-Visualization:

The following is a meditation or visualization exercise to try, while on a break at work, or simply anytime at home, Begin by sitting on the floor with one's legs crossed. Alternatively, sit on a chair or lay on a couch or bed if that particular position on a hard surface is too difficult or painful. Relax by taking slow, deep breaths, counting silently for twenty breaths. Remember to breathe in and out through the nose, not only from the lungs, but from the heart as well. Place a flower in front of you so it can be seen. Carefully observe it; notice its beauty and texture. Rub it gently against a cheek. With eyes closed, imagine that flower in the garden with the morning sun shining down upon it. Visualize the flower's response - how it opens slowly and softly. This visualization can be done with almost anything and anywhere: listen to a favorite song or concentrate on the flickering flame of a candle; or if one is out in the garden, dig in the ground and crumble the earth between one's fingers, taking time to observe its texture. In the kitchen, take a biscuit or piece of bread and slowly break it apart. Smell it, taste it, savor every aspect of its essence.

Visualization techniques are often used in healing: breathing, soft music and a soothing voice on a CD or cassette tape work well. Tape someone special; a child or a friend, and have them help to give directions to a place in your subconscious that is safe for you. Meditation CDs[1], many with soft music and spiritual messages are available in many book or music stores. This process becomes essential during those more difficult times, such as the bone marrow testing cited earlier in this book. Allow the mind to transport the body to a tropical island or secret destination with that special someone in your life. Use visualizations that are close to your heart. Imagine a tumor dissolving and leaving the body or have a jet fighter blow that plaque out of those clogged arteries. Use whatever works.

The following is a passage from the New Testament that delivers a great spiritual lesson that to be well we must both always think and act well, and believe in God and oneself. "On the Sabbath, Jesus came upon a paralyzed man who had been sick for thirty-eight years. Jesus said to him: 'Get up, pick up your mat, and walk.' Immediately, the man became well, picked up his mat and began to walk." (John 5:8)

Get out of the box: What would be daring to do in a year if it were one's last? Make today count! Taking risks can be beneficial in different ways: an achievement or triumph can be a happy event, whereas a loss or failure can be an opportunity to learn from that mistake.

Be present in your life - do whatever it takes. Remind yourself to listen to the birds, watch clouds, feel the gentle breezes. Stop making lists and over-scheduling your life.

---

1. A series of four meditation CDs, each with relaxing music and a spiritual message, entitled *The Journey* Series by Jackie Haverty, is available on-line from the publisher, author, or major on-line bookstores. For more information, see pages 334 of this publication.

"Don't die with the music still in you".

Read the poem slowly and let it enter your spirit, mind and body.

Slow Dance

Have you ever watched kids on a merry-go-round?
Or listened to the rain slapping on the ground?
Ever followed a butterfly's erratic flight?
Or gazed at the sun into the fading night?

You better slow down. Don't dance so fast.
Time is short. The music won't last.

Do you run through each day on the fly?
When you ask, "How are you?" Do you hear the reply?
When the day is done do you lie in your bed with the next
hundred chores running through your head?

You better slow down. Don't dance so fast.
Time is short. The music won't last.

Ever told your child, we'll do it tomorrow?
And in your haste, not see his sorrow?
Ever lost touch, let a good friendship die
Because you never had time to call and say "Hi"?

You better slow down. Don't dance so fast.
Time is short. The music won't last.

When you run so fast to get somewhere
You miss half the fun of getting there.
When you worry and hurry through the day,
It is like an unopened gift... thrown away.

Life is not a race. Do take it slower.
Hear the music before the song is over...
David L. Weatherford[1]
(child psychologist)

One's spirit is important;
take care of it; take care of your life;
make today count!

---

1. Used with the kind permission of the author. For more on David L. Weatherford, his poetry and work, visit his web site at: www.davidlweatherford.com

CHAPTER SEVEN SUMMARY

1. Make the circle of concern and circle of influence a part of solving problems. Today is the time to do just that.

2. Read any good books lately?

3. Take time to prepare a "laugh toolbox"; have fun putting one together. Don't forget to invite friends over for a few laughs.

4. Perform volunteer work within the community, make today count!

5. Learn to relax, breathe and visualize using the suggestions outlined in this chapter or take a course on Yoga, Tai Chi, or Qi Gong.

6. Raise your Spirit. What is important to you? Take time each week to do what you deem important or valuable in your life.

7. Ask yourself what did an illness (whether cancer, a heart condition, fibromyalgia, etc.) give one permission to do? Why was the conscious self unable to find the strength to do that? Where was that learned as a child?

8. Look into your past – find the link to the present and move forward in wellness.

9. Step out of that box, life is too short not to take risks. Don't die with the magic still in you!

10. Slow Dance

'Attitudes are more important than abilities
Motives are more important than methods
Character is more important than cleverness
And the Heart takes precedence over the head'

Dennis Burkitt

*BALANCE is essential
in all aspects of one's life,
including one's body.*

Chapter Eight

Exercise

Introduction:

Although the value of exercise had been entrenched in many primitive cultures, as well as in most advanced civilizations, both Western and Eastern, for at least three to four thousand years, that message seems to have been lost in our modern world. It was an important part of North American educational systems until the sixties, a time when spectator sports seemed to replace active participation; when physical education programs were downgraded in public schools; and the terms 'couch potato' and 'remote control' became entrenched within our lexicon. About that same time, fast foods, soda pop and chocolate bars were marketed to consumers via slick radio and television commercials. Unfortunately, the connections between obesity and declining health with low levels of physical activity and poor dietary habits were either not made, or were not disseminated to the population at large. Certainly there was no impetus for mass-market producers or those who sold passive entertainment to spread the message as that might have reduced profit margins! The only changes that occurred were superficial (questionable low fat chips and diet pop were introduced with no change in profits), but nothing of significance happened with respect to exercise for children or, indeed, in promoting an active lifestyle among an aging population. Today, that seems to be changing with an emerging concern on the part of health professionals and the general public that far too many children are obese, and with *type II diabetes* at near epidemic proportions. Indeed, many segments of our society are finally awakening to the reality, indeed to what can only be termed a crisis of poor health that has been largely self-inflicted. As Pogo, the famous swamp cartoon character of the 60s and 70s stated, "Today we have met the enemy, and the enemy is us!"

To be sure, a small, more literate segment of the population has intuitively known the above all along, and wisely chose exercise and quality nutrition as a way of life for their families. Unfortunately, they were and still are, a disproportionately small percentage of society as a whole. However, there may be light at the end of the tunnel as the links between poor nutrition and exercise on one hand, and society's over-stressed health care systems on the other, seem to become more obvious every day. Perhaps it has finally appeared 'above the radar' as governments, health officials and educators rush to formulate plans to include exercise as a vital component of a healthier population.

A rationale for a chapter on the role of exercise in healing:
This chapter presents additional information on the lymphatic system and the role of exercise in the removal of 'trash' from the body. As stated earlier, the lymphatic system does not have a pump like the heart to move this fluid throughout the body and dispose of the body's 'trash' on a regular basis. Humans require a regular program of exercise to maintain a healthy body. That might simply be as little as a thirty-minute walk, five times a week to prevent illness and maintain or reduce one's weight. Do what is enjoyable, but get off the couch and out of the car! The only caution would be to reduce one's level of activity when illness is present as under those conditions nutrients are scarce, oxygen in the blood is low, and the body may still have issues with absorption or low energy levels. Then those thirty minutes may have to be reduced to fifteen, twice daily, but always try to do some exercise within the limits of one's level of energy and wellness.

Proper breathing also helps move lymphatic fluid; that is why aerobic exercise is important to the body. Remember that aerobic means "in the presence of air". Aerobic exercise prior to entering a sauna will also stimulate the blood, move lymphatic fluid and help to draw toxins from deep within the body. Remember, some research has shown that just ten minutes of extra physical activity a day can equate to an eighty percent reduction in heart disease.

Exercise that involves use of the arms and legs also strengthens the thymus and, therefore, the immune system. Swimming, walking while swinging the arms, rowing, step class and jumping jacks are all good exercises to achieve this goal. Individuals may spend hours on a treadmill, when all that is necessary for basic fitness is the afore-stated thirty minutes of moderate exercise a day, for at least five days a week, especially if that exercise includes a combination of cardiovascular activities and weights. Weights apply resistance to tone the body; and when increased gradually with proper nutrition, will actually increase metabolism and reduce one's weight.

Re-bounding:

In Chapter Three, rebounding was briefly touched upon. It is an important exercise for the body and is vital to wellness. Rebounding is done on a mini-trampoline.

The process of re-bounding:

1.) At the bottom of the bounce, all of the one-way valves of the lymphatic system are closed.

2.) At the top of the bounce, all of the valves open at the same time to permit the stimulation and flow of lymphatic fluid. The gravitational pull also can help the fluid, filled with metabolic waste products, to move toward its dump site.

3.) Waste products moved during this process include dead and cancerous cells, nitrogenous waste, fat, viruses, and toxic metals such as aluminum, lead and mercury.

4.) Re-bounding should be performed for fifteen minutes a day, but even as little as five or six minutes a day is of value.

5.) Re-bounding can also be done for two to three minutes with a rest in between and performed as another set later in the day. That process will still be of value and enable one to reach the daily goal.

6.) If it is difficult for a person to bounce, let the trampoline do most of the work.

7.) Re-bounding is not only an excellent way to move lymphatic fluid, but it also strengthens vital organs, including the bladder and bowel. It also promotes better digestion in the stomach and helps to build stronger bones.

It is suggested that one make a trip to the bathroom before beginning a vigorous or lengthy session on the re-bounder, as this process can affect the bladder and bowels. Individuals with hardening of the arteries may experience discomfort, especially with a feeling of tightness in the calves. Even those who consider themselves fit may find rebounding difficult at first, especially on their butt and thighs.

Muscles:

Since many individuals begin to lose muscle mass between the ages of twenty to twenty-five, it is important to continually build muscle strength through proper exercise throughout one's life. The greater the muscle mass of the body, the more food can be eaten without gaining weight.

While I conducted research of the literature related to my own health, as well as for this publication, I experienced muscle wasting due to the catabolic action of my body during the fourth stage of cancer. Subsequent research indicated that this was a process known as *cachexia*, a cellular starvation involving protein/calorie malnutrition. Ninety percent of patients with advanced stage cancer experience this form of 'starvation', with a death rate of approximately fifty percent. This is the body's reaction to the presence of cancer cells, an inflammatory immune response. I first noticed this response in my legs and initially thought little of it. When the leg was held up the calf sagged, with a deep depression on the top of the leg as if the muscle was not being held in place properly. However, I really took notice when my 'butt' bounced when I rebounded; there was nothing left to hold it in place anymore. If I had realized earlier that approximately ninety percent of individuals in fourth stage cancer experience this phenomenon, I would have paid much closer attention to it and worked at reversing this condition sooner.

Rather than contact an oncologist, I decided to visit a naturopath immediately. After two weeks, a better balance was achieved. My protein intake was increased slightly and extra weights were added to my exercise program. Unfortunately, I exceeded my target with two repetitions of each exercise routine, subsequently increased my metabolism, and actually lost weight. The exercise program was adjusted to single repetitions only and my caloric intake was increased, resulting in the lost weight being regained. Another visit was arranged with the nutritionist to ensure that I was on track with my diet. The experience of *cachexia* frightened me, but also forced me to do more research on the importance of the partnership between the liver and the pancreas.

While working through a program such as B.A.L.A.N.C.E., readers are advised that it is quite likely that the liver and pancreas may have become damaged due to an excess of toxins in the body, and that it is essential the liver be detoxified. Toxins can fill the liver, preventing important functions, which in turn, can create a chain reaction with the pancreas. This process prevents the production of much needed pancreatic enzymes, thereby permitting cancer cells to develop. It is crucial that the liver and pancreas be restored to a level of vital functioning.

Exercise is a part of this process. It is also important to add enzymes as soon as the body can handle them. Two months of exercise and strength training, on alternating days, will add about one kilogram (two pounds) of muscle and induce a loss of 1.5 kilograms (about three and a half pounds) of fat on the average thirty-year-old woman. It will, in turn, increase the resting metabolic rate by about seventy-five calories per day. So, while the weight loss is minimal due to the trade-off between gaining muscle mass and the reduction of fat, as muscle weighs more than fat. The added bonus will be better fitness, as well as improved body shape and appearance.

One set of twelve to fifteen repetitions per weight or exercise machine works the muscle to the point of fatigue and is quite sufficient. B.A.L.A.N.C.E. again, is vital in everything one does. "To grab a fifteen pound weight and do fifty repetitions is of little or no benefit," says Stephen Todd, director of personal training with *Bally Total Fitness* (Detroit, Michigan and Toledo, Ohio). "Generally, if a person is not tired after twelve to fifteen repetitions, the weight is too light. It's not enough of a challenge to stimulate any type of improvement in the muscle." If a person whistles through fifteen repetitions, it is time to increase the weight. In addition, working the same muscle groups on consecutive days is actually counterproductive, says Jon Holmes, a personal trainer at *Lifetime Fitness* in Rochester Hills, N.Y. "One of the biggest mistakes I see is over-training. Some people think if they work a muscle back to back, they'll get results quicker, but that's not the case. To a certain degree, over-training is worse than no training at all, because you're not allowing your body to rest." Being a bit sore after an intense workout is normal, but if the soreness occurs after every workout, or persists for more than a few days, then reduce the repetitions or the amount of weight used.

Muscle loss occurs in less than a week once work on those muscles ceases. To take a week off from exercising while on vacation is not productive in the long term. Simple workouts during that week will help maintain one's fitness level. To build muscle, protein levels must also be increased, but beware of extremes. At this point, perhaps it is would be useful to recall what was learned in Chapter Two regarding protein and B.A.L.A.N.C.E. And remember not to give up eating carbohydrates while building muscle, as they are required to maintain the body's energy levels.

Several newer studies indicate that strength training can also help to keep blood pressure in check, lower *LDL* ('bad') cholesterol and boost *HDL* ('good') cholesterol. Developing muscles also helps keep bones strong; helps prevent diabetes by increasing glucose utilization; eases arthritic pain and strengthen joints; and reduces the symptoms of depression.

In 1998, during an earlier period of illness, I experienced extreme anxiety, depression, and agitation. It wasn't until I read Dr. Andrew Weil's books that I discovered that exercise could benefit me. After that, when I experienced an episode of depression or anxiety, I would head to the YMCA to ride a stationary bike for twenty minutes. If I could not get to the gym, I performed jumping jacks at home for the same length of time. The exercise helped reduce my depression and agitation! Now, thanks to detoxification, my anxieties have completely disappeared. However, I still enjoy the YMCA three mornings a week: I walk to the gym, ride the life cycle, lift weights and conclude my visit with a sauna. I avoid treadmills due to my personal concern for the potential negative influence of electromagnetic fields.

Avoiding muscle injuries:

Stretching is the key to avoiding muscle injury! Simple stretches before, during and after a workout or sporting event can eliminate a considerable number of sports' injuries. Stretching should also be performed during a long drive in a car or a flight in an aircraft. Doctors cannot fully agree on what causes muscle cramps, but most believe it is a result of poor stretching and muscle fatigue. Dehydration and depletion of salts, minerals or electrolytes can also play a significant role. This is especially true if individuals cannot absorb calcium-magnesium well or have lower potassium levels.

At least twenty-four hours is required before the same muscle groups in the body should be worked strenuously, or injuries could occur when those muscles become fatigued. Most cramps occur in the muscles of the lower leg or calf, in the back of thigh/hamstrings and front of the thigh or quadriceps. It is also possible to get cramps in the muscles of the feet, hands, arms, abdomen and ribs.

"Exercise should mirror life!"[1]

Jordan S. Rubin, The Maker's Diet

---

1. Historically, societies which have had the greatest longevity among its members have always walked everywhere they travelled. They were masters of anaerobic exercise.

A simple acronym - **RICE** – will help one remember the best approach to muscle pain or fatigue:

Rest: it is important to halt the exercise that is the cause of the cramp;

Ice: apply ice for fifteen to twenty minutes to relieve any swelling;

Compress: wrap the injury for support, if possible; and

Elevate: keep the injured arm or leg raised above the heart.

Apply heat to tense or tight muscles and cold to sore or tender muscles. If one is prone to muscle cramps, try to extend the stretching period. Drink plenty of fluids. Nutrition may also be a contributing factor in the onset of muscle cramps - the body may require *pantothenic acid*, potassium or additional calcium-magnesium. A check of one's thyroid functioning may also be in order, so it would be appropriate to consult a competent health care practitioner at this time.

Travel:
Upon arrival at a destination, schedule one half-hour for exercise, as it can re-vitalize the body and ease any tension that may have been created during the journey. Other good ideas include maintaining a membership in a health club in your hometown, such as those offered by the YMCA/YWCA, which may entitle a member to use of equipment and programs in other cities or countries; purchasing a guest pass at a local gym; or simply packing a jump rope or rubber tubing in one's suitcase or overnight bag to perform resistance workouts in one's hotel room.

Make Exercise a Habit:
What can one do when the enthusiasm for exercise begins to wane, perhaps simply because results haven't occurred quickly enough, or when one is pulled in too many directions due to a lack of time?

1. When an exercise program is begun, remember not to focus on weight loss too much. An increase in muscle mass will cause an increase in weight. In the beginning, when muscle is being built, weight may actually increase, or the loss may be slower than anticipated.

2. Begin slowly. Stay at a level for a week or two before the addition of a piece of new equipment or more repetitions on the original equipment. This will help increase the metabolism in stages, as well as reducing the possibility of becoming bored too quickly.

3. Weight loss is very different for each person, so do not make comparisons with others. Stay focused on personal goals and not those of a friend.

4. If boredom or thoughts of quitting creep in, remember to focus on the other benefits of exercise, other than weight loss, such as increased energy, quality sleep, improved self-confidence, or improved health and appearance.

5. If exercise for the sake of exercise seems to be rather boring, no matter how important or valuable, then take up a sport that will provide you with a competitive goal, as well as the required exercise. Golf (walking, not riding), hiking, badminton, or racquet sports are appropriate for both younger and older persons. This will ultimately help to achieve the fitness level you desire with all of the same benefits.

Try the following exercise to maintain motivation. Check the box that validates your situation. Make a list of favorite exercises; write in one's personal reasons for enjoying that particular activity.

What was enjoyable about exercise?

☐ Personal time for oneself;

☐ Building confidence;

☐ Feeling better; increased energy, healthier, and so on;

☐ Other _____
              (fill in)

How can workouts become more enjoyable?

1. Always stretch the muscles first.

2. Connect with someone at the gym or bring a friend for motivation. Be cautious, if they are less motivated and might tend to quit, make sure that it does not become an excuse to quit as well. Rather, find another person to join in.

3. Perform more activities out-of-doors, especially if the gym is not one's best venue.

4. Take up a sport or another aerobic or cardio exercise that allows one to do something really enjoyable.

List favorite exercises; write in reasons why the activity was enjoyable

aerobics _____

running _____

cardio equipment _____

racquetball/tennis _____

golf (without electric carts)_____

skating_____

other _____

What kind of sport or activity might be great to attempt, if only one were in better physical condition? Set a goal to do something special when that level of conditioning is reached.

☐ ballroom dancing   ☐ skiing or hiking

☐ running a marathon   ☐ taking fitness classes

☐ rock climbing   ☐ other_____

What are or were the major obstacles, both now and in the past, for not setting goals?

 The inability to schedule workout time.

 Not putting oneself first.

 An inability to do it alone - find a workout buddy.

 Become too tired, and attempt to put it off until tomorrow.

☐ Other (describe the reasons) _____

_____

What kind of reward would be necessary to help one set goals and maintain them?

If exercise goals are met, reward oneself with one of the following:

    1.) a massage once a month;

    2.) new clothes or _____ (for others) - be specific and be sure it is posted somewhere to enforce it;

    3.) a night out with friends;

    4.) playing or watching your favorite game or sport;

    5.) dinner and a movie; or

    6.) other _____.

Although being positive is always the best choice, some individuals may also require a negative consequence to stay on an exercise program.

What was noticed while performing the above exercise? Were any weaknesses observed? What would be necessary to ensure that this does not happen again? Write it down; make it a contract with oneself. Remember, for changes to occur, changes must have begun!

_____

_____

_____

_____

_____

_____

_____

_____

Exercise is important to one's overall health, as it . . .

a.   moves lymph fluid and helps the body run smoothly;

b.   helps to build strong bones;

c.   preserves muscle mass in order that the metabolism will not decrease;

d.   lessens weight gain with a regular exercise program;

e.   reduces the risk of heart disease;

f.   improves physical appearance, e.g., straighter shoulders and back, as well as a firmer behind,

g.   helps to keep the body energy and builds endurance;

h.   helps to overcome depression; and

i.   helps toxins move to their place of elimination positions, and is a positive thing to do before one begins a detoxification therapy to ensure that more toxins will exit the body.

A morning stretch and exercise program ensures that one's metabolism is enhanced during the day and also induces better sleep. However, exercise later in the day may aggravate one's sleep pattern, so be careful to schedule an exercise program earlier in the day.

"The prize is the journey, not how fast one gets there."

Today, obesity is rampant in North America, and unfortunately, includes far too many children. Lack of exercise and inappropriate nutrition are major factors in obesity, as refined sugars are rapidly converted to fat and accumulate in the body. The more body fat, the greater the chance for disease to occur, including heart, cancer, *type II diabetes*, stroke, *arthritis*, breathing problems, depression, and more. If one is already obese and has difficulty losing weight after adjusting one's nutritional intake and adding appropriate exercise, toxins may still have to be removed. It is important to remember that toxins accumulate in body fat making it more difficult to eliminate them naturally. The lymphatic system does not have time to work on the toxins the body has acquired from external sources, if it has to spend most of its time on eliminating excess fat that has accumulated within the body.

Body Mass Index:

Body Mass Index (BMI) is a general guide commonly used to indicate excess weight and obesity. However, this chart does have limitations for individuals who have lost muscle mass, such as the elderly or the ill, as well as for those who have a very muscular body. Either of these groups may not get proper readings from a BMI chart. In the chart below, **height is measured in inches, while the weight is listed in pounds.**

Body Mass Index (BMI)[1]

Height	Weight													
58	91	96	100	105	110	115	119	124	129	134	138	143	167	191
59	94	99	104	109	114	119	124	128	133	138	143	148	173	198
60	97	102	107	112	118	123	128	133	138	143	148	153	179	204
61	100	106	111	116	122	127	132	137	143	148	153	158	185	211
62	104	109	115	120	126	131	136	142	147	153	158	164	191	218
63	107	113	118	124	130	135	141	146	152	158	163	169	197	225
64	110	116	122	128	134	140	145	151	157	163	169	174	204	232
65	114	120	126	132	138	144	150	156	162	168	174	180	210	240
66	118	124	130	136	142	148	155	161	167	173	179	186	216	247
67	121	127	134	140	146	153	159	166	172	178	185	191	223	255
68	125	131	138	144	151	158	164	171	177	184	190	197	230	262
69	128	135	142	149	155	162	169	176	182	189	196	203	236	270
70	132	139	146	153	160	167	174	181	188	195	202	207	243	278
71	136	143	150	157	165	172	179	186	193	200	208	215	250	286
72	140	147	154	162	169	177	184	191	199	206	213	221	258	294
73	144	151	159	166	174	182	189	197	204	212	219	227	265	302
74	148	155	163	171	179	186	194	202	210	218	225	233	272	311
75	152	160	168	176	184	192	200	208	216	224	232	240	279	319
76	156	164	172	180	189	197	205	213	221	230	238	246	287	328
Mass	19	20	21	22	23	24	25	26	27	28	29	30	35	40

1. Body Mass Results: 18.5 - 24.9 =Healthy; 25-29.9 = Overweight; 30+ = Obese

Recent information in the public media:

Changes in any important segment within a society usually do not occur in a timely fashion without the support and participation of all major players / sectors acting in concert with one another. It is critical that the media, as well as educational systems, medical associations and government departments, be on the 'same page' with respect to messages relating to the value of exercise in regaining and maintaining a healthy body and a better quality of life. It is our belief that this important collaboration is beginning, albeit somewhat slowly, to occur. For example, during the past three to four years, a large number of studies (double-blind, clinical and anecdotal) have been reported in the public media related to the role of exercise in improving health. Indeed, in the past year, such reports are heard almost every other week, including the announcement of the return of the *"Participaction"* program at the federal level. (Feb., 2007)

One such account was reported upon in *Chatelaine* (March, 2006). The article told the story of three women who benefited from exercise for a wide variety of illnesses. One used exercise to combat postpartum depression; another reduced her pain from a whiplash injury as the result of a car accident with yoga; while a third had a second stage cancer, actually *non-Hodgkin's lymphoma*, the same kind as the author of this book. While this cancer was second stage (compared to the author's stage 4b) eight years ago the prognosis for recovery was only fifty percent for stage two of this particular cancer, even with a massive intervention involving intensive chemotherapy and radiation, as well as surgery for tumors in her chest. She chose conventional medical intervention, and although only twenty years old at the time, instinctively knew those invasive therapies would be difficult for her. As someone who exercised regularly, she wanted to continue exercising to "keep her mind off the endless visits to doctors", as well as to increase her endurance and mental toughness. It worked! The exercise increased her endorphins, which not only helped her cope mentally, but it also decreased her toxic burden by eliminating toxins through sweating, the increased movement of lymphatic fluid, as well as additional flushing through an increased consumption of water. Each of these actions reduced the impact upon her body, while allowing her to withstand the rigors of this massive chemical assault, both physically and emotionally. Today, she is a healthy twenty-eight year old with a family.

Even more recently (July, 2006), a segment on *Lifeline (CTV Evening News)* reported on a study of post-heart surgery patients, some who exercised for a minimum of six hours per week, while others did little or nothing. Six months later the survival rate for the group that exercised was a very significant fifty percent (50%) higher than those who exercised minimally or not at all! It is not possible just to have surgical intervention, without making changes in the lifestyle that contributed to this condition in the first place. Appropriate exercise and nutrition are critical factors in long-term survival, as well as to regain a quality of life worth living.

It is especially heartening that these reports are becoming more common within mainstream media, as only through the combined efforts of all segments of society can issues of obesity, malnutrition and disease be conquered. It is also hoped that this publication will be one more contribution to that effort.

Finally, it is important to take note that rest is essential for cellular growth. Diseased individuals require lighter forms of exercise, such as walking or rebounding at a slower pace. Being present and cognizant of one's breathing will help keep one in the present as well!

Begin Your Journey Toward Wellness Today!!

CHAPTER EIGHT SUMMARY

1. Exercise is important for mental and physical health. Schedule time for thirty minutes of exercise, at least five times a week.

2. Muscle is important to one's physical appearance, as well as to one's body composition. Whether one works out at home with rubber bands or tubing, or at a local gym, ensure that resistance training is included in these weekly activities.

3. Travel can be fun and exciting or it can tire the body. Spend time stretching upon arrival at any destination (by car or plane) and don't forget to work each muscle at least once during the week or the gain will be lost.

4. Make exercise a habit. Find reasons to be at the gym or play a sport. Also set goals and rewards for each accomplishment.

5. Take the quiz and use this format to commit to a specific goal.

6. Check your body mass index (BMI).

7. Exercise plays a critical role in the removal of toxins!

Appendix A

Anatomy of illness and the development of cancer: a chronology

Introduction:
This appendix was originally part of Chapter One, but since the content substantially overlapped *Susan's Story*, it was decided to move it to this location. Readers now have a choice: they can go directly from Chapter One to this appendix before proceeding to Chapter Two, or read it as a summary of Susan's ordeal, which documents a steady and seemingly inevitable progression through Harvey Diamond's *Seven Stages of Disease.*

This summary also chronicles the failure of modern medicine's approach to health care, one that treats each incident or problem or illness as singular events, without ever noting the connections between and among the various incidents or symptoms along the way. Readers will note that the 'treatments' or 'solutions' offered involved either medication or surgery, neither of which dealt with the systematic and systemic decline in health as the result of an accumulation of toxins in my body. It was misdiagnosis at its worst, as the symptoms were simply suppressed or masked, and root causes were never sought - never looked for - as each specialist independently 'repaired' or removed the offending part of my body.

I found myself on a slippery slope of illness and disease that became steeper as time went on, with an inevitable progression into advanced stage cancer at age fifty-three. But it did not have to happen. Had the steady decline in my health, as noted in the individual medical tests, been charted, or had other tests and evaluations been employed, the 'seventh stage' might never have been reached.

However, in many ways the diagnosis in **December 2002** was a blessing, as without this dramatic event I might never have had the impetus to change a lifetime of habits, as well as the strength and courage to do what I had to do to save my life. Today I am thankful for that, as my health and the quality of my life have never been so good, so enriched. And without that traumatic day, I likely would not have been able to tell this story to each reader of this book.

The Chronology:

1976: The beginning of a benign tumor on my right thyroid, which was surgically removed two years later. [Cause: possible adrenal fatigue due to shift work at a job that I did not like, a poor inter-personal relationship and being a single mom living far away from family.]

1980: Food poisoning and allergies caused by animals, pollen and specific over-the-counter medications. [Cause: a weakened immune system due to lack of sleep, improper diet, overwork and excess levels of stress.]

1990: Three episodes with kidney stones.
[Cause: an indicator of an acidic pH due to an improper diet, as well as the presence of environmental and emotional toxins.]

1993: *Mononucleosis.* [Cause: *Epstein-Barr virus (EBV)* - an immune suppressor.] It was not until several years into my journey toward wellness that I met a wonderful surgeon, Dr. Alan MacDonald, who shed new light on this virus. My oncologist had concerns that a blocked lymphatic capillary in my neck (See photos in Appendix H, pp. 294-5) required a biopsy. I agreed to a needle biopsy, but not surgical removal. Dr. MacDonald, the assigned surgeon, agreed with what I was doing, as the process was working and, therefore, required no intervention on his part. Dr. MacDonald explained, in great detail, the relationship between the *Epstein-Barr virus* and lymphomas. Dennis Burkitt, a noted surgeon, conducted research that had a significant impact on the association of certain types of *beta-cell lymphomas* with the *Epstein-Barr virus (EBV)*. This conversation and subsequent research led me to conclude that environmental and emotional toxins were likely triggers in reactivating the *EBV* and precipitating *non-Hodgkin's lymphoma.*

1994: removal of a new benign tumor on the right lobe of my thyroid gland, which ultimately resulted in the complete removal of the right lobe. I was rather fortunate not to have required thyroid medication, as I have since learned that certain medications could, over time, actually destroy the remaining portion of my thyroid. [Cause: *adrenal fatigue* and decreased *immune response* issues.]

1994: Anxiety attacks, for which I was prescribed the medication, Ativan ™· [Cause: overload of toxins, actually increased by anesthetics used in surgery, as well as other medications.]

1996: Fibroid surgery was performed to correct profuse bleeding while menstruating. [Cause: *estrogen dominance* due to a nutritional imbalance.] **Note:** Subsequently, I was able to pass this information on to a close friend and prevent her unnecessary surgery. Her fibroids dissolved and her system returned to normal after dietary changes. *Wobenzym N*™ is a supplement that is known to remove the fibrin from cancerous tumors, which allows the immune system to recognize and destroy these rogue cells. It is also helpful in destroying fibroid tumors.

1996: Following the earlier surgery, I progressed from anxieties to full-blown panic attacks, sleep deprivation, depression, and diarrhea from foods containing *mono-sodium glutamate* (*MSG*). This was in addition to a series of rather frequent food poisoning episodes. At that point, my blood pressure became so low that I literally fell over and had to ingest a handful of salt in a glass of water to remedy the problem. [Cause: toxic overload, as well as *adrenal fatigue.*]

1998 to 2002: My body experienced many symptoms that could not be identified or diagnosed by conventional allopathic medicine. I was bounced from one specialist to another, as my symptoms worsened and my life deteriorated. Symptoms included: *cataracts*, formed as the result of a very acidic pH leaching calcium from bones and teeth producing free floating calcium, as well as a selenium deficiency; painful knee and hand joints, produced as a result of an allergic reaction to peppers, potatoes and other nightshade plants due to an immune deficiency; as well as hot flashes and depression caused by a toxic overload. I also experienced severe colds from an immune deficiency; a lack of energy, headaches and anger as the result of an impaired liver filled with toxins; *dental plaque* caused by a *vitamin C deficiency*; extreme thirst as a result of low potassium levels; a severe back itch produced by a toxic overload in my lymphatic system; and dry eyes, originally suspected to be *Sjorgens disease*, produced as a result of a *vitamin A deficiency*.

Environmental toxins will block the absorption of vitamins and minerals, but I did not know that at that time. I had put my faith in 'modern' or allopathic medicine for over fifty years, and other than brief conversations with friends, as well as the books by Dr. Andrew Weil, complementary medicine was not a significant factor in my life. However, I had lost trust in the conventional medical approach following four years of searching for causes of my deteriorating health - all to no avail.

Consequently, I learned how to observe, assess and listen to my body, and to take responsibility for its care. This was accomplished through research, returning to God, trusting my heart and following my intuition

2000: I had extreme pressure in my chest, caused by an impaired thymus (another portion of the endocrine system), resulting in a rather serious immune deficiency. After mentioning the pressure that I felt to my naturopath, he resolved the pressure on my chest within five minutes by simply having me tap on the breastbone, thereby activating an *immune response* in my *thymus*. My doctors had suspected a heart condition, and had spent many hours and taxpayers' dollars with x-rays, *EKGs*, and treadmill tests that only eliminated possible medical conditions, but were no closer to finding answers. Again they were being thorough according to their tradition and training.

This was followed by '*creepy-crawly feelings*' up and down my arms produced by electromagnetic fields as a result of a weakened system from fourteen years of ill health. Unfortunately, this was just another set of symptoms viewed by my doctors as individual health issues, rather than a systemic breakdown due to a toxic overload and a suppressed immune system. So I eliminated electromagnetic fields (*EMFs*) in my bedroom, including shutting the electric heat register off at night and moving the electric alarm clock away from the bed. My naturopath suggested that mold may well be a likely culprit in these latest symptoms, and after a thorough search of our bedroom, we found a black spot on the wall near the head of the bed. Previously, my medical doctors had indicated these 'crawly feelings' were more than likely hormonal or a result of depression, and consequently prescribed anti-depressants. However, I refused to take them. When the body is loaded with toxins, any minute addition in the form of mold spores can drastically affect the body.

June 2001: I was prescribed antibiotics for a chest infection, fever, cold and swelling under my right jaw. By **July** I was experiencing tightness in my chest, blurred vision, flashing white light in my right eye, and a metallic taste in my mouth, all as the result of an impaired liver functioning. I also had continued swelling in the right jaw from the cancer. An independent visit to an *optometrist* confirmed that everything was structurally fine with my eyes.

October 2001: I was referred to an *ear, nose and throat specialist* (*ENT*) who speculated the lump under my right jaw might be a cyst and sent me for a *CT scan*. In the meantime, I went for an appointment with an *ophthalmologist* who also confirmed earlier diagnoses that my eyes were, indeed, healthy. The *CT scan* showed no issues of concern and the *ENT* specialist sent me on my way. I later learned that the scan had not been taken of the lump in the jaw, but further down the neck near my thyroid. The *ENT* specialist had missed this important information in the report. Readers can imagine how frustrated I was at this point, with no concrete answers, and a large lump causing pressure and pain as it pushed against my jawbone. Again, I was so conditioned by the standard approaches to medicine that I did not see these symptoms as part of some larger, more serious issue. Unfortunately, I did not bring this additional information to my naturopath's attention at the time.

Although I did not know it at that point in time, what was happening was a complete systematic and systemic breakdown in my bodily systems and functions, which finally resulted in a rapid slide into what Harvey Diamond termed as the sixth and seventh stages of disease, eventually concluding with the diagnosis of **cancer!**

Early in 2002: I returned to the ophthalmologist to determine if I, indeed, had *Sjorgens disease*, but the results were inconclusive. My eyes were still extremely dry and no one suspected a vitamin A deficiency, linked to mal-absorption, as well as to the overload of toxins. The month of **April** included a trip to the surgeon for a biopsy of the lump in my jaw. At the time, the surgeon felt that it could be an issue with excessive amounts of plaque (caused by a *vitamin C deficiency*) on my teeth, and consequently referred me to a dental specialist without performing the biopsy.

In **May of that same year**, I was tired of being poked and prodded and took a well-deserved break from doctors and tests. On impulse I flew to England with my sister, Cathy, putting the expense on my credit card, normally something quite out of character for me. We decided to retrace our parent's footsteps with video and photos, especially related to when and how they met during World War II. They subsequently married and had their first child in England before Dad returned home. Our mother followed later as a war bride. The trip was phenomenal. We not only enjoyed the history and beauty of this wonderful country as we re-traced our parents' steps, but were able to locate my mother's 'lost' family members as well. Unfortunately, her sister had passed away earlier in the year from ovarian cancer, but we were able to find her step-brother who was then a sprightly 92 years of age.

The only negative part of the journey occurred on the return trip home; I had eaten some salad just before boarding the plane and within an hour became violently ill. The first four hours of the flight were spent in the washroom with diarrhea and vomiting. As those who have traveled by plane can well imagine, that was quite a feat, as there are only four washrooms to be shared among a couple of hundred travelers. Pride was not a consideration as I pushed people out of line to enter the pint-sized bathroom before elimination from either end created a disaster.

On my return I was fortunate to get a **July** appointment with a *periodontist*, who suggested the lump in my jaw might be the result of a build-up of calcium blocking a drainage duct. He suggested an oral surgeon, stating that his office would contact me with an appointment. After several months of waiting, I contacted his office to ask about the delay, and was shocked to be informed that my file had been mislaid and that the appointment had not been booked as yet!

In **October 2002**, while performing leg presses at the YMCA, a lump suddenly appeared in my left groin. I assumed it was a hernia, but immediately made an appointment with my family physician. He ordered more blood and urine tests to ensure this was not simply another infection. I was also put on an emergency list to see an internal medicine specialist, who immediately requested a biopsy. The biopsy (the removal of a lymph node in my left groin) occurred as an outpatient at the hospital. The node was the size of a golf ball and pink in color, which I mistakenly assumed meant it was healthy. What I did not understand at the time was why the surgeon had only removed one node, when I actually had three rather large nodes in the same area. Later, after conducting research on the role of the lymphatic system, I was very happy to have had only one node removed. In fact, if I had known then what I now know, I would have only had a needle biopsy performed, rather than removal of the node. Loss of lymph nodes through surgery reduces the pathways available for the removal of toxins from the body, eliminating an important line of defense for the body.

The time from **October to December 4, 2002** was spent waiting for the results: **the final diagnosis - TERMINAL CANCER!**

Appendix B

Review List for Naturopath and/or Nutritionist

1.   Subconscious:
      a.   **"It is safe for me to be well"** and/or **"I believe I can be well."** These affirmations may be useful in uncovering the subconscious with the use of *MRT*.
      b.   Your body requires acceptance of the illness/disease before healing can take place. This also can be checked via *MRT*.

2.   Electrolytes - **sodium/potassium** and **calcium/magnesium:** Too much sodium has been known to reduce the body's potassium, while adrenal fatigue or tumors may also affect potassium levels. Too much calcium will do the same with respect to magnesium, as will excess toxins. Research indicates cancer and diabetic patients generally have a potassium and/or magnesium deficiency.

3.   Thyroid – **iodine** deficiency.

4.   **Adrenal fatigue** - affects four hormones; emotions, elimination processes, the immune response, fluid levels, potassium, magnesium, and sex drive. It can also be affected by high *lactate dehydrogenase (LDH)*; this cycle must end.

5.   Acid-Base Balance (carbon dioxide/bicarbonate buffers) acts as a buffering system to regulate **blood pH**. When out of alignment, this situation can create a fertile ground for a yeast infection, leading to digestive problems and eventually, auto-immune disease.

6.   Liver - **detoxification supplements, toxin pathways, coffee enemas,** (too many coffee enemas can affect the adrenals in

certain individuals) **energy balance cellular detoxification, desiccated liver supplements, spirulina powder, and castor oil packs.** The liver needs to be in the foreground of recovery, not the disease, as it is only through the liver that tumors can be dissolved, absorbed, eliminated and the body restored.

7. *Candidiasis - yeast infection*; is affected by high levels of CO_2 and creates digestive and elimination issues, eventually leading to systemic yeast infection and autoimmune disease. Excess chlorine, birth control medication, as well as antibiotics are other contributors to *Candida*.

8. Parasites - nutritional deficiencies contribute to parasitic infestation. Cancer is a symptom of malnourishment - cells no longer retain important nutrients. Parasites can multiply in this environment and devour essential nutrients required for the body to heal.

9. *Lactate Dehydrogenase (LDH)* - is an enzyme found in all tissues of the body and if it is too high this can indicate the presence of disease or parasites). High *LDH* creates a cycle where the liver turns excess *LDH* into glucose creating even more *LDH*, which may eventually destroy the liver.

10. Vitamins - **C, B$_3$, B$_6$, B$_{12}$** are important essential vitamins to check.

11. *Essential Fatty Acids (EFA)* - **flax liquid and ground forms. Hemp or fish oils** may be used if the body finds flax to be difficult to take. Flax should be consumed with one-quarter cup of **organic quark** for more sufficient absorption into the cells. *EFAs* are required to strengthen weakened cells.

12. Amino Acids - the body cannot make eight (8) of these: *lysine, isoleucine, leucine, methionine, phenylalanine, threonine, tryptophan* and *valine.*

13. Emotions - **check important ones such as fear of the disease, finances, relationship issues, children, and more.** It is also a good suggestion to check one's emotional status via *MRT* to determine if one is emotionally compatible with one's partner, children or caregiver and have this situation remedied through *N.A.E.T.*

14. Enzymes - *betaine hydrochloric acid, pancreatin, pepsin, bromelain,* and *papain* or plant enzymes may be lacking. Also have the body evaluated for the status of *brush border enzymes* in the small intestine.

15.   **Immune builders** – *Noni Juice, ESSIAC, Moducare, Aerobic oxygen, Aloe Vera Juice, Goji juice,* and high potency *echinachea* most likely will need to be added to one's daily regimen. [Removal and replacement of *mercury amalgam* fillings by a dentist may be the path to follow, especially where persistent sinus problems are an ongoing issue].

16.   Other supplements that may be necessary during an illness or disease:

   a.   **Kelp** - especially important following an x-ray or bone scan. This is recommended in order to remove toxins that are created through these processes.

   b.   **Kyolic garlic** - is an antibacterial, as well as providing support for the immune system.

   c.   **Wobenzym N**^{TM} - helps in dissolving the fibrin coating on tumors to permit the immune system defenders to locate and destroy them.

   d.   **Vitamin E, A** (beta-carotene).

   e.   **Acidophilus - the 'good' bacteria -** for the colon and stomach.

   f.   **Shark cartilage** - helps to heal damaged cartilage and is linked to decreasing blood flow to the affected areas , thus limiting growth.

This checklist is provided to ensure that readers get value for their dollar and to ensure that they are on the right path. Remember, even the most qualified naturopath or nutritionist can settle on the reduction of symptoms rather than searching for the root causes of illness. This can create a lengthy, ongoing cycle in search of balance or resolution. It is the client's responsibility to ensure visits are kept on track, as well as to chart their own progress. Inform all practitioners of any current symptoms, as well as any changes, including the most recent blood and urine test information.

Appendix C

pH defined[1]

pH is a measurement of the relative amount of acidity/alkalinity in any system, including blood. It is a technical, mathematical term used by chemists and medical personnel, who created a simplified scale ranging from 0 (maximum acidity) to 14 (maximum alkalinity) for ease of understanding. Technically, 'p' stands for 'negative logarithm' and 'H' stands for the 'hydrogen ion concentration', which is a measure of the relative acidity of a system. The use of 'p' eliminates negative numbers, as well as compound fractions and, therefore, makes the scale much easier to read for laymen and scientists alike.

A pH of seven (7.0) is the neutral point (e.g., distilled water is very close to 7). pH is also a logarithmic scale, quite similar to one that measures the strength of earthquakes (the Richter Scale, which ranges from 1-10) where each successive number on the scale is a multiple of ten. For example, an earthquake reading of five (5.0) in quite noticeable; while a reading of 7.0, which is 100 times stronger than an earthquake at five (5) on the scale, can be very dangerous. In December 2004, the devastating tsunami that hit Indonesia was triggered by an earthquake that exceeded nine (9) on the Richter Scale. That particular earthquake was more than 10, 000 times stronger than one with a reading of five (5).

The same is true for pH. An example: anything with a pH of two (2) has 10 times greater acidity than something with a pH of three (3); while that same pH of two (2) is 1000 times more acidic than a system with a pH of five (5). Correspondingly, pH concentrations above seven (7) are considered 'basic' or 'alkaline'. Similarly, a pH of eleven (11) would be 1000 times more basic (or more alkaline) than a pH of eight (8). Thus higher levels of acidity range from 0 to 5; while higher levels of alkalinity range from 10 to 14. A pH of 5 - 7 is weakly acidic; while a pH from 7 to 9 is considered weakly basic or alkaline. Blood, with a pH of 7.3 - 7.4 is weakly alkaline, and, interestingly, is not much different than the pH of seawater, in which all multi-cellular life evolved. **Since pH is a logarithmic scale, it is very important to understand that what may appear to be a relatively small change in pH of 0.3 to 0.5 actually represents a very significant change in the alkalinity/acidity of human blood.** When the mineral reserves of the body are depleted, the alkaline buffers, such as the all important carbonic acid/bicarbonate buffer system, cease to regulate the blood properly. Homeostasis is then lost, and one's pH can drift out of the optimal range. Acidic blood pH readings are quite serious for human health and need to be corrected as soon as possible. Sustained high readings above eight (8) also are indicative of potentially serious health problems.

The preceding material simply outlines and defines some basics of pH chemistry to assist readers in understanding the importance of blood chemistry and blood pH, which play such a significant role in human health. In fact, this topic was considered so important that it merited an entire chapter in this publication (see Chapter Three).

Sample pH Scale:

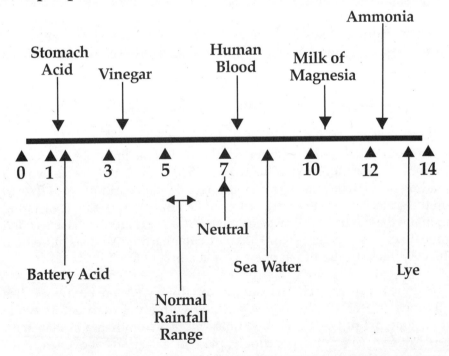

---

1. The concept of pH is usually a whole chapter in an introductory course on chemistry Readers wishing to learn more about the importance of blood chemistry and pH, may wish to search for information on the Internet, especially information related to 'buffering agents'.

APPENDIX D

Epstein-Barr Virus (EBV)[1]

EBV, also known as HHV-4, is one of the six principal classes of human herpes viruses. It is also one of the most common human viruses worldwide. Although symptoms of infectious *mononucleosis* caused by *EBV* typically subside in one to two months, *EBV* remains dormant in the blood, throat, saliva and the immune system. Most adults have had some exposure to *EBV*, even if they are asymptomatic, and periodically this virus can be reactivated.

Since *EBV* is an auto-immune condition, revitalizing the immune system is the only way to treat the condition's root cause and keep symptoms at bay. *Chronic fatigue syndrome (CFS)* may well be a sustained or chronic manifestation of *EBV*.

The structures of viruses are too simple for them to be classified as living organisms, as they cannot reproduce on their own. However, they are able to replicate by invading a host's cells. Anti-viral medication can interfere with the viruses ability to reproduce, but antibiotics and other medications are essentially useless against viruses. Suppressing viral conditions with drugs or medication may also lead to severe, chronic and/or degenerative symptoms. The more toxic a person's blood and emotional state, the faster viral infections will replicate and the more severe, or virulent, will be the symptoms. In addition to improving one's immune system, there are natural substances which may help. Native American tribes used *larrea tridentate* almost exclusively as their "medicine chest" plant. *Larrea* plants have been identified as being 12,000 years old. Check http://herb.umd.umich.edu/

Herpes strain viruses related to various diseases include:
   a. *Lupus* - linked with previous Epstein-Barr viral exposure, as are certain forms of arthritis and rheumatism;
   b. *Alzheimer's;*   c. *Multiple Sclerosis (MS);*
   d. *Kaposi's sarcoma;*   e. Bells palsy;
   f. Heart disease, hypertension;
   g. Lymphomas, cancers - linked with the *Epstein-Barr virus;*
   h. Shingles - from dormant "chicken pox" or *VZV*, a herpes virus.

---

1. Read more on viruses/viral symptoms/viral conditions/disease at www.hzworldgroup.com

APPENDIX E

Adrenal Function

The adrenals are part of the endocrine system and are walnut size glands that sit on top of the kidneys. The adrenal glands drip hormones into the kidneys, and from there they enter the blood supply. Abuse from cumulative stress reduces the ability of the adrenals to drip fluids, somewhat like a sponge, while the excessive use of stimulants such as caffeine can cause them to twist, subsequently creating major health issues such as *fibromyalgia, chronic fatigue, depression*, thyroid problems, as well as symptoms related to *diabetes* In addition, adrenal malfunction can also play a role in the development of cancer.

The adrenal glands contain and secrete four separate hormones that perform a rather amazing range of functions:
1. *Adrenaline (epinephrine)* - the "fight or flight" hormone.
2. *DHEA* (a sex hormone precursor) - which is responsible for tissue repair, anti-aging and sexual stimulation.
3. *Cortisol* - a blood sugar regulator, which regulates the opening and closing of blood vessels and capillaries, the anti-inflammatory immune response, regulation of the heart beat, and it affects the nervous system. Protein is burned to create *cortisol*.
4. *Aldosterone* - regulates sodium, potassium levels and fluid volumes in the body.

When a person is stressed, three separate glands are affected in sequence: the *hypothalamus* affects the *pituitary*, and then the *pituitary* in turn, affects the *adrenals*. This creates a domino effect. First *cortisol* levels are increased, which consequently decrease certain detoxification pathways, while increasing sodium levels in the body, which in turn, decreases potassium levels and raises blood sugar.

Cortisol is a hormone that is essential for the body's proper functioning, but not on a constant basis. Laughter lowers *cortisol* levels, while excessive exercise can reduce it too much. Rest is the only cure for recovery from adrenal fatigue. The acronym, ARE, refers to alarm, recovery, and exhaustion, which in medical language is known as *Addison's disease* or *Selye's general adaptation syndrome*. Craving salt is one of the first signs of low levels of *cortisol* or *adrenal fatigue*. These symptoms are general precursors to a more chronic syndrome that will require additional time and rest to reverse. Conventional medicine refers to adrenal fatigue as *Cushing's disease* (hyperactivity), *Addison's disease* (shut down) or *hypodrenia*, a condition where one is functioning below what is optimum for that individual.

Symptoms of *adrenal fatigue* include: salt cravings, increased thirst, muscle weakness, decreased force of one's heart contractions, irregular heartbeat, light headedness, low blood pressure, lethargy, respiratory infection, *fibromyalgia,* increased *PMS, hypoglycemia,* fuzzy thoughts or memory issues. It also is reflected in being easy to anger or/and loss of control, decreased productivity, auto-immune disease, *alcoholism,* allergies, *asthma, arthritis,* decreased immune response, *insomnia, chronic fatigue,* being tired upon waking and/or difficulty getting up in the morning, energy lows between three and four PM, feeling better after supper, depression, anxiety and being fearful. Note: many of these symptoms may also have other causes or reasons; not all are necessarily symptoms of adrenal fatigue, but they may well be.

To recover from adrenal fatigue it is essential to rest. The body needs to be prone between six and seven am when it produces more *cortisol.* It is also a benefit to do the same for fifteen minutes in the morning and afternoon.

Three Easy Tests

1. The first test is to check the contraction of the iris. To perform this test, one requires a flashlight and hand mirror to be taken into a closet. Give the eyes a few moments to adjust to the light, or lack thereof, in the closet. Shine the flashlight past the eye (not in them) and watch in the mirror for the centre of the eye to contract. If it does not contract within 30 to 45 seconds, one may well have an adrenal issue.

2. The second test requires the use of a blood pressure monitor. Take the blood pressure while at rest in a seated position, and then take it immediately after the first reading, while standing.

The standing reading should be higher not lower than the first one. If it is lower, that may indicate an adrenal problem.

3. Scratch the surface of your arm with a fingernail. This action should leave a visible white line. If, after 30 to 45 seconds, the line does not disappear, that could be suggestive of an adrenal issue.

A more **scientific adrenal evaluation** employed by many natural health practitioners involves a rather basic urine test. Ten drops of urine are placed in a test tube containing potassium chromate (K_2CrO_4)[1] causing a reaction, which precipitates salts in the urine and the silver nitrate solution, causing the solution to turn a reddish-orange. The level of adrenal function is determined as drops of a titrating agent (silver nitrate), which are counted as added until the mixture reaches the designated end point color. Normal test results fall within the range of 17 to 25 drops. Above or below that range likely suggests problems with adrenal functioning. If only MSI (Nova Scotia) and other provincial government health programs paid for such tests, what a healthier country Canada could be! It should also be a consideration for many of the private insurers in both Canada and the United States - it would even save them significant dollars in the long run.

There is also an '*adrenal recovery soup*' that supplies all the nutrients required to help in one's recovery from this condition. Check the reference to Dr. James Wilson listed below for more information on this topic. Lifestyle changes may also be necessary. Stress also comes from worrying about things one cannot change. If this is the case, then priorities must be changed. Make a list of people or things in life that rob energy, as well as a list of those that increase one's energy levels. Then, either change the situation or change yourself to adapt to the situation . . . or leave!

Adrenal fatigue also creates fluid (water) loss, which in turn reduces magnesium levels in the body. Another interesting fact: "The Federal Government employs the largest number of persons who regularly use sick leave due to stress or adrenal failure."

REFERENCE: Dr. James Wilson, DC, N.D., PhD wrote a wonderful book called *Adrenal Fatigue: The 21ˢᵗ Century Stress Syndrome* (© 2001). His web site is www.adrenalfatigue.org

---

1. **IMPORTANT SAFETY ISSUE**: Potassium chromate is a yellow chemical indicator used for identifying concentrations of chloride ions in a salt solution with silver nitrate ($AgNO_3$). It is a **class two carcinogen and can cause cancer upon inhalation.** Do not attempt this procedure yourself; consult a reputable, trained technician, chemist or qualified health professional.

–

APPENDIX F

Essential Fatty Acids

Chronology of research on Flax (or Linseed) Oil:

1899-1902: Rosenfeld's research found conclusive evidence for the value of flax (linseed oil) in human diets. His research illustrated that a diet high in carbohydrates, but low in protein, creates fat deposits within the body. Correspondingly, he also discovered that diets high in both carbohydrates and protein also created fat deposits, but if high quality fats (*EFAs*) were added, the excess fat deposits actually decreased.

1920:Otto Meyerhof, a Nobel Prize winner, discovered that when flax (linseed) was combined with sulfur rich proteins (e.g., quark, cottage cheese, certain soy products), they form a partnership in the body.

1929: G.O. Burr and M.M. Burr isolated and identified essential fatty acids. Their research discovered that rats deficient in *EFAs* died, while other rats, in advanced states of disease, actually recovered when the EFAs were re-introduced into their diets.

1930: Otto Henrich Warburg, another Nobel Prize winner, found that a person with diabetes or cancer had depressed levels of oxygen in their body. He also found that flax (linseed) combined with sulfur stimulated the oxygenation process and increased levels of oxygen within the body.

Unfortunately, after the 1930s, scientists only studied amino acids (proteins) and left *EFAs* alone, until:
1950: Joanna Budwig, Germany's leading biochemist at the time, was the first to separate and identify fats from a single drop of blood. Earlier

scientific leads now could be followed. Blood samples from those with cancer, diabetes, and certain types of liver disease consistently were deficient in *linoleic acid (LA)*. Dr. Budwig discovered the appropriate combination of *EFAs* and *sulfur-rich proteins* that permitted oxygen levels to increase within the body, thereby enabling individuals to recover from that disease. She claimed that all healthy individuals have *EFAs* present in their blood.

William Fischer, in *How to Fight Cancer and Win* describes Joanna Budwig's methods. Although dated, it is a knowledgeable read. However, Dr. Budwig's work is also published in *Cancer-A Fat Problem* and *The Death of the Tumor*. And Budwig's research was not only about cancer. The approach she took involved undissolved fat deposits that accumulate to form a host of degenerative diseases, including cancer, heart infarction, stroke, arteriosclerosis, and arthritis. For example, victims of the latter have fat deposits in their joints and muscles, while healthy persons do not have such deposits in their body. In those situations, saturated or hydrogenated fats can actually act as a chemical carcinogen within the body. Budwig's work illustrated that, margarines, shortening and hydrogenated oils cause damage to the body, as they block circulation, damage heart action, inhibit cell renewal, as well as impede the free flow of blood and lymphatic fluid. She worked with terminally ill patients for many years with life saving results, using a regimen of *high sulfur proteins* along with *electron-rich linseed oil*. Within two weeks, improvement was evident in most patients using this regimen.

Blood samples taken from people with cancer, diabetes, and certain types of liver disease consistently lack linoleic acid. Lipoproteins, which contain *linoleic acid* combined with *sulfur-rich protein*, are not present in the blood of such persons either. To her surprise, Budwig found yellow-green protein instead of *hemoglobin*. That helped to explain why anemia, depressed levels of oxygen, as well as a lack of energy, were commonly found in patients with cancer, diabetes and liver disease. *Hemoglobin* carries oxygen and if levels of oxygen are low, then that individual's life energy is reduced. What was significant about Dr. Budwig's research and practice was that "the cure" she used for more than fifty years was simply the addition of flax oil to otherwise 'normal' diets. For reasons, unknown at the time, the flax oil had combined with *sulfur-rich proteins* to inhibit tumor growth. As such, it was a natural treatment for cancer. To enable *EFAs* to work efficiently in the body, specific nutrients were required, but Dr. Budwig did not use supplements. She felt strongly that humans need to return to a more natural way of eating in order not to become ill in the first place.

Hemp oil is dark-green oil with a light nutty flavor. Hulled hemp will supply the body with forty percent (40%) digestible protein plus *EFAs* in a 3:1 ratio of *Omega 6* to *Omega 3*. Cooking is not recommended with this oil as it has a low 'smoke point'. It contains *Gamma-Linoleic acid (GLA)*, which is not found in either fish or flax oils. The latter reduces *PMS*, depression, irritability, and breast pain.

Light, air and heat destroy *EFAs* in the form of oils, but seeds keep for years under the proper circumstances. Light produces free radicals, rancid oil and toxic effects, while oxygen makes oil rancid and toxic through the process of oxidation. Heat used to deodorize, for hydrogenation, or for commercial frying also destroys *EFAs*. Oils that contain *EFAs* must be shelf-dated, stored in opaque containers, and be expeller or cold pressed. Being frozen also protects *EFAs* longer.

Whole Seeds:
Whole flax seeds contain *EFAs*, vitamins, minerals, protein and fiber; are nutritionally balanced and highly recommended. A good choice would be to sprinkle them on your whole grain cereals. Flax seeds should be ground to be effective or soaked in pure water and left to germinate. Grind no more than half a cup (125 ml) at a time as once ground or germinated, the seeds lose nutrients and begin to become rancid. Small coffee bean grinders are an excellent and inexpensive choice for grinding nuts and seeds. Most melon and fruit seeds are good to eat; but a few are not. For example, papaya seeds can create a toxic effect on the nervous system, while apple seeds contain small amounts of cyanide. (See more on *laetrile* in Chapter Six

Other great oils:
Almond oil, rich in vitamin E, is great when applied to the skin. Apricot and/or prune oils are also good for the skin. Neem oil is excellent for the treatment of fungal infections, such as athlete's foot, or for bites/infestations from mosquitoes, lice, or fleas. It can also be used as an antiseptic and to reduce fever. Neem oil has been used for over 4500 years for a variety of ailments. Tea Tree oil is similar to Neem oil.

Pure virgin olive oil, is a mono-unsaturated oil, but is low in *EFAs*, containing only one percent *LNA* and ten percent *LA*. However, approximately eighty percent (80%) of its *vitamin E* is retained, and it is also rich in magnesium and chlorophyll. Used with fresh lemon it will flush toxins from the liver. Use olive oil for salads and baking, but ensure that the baking temperature is less than 400 °F (200 °C). Baking at temperatures over 400 °F (200 °C) destroys the value of olive oil, although it is still better than hydrogenated oils at this temperature. Never allow oils to become hot enough to smoke. Olive oil should always be stored in opaque glass containers.

Poorer Quality Oils:

Rapeseed oil contains a small quantity of *EFAs*, but also includes up to forty percent (40%) uric acid. The latter can cause heart damage in excessive amounts. Mustard seed oil contains essentially the same ingredients as rapeseed. Canola oil has low uric acid levels, but is usually partially hydrogenated, so it is recommended that one buy only organic expeller-pressed Canola oil. Peanuts contain a fungus, which can also become carcinogenic for some individuals. All hydrogenated oils and margarines contain trans-fats, a fact upon which all nutritionists agree. Even government nutrition agencies, such as those which produce the *Canada Food Guide*, recommend that *trans-fats* need to be avoided or eliminated entirely in modern diets.

Hydrogenated fats are oils that have been altered through a chemical process to increase the solidity of the liquid oil at room temperature. *Partial hydrogenation* hardens oils, but does not make them fully solid. The latter are often found in soft margarine spreads. In *fully hydrogenated oils*, the natural saturated fats have been left intact, while all of the mono and *poly-unsaturated fatty acids* that remain are converted from a fluid state to *trans-fat solids*. The process of *hydrogenation* uses high heat, and a metallic catalytic agent such as nickel, zinc, or copper, plus hydrogen gas. This process is performed to make the oil into a solid, as well as to ensure that the resulting product does not become rancid, thereby extending its shelf life. This process, however, forms trans-fats, which are very detrimental to human health.

Trans-fatty acids, commonly referred to as *trans-fats*, are synthetically saturated fats that are primarily man-made. However, they can occur naturally in cow's milk, as well as in vegetable fats through this same hydrogenation process. Most margarines and vegetable shortenings have been changed to trans-fats by the full or partial hydrogenation process. A high intake of trans-fats is strongly linked to increased cardiac disease risk, and is likely to contribute to increased cancer risks as well. Trans-fats in the diet have also been recently linked to gallstone formation. They have also been shown to increase total cholesterol, *LDL cholesterol*, and *triglyceride* levels more than naturally saturated fats, such as those found in animals. Furthermore, *trans-fats* reduce levels of *HDL cholesterol* (the good kind), a type of cholesterol believed to protect against gallstone formation, as well as many other health benefits. The findings add to a growing list of reasons for recommending that trans-fats be eliminated from the diet as much as possible. It is interesting to note that new (circa 2006) packaging regulations / guidelines in the USA now require *trans fat* content to be put on the labels of most processed foods. It is a welcome improvement.

Trans-Fatty Acids[1] increase blood insulin levels in humans in response to an increased glucose load from the fat itself. They also affect the immune response; decrease the response of red blood cells to insulin; inhibit the function of membrane-related enzymes; create alterations in physiological properties of biological membranes; as well as cause alterations in adipose cell size, cell numbers, lipid class, fatty acid composition and more! The presence of *trans-fatty acids* creates an even greater *EFA* deficiency and they are difficult to eliminate from the body.

Pan-frying:
Organic butter, tropical fats (coconut, palm, cocoa and shea oils) are among the safest to fry foods in if they are *non-hydrogenated* and are used in smaller quantities. They all contain small amounts of *EFAs*. As mentioned earlier, non-hydrogenated canola oil is also great for frying.

Prostaglandins:
The body metabolizes *prostaglandins* from *EFAs*. *Prostaglandins* are essential for a number of physical effects as mentioned in chapter two, but there are also a variety of physiological effects including:

1. Activation of the inflammatory response, production of pain, and fever. When tissues are damaged, white blood cells flood to the site to try to minimize tissue destruction. *Prostaglandins* are produced as a result.

2. Blood clots form when a blood vessel is damaged. A type of *prostaglandin* called *thromboxane* stimulates constriction and clotting of *platelets*. Conversely, *PGE2,* is produced to have the opposite effect on the walls of blood vessels where clots should not be forming.

3. Certain *prostaglandins* are involved with the onset of labor for the birth of a child, as well as other reproductive processes. *PGE2* causes uterine contractions and has been used to induce labor.

4. *Prostaglandins* are involved in several other organs such as the gastrointestinal tract (inhibit acid synthesis and increase secretion of protective mucus), increased blood flow in the kidneys, and *leukotriens* promote the constriction of bronchi associated with *asthma*.

---

1. Reference: The Journal of the American Heart Association

APPENDIX G

Meridian Organ Clock

There are two major cycles at work in our bodies - the meridian clock cycle and the acidic/alkaline balance, as measured by the pH of our body. The meridian organ clock provides us with bio-energetic insights, while the acid/alkaline cycles are the basis of our biochemical life processes. Essentially, there is a time to eat, a time to live, and a time to sleep.

The Chinese acupuncture 'meridian clock' is an example of a 24 hour cycle that explains the body's complete sets of functions, as well as its relationship with diet. These cycles occur automatically. There are twelve meridians, each 'taking the lead' for two hours during the 24 hour period. Each one involves a flow of energy, either moving away from or moving towards the body. The former is referred to as *yin*, the energy of earth, while the latter is *yang*, the energy of heaven. Between the two, they create a vital force of energy within the body. This energy travels within the body and is responsible for much of the communication among the various parts. As there is no beginning or end to this flow, the order can be represented as a wheel[1]. Each meridian runs on both sides of the body, thereby mirroring itself.

Every organ and every part of your body is directly linked to a specific tooth or area of the mouth through these meridians, or energy highways. This connection is so strong that a biological dentist can often accurately predict one's dental history simply by reviewing one's physical symptoms. Root canals often create disturbing energetic roadblocks in the body, which short-circuit essential pathways leading to the breakdown of essential organ functions. If a person has a weakened organ, a root canal performed on the associated meridian tooth can make it even more problematic. Balancing and strengthening the organ can allow a person to handle the tooth problem temporarily.

These energy flows have been measured and mapped by modern technological methods: electronically, thermally and radioactively. With practice and awareness they can be felt by everyone. Through these meridians, passes an invisible nutritive energy known to the Chinese as Chi.

It is the pure, harmonizing and free-flowing energy that sustains all of life. Chi holds the organs, glands, blood vessels, and other bodily parts in place, with harmony.

The Body's Food Processing Cycle:

7 AM to 3 PM – process nutrients

3 PM to 11 PM – use the nutrients

11 PM to 7 AM – cleansing of cellular wastes

The lymphatic system sleeps when you sleep. When proteins are eaten later in the day, the time during which metabolism takes place coincides with the body's sleep cycle, affecting it while it is in a cleansing mode. This can cause interference with sleep patterns; and food can become toxic waste, creating congestion in the lymphatic system. This includes meats and complex vegetable proteins.

Meridian Organ clock (wheel):

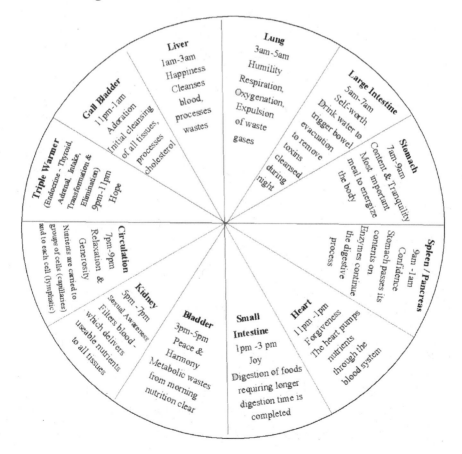

APPENDIX H

Blocked Lymphatic
Capilliary (cell debris)

July 2005	August 2005
	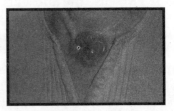

September 2005 (looks like a rose)	October 29, 2005 (skin breaking down)
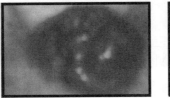	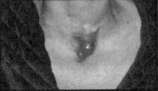

Physical Reasons:

I contracted anemia from arsenic contained in bottled water. North American standards for water quality related to arsenic levels are quite low, such that a weakened body (i.e., someone in the state of reversing disease or in any diseased state) can absorb more arsenic and become anemic. This process caused the interstitial fluid, normally regulated by the thyroid and blood pressure, to produce a blocked lymphatic capillary. This blockage also created further anemia as the capillaries and blood vessels transfered fluid between these systems. In addition, the natural detoxification of the left side of my lymphatic system had become a real issue for me.

Emotional Reasons:

One of the primary Chakras is the area of communications. I always had difficulty saying no to people even when I was ill, thus the placement of this blockage was a visual sign for people to understand that I was ill and, therefore, should not ask me to help them at this time. Specifically, this involved my husband, eldest daughter, and youngest sister, as well as a friend. I had not only helped, but had actually navigated their lives in the past. This enabled rather than empowered them. However, the process of empowering actually permitted them to move forward with my support, but not with my energy. The lesion had held the anger towards my family within my body, as well as for not allowing the empowerment to occur.

Physical Actions:

The healing required additional rebounding and walking to help open and close the lymphatic capillary valves; eating non-hydrogenated potato chips with sea salt to increase blood pressure; plus a visit to the naturopath to balance my thyroid. Homeopathic solutions to drain the lymphatic system were also used: one week with one kind, and a second week with another. Gentle massage under the lesion (a type of pumping action) was performed, and castor oil packs helped in the final stages. The combined actions helped stop the debris from accumulating into a larger growth, but did not reduce the overall size of the mass. However, when combined with emotional work through *MRT*, these actions helped reduce further build-up.

Emotional Actions:

After using *MRT*, I met with the four persons involved to determine which emotions were involved, as well as to ascertain who among the four were involved with each emotion. We agreed that they had come a long way on their own since first discovering they were one of the contributing factors for the development of the cancer itself, but that we had all slipped back somewhat due to old habits. They had relied on me in the past, and I let them do so, as it made me feel good as well. Following this emotional work, and utilizing *The Way of the Heart* ™ program, the lump was reduced in size by over ninety per cent. Reviewing emotional issues had helped to resolve this problem and it had increased the physical action on the cell debris as well.

November 7, 2005	**November 22, 2005**
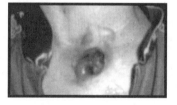	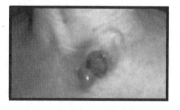
December 10, 2005	**December 19, 2005**
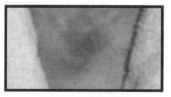	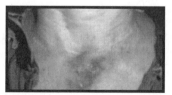

As anyone could readily see, the process was working - the body can heal itself when given the proper tools to do so!

> **It is crucial that one be aware of the precise level of arsenic contained in bottled water produced within North America or choose well known European brands such as Evian™.**

APPENDIX J

Healthier Recipes & Remedies

Natural Children's Remedies

Colic or indigestion:

Chinese mothers traditionally use fennel, while Lebanese use dill, but in North America it is common to use Gripe Water, a syrup made from seeds of fennel and dill. A few such solutions may also contain ginger. Care needs to be taken not to purchase products with alcohol, or preservatives, and the like.

Peter Rabbit's Tea

2 cups (500 ml) boiled water
½ teaspoon (2.5 ml) catnip leaves
1 teaspoon (5.0 ml) chamomile flowers
½ teaspoon (2.5 ml) fennel or dill
1 teaspoon (5 ml.) lemon balm leaves

Gia

Steep for ten minutes, strain the herbs and allow the tea to cool. A child should only sip the brew as very little is required to do the job. For babies, it is suggested that one dilute the finished tea with an equal amount of water to make approximately one quarter of a cup (60 ml) in total.

Other ways to soothe a child and help with indigestion, include:

Herbal Bath

Two drops of a lemon grass essential oil plus one drop each orange and chamomile essential oils. Add essential oils directly to bath water. Stir to distribute before a child is placed in the tub. (Caution: essential oils will burn the skin if not diluted.)

Tummy Rub

Six drops lemon grass essential oil; one drop of fennel essential oil; one drop chamomile essential oil; and two ounces (60 ml) virgin olive oil Mix together and rub on every hour, or as needed. Lemon balm is cheaper, but not as effective as the lemon grass essential oil.

Teething Naturally

Try a cold carrot or a frozen banana for a child that does not have teeth yet. If a child has teeth, they might choke on a piece. As always, when a baby is being fed, close supervision is necessary.

Wet face cloths (natural white have fewer chemicals) placed in a freezer for a bit are also helpful, as is very clean finger joint.

Teething gels (caution required)

Experts' caution against the excessive use of teething gels as they usually contain *benzocaine*. There is a risk of allergic reaction. In addition, *benzocaine* can cause the throat to numb and could cause a child to choke. Consult a medical doctor, naturopath or nutritionist for help to relieve a child's pain.

Motion sickness

Use one 750 or 1000 gram ginger capsule over a twenty-four hour period for adults or children twelve years and older. For younger children please consult a qualified health practitioner, such as a medical doctor, naturopath, or certified nutritionist.

As a child when I became ill, my parents would give me 'flat' ginger ale to help calm my stomach. The problem with that today is the knowledge that the amount of sugar in a can of soda pop can shut down the immune system for up to six hours.

In chapter four I related a story about ginger and how one pill worked within twenty minutes for sea sickness, nausea caused by the flu, as well as for the intense nausea from chemotherapy. I also place a small amount of ginger powder in turkey stuffing, beans or chicken soup to prevent indigestion when I prepare those dishes for company,

Peppermint often prevents nausea as well.

Peppermint Tea

1 cup (240 ml) boiling water
1 teaspoon (5.0 ml) peppermint leaves

Pour boiled water over the leaves and let them sit approximately five minutes. Strain and serve about half a cup (125 ml).

Herbs

Parsley: The world's most popular herb has the ability to ease digestion, cleanse the breath and act as a mild, natural laxative. It contains essential oils: luteolin (antioxidant), folic acid, vitamin A, E, and C.

Sage: It has a long history of medicinal use such as the reduction of inflammation, and as a memory enhancer. It is also easy to digest.

Rosemary: It is known to improve memory as Rosemary increases blood flow to the brain. It also stimulates the immune system and improves digestion.

Thyme: It is a good herb to use with orange vegetables such as carrots, squash and sweet potatoes. Thyme is an immune booster and as a tea will soothe chest infections and coughs.

Fresh herbs should be wrapped in wet unbleached paper towel and placed in a glass container in the refrigerator where it will keep for approximately two weeks.

Main Dishes

Research varies on the inclusion of poultry or fish during the process of healing the body. If the choice is to include those products, then ensure that one consumes wild fish and not those that are farmed. Ensure that any poultry is free-range and not fed grains grown with pesticides. The poultry dishes provided are simple and include ingredients that provide nutrients for healing and comfort.

Bean dishes provide sufficient protein for the body, but require more thought when preparing such meals. Large cities enjoy variety in their natural food stores and have prepared dishes such as three bean chili that can just be taken home and heated. (Use of a microwave is not recommended as this process can change the chemical make-up of foods. This can confuse cells and improper absorption of nutrients may occur.)

Most recipes call for unpasteurized honey or stevia. Unpasteurized honey is not heated (as in the pasteurization process) and retains its full nutritional value. These recipes also suggest whole wheat or unbleached flours, but these can be replaced with 'historic' grains that are better utilized by our body, such as *kamut, quinoa, spelt*, or *rye*. Celtic sea salt is the salt of choice, as it is absorbed more efficiently by the body, as well as alkalanizing it. It is also important to stay away from heavy metals, and therefore, it is recommended to use aluminum free baking soda and baking powder.

Garlic & Honey Chicken

Chicken legs should be steamed in water for approximately fifteen minutes on top of the stove. Mix in the following ingredients:

1 tablespoon (15 ml) unpasteurized honey
2 tablespoons (30 ml) virgin olive oil
1/3 cup (80 ml) *Braggs*™ soy sauce
4 garlic cloves (sliced thin)
1/2 cup (125 ml) water
2 teaspoons (10 ml) minced ginger

Place steamed chicken in a casserole dish and pour the above mix over the chicken. Cook for forty minutes in an oven at 350 °F. (175 °C) Turn once and baste from dish.

Tortillas
1 cup (250 ml) corn meal
1 cup (250 ml) unbleached flour
1 cup (250 ml) whole wheat flour
1 teaspoons (5 ml) Celtic sea salt
4 - 6 tablespoons (60 - 90 ml) expeller pressed canola oil
1 - 1/4 cup (310 ml) warm water

Mix and make twelve small balls. Let sit ten minutes. Flatten and cook in flat round slightly oiled pan on medium heat. Cook about two minutes on each side. Tortillas should be warmed in the oven before use. **Optional:** Use one teaspoon (5 ml) of aluminum-free baking powder to make lighter tortillas

Fajitas are quick and easy once the tortillas are prepared. Fill separate bowls with the vegetables of choice, then invite friends and family in for lunch or supper. Salsa is a good way to moisten the vegetables; in addition soft tofu with added herbs can be daubed on rather than sour cream. Hummus is also a wonderful topping. A side order of beans or rice can top off this wonderful meal.

Notes:
Most veggie cheese has casein, a milk product. Iceberg lettuce often draws metals from the ground. Use field greens, romaine, leaf lettuce, or spinach instead.

Chicken Torrie
4 boneless, skinless chicken breast halves
1/2 teaspoon (2.5 ml) Oregano
One 19 ounce can or jar (300 ml) of stewed tomatoes
1/2 teaspoon (2.5 ml) Basil
1/4 cup (60 ml) green pepper strips
4 teaspoons (20 ml) of powdered potato starch to thicken the sauce.

Steam the organic chicken breast halves for fifteen minutes in a Dutch Oven. Dissolve the potato starch in the tomatoes; add spices and pepper. Add this mixture to the chicken and place in the oven at 350 °F (175 °C) for twenty minutes. Cook pasta in boiled water until tender. Serve chicken on the pasta. Side salads and garlic bread are optional.

Eating out can be quite a challenge in many towns compared to most cities. One particular trip to a restaurant for me created several issues - the meal was a turkey dinner which I choose without the cranberry sauce (as it contained refined sugar), no mashed potatoes (which contained milk and butter), and no gravy (made from bleached flour). I did have the turkey and carrots. The turkey was likely not free-range, but at that point I had to eat something. Many foods may also contain *MSG*, hydrogenated oils, refined sugars, or bleached flours, not to mention the inclusion of hidden dairy products. Some restaurants may not even stock virgin olive oil or fresh lemons, so be prepared by taking a pocket size container to such places, including apple cider vinegar or a mixture of oil and lemon.

Recently a new vegetarian restaurant opened that has healthy choices, and it is only thirty minutes from where I live. When I visit the naturopath, there is place nearby which offers excellent take-out foods. Here one can create one's own salad as they do stock olive oil and fresh lemons. I usually choose spinach rather than lettuce, then add red onions, tomatoes, chickpeas, green peppers, sunflower seeds and egg, along with a veggie lentil soup and a healthy homemade roll. The latter is made with olive oil, unbleached flour, added grains and unrefined cane sugar. Farmers' markets have also been a blessing - just recently I ate some homemade brushetta on spelt bread with fresh carrot, and apple juice.

The reason I felt a need to write the above paragraphs was to help readers to understand that the removal of unhealthy foods is not always an easy thing to do. One must create a new mind-set that these changes are important, as well as being satisfying ways to attain good health. In the beginning I was angry, followed by frustration, but today, enjoy the challenge of finding healthy food choices. Once in awhile, just when one thinks it is safe, there can be a mix up, as when I ordered a glass of tomato juice and they put ice in the glass. Remember that chlorine, and in some cases fluorides, are often added to municipal water supplies.

French Fries, without trans-fats, are easy to make. Cut the peeled or unpeeled, but washed, potatoes or yams into fries and dip in egg white or virgin olive oil and place on unbleached parchment paper on a cookie sheet. Bake for forty minutes at 350 °F, (175 °C) turning the fries at least once. If crunchy fries are not preferred, place the fries in a covered casserole for approximately five to ten minutes to soften them. Purchase organic ketchup or make your own.

Veggie burgers are also great alternatives, but shop around, as it can take a few tries to find a brand without dairy that one enjoys. A bread machine comes in handy to make the buns. **Spelt bread crumbs** are a great way to coat fish and chicken pieces to bake in the oven. First dip the protein choice in pure olive oil or free-range egg, and season with spices to taste.

Minestrone Soup
1 large leek and zucchini sliced thin; 2 carrots diced
4 ounces (125 ml) halved wax or green beans
14 ounce can or a jar (185 ml) of stewed tomatoes
3 tablespoons (45 ml) expeller pressed virgin olive oil
1/2 cup (125 ml) whole-wheat, rice or kamut pasta
1 tablespoon (15 ml) chopped basil
19 ounce can (300 ml) or cooked kidney beans, plus a sprinkle of thyme
with a pinch of sea salt; 1 minced garlic clove; 5 cups (1¼ liters) water
1 ½ cups (375 ml) organic vegetable broth

Simmer the covered vegetables in the oil for ten to fifteen minutes. Add water, tomatoes, herbs and seasoning and bring to a boil. Simmer for thirty minutes. Add the beans and pasta and simmer for another ten to fifteen minutes. Serve hot or cold. Rather than using canned tomatoes, try the recipe below. It is simple, easy and larger batches can be made and preserved in glass mason jars for future use.

Stewed Tomatoes
Use eight (8) lbs. [4 kg] of tomatoes; one chopped red onion and one minced garlic clove; 2 teaspoons (10 ml) unrefined cane sugar; a dash of Celtic sea salt and oregano; plus one tablespoon (15 ml) of dried basil.

To peel the tomatoes, place them in boiled water for half a minute. Rinse in cold water and remove the skin. Place the peeled tomatoes and the remaining ingredients in a large pot and bring to a boil. Reduce the heat and simmer for ten minutes. Spoon into hot jars, but leave one inch of space at the top of the jar for expansion.

Vegetable Chili

Cut up ½ cup (125 ml) chopped celery; 2 garlic cloves, sliced thin; plus one diced medium red onion. Sauté celery, onion and garlic in expeller pressed canola oil in a deep pan (e.g., a Dutch Oven).

Add:

½ cup (125 ml) each of diced red, yellow and green peppers
1 cup (250 ml) diced carrots
1 medium zucchini (with peel) sliced thin and diced
1 cup (250 ml) of each – drained: red kidney beans, chickpeas, pinto beans
1 cup (250 ml) of diced or stewed tomatoes with juice
1 cup (250 ml) of tomato sauce
1 or 2 tsp (5 to 10 ml) chili powder
½ tsp. (2.5 ml) each of ground cumin and dried crushed oregano

Cover and simmer for one hour or until carrots are barely tender. Stir occasionally. This dish serves four to eight people depending upon the serving size. **Optional**: add 1 to 2 cups (250 to 500 ml) fresh shiitake or maitake mushrooms - do not use button mushrooms.

A few suggestions to serve healthy food at a party:

- Fruit tray with soft tofu or fruit soy yogurt as a dip.
- Veggie tray - use hummus or herbed tofu dip.
- Dukkuah and olive oil with a tray of sliced European breads.
- Homemade breads (zucchini nut, banana, etc.)
- Brushetta made with olive oil, garlic, tomato and herbs.
- Chocolate coated almonds or strawberries. Use only high quality
  dark chocolate, such as dark organic Belgian chocolate.
- Organic carbonated white grape juice or apple juice without added sugar. **Caution**: If juice contains added vitamin C, it may cause diarrhea.

Dukkah (pronounced doo-kah)

This is a mixture of finely ground nuts and spices that hail from the Middle East and is traditionally eaten with a variety of fresh breads along with a small dish of extra-virgin olive oil. Dukkah makes a complete meal. Dip the bread into the oil, and then touch the bread into the dukkah before each mouthful.

Mix one cup (250 ml) each of sesame seeds and hazelnuts; 1/3 cup (80 ml) fennel seeds; ¼ cup (60 ml) large coriander seeds; ¼ cup (60 ml) cumin seeds; add one tablespoon (15 ml) each of black peppercorns, Celtic sea salt and sweet paprika.

Put the sesame seeds on a baking sheet and toast in a pre-heated oven at 355 °F (180 °C) for ten minutes or until pale golden brown. Cool. Place the hazelnuts on a baking sheet and toast in a pre-heated oven at 355

°F (180 °C) for ten to fifteen minutes. Rub the skins off the nuts with a clean cloth. Cool and place the toasted hazelnuts in a food processor and grind until fine. Stop before they become paste.

Place the remainder of the spices on a baking sheet and toast for five minutes at 320 °F (160 °C). Cool and grind in a food processor until fine powder. Grind or pound the peppercorns until they become a course powder. Add paprika and mix well. Place all the ingredients in a bowl and stir until mixed well. Store the dukkah in a well sealed glass jar until it is time to serve it. Use as above.

Sunshine Muffins
One cup (250 ml) each of whole wheat and unbleached flours
3/4 cup (185 ml) unsweetened applesauce
2 teaspoons (10 ml) aluminum free baking soda
1/2 teaspoon (2.5 ml) cinnamon; 2 cups (500 ml) grated carrots
1/3 cup (80 ml) diced cranberries; 1 mashed banana; 3 free-range eggs
1/2 cup (125 ml) extra-virgin olive oil; 2 teaspoons (10 ml) vanilla

Combine flour, applesauce, soda and cinnamon; mix well. Stir in carrots, cranberries and banana. Beat together eggs, oil and vanilla. Stir lightly into the flour mixture. Spoon this mixture into greased muffin cups and bake at 375 °F (190 °C) for fifteen to twenty minutes. This recipe makes approximately eighteen large muffins.

Fruit Muffins
¼ cup (60 ml) extra-virgin olive oil
¼ cup (60 ml) pure cane sugar or 1 to 2 teaspoons (5 to 10 ml) of stevia
1 egg (well beaten); 1 ½ cups (375 ml) flour (whole wheat, unbleached white, kamut, spelt); 2 teaspoons (10 ml) aluminum free baking powder; ½ cup (125 ml) soy or rice milk; 1 cup (250 ml) fruit (e.g., blueberries, or wild berry mix).

First combine the oil, sugar and egg, then alternately add flour and baking powder with soy milk to the oil mixture. Gently stir in fruit, then bake at 375 °F (190 °C) for twenty to twenty-five minutes.

Date and Apple Breakfast Bars
1 cup (375 ml) organic rolled oats; 2/3 cup (205 ml) dates, chopped; ¼ cup (60 ml) whole-wheat flour; ½ cup (125 ml) walnuts, chopped; ¼ teaspoon (1.25 ml) Celtic sea salt; 1 ½ cups (375 ml) apples, shredded; and ¼ cup (60 ml) orange juice.

Combine all ingredients and let stand five to ten minutes. Press into an 8" x 8" baking dish then bake at 375 °F (190 °C) until light brown (about twenty minutes). Cut into bars and serve hot or cold.

JUICE RECIPES

NOTE: The recipes listed here are for educational purposes only - they are not meant to replace the advice of a nutritionist or your medical advisors. If fact, if one is planning to use any of the detoxification recipes listed here, it is crucial that one seek the advice of a qualified practitioner. Many of the detox and immune support recipes often require a number of repeats, so make sure you consult a knowledgeable and experienced complementary health professional - and always discuss your plans with your family physician and pharmacist if you are on any medications.

For cancer patients: 6 carrots, one beet, a clove of garlic; 2 cabbage leaves, a few red grapes; 2 granny smith apples; and the juice from one lemon

For constipation: 4 carrots and one apple cup (250 ml) each plus raw sauerkraut and leafy lettuce

Note: Another great drink for constipation is one-half lemon in warm water in the morning - this will also help to alkalanize the body. Lemons should be real, not from a concentrate, as the latter may include sulfites.

For one's eyesight: 6 carrots, one apple and 4 apricots, plus one cup (250 ml) of blueberries

As a Gall Bladder cleanse: 6 carrots, 1 beet, one-half lemon and 6 radishes
Note: There is also a three day *gall bladder protocol* (*Appendix M*, p. 321) that is recommended prior to considering *gall bladder* surgery.

For the immune system: Use 2 large pomegranates, 4 carrots, one half lime plus one tablespoon (15 ml) of organic maple syrup

To increase chlorophyll levels: Combine one half cup (125 ml) water, 4 teaspoon sunflower seeds, 7 almonds and 4 pitted dates with one pound (1/2 kg) of dark green leaf vegetables (i.e. spinach, parsley, etc.) Soak the nuts and dates overnight in pure water. Run the mixture through a juicer. Remove the pulp and add a small amount of water and rerun the pulp through the juicer again.

To enrich one's blood: Combine 6 tomatoes and one cup (250 ml) of chopped beet leaves with one slice of lemon.

When I became anemic and a transfusion was required according to allopathic medical protocols, I chose to juice one cup (250 ml) of beet juice; using beets and greens instead. Every two hours I would consume two tablespoons (15 ml). I also juiced turnip and alfalfa or fennel and carrot. Within ten days my blood was back within a normal range and I did not require a transfusion.

One ounce (30 ml**) of wheat grass**, added to eight ounces (one cup) of carrot juice is also great for building blood. Try also forty percent (40%) apple, forty percent (40%) grape with twenty percent (20%) blueberry.

Pomegranate juice inhibits the enzyme *aromatase* by up to eighty percent - without the side effects of most drugs. It is of value in the prevention and healing of breast cancer, and is suggested as a more natural enzyme than the drug, *Tamoxifen*TM. It also provides calcium, iron and magnesium.

For the kidneys: Choose watermelon, including the rind and seeds.

For bone marrow: Eat beets, beet greens and carrots

Liver Cleanse: (also valuable for kidney cleanse and arthritis): Choose citrus with the rind. Radish is also good as a liver cleanse, as are carrot with apple or carrot with pear.

For improved digestion: Eat cabbage.

Favorite recipes are easy to transform to benefit health:
a. Change vegetable oil and shortening to olive or canola oil (expeller or cold pressed only), cup for cup or milliliter for milliliter. Make sure they are purchased in dark glass (green or brown) containers.

b. Switch from dairy to soy (powder or liquid); or rice and/or nut milks if one cannot digest soy or is allergic to it.

c. Use unsweetened applesauce or mashed banana in exchange for sugar when possible. Again, cup for cup or milliliter for milliliter.

d. Use cane, maple syrup and unpasteurized honey or stevia rather than refined sugar. Reduce the amount of sweetener required for the recipe by one half or more

e. Use unbleached rather than white flour, but ensure that it is organic.

Healthy Breakfasts:
Try vegetable omelets; eat porridge, using organic oats with soy or rice milk; then sprinkle with raisins, dates, sliced bananas or apple chunks; homemade waffles with blueberries or raspberries as toppings rather than syrups. There are quite a variety of organic cereals available now, but be careful - always read labels. Try to purchase unsweetened fruit juice rather than those sweetened with cane or corn sugars. Toast, served with almond butter, or homemade raisin bread are other possibilities.

Lunch:

In addition to minestrone, there are a variety of homemade soups that can be made in advance. Combine frozen organic vegetables with pasta, rice or lentils to thicken the mixture and make a quick soup out of any leftover chicken or turkey broth from supper. Add plenty of quality salads with lots of protein such as eggs or chickpeas. And one can always throw a quick sandwich together, using free-range chicken or eggs, almond butter, or 'wild' salmon.

Miso soup is another suggestion - the taste is similar to French onion soup. Miso is a bean paste (fermented soybean) that has the consistency of peanut butter and is rich in essential amino acids and enzymes that aid digestion, as well as food assimilation.

Suppers:

Remember how important vegetables are; add plenty to make up for any lack at lunchtime. There are chicken stews, curries, pasta recipes, homemade veggie pizza and lots of dishes to make with salmon, halibut or haddock. Have a treat with scallops on occasion as they have a fantastic taste with bread crumbs and herbs. Homemade Chinese food, such as egg foo young, egg rolls, chicken fried rice, and stir fry are special treats. Always make extra portions and freeze them for those days when life is hectic.

I learned to steam leftovers rather than use a microwave, and choose a hot-air popcorn maker for snacks. My aluminum pots and utensils have been exchanged for stainless steel, glass or wooden items, along with the removal of all *Teflon*™ or *Tupperware*™. Currently, I store leftovers in the refrigerator or freezer in glass or stainless steel containers. It took about three years for the complete transition, including replacing charcoal briquettes in the barbecue with ceramic blocks.

Notes: The white skin and vein sections of oranges and grapefruit need to be eaten to obtain Vitamin P. This vitamin is excellent for the repair of capillaries such as varicose veins.

This was a sample section of recipes to begin the concept of healthy cooking and eating. The choice, of course, is up to each reader.

Watch for a future healthy recipe collection/cookbook by another member of the Manion - MacDonald family.

Make Today Count!!!

APPENDIX K

Preparation of a coffee enema [1]

An enema kit will be required, consisting of ground organic coffee, an enema bag (water bottle) or bucket, a colon tube, and a natural lubricant. Look for an appropriate herbal lubricant without chemicals or use cold-pressed virgin olive oil. Chemicals, especially pesticide residues found in many commercially grown coffees, could damage the liver when used as a coffee enema. **Use only organically grown coffee!** Add one to three heaping tablespoons of organic medium ground coffee to approximately one liter (about one quart) of pure water. Boil the water and coffee lightly for three minutes, then cover and simmer for approximately twenty minutes. Strain the mixture and use at body temperature (37 C or 98.6 F).

Find a comfortable area, such as the bathroom or bedroom floor. Use an old blanket or towel; have a clock handy, as well as a book or some favorite music to pass the time. The process takes fifteen minutes before the liquid can be expelled. One may wish to expel the solution earlier if too much pressure builds and results in cramps or pain. With practice, this should not be an on-going difficulty. The enema bag should not be more than two feet above the body while lying on the floor. Remember to lubricate the tube before insertion. Two to three inches should be sufficient for most, but in some cases the tube can be inserted a bit further. Whatever works and is comfortable without coffee leakage is the goal. The insertion tube should be short (3-5" maximum); too long and it could damage the colon wall.

To begin the process, lie on either the left or right side; draw both legs up close to the abdomen, as in a fetal position. During the process, it is suggested that one spend five minutes on the left side, five on the back and five on the right. For maximum benefit it is also recommended that a gentle massage be performed on the abdomen during this procedure, while in each of these positions. This massage should be done from right to left in counterclockwise circles so as not to back up the digestive process. Bowel movements should never be forced and that includes during an enema. If it becomes necessary to eliminate before the fifteen minutes is up, then do so.

1.Remember that coffee enemas are primarily recommended for more serious cases requiring rapid detoxification, and that other detox methods such as more traditional bowel and liver cleanses, saunas, soaks, or the cellular detoxification foot baths described in Chapter Four would likely be more appropriate for many individuals.

APPENDIX L

Movin' the Mercury
by Helke Ferrie[1]

If you haven't thought of your mouth as a toxic dump requiring high-tech clean-up procedures, you should! Mercury amalgam is dangerous when being placed in your mouth and deadly when being removed – to your nervous and immune systems, as well as to those of your dentist and the dental assistant.

So, what should you know when you want to have your 'silver' fillings taken out?

Depending on your individual susceptibility, as reactions differ, but no living organism can tolerate mercury. The *International Academy of Medical and Oral Toxicology (IAMOT)* developed a safety protocol for mercury removal. Many Canadian dentists are members of that association. Fillings should be removed either by dentists who have never used mercury fillings (those rare, enlightened types do exist!), or *IAMOT* trained dentists.

Dr. Rick Riley of Huntsville, Ontario, is one dentist who specializes in amalgam removal in ill persons. He uses devices that continually bring clean, compressed oxygen to the patient, himself and his assistant during the procedure. A rubber dam is placed in the mouth to prevent mercury vapour from reaching the brain. A carbide drill, rather than a diamond one dissects (not grinds) out the mercury filling, thereby minimizing the production of toxic micro-particles, which could damage the lungs and kidneys.

The Long Road To Banning Mercury Fillings

In the 1970s, Health Canada scientists presented overwhelming evidence that mercury amalgam fillings caused or triggered most of the chronic illnesses [that were] on the increase world-wide. They urged the government to investigate this under the Canada Health Act, which requires that all implants pass safety standards. For their trouble, they were fired or "eased out", while the Canadian Dental Association lobbied the government for more than a decade to prevent this investigation. A 1992 United Nations report singled out dental fillings as the world's largest source of toxic contamination in people, while scientists were finding links between dental fillings and *multiple sclerosis, muscular dystrophy, Lou Gehrig's disease, chronic fatigue syndrome, arthritis,* and *Alzheimer's* disease.

Many countries have banned the use of mercury amalgam or are phasing it out. A major study was released [in 1998] in Sweden, which stated unequivocally that amalgam fillings can cause brain damage in children, and may damage the brain, kidneys and the immune system of a great number of others. The Swedish government announced a total ban of dental amalgams, which [took] effect in 2001.

In 1996, Health Canada also responded to public pressure, at least in part, and therefore, readers will routinely find new questions on dental questionnaires, asking if one is pregnant, or suffers from allergies, kidney or auto-immune diseases. Patients will be informed that children under six years of age are not to have "silver" fillings, and that everyone else may not have more than four amalgam fillings and never in conjunction with other metals (e.g., braces, gold teeth) in one's mouth. Non-compliance runs the risk of legal liability. Today, many dentists are taking courses to learn new safer methods.

At the end of March, 1998 a citizens' group called Canadians For Mercury Relief filed a lawsuit on behalf of Canadians who have had mercury amalgams installed and not been informed of the potential health and environmental risks. Contact: Canadians For Mercury Relief http://www.talkinternational.com

---

1.Helke Ferrie is a free-lance science writer who lives in Alton, Ontario. She has authored, co-authored and published several ground-breaking books on the politics and science of alternative medicine, as well as environmental health in Canada. Contact her at helke@intersonic.com or through KOS Publishing at info@kospublishing.com

© 2005 Life Media - In *Natural Life Magazine*, May-June,1998
Reprinted with the kind permission of Helke Ferrie (July, 2006)

Mercury Amalgam Fillings (photo):

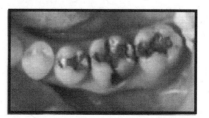

Resource List I
Books

Cancer related publications:

How to Fight Cancer and Win
William Fischer, ©1987, Fischer
Publishing Corp., Canfield, OH, USA
[ISBN: 1-891434-01-2]

Alternative Medicine: Definitive Guide to Cancer -
W. John Diamond, M.D. and W. Lee
Cowden, M.D. with Burton Goldberg,
©1997, Future Medicine Publishing,
Inc., Tiburon, CA, USA
[ISBN: 1-887299-01-7]

Cancer Battle Plan Sourcebook -
David Frahm, © 2000,
Jeremy P. Tarcher
Putnam, © 2000, New York, NY, USA
[ISBN: 1-585420-02-6]

Raw Food Treatment of Cancer
Dr. Kristine Nolfi, ©1945, Humlegaarden
and Dr. Kristine Nolfi, Re-published
with additions by Teach Services Inc.,
© 1995 [ISBN: 1-572580-57-7]

A Cancer Therapy – results of fifty
cases and *The Cure of Advanced
Cancer by Diet Therapy (a summary
of 30 years of clinical experimentation)*
- Max Gerson, M.D., Gerson Institute
P.U.L.S.E., Barrytown, NY, USA
[ISBN: 0-88268-105-2]

One Answer to Cancer -
Dr. William D. Kelly, D.D.S., M.S., ©
1967 to 1998, Cancer Coalition for
Alternative Therapies Inc., USA
[ISBN: 0-7873-1262-2]

Your Life in Your Hands - Dr. Jane
Plant, © 2001, Thomas Dunne Books,
New York, NY, USA
[ISBN: 0-312275-61-7]

*Lance Armstrong: It's Not About the
Bike* and *My Journey Back to Life* Lance
Armstrong with Sally Jenkins © 2000,
2001, Berkley Books, New York, NY,
USA, [ISBN 0-425-17961-3]

The Healing Journey and *Overcoming
the crisis of cancer*
Alastair J. Cunningham, Ph.D.,
©1992, 2000, Key Porter Books,
Toronto, ON, Canada,
[ISBN:1-55263-107-9]

*The Complete Natural Medicine Guide
to Breast Cancer*
Sat Dharam Kaur, N.D., © 2003,
Robert Rose Inc., Toronto, ON,
Canada, sdk@log.on.ca
[ISBN 0-778800-80-6]

Nutrition, Natural Healing, and Wellness:

Free to Fly: a journey toward wellness
(#1 Canadian Best Seller) Judit Rajhathy,
BA, RNCP, D. Ac., © 1996, 1999 New
World Publishing, PO Box 36075,
Halifax, N.S., B3J 3S9 Canada
Toll free orders: 1-877-211-3334
[Original Ed: ISBN: 1-895814-04-9]

Free to Fly, 2nd Edition, © 2003
Toll free orders: 1-877-211-3334
[ISBN: 978-1-895814-15-6 and
1-895814-15-4] $27.95 CAD

Spontaneous Healing [ISBN 0-8041-
1794-2], *8 Weeks to Optimum health*
[0-449-00026-5], and *Eating Well for
Optimum Health* [0-375-40754-5]
Andrew Weil, M.D., © 1995, 1997,
Ballantine Books; and Borzoi by
Alfred A. Knopf, New York, N.Y., USA

Eat Right For (4) Your Type - Dr. Peter
J. D'Adamo with Catherine Whitney,
© 1996, Published by G.P. Putnam's
Sons, New York, NY, USA
[ISBN: 0-399-14255-X]

Digestion: Inner Pathway to Health, © 1995 and *Endocrine Harmony : The Mind-Body-Nutrient Connection,* © 1996, [ISBN: 1-896651-08-9] David W. Rowland, PhD, Rowland Publications, Parry Sound, ON, Canada [ISBN: 1-896651-05-4]

Herbs for Health and Healing - Kathi Keville with Peter Korn, © 1996, Rosdale Press, Berkley Books, New York, NY, USA; Kokko, JP, [ISBN: 0-87596-293-9]

Dr. Whitaker's Guide to Natural Healing Julian Whitaker M.D., and Michael T. Murray, N.D., © 1996-07-24, Three Rivers Press [ISBN: 0-761506-69-1]

Diet for a Poisoned Planet – How to Choose Safe Foods for You and Your Family - David Steinman, ©1998, Harmony Books [ISBN: 0-34537-465-7]

The Nutritional Bypass – Reverse Atherosclerosis without Surgery - David W. Rowland, PhD, © 1995, Rowland Publications, Parry Sound, ON, Canada [ISBN 1-896651-02-X]

The Miracle of Pi-water (A Gift from the Cosmos) Shioyi Makino, PH.D., © 1999, IBE Company Ltd or Bio-Water 2000 Inc. [ISBN: 0967057108]

The Juicing Bible - Pat Crocker & Susan Eagles, © 2000, Robert Rose Inc., Toronto, ON, Canada. [ISBN: 0-7788-0019-9]

The Wheatgrass Book - Ann Wigmore, ©1984, Avery Penguin Putnam. [ISBN: 0-89529-234-3]

Dining in the Raw Rita Romano, ©1992, Kensington Bks, NY, NY, USA, [ISBN 1-57566-192-6]

Applied Kinesiology, Volume I - David S. Walther, © 1981, Systems DC, Pueblo, CO, USA

The Book of Macrobiotics – The Universal Way of Health and Happiness Michio Kushi © Japan Publications, Inc., Tokyo, Japan & New York, NY, USA. [ISBN 0-87040-381-8]

Dr. Wright's Book of Nutritional Therapy Real- Life Lessons in Medicine with Drugs - Jonathan V. Wright, M.D., © 1979, Rodale Press, Inc., Emmaus, PA, USA. [ISBN 0-87857-270-8]

The Complete Handbook of Natural Healing - Marcia Starck, © 1991, Llewellyn Publications, Inc., St. Paul, MN, USA. [ISBN 0-87542-742-1]

Love Medicine & Miracles - By Bernie S. Siegel, M.D., © 1986, Harper and Row, New York, NY, USA, and Fitzhenry & Whiteside Ltd., Toronto, ON, Canada. [ISBN 0-06-015496-9]

Natural Cures What They Don't Want You to Know About Kevin Trudeau, © 2004, Alliance Publishing Group, Inc., Elk Grove Village, IL, USA. ISBN 0-9755995-1-8]

Say Good-bye to Illness (3rd edition) Devi S. Nambudripad M.D. D.C., L.Ac, PhD © 1993, 1999, 2002, Delta Publishing Company, Buena Park, CA, USA [ISBN 0-9704344-8-0]

The Detox Book (How to Detoxify Your Body to Improve Your Health and Reverse Aging) Bruce Fife, N.D., © 2001, Piccadilly Bks Ltd, Colorado Springs, CO, USA. [ISBN 0-94159-932-9]

Essential Fatty Acids:

Fats That Heal, Fats That Kill
Udo Erasmus, BSc, MA, PhD, ©1993,
Alive Books, Burnaby, BC, Canada
[ISBN: 0-920470-38-6]

*The Oil That Heals: a Physician's
Successes with Castor Oil Treatments*
William A. McGarey, M.D., 2004,
A.R.E. Press, (10th printing),
Virginia Beach, VA, USA
[ISBN: 0-87604-308-2]

Disease, Stress and Fatigue:

Fit For Life 3
Harvey Diamond, ©1998,
P H Canada, Scarborough., ON, Can
[ISBN: 0-13-975376-1]

Survival into the 21st Century -
Viktorias Kulvinskas, © 1981,
Twenty-First Century Books. [ISBN:
0-93327-804-7]

*Toxic Overload: A Doctor's Plan for
Combating the Illnesses Caused by
Chemicals in Our Foods, Our Homes,
and Our Medicine Cabinets -*
Paula Baillie-Hamilton, MD, Ph.D. © 2005
Avery (Penguin Gp.), NY, NY, USA 10014
[ISBN: 1-58323-225-1]

The Yeast Connection and the Woman -
William G. Crook. M.D., © 1995,
Professional House, Jackson,
Tennessee, USA.
[ISBN :0-933478-22-4]

Blood Never Lies - Ted Aloisio, © 2004,
Media Creations, Seattle, WA, USA
[ISBN: 1-932560-94-7]

*Adrenal Fatigue: The 21st Century Stress
Syndrome -* Dr. James L. Wilson, ©2001,
Smart Publications, Petaluma, CA, USA
[ISBN: 1-890572-15-2]

Beating Alzheimer's - Tom Warren,
© 1991, Avery Publishing Group, Inc.,
[ISBN: 0-89529-488-5]

Anatomy of an Illness
Norman Cousins, © 1979,
Bantam Book, New York, NY, US
[ISBN: 0-553-01293-2]

Death by Modern Medicine,
Dr Carolyn Dean, MD, ND and
Trueman Tuck, ALL ABOUT BOOK
SERIES, © 2005 Matrix Verite, Inc., PO
Box 22070, Belleville, Ontario K8M 5V7
www.deathbymodernmedicine.com
[ISBN: 0-9737392-0-7]

*Why Animals Don't Get Heart Attacks
… But People Do!*
Matthias Rath, M.D., © 2003, MR
Publishing, Inc., Fremont, CA, USA
[ISBN: 0-9679546-8-1]

Healing the Planet: one patient at a time:
a primer in Environmental Medicine-
Josef J. Krop, © 2003
KOS Publishing, 1997 Beechgrove
Road, Alton, Ontario L0N 1A0
Canada. www.kospublishing.com or
Phone: (519) 927-9542

Chemical Additives:

*Additive Alert (A Guide to Food
Additives for the Canadian) -* Linda
R. Pim, © 1979, 1984, Doubleday,
Toronto, Canada
[ISBN: 0-4401-0104-2]

The Toxic Science of Fluoridation - Paul
Connett, PhD, © 2005, ACRES U.S.A.
www.acresusa.com / Acres-U-S-A
1-800-355-5351; fax: (512)892-4448

AEHA Guide to Less Toxic Products
Susan Bone; Tina Conrad, © 1997, 1999
Contact: New World Publishing,
Halifax, NS, Canada B3J 3S9
Toll free: 1-877-211-3334
[2004 ISBN: 1-895814-17-0] $6.95

Psychological and Spiritual:

God helps those who help themselves
[ISBN: 1-883713-11-0] and *Parasites
The Enemy Within* -
Rev. Hanna Kroeger, Ms.D.,
H. Kroeger Publications, Boulder, CO, USA
[ISBN: 1-883713-07-2]

The 7 Habits of Highly Effective People
[ISBN:0-671-70863-5] © 1989, and
First Things First - ©1994, 1995 ,
Stephen R. Covey, Simon and Shuster,
New York, NY, USA
[ISBN: 0-684-80203-1]

*Life Strategies and Life Strategies
Workbook* - Phil McGraw, ©
2001,Simon & Schuster, NY, NY, USA
[ISBN: 0786887435 and 0786885149]

Self Matters Book and *Companion* © 2002,
Dr. Phil McGraw
Simon & Schuster, NY, NY, USA
[ISBN: 0-74322423-X and 0-7432-4296-3]

The Celestine Prophecy
James Redfield, © 1993, 1996, Warner
Books, Inc., New York, NY, USA.
[ISBN: 0-446-67100-2]

Power of Intention, *Learning to Co-
create Your World Your Way*
[ISBN: 1-4019-0216-2]; *Getting in the Gap*
- Book and CD, [ISBN: 1-4109-0131-X],
Dr. Wayne Dyer, © 2004, Hay House
Inc., Carlsbad, CA, USA, and
Inspiration, Your Ultimate Calling, © 2006
[ISBN 13: 978-1-4019-0721-1]

*Heal Your Body – The Mental
Causes For Physical Illness and the
Metaphysical Way to Overcome Them*
Louise L. Hay, © 1988, Hay House
Inc., Santa Monica, CA, USA
[ISBN: 0-937611-35-2]

Handbook for Today's Catholic
Liguori Press, © 1978, 1991 and 1994.
[ISBN 089243-671-9]

Let the Magic Begin
Cathy Lee Crosby, © 1997,
Dell Publishing Group Inc., New
York, NY, USA.[
ISBN 0-440-22566-3]

Tuesdays with Morrie
Mitch Albom, © 1997,
DoubleDay, New York, NY, USA.
[ISBN 0-385-48451-8]

Legacy of the Heart
Wayne Muller, 1992, Simon & Shuster,
© 1992, New York, NY, USA
[ISBN 0-671-76119-6]

*Home Coming - Reclaiming and
Championing Your Inner Child*
John Bradshaw, © 1990, 1992
Bantam Books, New York, NY, USA;
and simultaneously with Random
House in Toronto, ON, Canada
[ISBN 0-553-35389-6]

The Positive Principle Today -
Norman Vincent Peale, © 1977,
Fawcett Crest Edition, 1983,
1994, The Ballantine Publishing
Group, New York, NY, USA; and
simultaneously with Random House
in Toronto, ON, Canada.
[ISBN 0-449-20029-9]

Minding the Body Mending the Mind
- Joan Bosysenko, PhD., © 1987, 1988,
Bantam Books, with Addison-Wesley
Publ. Company Inc., Reading, MA,
USA. [ISBN 0-553-34556-7 -895]

Not All in the Mind
- Richard MacKarness, M.D., © 1976,
Pan Books Ltd., with 1994 reprint
by Thorsons. [ISBN 0330313541]

Miscellaneous:

Essentials of Human Anatomy &
Physiology (8th edition)
Elaine N. Marieb, R.N., PH.D., © 2005,
Benjamin Pearson Cummings,
San Francisco, CA, USA.
[ISBN: 0-8053-7328-4]

The Atlas of the Human Body
Prof. Peter Abrahams, © 2002, 2003,
Bright Star Publishing Plc., Desford
Road, Enderby, Leciester, UK.
[ISBN 0-8053-7328-4]

An Owner's Guide to the Human Body
Dr. Jim Walkenbach, D.C., © 2001,
D J W Publishing Inc., 1-800-527-8611

Creative Yoga Companion: A Workbook
for Beginners and Intermediate Levels
Jodie Myers, © 1999, Glen Margaret
Publishing, Tantallon, NS, Canada
Phone: 1-902-823-1198
e-mail: gmp@eastlink.ca
[ISBN: 0-920427-47-2]

Dispatches - from the war zone of
environmental health,
Helke Ferrie, © 2004,
KOS Publishing, 1997 Beechgrove
Road, Alton, ON L0N 1A0 Canada
www.kospublishing.com
Phone: 1-519-927-1049
[ISBN: 0-9731945-3-7]

The Canadian Green Consumer Guide
(revised and expanded) ©1989 and 1991
McClelland & Steward Inc.
The Canadian Publishers *(M&S)*,
[ISBN: 0-7710-7147-7]

The Art of Dowsing
Richard Webster, © 2001,
Castle Books a division of Book Sales
Inc., Edison, NJ, USA
[ISBN: 0785814302-0]

What Your Doctor Didn't Learn in
Medical School - Stuart M.Berger.
M.D., © 1989, Avon Books, New York,
NY, USA. [ISBN 0-380-70319-X]

The Maker's Diet
Jordan S. Rubin © 2004,2005
Siloan - a Strang Company, 600 Rinehart
Rd., Lake Mary, Florida 32746 USA
[1-59185-714-7]

Resource List II
Web Sites

www.alkalizeforhealth.net - saliva pH test, alkalinity information, immune building, cancer prevention and eight step program to better health, exercise, meditation, enzymes, and much more.

www.excelex.com - alkaline - living water

www.healthworks2000.com - *Health Works* 2000's products have been developed with the singular objective of helping optimize one's health and well-being using the vast resources of nature.

www.healthfree.com – *Health Freedom Resources; products, cleansing programs and Incurables Program* (Dr. John Christopher and Dr. Richard Schulze - herbalists and healers)

www.nomorecandida.com - explains Candida (yeast); an endorsement for the product, *Threelac* ™

www.pollutionprobe.com *What Have They Done To Our Food? A Consumer's Action Guide* by Pollution Probe

http://science-education.nih.gov/home2.nsf/Educational+Resources - *Prions: Puzzling Infectious Proteins* - Ruth Levy Goyer, Ph.D.

www.mypyramid.gov.downloads/miniposter.pdf - USA Food Guide Pyramid

www.healthcanada.gc.ca/foodguide - Canada's Food Guide Rainbow

www.alive.com - *Alive Magazine* - beauty, environment, health, fitness, food and nutrition, holistic healing, recipes, and more.

www.rawbc.org - living food recipes, lists of raw food books, links and articles related to natural healing.

www.naet.com - information on treatments with NAET and location of practitioners

www.neuromodulationtechnique.com - information on the NMT technique and conditions treated via NMT.

www.caps.20m.com -*Canadians Against Pesticides*

www.lightangels.com -information on the "Journey series" CDs and workshops for spiritual meditation and relaxation

www.toxicteeth.org - role of mercury amalgams in a range of diseases or conditions

www.mercola.com - articles on safe mercury removal as well as other toxic materials http://www.talkinternational.com - locate dentists who do not use amalgams and/or are trained in their proper removal.

www.tuberose.com/meridians - information of the *Meridian Organ Clock*. This self-help alternative medicine site offers extensive educational information on the topics of natural healing, holistic and biological dentistry, herbal medicine, cleansing and detoxification, heavy metal detoxification, diet, nutrition, weight loss, and trusted health equipment and products available for the natural management of health.

http://hippocratesinst.org - *Hippocrates Health Institute*; programs on life changes, growing wheatgrass and sprouts, Ann Wigmore / Viktoras Kulvinkas co-founders. *"Let food be our medicine"*.

www.cancertutor.com - *Cancer Tutor* focuses on alternative cancer treatments to deal with cancer patients by orthodox medicine. (Key protocols for free - be cautious, always ensure what is right for your body)

www.cancercontrolsociety.com - education, prevention, control, conventions, and more.

www.davidlweatherford.com - website of child psychologist and poet David L Weatherford, author of the poem "Slow Dance", reprinted in the chapter on "Coping" [pp. 252-3]

www.hayhouse.com - Self improvement, inspirational, healing, spirituality, astrology, feng shui and more.

www.gerson.org - 60 years of success for proven nutritional programs for cancer and other serious illnesses. Toll free: 1-800-838-2256 (USA & Canada)

www.herbaled.org. – safe and effective use of liquid herbal extracts

www.nonscentedtoxicfree.com - information on toxins and sale of products that are 100% toxic-free and devoid of artificial scents. Products are imported from three countries, plus three Canadian provinces to offer a complete line of products for personal care and household cleaning, including world's best sunscreens for babies, swimmers and golfers.

www.jtwnaturalhealth.ca - Information on energy balance cellular detoxification therapy. Natural products to facilitate balance, including Champion juicers, Nikken products, Threelac™, Rascal/parasitic products, Bernard Jensen dry brushes, and more. Course and lecture dates with venues on *B.A.L.A.N.C.E.: nature's way to heal your body*. Natural consultation and guidance. Links to: Armadale Farm ltd, Roachville, N.B., processors of 100% natural quark; and *Nature's Own* all natural handcrafted soap and skin care products.

www.oliviersoaps.com or www.savonolivier.com - Award-Winning Soapery. A living family country soapery dedicated to the preservation of our Canadian heritage of natural therapeutic treatments, the art of making soap and the creation of botanical, economical and ecological skin care products.

www.who.int/peh-emf/en/ - World Health Organization web site

Resource List II

Magazines, newspapers, newsletters and pamphlets:

HealthExcel Detox Packet, © 1986

Healing Newsletter, #13, May-June, 1986

Halifax Daily News, April 16, 2002, Toronto: Canadian Press and Health Canada – Lead Poison

Get Your Lawn Off Drugs, a project of the Ecology Action Centre (Halifax, NS), the Nova Scotia Department of Health (Community Health Promotion Fund), CESED (NS) and Edmonds Environmental Services. (pamphlet)

Health Effects of Microwave Radiation – Microwave Ovens - Dr. Lita Lee, Ph.D., 1989, in *Lancet, the British Medical Journal*

Electrical Magnetic Fields (EMF) Associated Press, Boston, August, 21, 1996 – The human body is electrical; mutant cells are produced by exposure to EMFs; even a watch battery can produce EMFs.

What on Earth is ORGANIC? Maritime Certified Organic Growers, OCIA-PEI, NSOGA, and Speerville Flour Mill. (pamphlet)

Parasites are a Serious Health Concern - Brenda Watson, N.D., C.T., *Renew Life Canada* (pamphlet)

OPRAH Magazine, April 2003

Fluoride - The Battle of Darkness & Light - Mary Sparrowdancer, © 2003; Rense.com

Bone Cancer-Fluoride Link - Harvard University; Rense.com

Movin' the Mercury, Helke Ferrie © 2005, Life Media- *In Natural Life Magazine,* May-June, 1998.

Natural healing can cure the medically-incurable; Immune System Formulas for pneumonia, killer viruses, cancer and AIDS; Aggressive Cold and Flu Treatment Program - Dr. Richard Schulze, N.D., M.H.

"Not in My Water Supply", TIME Magazine, Canadian Edition Oct. 24, 2005 pp.38-9

Resource List IV

CDs ,cassettes and videos:

Pi-water: a concise introduction, Dr. Jim Walkenbush, ©2001, DJW Publishing, Inc. (Video)

Journey to the Crystal Palace (Vol.1) Jackie Haverty © 2002 [ISBN: 1-895814-25-1] (CD) First in the 'journey series' involving four spiritual meditation and relaxation CDs complete with music by noted artist Paul Armitage.

Other CDs include: *Journey to the 5th Dimension,*© 2003 [ISBN: 1-895814-30-8]; *Journey Through the Chakras,*© 2005 [ISBN: 1-895814-26-X] and *Infinite Healing, for Body, Mind and Spirit* © Nov. 2006 [ISBN: 978-1-895814-33-0] Contact: www. lightangels.com or call toll-free to order with credit cards: 1-877-211-3334 or visit www.newworldpublishing.com.

Chakra Clearing - CD - Doreen Virtue, Ph.D., MA., B.A., © 2004, Hay House Inc., [ISBN 1-4019-0277-4] Information and guidance about the opening, cleansing and balancing of the body's energy centers (chakras).

Getting Started on Getting Well Series of Health Videos: "Cancer Doesn't Scare Me Anymore", "You Can't Improve on God", "Turn on The Light" and "Disease Doesn't Just Happen" - Lorraine Day, M.D. © 2003, Rockford Press.

Judit Rajhathy Live! audios:
V.1 Raising Healthy Children [ISBN 1-895814-06-5]
V.2 -Boosting Your Energy [ISBN 1-895814-08-1].
Boxed set [ISBN 1-895814-07-3] Order via credit card from Amazon.com, Indigo. ca or directly at newworldpublishing.com.
Individual cassettes only - available from www.newworldpublishing.com or phone toll-free 1-877-211-3334

What The Bleep Do You Know? - Dr. Joe Dispenza, www.whatthe bleep.com A controversial idea suggesting change to the current paradigm, inviting viewers to ask themselves "What do I know?" Includes information on water crystal work and quantum physics in a stimulating learning format.

Resource List V:

Organizations and People

A. Organizations:

Consumer Health Organization of Canada (CHOC) - a not for profit organization, was begun in 1973 by three individuals who chose to dedicate their live to spreading awareness about the holistic natural approach to improving our health. They emphasize prevention of disease via nutrition, whole foods, dietary supplements, herbs and other healing modalities. Practicing prevention creates a healthy individual, and when the individual is healthy, the whole of society benefits. www.consumerhealth.com

The World Health Organization EMF Project - www.who.int/peh-emf/en
Health Canada *"It's your health"* www.hcc.gc.ca/english/iyh/environment/magnetic.htm

Sierra Club Canada - A well-trained grassroots network, working to protect the integrity of our global ecosystems. Mission focuses on five overriding threats: loss of animal and plant species; deterioration of the planet's oceans and atmosphere; the ever-growing presence of toxic chemicals in all living things; destruction of our remaining wilderness; spiraling population growth and over consumption. www.sierraclub.ca

Pugwash Peace Exchange - part of a world wide effort to create a more civil society that acts under the patronage of Lieutenant-General, the Hon. Romeo Dallaire with an Advisory Council of distinguished individuals, chaired by the Hon. Senator Douglas Roche, Q.C. www.pugwashpeaceexchange.org

YMCA/YWCA – a charitable organization offering a variety of opportunities for all members of the community, designed to enhance the quality of their lives through health and wellness. For information; on a center near you, saunas, exercise programs, sponsored membership, contact: Canada – www.ymca.ca USA – www.ymca.net/index.jsp International www.ymca.int/ymcascountry/addresses.htm

The Way of The Heart - www.thewayoftheheart.com The vision of *The Way of the Heart* is a world where every person holds as self-evident that they are here for a reason, and that it is important to create that in our world. It is the passing from one view of living your life to another by simply following your heart.

The Nova Scotia Environmental Centre, Fall River, Nova Scotia: environmentally safe personal and home care products.

B. Professional Resources:

Dr. Bruce Hayhoe, D.C., N.D.
123 Hazen Street
Saint John, New Brunswick, Canada

Rose Marie Saulnier, B.A.Sc.,
R.N.C.P., C.R., n.d., C.I.
Natural Choice Nutrition Center
92, rue Oliver Street, Dieppe, N.B.,
Canada

Lise Fournier, R.N.C.P. *Canadian
School for Natural Nutrition*
7 Beach Street, Dieppe, N.B., Canada

Dr. Pamela Purcell, N.D.
Naturopathic Solutions Health Clinic Ltd.
2625 Joseph Howe Drive, Suite 26
Halifax, N.S., Canada

Stephanie Allen, B.Sc. Kinesiology,
R.M.T. & Connie Fisher, B.A.
Communications, M.A. *Psychology
DreamField Consulting Group* (Atlantic
Canada representatives for *The Way of
the Heart*) (902) 694-3098
or (902) 660-2026;

Cheryl Marr R.N.C.P., D.Ac
Inner Oasis Ltd.
92 Oliver Street, Dieppe, N.B.,
Canada

APPENDIX M

Gall Bladder Protocol/Flush

This is a safe, time-tested technique for removing gallstones from the gall bladder - without surgery;

For three days, adult males should consume nothing but apple juice or apple cider (four liters [4000 milliliters] daily; reduce to three liters for women. No other food or liquid is to be consumed except for water, if desired. In the late afternoon or early evening of the first and second days, mix two ounces (60 ml.) of virgin olive oil and two ounces (60 ml.) of freshly squeezed lemon juice in a blender and drink this mixture down, pinching one's nose if necessary, as some will find this mixture somewhat nauseating to drink.

On the evening of the third day, drink four ounces (120 ml) of olive oil mixed with four ounces (120 ml) of lemon juice. (*At least once each day to keep the bowels moving it is recommended to take a heaping tablespoonful of a supplement with psyllium or a herbal-fibre blend (psyllium, pectin, peppermint, acidophilus, garlic, guar bark, red clover, senna, ginger, buchu, cascara sagrada, burdock, buckthorn, yellow dock, rhubarb, cinnamon, barberry and plantain).* On the third day of this protocol, about 400 green triglycerides from the gall bladder have been observed during elimination.

By the fourth day or sooner, stones should appear in the toilet bowl, mixed with one's fecal matter. There may be hundreds of tiny ones, a few larger ones, or simply some sludge. Colors can range from dull, pea green to emerald green - to almost black.

NOTE: There is always a chance a large stone might get stuck in the bile duct and would have to be removed through surgery, although this has never been reported in thousands of cases. This procedure would, however, save one's gall bladder. Most gallstones are solidified cholesterol and this procedure makes them very soft before squeezing them out the bile duct. Stones as large as three quarters of an inch in diameter have been safely passed in this manner, without surgery. Many naturopaths, holistic medical doctors and registered nutritional consultants use this procedure regularly with their clients and they should be consulted before proceeding with a gall bladder flush.

Removal of the gall bladder has also been associated with some types of colon cancer. Additionally, those individuals without a gall bladder may wish to increase their EFAs, as well as their egg consumption (with runny yolks) to add lecithin to the body and to protect the colon.

BALANCE Index

H

I

J

K

L

Lactate (Lactic Acid) *Dehydrogenase* - 45–76;
LDH - 45–76, 49–76, 220–258, 245–258, 248–258, 278–280, 279–280
lactic enzymes - 245–258, 246–258
lactobacillus acidophilus - 131–141
lactobacillus sporogenes - 131–141, 132–141, 135–141
lactose intolerance - 65–76
laetrile - 289–291
Larrea Tridentate - 283
Live Blood-cell Analysis (LBA) - 46–76, 47–76, 74–76
LDL (low density lipoproteins) - 75–87, 117–141, 261–271, 290–291
lead poisoning - 169 –188
"leaky gut" syndrome - 129–141, 130–141, 207, 226–258
lecithin - 54–76, 204–258, 207–258, 300–301
leucine - 62–76
leukotriens - 291
linoleic acid - 56–76, 57–76, 288–291
linseed oil - 58–76, 59–76, 287–291, 288–291
lipase - 71–76, 101–141
lipoprotein - 194–258
lipotropic factors - 204–258
Lithothamnium Calcareum - 84–87
liver - 4–5, 18–33, 44, 45–76, 53–76, 54–76, 55–76, 56–76, 58–76, 62–76, 63–76,
    102, 279–280, 288–291, 289–291, 301 (+ 70 other references)
liver (**diagram**) - 106
lunula (half moons) -37–76, 58–76, 191–258
lurium usitatissimun - 59–76
lymphatic fluid - 22–33, 94–141, 96–141, 97–141, 101–141, 116–141, 126–141,
    140–141, 258–271, 259–271, 269–271, 288–291 (plus 10 more)
lymphatic system - 40–76, 72–76, 85–87, 93–141, 41, 267–278, (plus 15 more)
lymphatic system (**diagram**) - 92 ; **Appendix H** (294-295)
lymphocytes - 44, 93–141
lymph nodes - 96–141, 137–141, 277–278
lysine - 62–76

M

M.S (*Multiple Sclerosis*) - 128–141, 144–188, 304–308
mad cow disease (*spongiform encephalopathy)* - 171–188
Mad Hatter (mercury nitrate) - 144–145; **sketch** - 145
malnutrition - 260–271, 270
maltose - 71–76
Material Safety Data Sheets (MSDS) - 165–188
MDF board - 176–188
Medical Doctor (MD) -18, 29, 43-44, 49-50, 64, 75, 89, 91, 94, 96, 113-14, 117, 130,
    132-137, 149, 166, 185, 196, 206, 222, 276, 294
meditation - 89, 108–141, 236–258, 237–258, 239–258, 250–258, 251–258, 309–314,
    310–314, 312–314; meditation CDs - 251, **
menopause - 94, 190, 197, 203

N

O

P

Q

R

Other Quality Books on Health, Wellness and Self-esteem

Free to Fly: a journey toward wellness (Second Edition) © 2003 (352 pp.; 6x9 perfect/laminated cover)   ISBN (978-189581415-6)

#NWP 126 . . . .$27.95CAD/25.95 USD. With over 36,000 copies sold in Canada alone and thousands more internationally, this 352 page book by international author Judit Rajhathy is a wonderful success story. It is Canada's **number one best seller on holistic health** with a focus on natural and complementary approaches to healing; health issues at school; in the workplace and in your home; proper nutrition; and taking responsibility for your own health! Written in a narrative form, it's a story of one family's search for wellness and provide readers with complex information in an extremely readable, enjoyable and understandable form. *The main thesis is what you eat, drink and breathe on a daily basis has a profound impact on the quality of your health* - and consequently your life! If you or your child suffers from **asthma, ADD, hyperactivity, aggression or depression, mood swings, memory loss, PMS or prostatitis, bowel or bladder problems, fatigue, nausea, migraines, allergies, yeast or ear infections, acne, eczema or arthritis - then this is the book for you!** The **Second Edition** contains new information on the testing and successful treatment of allergies and other underlying conditions which are the cause of much ill-health in our society today - and includes all updated resource lists, complete with toll-free numbers and web sites to assist readers with additional research.

Judit Rajhathy Live! (boxed double cassettes: 3.25 hours run time) 978-1-895814-07-3 © 1999 - #NWP116 . . . $17.95 CAD/$14.95USD Two full-length audio-cassettes of keynote lectures by Judit Rajhathy, one of

Canada's most sought-after speakers on health and wellness . These tapes were produced in response to hundreds of requests from those who attended her lectures and workshops over the past three years. Many simply wanted to "take Judit's words home" to share with their partners, family members and friends, or to use it as a refresher course for themselves. Digitally recorded live, with 45 or more minutes per side, they are easy to listen to as you drive to and from work; use as an *aide memoire;* or as a focal point for discussions in the staff room or office - or at home with your friends. The focus of *Vol. # 1 - NWP113 (Raising Healthy Children:* (978-1-895814-06-4) is on family health and wellness in the new millennium - with an emphasis on factors

that affect the attention, learning and behavior of children. *Vol.. # 2 - NWP114 (Boosting Your Energy:* (978-1-895814-08-8) features a presentation on adult health and energy concerns with a special focus on issues related to chronic fatigue, anti-aging and vitality - for use in the home and the workplace. **Individual cassettes are available at $9.95 CAD/USD each. (. . . over 90 minutes each).**

AEHA guide to less toxic products (140 pp., 5x8 paper cover) ISBN (978-1-895814-17-0) -#NWP117. . . . .$6.95 CAD/USD

An inexpensive and invaluable guide for locating and substituting safer, non-scented personal care and cleaning products, as well as locating information on pest control, indoor air quality devices, low-toxic building materials and school supplies. Also includes tips on food preparation and storage, plus a short listing of useful books. The personal care and alternative home cleaning products sections are quite extensive. Produced by the *Allergy and Environmental Health Association (N.S.)*, the final section lists product sources, supporting those who sell healthier and safer personal care products, as well as for sources of regional organic produce.

WORTH: a story about love and self-esteem by Joseph Britto (160 pp., 6x9 perfect/laminated cover, poems incl..) ISBN (978-1-895814-12-0) © 2000, #NWP123 . . . . $16.95 CAD/$14.95 USD

Gray Hassett, aspiring poet, is consumed by a single word: *Worth*. When he meets Christie Phelps, her sense of self-worth intrigues him. With the help of his kindred spirit, Gray embarks on a personal journey that just could change his life. . . if he lets it. *Worth* is a story of personal growth, self-esteem and change that offers us all the opportunity to hold destiny in our hands and live life as it was meant to be lived. Sparkling with warmth, emotion and humour, *Worth* is the kind of book you'll treasure and want to share with the most important people in your life. **Self-esteem for adults!!**

George, the friendly dragon by E. T. Matthews (40 pp., 3 part story, 8.5 x11, 12 point perfect/laminated cover, full color) ISBN (978-1-895814-02-6) #NWP112 . . . . $15.95 CAD/12.95 USD

A heart-warming story about being different and all that it entails, especially for someone growing up wanting to be understood and seeking acceptance from others. This story is about believing in oneself and developing tolerance for others, and addresses the important concept of self-esteem for children. It was field-tested with hundreds of school children and reviewed by dozens of classroom teachers prior to its release. Parents and grandparents enjoy reading *George* aloud or using it as a dramatization. Teachers find that younger children love having it read to them, while older ones can read it on their own. Full of wonderful rhyming conversations between the principal characters, George and a little girl named Amber, it makes a great gift, as well as an economical school resource. Each page resonates with rich, vibrant colors and cartooned characters by Gizelle Erdei. Add 100 lb. paper/12 pt. laminated cover and you have a very durable, **"nearly kid-proof"**, book. Officially adopted by the Nova Scotia Department of Education; used in all schools throughout Bermuda, and in many US states and provinces of Canada.

Spiritual & Meditation CDs

Journey to the Crystal Palace: An Extra-Ordinary Guided Meditation, ©
2002 Vol. 1 #NWP125 ISBN: 978-1-895814-25-5 . $21.95 CAD/$17.95 USD

This extraordinary sixty minute guided meditation was created to provide the listener with a profound, multi-dimensional experience in which our Guides and Angels are accessed for mystical insight and true healing in the Crystal Palace. The spontaneously composed, celestial music of Paul Armitage, combined with the soothing voice of Jackie Haverty, weave together a tapestry of transcendence where words and music become one. The heart is opened to the timeless gifts of transformation and unconditional love from our Divine Self. This journey provides true liberation of your body, mind and spirit. There is a peaceful interlude of spirit-filled music while you receive the gifts requested in this luminescent space. Next, you will be filled with the golden light of Christ Consciousness and be gifted with a profound sense of peace and unconditional love.

Journey to the 5th Dimension: An Extra-Ordinary Guided Meditation
©*2003 Vol 2#NWP130 ISBN: 978-1-895814-30-9. $21.95 CAD/$17.95 USD*
This guided meditation was created to guide the listener beyond the limits of one's body and ego consciousness to the higher levels of the 5th dimension. The words were created from visions received by Jackie while in deep meditation. The beautiful artwork used for the labels and inserts was also spontaneously composed by Diane Parks. Through intent, the body, mind and spirit absorb and integrate the highest vibrations of the platinum/violet light of Cosmic Consciousness. This awakens the DNA and transforms all negativity into the higher vibrations of pure unconditional love, acceptance, compassion and forgiveness. It provides a truly remarkable experience with a shift in consciousness that occurs on all levels and prepares the body, mind and spirit for ascension into the 5th dimension.

Journey to the Chakras: A Guided Meditation, Vol 3, ©*2005 #NWP135*
ISBN: 978-1-895814-26-2 .... $21.95 CAD/$17.95 USD
Volume three was created to provide the reader/listener with a profound, multi-dimensional experience where the energy centers, called chakras, are accessed for the balance, assimilation and transmission of vital life energy. Together, the seven chakras form a profound formula for wholeness by linking our physical, emotional, mental, and spiritual selves into one divisible whole.

Infinite Healing: for Body, Mind & Spirit, Vol 4, ©*2006 #NWP133 ISBN: 978-1-895814-33-0 [Contains booklet & two full tracks*] ... $24.95 CAD/$21.95 USD*
Prepare for a powerful healing experience that transcends time and space. Using these incredible tools will create the highest expression of Love in every aspect of your life. The enclosed booklet provides necessary information for self healing on a conscious level exploring how acceptance, forgiveness, love, faith and intent play an integral part in the healing process. Next, transform your life with a harmonic resonance of Divinely inspired words and music that integrate quantum physics with Divine Love for Infinite healing   * **[2 separate messages]**

Books from/about Atlantic Canada

*Timeless Treasures: Historical Newfoundland in Art (Vol. 1)©2004 - NWP 127
ISBN: 978-1-895814-18-7 (54 pp., full color, coil, address book)....$18.95 CAD*
.
*Timeless Treasures: Historical Newfoundland in Art (Vol. 2)©2005 -NWP 128
ISBN: 978-1-895814-19-4 (54 pp., full color, coil, 'guest' book).....$18.95 CAD*
Two formats of thirty plus timeless paintings of Newfoundland & Labrador
architecture and communities by celebrated artist Virginia Houston. Some of
these depictions are of places lost in time, but still remembered by their inhabitants
and descendants. Paintings depict dates from the later 18th Century to the early
1950s. Complete with historical accounts, descriptions, maps, TOC and indices.

*Success on the Edge: portrait of a small town ©2000 - NWP 122 ISBN: 978-1-
895814-11-8 (128 pp., photos, maps , records) E.E. Cran . $12.95 CAD/9.95 USD*
Using Tignish, PEI as a model, the author analyses the factors that allow small
communities to thrive and grow - and to retain a measure of independence
in an age of globalization. Citizens and governmental officials in small towns
anywhere will find much food for thought in this well written little book

*Ballerina, the dancing angel ©2000 - NWP 121 ISBN: 978-1-895814-10-1 (36
pp., full color, poetic verse, ballet) Ray Saunders.........12.95 CAD/9.95 USD*
A picture storybook for children and all those who love music and dance.
Inspired by the *Old Testament 'Creation Story'* and a celebrated *'prima ballerina'*,
it's a story that will warm your heart and inspire children to dance. Illustrated
by Nuri Guerra. Suitable for pre-school and early elementary grades.

*Leslie Braes: Scottish dance music ©2004 NWP 108 - ISBN: 978-1-895814-03-3
(54 pp., illust., original scores, dance sets)...............15.95 CAD/13.95 USD*
Sixty original scores and 17 tunes arranged in five dance sets by Scottish-born
Canadian composer Murray Shoolbraid - the best of over 400 scores in 30 years
of work by this prolific musician-composer. Jigs, reels, strathspeys, airs, laments,
two-steps and waltzes for mandolin, accordion and all fiddle styles.

*An Unfortunate Likeness (novel) ©1998 NWP 115 - ISBN: 978-1-895814-05-7
(144 pp., photos, illust., original painting cover)........ $12.95 CAD/9.95 USD*
Second of three historical novels with a connection to a Nova Scotian fishing town by
Anna Careless. A novel of romance and the supernatural where a vengeful act of the
past plays itself out in the present - combining intimacy, suspense and intrigue that
holds your interest until the very end **Limited copies of her other novels remain.**

*Quarantine, What is Old is New : Lawlor's Island Quarantine Station 1866 -1938
©2007 NWP 145 - ISBN: 978-1-895814-34-7 (240 pp., hist. photos, maps, TOC,
footnotes, indexed) Ian Arthur Cameron, MD..............$19.95 CAD/USD*
After a long love affair with Lawlor's Island, clinician/historian Ian Cameron,
MD, reveals the ghosts of its medical past. The story is of tragic events and
unimaginable hardships, public health successes and failures, remarkable
bravery and unforgivable incompetence. As new epidemics threaten , we must
learn lessons from the past. This book is an important contribution to medicine,
public health and maritime history, as well as an intriguing history of Halifax
and some of its more prominent citizens.

Ordering Information

This book and the other publications listed on the preceding pages are available at selected **retail outlets in Canada**, as well as many **on-line retailers worldwide**. If they are not available in your community ask your local bookseller to order copies for you from the publisher or contact New World Publishing toll-free to find the nearest bookseller in your region. Inquiries from distributors and library supply houses are also welcomed

Mail, phone or internet ordering:

If there are no local booksellers in your area, you may purchase copies directly from the publisher at competitive prices. Please contact the publisher in **writing, or by phone, fax, or e-mail** at the addresses and numbers listed below. The publisher also provides a gift order service with payment by **certified cheque, money order, VISA, MasterCard or American Express**. All book prices are listed in both Canadian and US dollars. **Check for monthly specials on-line.**

Introductory offer for direct mail order or phone order pricing for BALANCE:

    Single book = $24.00 CAD/USD plus tax and shipping
    2 - 4 books = $22.00 CAD /USD each plus tax and shipping
    5 - 9 books = $21.00 CAD/USD each plus tax/free shipping
    10 + books   = $19.00 CAD/USD each plus tax/free shipping

Toll-free phone orders with credit card: 1-877-211-3334
Web-based on-line orders: Health/Wellness Books & Meditation CDs:
www.nonscentedtoxicfree.com

Shipping and taxes for all books and CDs:

Shipping rates are quoted in Canadian dollars or USD for orders shipped to the continental USA. For pricing and rates for other countries or remote locations, please contact the publisher. Typical shipping rates (*subject to change*) are $5.00 CAD/USD (non-tracked pkgs.) for **single items** under one-half pound; over that weight: $8.00 in Canada or $12.00 to the continental USA (tracked packages). Express shipping extra. **Free shipping for orders over $100. In Canada, add GST; all others are tax-free.**

Schools, Libraries, Professional Associations:

In addition, discounts are offered to selected groups who wish to purchase copies of the books listed in this publication. These discounts apply to libraries, schools, health, environmental and self-help groups, or professional associations. Contact the publisher for shipping arrangements and rates. Our popular health, self-help, children's and Atlantic Canadian publications are currently shipped world-wide.

New World Publishing
P.O. Box 36075
Halifax, Nova Scotia
B3J 3S9 Canada
(902) 576-2055   Fax: (902) 576-2095
Toll free orders: 1-877-211-3334
e-mail: nwp1@eastlink.ca
www. newworldpublishing.com